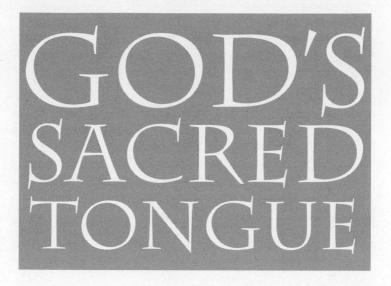

GOD'S
SACRED
TONGUE

Hebrew Idioms

Gen. 16. 2. It may be I shall be BUILT UP
by her. אִבָּנֶה i.e. I shall obtain children

Gen. 16. 11. The Lord hath HEARD thine affliction
i.e. hath regarded thine affliction.

Gen. 16. 12. and He shall be a a WILD ASS
man. i.e. a wild man.

Gen. 18. He hastened to make it Lagnahshoth. i.e.
to dress it. also v. 8.

Gen. 18. 11. old & ~~&~~ COMING to days i.e.
well stricken in years age

Gen. 19. 4. mikkātzeh. ~~from~~ ab extremo
~~from every Quarter~~ from the EXTREME
the LIMITS or UTMOST
Part. i.e. from every ~~Quarter~~.

Gen. 19. Koráthō.. ~~Rafter~~ RAFTER
BEAM or Timber. i.e. ~~the~~
~~have~~ Roof.

Gen. 19. 21. I have ALLESPITED thy FACE
for I have accepted Thee

Gen. 19. 28. to the FACE of Sodom. i.e
towards Sodom. so to the Face of all the Place
v. 29.

Gen. 20. 9. ~~was~~ deeds which SHALL not be
done i.e which ought not to be done

Gen. 20. 11. ONLY the Fear of God is not in
this Place. i.e surely the Fear &c —

Gen. 20. 13. Say of me he is my Brother
i.e. of me.

Gen. 21. 11. Grievous ~~&~~ Been for the Cause of
his son.. i.e. because of his son or on the account of his son

GOD'S SACRED TONGUE

Hebrew & the American Imagination

SHALOM GOLDMAN

The University of North Carolina Press   Chapel Hill & London

© 2004
The University of North Carolina Press
All rights reserved
Set in Carter and Cone Galliard and Charlemagne types
by Tseng Information Systems, Inc.
Manufactured in the United States of America

The publication of this book
was supported by a subvention from Emory College
and the Graduate School of Arts and Sciences of
Emory University.

Library of Congress Cataloging-in-Publication Data
Goldman, Shalom.
God's sacred tongue: Hebrew and the American imagination /
Shalom Goldman.
p. cm.
Includes bibliographical references (p.) and index.
ISBN 0-8078-2835-1
1. Hebraists, Christian—United States—Biography.   2. Old
Testament scholars—United States—Biography.   3. Hebrew
philology—Study and teaching (Higher)—United States—
History.   4. Christian Zionism—United States—History.
5. Christianity and other religions—Judaism.   6. Judaism—
Relations—Christianity.   I. Title.
PJ4533.G65   2004
261.2'6'0973—dc22   2003017453

08 07 06 05 04   5 4 3 2 1

TO LAURIE

Poet, Scholar, Muse

Moses turned, and went down the mountain, and the

two tablets of testimony were in his hand. The tablets

were inscribed on both sides; on the one side and on

the other side they were inscribed. The tablets were

the work of God, and the writing was the writing

of God, engraved on the tablets.

EXODUS 32:15–16

I was harkening back to my Puritan forbearers

by studying "God's sacred tongue."

EDMUND WILSON

CONTENTS

ILLUSTRATIONS

ACKNOWLEDGMENTS

As *God's Sacred Tongue* is an intellectual history of American Hebraism, it relies on the work of many earlier researchers. To them I owe a considerable scholarly debt. Hebrew was taught at many of the American colleges founded before the Revolution, and to the librarians and archivists at those colleges discussed in this book—Dartmouth, Columbia, Harvard, Princeton, and Yale— I owe thanks. In Israel, librarians at Tel Aviv University, Hebrew University, and Hebrew Union College stretched available resources to uncover rarities of American Hebraism.

Scholarly organizations that supported and encouraged my work include the National Endowment for the Humanities, the American Jewish Archives, and the American Jewish Historical Society. My home institution, Emory University, has been generous in research and publication support and I especially want to thank the present and former chairs of Middle Eastern and South Asian Studies, Devin Stewart and Gordon Newby. Deans Gary Wihl and Robert Paul provided support for research assistance and manuscript preparation.

Scholars of my generation rely on quiet cafes almost as much as we rely on research libraries. While thanking librarians and archivists I also want to thank the owners and staff of the Hungarian Pastry Shop in New York City, Emory Starbucks in Atlanta, Duvshanit in Jerusalem, and last but not least T'mol Shilshom, Jerusalem's literary cafe.

Readers who were generous with their time and comments include my brothers Ari and Dov and my son Daniel. To have such critical acumen present within the family is both a challenge and a constant pleasure. To Patrick Allitt, Sheri Katz, and Brian Mahan, many thanks for comments on individual chapters. Tony and Chris Patton braved their way through the complete work, and I am particularly thankful to Tony Patton for his suggestion that I add an epilogue that ties the intellectual issues raised in the book to current events in the Middle East and the United States.

Many of the book's biographical portraits were first presented as lectures at Emory, Ohio State, Case Western Reserve, and Dartmouth, and I hope my students and colleagues find that these portraits have been improved by their questions and comments. I have also benefited from comments by participants at the National Association of Professors of Hebrew conferences, where some of this material was presented. The Jewish Studies Colloquium of the University of North Carolina and Duke University, whose members heard my presentation on Edward Robinson and Moses Stuart, helped refine my understanding of the nineteenth-century "rediscovery" of the Holy Land. The convener of that colloquium, Yaakov Ariel, was very generous with comments and suggestions, as was New Testament scholar Bruce Chilton of Bard College.

During my research sojourns in New York I benefited from the hospitality of Lou Solomon and Beth Goldman. My work at Yale was facilitated by the generosity of Jack Goldman and Rhoda Miller. In Jerusalem, Danny Rubinstein and Uri Katz invited me to join their fabled walks in the Old City and Ruth Kark shared her encyclopedic knowledge of the city. David Ehrlich of T'mol Shilshom and Yishai and Rivka Elder, also of Jerusalem, shared their love of adventure and intellectual engagement. Yaakov and Esther Gindin gave me homes away from home in both Tel Aviv and Gedera.

Nick Fabian, careful reader, skillful editor, and computer guru, helped bring the manuscript into the twenty-first century. Loretta Anderson brought her typing and organizational skills to the project. Patrick Graham and the staff at Emory's Pitts Theology Library were of great help throughout the project. Elaine Maisner of the University of North Carolina Press saw the promise of the project from its beginnings. My partner and first reader, Laurie Patton, helped me see the intellectual and literary connections, and it is to her that this book is dedicated.

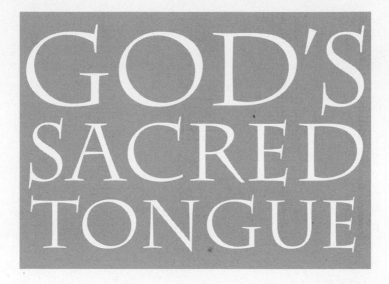

GOD'S
SACRED
TONGUE

PROLOGUE

On New Year's Day of 1812, John Adams and Thomas Jefferson resumed a correspondence, and a friendship, interrupted by eight years of personal and political antagonism. Their dramatic reconciliation was achieved through the efforts of their mutual friend Dr. Benjamin Rush, physician and fellow signer of the Declaration of Independence. In 1809 Rush had written to both men, telling of a dream in which the former presidents were reconciled. "I am sure an advance on your side will be cordial to the heart of Mr. Adams," Rush wrote to Jefferson. "Tottering over the grave he now leans wholly upon the shoulders of his old Revolutionary friends." Other mutual friends joined Rush's call for peace between the heroes of the Revolution, and eventually Adams and Jefferson wrote to each other. Both men saw this renewed exchange of ideas and views as an opportunity to explain the origins of American democracy to a new generation. Adams wrote to Jefferson, "You and I ought not to die before we have explained ourselves to each other." Adams was then seventy-six years old; Jefferson was sixty-eight. An eminent historian of the American Revolution noted, "This correspondence is generally regarded as the intellectual capstone to the achievements of the revolutionary generation and the most impressive correspondence in all of American history."[1]

Early in the renewed correspondence Adams raised questions about what we might today call the anthropology of the Native American tribes. How were the Indians organized? Did they have a system of government? And, most intriguing to Adams, "Have they any order of Priesthood among them, like the Druids, Bards, or minstrels of the Celtic Nations?" In response, Jefferson, long interested in the Native Americans of his native Virginia, provided Adams with a comprehensive review of Western theories of Native American origins. He lingered on the theories of James Adair, author of the 1775 book *The History of the American Indians*. In Jefferson's words, "Adair believed all the Indians of America to be descended from the Jews: the same laws, usages, rites and ceremonies, the same sacrifices, priests, prophets, fasts and festivals, almost the same religion." Rejecting this then widespread notion, Jefferson was nonetheless intrigued, as he was sure Adams would be, by Adair's theory of language—that the Indian dialects of North America were descended from "a common prototype," the Hebrew of the Bible. Observing that Indian ritual chants invoked God as "yohewah," later supporters of this "Jewish-Indian theory" were convinced that the Indians were chanting the name Jehovah, or Yahweh.

That Adams and Jefferson were intrigued by this theory should not surprise us. In an age of revolutionary upheaval, questions concerning "origins" and the definition of national groups had become central. In an era of premodern Christian belief, public figures debated whether a providential scheme governed the relationship between ethnic groups. For American Protestants, both the Jews and the Native Americans were objects of fascination. A theory that made sense of the role the American colonies played in the fate of both peoples was especially intriguing. When combined with inquiries into the origins of language and questions of how the world's languages were related one to another, the theory was well-nigh irresistible. The Hebrew language, thought by many to be the world's first language, was viewed as the key that would unlock the mysteries of the origins and fates of nations and peoples.

God's Sacred Tongue tells the story of American engagement with the Hebrew language and the Hebrew Bible. Through biographical portraits of scholars, clergymen, explorers, and public figures, it ties the history of American Hebraism to questions of national self-concept, religious identity, and the place of the American Republic in world affairs. A biblical self-concept dominated much of early American thought. Manifest in the first two centuries of European colonization and settlement, this self-concept has again come to the forefront in the religious revivals of modern times. The notion that the United States is a nation with biblical roots, a nation chosen by God to play a major role in world affairs, is very much with us.

The study of Hebrew in Colonial America and in the early Republic was, for the most part, a Protestant endeavor. The few Jews resident in the thirteen colonies (estimates range from one thousand to fifteen hundred) used Hebrew for liturgical and other religious purposes, but theirs was a Hebrew quite different from the language studied in the early American colleges and in the homes of Christian ministers, professors, and legislators. Christian Hebraism focused on biblical interpretation, and it utilized teaching materials written by scholars who were often clergymen. Colonial American Jews, whether of Sephardic or Ashkenazic extraction, used and studied a rabbinic Hebrew that had a long history of continuous development. Their Protestant counterparts were students of what a modern scholar has dubbed "Divinity School Hebrew, the original language of the text sacred to Protestants, a text created by a 'primitive people,' Jews, who were of little contemporary relevance except for millennial groups." The pedigree of Divinity School Hebrew was then approximately two centuries old. Its origins lie in sixteenth-century German Humanism and in the related Reformation ideal of *sola scriptura*, the notion that the text of the Bible was the only source of revealed truth.[2]

It is important at the outset of this book to make this distinction between Christian Hebraism and the Jewish use of Hebrew. It should serve as a corrective to the prevailing notion that Christian study of the Hebrew language and Hebrew texts in both Europe and America implied sympathetic interest in Jews, be they individual Jews or members of an established Jewish community. To the contrary, some Christian Hebraists, though they demonstrated the "Christian truth" through their study of Hebrew, were most vocal and active in their anti-Judaism. In some cases this anti-Judaism took the form of missionary activity; in other cases Hebrew learning was used to expose the alleged "iniquities of the Jews."

As the chapters in Part I demonstrate, these Christian Hebraists were participating in a cultural conversation that extended beyond the confines of their small academic circle. Protestant thinkers in Europe, England, and the American colonies were engaged in varied attempts to understand the function of the Jews in history. In his 1983 book *Israel in the Mind of America*, *New York Times* journalist Peter Grose noted, "Between the early American Christian and the early American Jew there hung an awkward ambivalence." A century and a half earlier President John Adams's great-grandson Henry Adams highlighted these distinctions between American Christians and traditional Jews in the opening paragraph of his now classic *The Education of Henry Adams*. As an Adams born on Boston's Beacon Hill in 1838, Henry was christened by his uncle, the minister of the First Church "after the tenets of Boston Unitarianism. Had he been born in Jerusalem under the shadow of the Temple and circumcised in the Synagogue by his uncle the high priest, under the name of Israel Cohen, he would scarcely have been more distinctly branded."[3]

As Part II reminds us, later in the nineteenth century a new form of Christian engagement with Jewish issues and images appeared: support for the recently emerged Zionist movement. This support was especially strong among dispensationalists, those Protestants who subscribed to a messianic belief that linked the Second Coming to the fate of the Jews. Believers in the imminent "Great Tribulation" that would precede the final redemption, dispensationalists, believing that history was divided into eras or "dispensations," read biblical prophecies as references to the Jews of their own time. While many earlier Christian thinkers sought to sunder the ties between biblical Israel and the Jewish communities of their own time, these modern Protestant writers reaffirmed that connection. This reading dovetailed with Zionist thought, which emphasized the Jewish connection to the biblical historical and territorial past.

In the mid- to late nineteenth century only small and often marginalized groups of American Protestants held these millennialist beliefs. But by the end of the century their influence was felt among the evangelical churches. As

Yaakov Ariel has noted: "In the late nineteenth and early twentieth centuries, dispensationalism became an important component of the worldview of the conservative camp within American Protestantism. It meshed well with the fundamentalist view, which criticized the prevailing cultural trend in society, and offered an alternative philosophy of history to the liberal post-millennialist notions that prevailed in American Christianity at the time."[4]

For some American Christian thinkers this new philosophy of history placed the fate of the Jews at center stage. The Millerites, mid-nineteenth-century Adventists who predicted the imminent return of Christ, predicted that the Second Coming would occur between Passover of 1843 and Passover of 1844. William Miller's response to the events of that year was a remarkable expression of Adventist interest in Jewish rituals and categories of thought. Miller had predicted the return of Christ at the end of April 1844. Thousands of people gathered outside of Philadelphia and other major cities to witness the Final Redemption. When the Second Coming did not arrive, Miller announced to the faithful that his calculations had failed to take into account the Jewish High Holy Days. Yom Kippur (the Day of Atonement), the most sacred day of the Jewish calendar, was the date of the redemption. That sacred day in 1844 would mark the culmination of the redemptive process. When that prophecy too failed, some of Miller's followers organized a voyage to Palestine, where they hoped to restore the Jews to their land.

In that same mid-century decade the Mormon Church was similarly engaged with questions of the Christian relationship to, and understanding of, Jewish history. Knowledge of Hebrew and Scripture would enable them to investigate further that relationship. Joseph Smith, the Mormon prophet, studied Hebrew with Joshua Seixas, a Jewish teacher from an esteemed New York rabbinical family. Smith's followers were among the first American Christians to call for the restoration of the Jews to the Holy Land. In the late nineteenth and early twentieth centuries these Christian theological grapplings with Jewish history had political implications, as many dispensationalists, and other Christians, became ardent supporters of Zionism.

As *God's Sacred Tongue* demonstrates, we gain a richer understanding of Christian Zionism and of current American thinking on Israel by looking at the histories of both Christian Hebraism and evangelical thought. In the mid-nineteenth century Christian support for the idea of the restoration of the Jewish people to Palestine manifested itself in some thoroughly unexpected ways. Between 1850 and 1880 at least three groups of American Christians journeyed to the Holy Land with the intent of settling the land and physically preparing the way for the return of the Jews. The first group, led by Mrs. Clorinda Minor, a "prophetess" of the Adventist movement who had witnessed the great disappointment of 1843 and 1844, established colonies in Jaffa and Artas, a town near Bethlehem. On his pilgrimage to the Holy Land, Herman Melville visited the remnants of this group. Fifteen years later 150 pioneers from Maine and New Hampshire joined their "prophet" George Adams on a voyage to Jaffa. The colony failed when Adams succumbed to drink and "Oriental lassitude." Most of those who survived the Jaffa debacle slowly made their way back to the United States. In *The Innocents Abroad* Mark Twain recounts his encounter with the remnants of this sorry group. In 1881 a small group of Americans joined with European Christians to found the American Colony of Jerusalem. This was the longest-lasting and most successful of American Christian attempts to establish Palestine settlements. The leadership of the Zionist movement acknowledged their practical and ideological debts to these American Christian pioneers. As early as 1917 David Ben Gurion wrote of American settlement efforts and praised the settlers for introducing modern agricultural methods into that corner of the Ottoman Empire.[5]

As Part III of this book demonstrates, some of the most prominent American intellectuals of the twentieth century were deeply engaged in puzzling out the relationship between America's self-concept and the set of ideas and practices they recognized as Judaic. Support for Zionism was one way that this relationship manifested itself. Today, at the beginning of the twenty-first century, American Christian support for Zionism is a political force to be reckoned with. Millions of church-going Americans regularly express support for the Jewish state and its policies. For the most part these Christian Zionists sympathize with the politics of the Israeli right and disdain the worldview of Israeli liberals. Since the late 1970s prominent evangelicals, among them Jerry Falwell and Pat Robertson, have formed a set of alliances with politicians of Israel's Likud Party. The prime ministers of that party—Menachem Begin, Yitzhak Shamir, Benjamin Netanyahu, and Ariel Sharon—have embraced evangelical support of Israel. In a December 2000 speech to a Christian Zionist conference in Jerusalem, Ariel Sharon told the fifteen hundred attendees, "We regard you to be one of our best friends in the world." Observers of the current political scene have noted that this synergy between the millennialist expectations of Christian Zionists and Israeli political needs is a potent force in the current administration's Middle East policy. Christian Zionism and Jewish Zionism have converged in a compelling and creative manner, and this convergence has had a profound influence on American life and on the lives of the citizens of the Middle East. The background to this development is to be found in the story of Christian Hebraism's encounter with the Jews.

I

ZION ON AMERICAN SHORES

SEVENTEENTH AND EIGHTEENTH CENTURIES

If the first chapters of the Bible tell of the origins of all the peoples of the earth, how does one account for the native peoples of the Americas, peoples with no apparent relationship to other known human cultures? This question vexed many Europeans and early American settlers. Chapter 1 of this book looks back at premodern European notions of identity, language, and culture and traces the manner in which these ideas influenced the American colonies and the early Republic. The subsequent chapters tell of additional American attempts to study the Hebraic and Judaic traditions and understand the American experience through a biblical and rabbinic lens.

Against the Puritan Old Testament background of American religious life, New England intellectuals and scholars were eager to study the Bible, both in translation and in the Hebrew original. The Pilgrims' engagement with Hebrew and biblical studies began long before they reached New England. Some of them had studied Hebrew with Continental European scholars—especially in the Low Countries. Others embarked on the study of Hebrew and the Bible through the use of Buxtorf's dictionaries and other study aids.

Two Hebraists, William Bradford and William Brewster, arrived in the New World aboard the *Mayflower*. Bradford, author of colonial America's first narrative history, *Of Plymouth Plantation*, was governor of the Plymouth Colony. Many regarded his colleague William Brewster, who was both teacher and preacher at Plymouth, as spiritual leader of the Pilgrims. Both men, busy as they were in the early years of settlement, set time aside each day for the study of the Bible and the sacred tongue. In the original manuscript of *Of Plymouth Plantation*, written in 1650, Bradford included eight pages of Hebrew vocabulary notes.[1] These "Hebrew Exercises" included a list of more than one thousand Hebrew words and phrases and their English equivalents. The exercises are graced by Bradford's charming hymn of praise to the study of the Hebrew language:

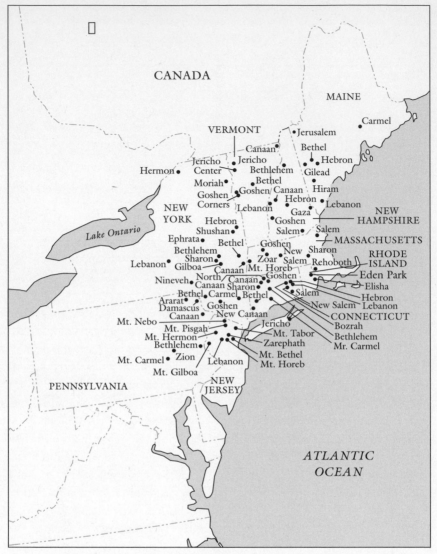

Biblical place names in New England (Adapted from Davis, America and the Holy Land; *used by permission of the International Center for University Teaching of Jewish Civilization, The Hebrew University of Jerusalem)*

Though I am growne aged, yet I have had a longing
desire to see with my own eyes, something of that most
ancient language, and holy tongue, in which the law
and Oracles of God were write; and in which God
and angels spake to the holy patriarchs of old
time; and what names were given to things
from the creation. And though I can not
attaine to much herein, yet I am refresh-
ed to have seen some glimpse hereof
(as Moyses saw the land of Ca-
nan a farr of). My aime and
desire is, to see how the words
and phrases lye in the
holy texte: and to
discerne somewhat
of the same,
for my owne
contente.

This early interest in the Bible and the sacred tongue was rapidly institu-
tionalized. In its early years Harvard, America's first college, was more closely
focused on the study of Hebrew and the Bible than any parallel institution in
Europe. The "learned languages"—Latin, Greek, and Hebrew—were at the
core of the curriculum. The model that influenced New England's clergy was
the curriculum of Cambridge University, from which almost two-thirds of
that clergy had graduated. Since 1549 Cambridge had required Hebrew training for all candidates for the Master of Arts degree. But at New England's
"Cambridge," Hebrew had special pride of place. Harvard historian Samuel
Eliot Morison has noted that in the early period "the most distinctive feature of the Harvard curriculum was the emphasis on Hebrew and kindred languages." Dunster and Chauncy, the college's first two presidents, were, according to Morison, both good Hebrew scholars who saw themselves as "primarily
orientalists." In addition to Hebrew, they studied and taught Aramaic, Arabic,
and Ethiopic. Chauncy, in fact, boasted that he knew more Arabic than any
other person in the American colonies.[2] When he was appointed president of
Harvard in 1654, Chauncy requested that a chapter of the Hebrew Bible be
read, in Hebrew, at morning chapel services.

Chapter 2 of *God's Sacred Tongue* tells the story of Hebrew at Harvard
through biographical portraits of the college's first Hebrew instructors and
professors. Harvard, the first of the early American colleges, was founded in
1636 to ensure that learning continued when New England's clergy "lay in the

dust." A few years later the College of William and Mary was established in Virginia. Eight more colleges were established on American soil before the Revolutionary War. In all ten of these institutions, the Bible, the "learned languages," and classical texts served as the core of the curriculum. With the classics, Christian theology, logic, and mathematics comprised the course of study. The study of the Hebrew language, though relegated to a lesser degree of importance than the core subjects, was too important to exclude from the curriculum of any new institution of higher learning. As late as the early nineteenth century, the founders of New York University, which was established in the early 1830s with the stated purpose of secularizing American higher education, felt it necessary to appoint a professor of Hebrew to the faculty. This was Professor George Bush, Protestant clergyman and ancestor of Presidents George Bush.

That the founders of Harvard emphasized Hebrew and cognate studies was in keeping with the standards and needs of their place and time. Many of New England's founders were enthusiastic and learned students of Holy Writ and its original languages—one of which, Hebrew (invariably studied in conjunction with Aramaic and Greek), was thought to be the original language of humanity, the "primitive language" with which God created the natural order and man named the animals. This idea of Hebraic originality was more than a scholarly abstraction. One eighteenth-century Harvard graduate, Jonathan Fisher of Blue Hills, Maine, was so inspired by this Hebraist understanding of Adam's naming of the animals that he carved the biblical Hebrew names of his farm animals over their pens. Fisher aspired to collect a "biblical zoo" of domesticated animals. He also published a charming book on biblical animals— each illustration accompanied by the animal's Hebrew name and by biblical quotations about that animal. Two hundred years later, in British Mandate Palestine, Jewish researchers emulated Fisher's efforts when they established Jerusalem's "biblical zoo." Although these researchers were likely unaware that a prototype of their zoo had been established in Maine two centuries earlier, this correspondence is an example of the many striking American–Holy Land correspondences that will figure largely in my later discussions of emerging American interest in the Middle East and in the fate of the Holy Land.

Because the aftermath of the English Civil War had caused a reaction against Puritan religiosity and scholarship, Cambridge University of the mid-eighteenth century was not as strong in biblical scholarship and Hebrew studies as it had been at the beginning of the seventeenth century. Many Puritan scholars emigrated from England to Holland and later to colonial New England, thereby strengthening Hebraic and biblical scholarship in the colonies and at the colonies' first college. England's loss was thus Harvard's gain. Those Puritan scholars who sojourned in Amsterdam before journeying to the New World had the opportunity to study with Dutch Christian Hebraists. Many of these Dutch and English religious dissidents availed themselves of the opportunity to observe Amsterdam's thriving Jewish community and on occasion to engage its learned rabbis in conversation. But these arcane matters were not of interest to the young students of America's Cambridge. They resented the imposition of yet another "dead tongue." Latin and Greek posed enough of a problem. The requirement that all entering students know Latin and learn Greek seems to have been honored only in the breach. That European visitors to the colonies were dismayed by the failings of American classical education is indicated by this amusing tale: In 1703 visitors from Europe tried to engage Harvard students in a conversation in Latin. "When they went into Harvard Hall they found ten scholars smoking tobacco in a room which smelled like a tavern. They tried Latin on these youths and were astonished at the sad result."[3]

At seventeenth- and eighteenth-century Harvard, all freshmen had to study Hebrew. As early as 1653, students began to complain about this requirement. The instructor in Hebrew, Michael Wigglesworth, author of *Day of Doom* and a figure who has been described by Perry Miller as "the embodiment of repulsive joylessness," wrote in his diary in 1653: "Aug. 29. My pupils all came to me this day to desire they might cease learning Hebrew: I withstood it with all the reason I could, yet all will not satisfy them. Thus I am requited for love; and thus little fruit of all my prayers and tears for their good." A little later he is heard contemplating resignation, in part because of "my pupils' forward negligence in the Hebrew."[4]

Yale, founded in 1701, offered Hebrew in its early years. The founders of the Collegiate School, from which Yale developed, stated that students would spend their first year in "practice of tongues," especially Hebrew. As I discuss in more depth in Chapter 3, Yale was to become a center of interest in Hebrew under President Ezra Stiles, who assumed leadership of the college in 1778. Stiles's study of the language deepened to include readings in rabbinic and kabbalistic literature; these endeavors led to his friendships with six European and Palestinian rabbis. This is not to say that he had an unprejudiced view of the Jews of his day; while admiring their culture, Stiles was suspicious of "Jewish designs" on the outcome of the American Revolution.

As Chapter 4 notes, among Yale's first students was Jonathan Edwards, a gifted young scholar from the nearby Connecticut town of Southington. First in his small college class, Edwards would later become the Yale College tutor, a position he left for the pastorate. While serving as a rural pastor, Edwards embarked on a remarkable career of self-education and self-mastery. His philosophical and theological writings enriched the American religious conversation, and their depth, style, and sophistication astounded his British and Continental readers. His early study of and interest in Hebrew and the biblical text are keys to understanding this complex American genius.

With the exception of the rare Jew who visited the Massachusetts Commonwealth and the even more rare convert from Judaism to Christianity, Puritan interest in Hebrew and the Bible had no relationship with the Jews as a living community. As historian Arthur Hertzberg has noted, "The Puritans of New England were obsessed by the Jewish Bible, but they were not hospitable to Jews, or to Judaism."[5] Sixteenth- and seventeenth-century European Christian Hebraists often had contact with Jewish scholars. But after the establishment of Hebrew teaching at European universities and the wide dissemination of Christian Hebraist grammars, dictionaries, and translations, Christian scholars no longer felt the need to turn to Jews for biblical knowledge. By the early decades of the eighteenth century, Christian Hebraism had developed a scholarly tradition of its own, independent of Jewish scholars and scholarship. Doctrinal issues intruded here as well. Some churchmen warned their flock against the pernicious effects that contact with Jews could bring. Hebrew knowledge received from Jewish scholars was thought to be suspect or tainted. This suspicion was reinforced by the reluctance of many Jewish scholars to engage Christian scholars in dialogue. These Jewish scholars feared (with considerable justification) that "dialogues" which quickly deteriorated into angry polemics could harm Jewish communities. The unequal power relation between the church and the synagogue was clear: the synagogue had been "vanquished." But though vanquished, it had not disappeared, and the refusal of the synagogue to accept the teachings of the church could not be forgiven or forgotten. Though Christian Hebraists might in some cases consult rabbis, they nevertheless regarded their answers to exegetical questions with suspicion. If Jewish scholars did not concede a doctrinal point, punishment might ensue.

Knowledge of Hebrew was, in the hands of some Christian missionaries, a conversionist tool. An 1823 *Hebrew Grammar*, written by Joseph Frey, a convert to Christianity and missionary to the Jews of the United States, alerts Christian students of Hebrew to the dangers of mispronunciation: "If Christian preachers were sensible of the good or bad effects produced upon the minds of the Jews, according as they pronounce the Hebrew language correctly or incorrectly, they would think no time too long, and no pains too great, to acquire the correct and accurate pronunciation." As Chapter 5 shows, many European and American missionaries studied Hebrew in order to sharpen their polemical skills and convince Jewish audiences that their language could be used to buttress Christian claims.

For Jewish scholars and their communities, there was a different doctrinal question to consider—the legality of "teaching Torah to non-Jews." As

[*Zion on American Shores*]

understood by many Halakhic authorities, rabbinic law forbids engaging in Torah study with outsiders. According to this view, the Torah, both written and oral, was given to the Jews and not to others. As part of their covenantal relationship with God the Jews were to study the law and observe it. But they were not to share it with others. Especially egregious to Jewish sensibilities were Gentile attempts to appropriate Jewish ritual. According to one Talmudic statement, "A non-Jew who observes the Sabbath is subject to capital punishment" (Sanhedrin 58b). Throughout Part II, I take up the question of Jewish-Christian scholarly cooperation in considerable detail.

How can we understand the relationship between Hebraism and higher education, a relationship that is a recurring theme throughout this and later parts of this book? During the first two centuries of American life Hebrew learning played a role beyond the philological. It also had a philosophical aspect. For beyond training students in the use of the Hebrew language, biblical and rabbinic institutions and structures of education served as models for the founders of American colleges. Cotton Mather, in *Magnalia Christi Americana or The Ecclesiastical History of New England*, dubbed Harvard the first of our "*midrashot*," borrowing from the rabbinic tradition the appellation of the Talmudic study hall. Eliezer Wheelock, founder of Dartmouth College in 1769, spoke of his new school as an institution built on the model of the prophet Elijah's "School of the Prophets." With this comparison, Wheelock was evoking biblical models and the legacy of Yale and Harvard. More than a century earlier Harvard's President Chauncy used similar language when he referred to Harvard students as "sons of the Prophets." For these American college founders the very idea of the university was linked to Hebraic origins.

The final chapter of Part I, Chapter 6, focuses on the use of Hebrew in the American Jewish communities of the eighteenth and early nineteenth centuries. Hebrew was, of course, used in prayer and in the liturgical readings of scripture. New York's Shearith Israel congregation organized a Hebrew school for its children in the 1730s; schools in other cities sprang up over the following century. But Jewish higher learning and the production of Judaic scholarship would not flourish on American shores until the twentieth century. The prehistory of the American Jewish success story can tell us much about later unexpected developments.

It would be an error, however, to consider New England Hebraism a direct antecedent of later American Jewish success in cultural and intellectual spheres. Twentieth-century attempts to tie the Hebraism of the New England Puritans to issues of American Jewish identity have little validity. For example, Yale's Hebrew-language insignia, now emblazoned on notebooks, coffee cups, and tee-shirts (and adopted by the Yale Hillel), was chosen by early eighteenth-century Hebraists who had no knowledge of—or interest in—Jews. As the

Yale founders understood it, the Yale insignia, "Urim Ve-Tumim," represents the "Christian Truth" as foreshadowed by the Old Testament description of the oracle worn by the High Priest of Israel on his bejeweled breastplate. That at the end of the second Christian millennium fully one-third of Yale's undergraduates are Jews would have surprised its early eighteenth-century founders. What early Puritan Hebraists like Ezra Stiles would have thought of the 1997 case of the "Yale Five" (five Orthodox Jews who sued Yale, contending that the college rule that all freshmen live in mixed-sex dorms violated their religious freedom) is an intriguing question for speculation.

1

LOST TRIBES

AND FOUND

PEOPLES

Sixteenth- and seventeenth-century Europeans understood exploration and discovery in the New World in biblical and Hebraic terms. This is, in effect, the earliest chapter in our history of American Hebraism, a Hebraism shaped within the context of the European history of ideas. For the Americas were thought to hold "Hebrew secrets." With the news of the European discoveries of the Americas, Christians and Jews sought ways to contextualize these astounding discoveries. Not surprisingly, a biblical worldview provided the context to explain the wonders of this New World. While Christians could accept that continents might remain unknown or forgotten for long periods of time, the enigma of unknown or forgotten peoples was more difficult to fathom. Had the Bible not accounted for the origin and spread of all of humankind? Genesis, Chapter 10, represents the three sons of Noah as the ancestors of all who live on the earth. For centuries the common Western understanding of the origins of the earth's diverse and far-flung peoples was that Europeans were descendants of Japeth, Africans descendants of Ham, and Middle Easterners the children of Shem or Sem. (Hence the designation "Semitic"—first applied to a group of Middle Eastern languages, later specifically to Jews.) The peoples of the Far East were variously assigned to one of the three sons.

But what of the peoples of the New World? To which son of Noah were they to be attributed? As historian of ideas Anthony Grafton noted: "The discovery of human beings in the Americas, after all, posed a hard question to scholars who believed that the world had a seamless and coherent history: where did they come from? Neither the Greeks, the Romans, nor the Jews had known of their existence. How, then, could Greco-Roman and Hebrew texts be complete and authoritative?"[1]

A ready-made solution to the enigma of the Native Americans was to link them to a people of biblical times who had long been lost to history: the "Ten

Lost Tribes" of the Israelites. For many European scholars the biblical account was authoritative. Few disputed the accounts in the Book of Kings that chronicled the emergence of the Hebrew monarchies. In the tenth century B.C. the United Kingdom had divided into a Northern Kingdom, "Israel," made up of ten tribes, and a Southern Kingdom, "Judah," inhabited by the tribes of Judah and Benjamin. The biblical account of the fall of the Northern Kingdom of Israel in 722 B.C. concludes with this explanation of the fate of the kingdom's inhabitants: "In the ninth year of Hoshea the King of Assyria took Samaria, and carried Israel away into Assyria, and settled them in Khalah and on the Khabur, a river of Gozan, and in the Cities of the Medes" (II Kings 17:6). The fate of these tribes would remain an unsolved mystery that would inspire fabulists and theorists from ancient times to the present.

A century and a half after the fall of the Northern Kingdom of Israel, the Babylonian armies destroyed the Southern Kingdom. Jerusalem was laid waste in 586 B.C. The exile to Babylon—the paradigmatic exile of the Jewish experience—followed. The Jewish sense of self was forged in this experience. As the Psalmist wrote, "By the waters of Babylon we sat and wept as we remembered Zion." For the exiled Judeans, who yearned for Zion, there was no inclination to remember the ten tribes of the Northern Kingdom. The northern tribes were lost to history and to Jewish memory, their dispossession punishment for their sins of idolatry and wantonness. The Hebrew prophets spoke vaguely of a time when all the Tribes of Israel would be reunited; but this was in the End of Days. Ultimately, it was the fate of Judah that concerned the biblical narrator and later biblical commentators. Stories of the Lost Tribes only began to appeal to both Jewish and Christian audiences much later, during the medieval period.

As Christianity made the Old Testament its own, fusing it with the emerging New Testament, the historical fate of the Lost Tribes was divorced from the issue of ethnic identification that Jewish writers and readers had brought to it. The Lost Tribes now became part of Christian history, and the stories found a new audience. History as told in the Hebrew Bible now served as a "universal history." Even before the advent of Christianity, the Hebrew Bible, in Greek translation, had circulated throughout the Greek-speaking world. Greco-Roman and early Christian cultures developed an interest in the fate of the "lost" Israelites. Perhaps these lost peoples were living among them? Perhaps they peopled distant and inaccessible lands? Perhaps some Christians were themselves descended from the Lost Tribes? For Christians this curiosity would serve to link them to Old Testament Israel in both the physical sense and the spiritual sense.

With the spread of Christianity, speculation about the fate of these tribes became widespread. For many, Old Testament narrative was not only a moral teaching, but also a narrative of sacred history. While Catholic thinkers emphasized the allegorical in biblical history, the Reformation—with its focus on *sola scriptura*, scripture alone, as the key to truth—looked afresh at that history. In a book on the Lost Tribes one scholar noted, "No other subject seems to have had such fascination for the fanciful theorist."[2] Such theorizing began in earnest with the publication of reports of the European discoveries. While a variety of theories emerged, the "biblical origins" theory was the most popular. As Grafton points out, "In 1614 Sir Walter Raleigh's magnificent *History of the World* still dealt at length with exactly the same enterprise, that of tying the Indians to the biblical history of man."[3]

The Jewish-Indian Theory

For more than three centuries Americans have been fascinated with the attempt to "tie the Indians to the biblical history of man." Most of the adventurer-scholars portrayed in this book were engaged with proving, refuting, or reflecting upon this "biblical origins theory." Writing in the 1980s, intellectual historian Richard Popkin dubbed this notion "the Jewish-Indian theory." An American scholar of an earlier generation, Allen Godbey, compiled and analyzed many of the legends concerning the "true fate" of the Ten Lost Tribes of Ancient Israel. While Godbey's 1934 book focuses on the proliferation and acceptance of Lost Tribe theories, I treat those theories as part of the history of Christian Hebraism, the study of Hebrew and the Bible by premodern Christian scholars.

One of the more remarkable episodes in the history of speculation on the fate of the Lost Tribes occurred in seventeenth-century Holland. In 1644 Antonio Montezinos, a Spanish explorer of Jewish ancestry (he was also known as Aaron Levi), returned to Amsterdam from an extended journey in the interior of what is now Eastern Colombia. Testifying in front of Amsterdam's Rabbi Menasseh Ben Israel, Montezinos stated that he had met on his travels "the remnant of the Tribe of Reuben." A group of Indians in the mountains of the New World had spoken to him in an archaic Hebrew. As Montezinos put it, "They greeted me with the *Shema Yisrael*." The report that these people knew the words of the Jewish creed, words as old as the Book of Deuteronomy, convinced many who heard Montezinos's account that this tribe was Israelite in some form. A close look at Montezinos's account reveals that he implied only that some lost Jews lived among the Indians, not that all of the local Indians were Jews.

The news of this report spread quickly through European Jewish and Christian communities. The notion that the Lost Tribes had been "found" had a profound impact on millennialist thinking and politics in the seventeenth and eighteenth centuries. For many Christians and Jews, finding the remnants of the Lost Tribes served as a sign that the end of time was approaching. From this point forward the ingathering of the exiles and their return to the Land of Israel became an integral part of both Jewish and Christian millennialist thought.[4]

The Jewish-Indian theory, though today associated with fringe groups, "catastrophists," and other practitioners of wild historical speculation, was once accepted by some of the most respected and authoritative members of English and American society. Like Christian Hebraism with which it is sometimes conflated, this theory had little or no relationship to the Jews of its time. The Ancient Israelites generally—and the Ten Northern Tribes more specifically—were the object of inventive speculation. But Christians speculated only about their fate, not the fate of the Jews. The history of the Southern Kingdom, the group from which the Jews had descended, was well known: the exile to Babylon in the sixth century B.C., the Return to Zion "seventy years" later, the Second Temple and the reestablishment of the Jewish commonwealth, and, finally, the destruction of Judea—and Jerusalem, its political and spiritual center—by the Romans in the first century A.D. From this Judean culture, both rabbinic Judaism and Christianity emerged. The meaning of Jewish history was, therefore, clear to Christians (and to Jews, in a different sense). But what of the meaning and the fate of the Ten Lost Tribes?

As so much of *God's Sacred Tongue* is devoted to writers who were engaged with this theory, we might ask what part did the study of Hebrew language and texts play in this heady mixture of scientific and theological speculation? Montezinos based his claims on the Colombian tribe's knowledge of Hebrew. Rabbi Joseph Hakohen had made a parallel suggestion earlier in his Hebrew-language *Universal History of the Franks and the Ottomans*. According to Rabbi Hakohen, the European discoverers of the New World found that "the Indians of the Americas were able to speak a little of the language of Ishmael." This story, which indicates that some Jewish scholars were interested in biblical explanations of New World discoveries, may have resulted from reports that Columbus's navigators attempted to speak Arabic to the Indians. To some readers it suggested much more: a "Semitic" origin for the American tribes. Christian and Jewish readers associated Arabic with its Middle Eastern origins. For Middle Eastern Jewish scholars Hebrew, Aramaic, and Arabic were languages that all exegetes and legalists had to know. Perhaps the American tribes, with their seemingly familiar language, were, in fact, of the children of Ishmael.[5]

That Columbus's navigators had a biblical orientation is not at all surprising, for Columbus himself was deeply imbued with a biblical worldview.

[*Zion on American Shores*]

Rembrandt portrait of Rabbi Menasseh Ben Israel, 1636

Biblical passages, among them the accounts of King Solomon's voyages to Ophir, were among the ancient writings that convinced Columbus that he could reach Asia by sailing to the west. As the classicist James Romm noted, "Columbus saw himself taking part in a grand reenactment of a glorious moment in the biblical past; and such returns to early mythic patterns confirmed his belief that the ancient prophecies were being fulfilled and that history was at last reaching its end."[6]

In the realm of the history of ideas, Rabbi Menasseh's *Hope of Israel* proved the most important expression of the theory. Menasseh had heard Montezinos's testimony as to Israelites in America in 1644. In the late 1640s he wrote an essay on the larger issue of the Jewish role in history. Published in 1650 in

Spanish, it soon appeared in Latin, Hebrew, English, and Dutch. "The English translation, *Hope of Israel*, excited minds on both sides of the Atlantic, with its most enduring legacy being its influence on early American ethnography and eschatology. . . . Not surprisingly, most readers saw what they wished to see in the *Hope of Israel*, rather than what Menasseh intended. *Hope of Israel* was an important piece of Jewish messianism primarily because of the notoriety Gentiles gave it."[7]

For some Christian readers *Hope of Israel* affirmed their expectation of the promise of the conversion of the Jews to Christianity. The Protestant Reformation had subverted the allegorical reading of Israel's fate. "Particularly among some of Calvin's followers, prophecies and statements dealing with Israel and Zion came to be understood at face value. Thus, the apostle Paul's promise that one day 'all Israel shall be saved' was taken literally as referring to scattered Jews and the Lost Tribes."[8] In Protestant America these promises would take on new meaning and force.

American Puritans, followers of Calvin, had a special affinity for the biblical and Hebraic, and this affinity survived in American culture after the decline of Puritan doctrine and political power. Thus, a process begun in the Reformation in which the Jewish content of Christianity was rediscovered and reevaluated found its culmination and fulfillment in an American setting. If we think of the first four Christian centuries as a period when Christianity distanced itself from Judaic texts and concepts, we might think of the past four centuries as a time when some Christian churches rediscovered Hebraic and rabbinic categories of thought and action. These rediscoveries, which enabled the emergence of both Christian Hebraism and Christian Zionism, did not necessarily bring about or translate into sympathy for the Jews. As we shall see in the following chapters, an unsettling ambivalence characterized early American Protestant attitudes toward Jews. As with other components of the Christian Hebraic endeavor, this too had its roots and parallels in English thought.

England, steeped in a biblical tradition that identified and correlated English history with Jewish history, was at the forefront of such speculation. As late as the mid-nineteenth century influential British aristocrats were influenced by such speculation and adopted a "British Israelite" ideology. Fanciful philology backed up their claims that the Anglo-Saxons were, in fact, the descendants of Israel. Was *Brit-ish* not a code for Hebrew "Brit," covenant, and "Ish," man? Thus, the English upper classes were the true children of the Old Testament covenant. Though this group later discredited itself with its reactionary politics and thinly veiled anti-Semitism, certain of its ideas still persist in the upper reaches of British society. For its outlandish idea rested on a firm British foundation, the coronation of the British monarch is replete with Old Testament language and ceremony. In the 1953 coronation of Queen Elizabeth II, the Archbishop of Canterbury placed oil on the skin of the Queen as he recited this prayer: "And as Solomon was anointed King by Zadok the priest and Nathan the prophet, so be thou anointed, blessed, and consecrated over the peoples, whom the Lord thy God hath given thee to rule and govern." Though this blessing and others in a similar biblical vein are generally understood as the assertion of a spiritual connection to biblical Israel, some insist on a biological connection between English royalty and the ancient Davidic kingship. Queen Victoria seems to have subscribed to this Davidic theory and had her male children circumcised by a Jewish ritual circumciser, a *mohel*. Both Edward VII, the duke of Windsor, and Charles, the current prince of Whales, were circumcised by a well-known London physician and *mohel*, Dr. Jacob Snowman.[9]

During an earlier period British colonialists in Asia had identified the Afghans and Pathans as lost Israelite tribes now found by their Christian brothers. This insight would be made to serve British missionary aims. Not only could it explain the intransigence of these warring tribes that resisted British incursion, but more importantly, it also provided British theorists with a scenario for the End Time that excluded American notions of specialness. For Sir William Jones and others "the millennial drama involved the true Christians of Europe locating the Afghan Lost Tribes, and so creating the final moments of history without need of any Americans, native or immigrant."[10]

European discoveries in the New World, and the dissemination of relatively accurate ethnographic information about the indigenous peoples of the Americas, led to the decline of these apocalyptic fantasies, but not to their demise. Among both Jews and Christians, variants of the Jewish-Indian theory continued to crop up throughout the eighteenth and early nineteenth centuries. In the English-speaking world two elaborate statements of the theory were published in the eighteenth century: Lord Kingsborough's nine volume work *The History of Mexico* and Samuel Adair's ethnographic study of the American Indians.[11]

Adair was an English explorer who lived with the Native Americans of the southeastern colonies for close to forty years. His 1775 work, *The History of the American Indians*, is still valued today for its ethnographic insights into the lives of members of Native American tribes soon to be displaced. No longer taken seriously are Adair's emphatic claims that the tribes he lived among—the Cherokees, Creeks, and Chickasaws—were descended from Jews. Nevertheless, in the eighteenth and early nineteenth centuries this claim was debated at the highest levels of colonial and republican American life. As explained in the Prologue, Thomas Jefferson and John Adams discussed Adair's claims. Other prominent Americans, such as Elias Boudinot, president of the Continental

Congress and first director of the U.S. Mint, firmly endorsed Adair's claims. Those like Jefferson and Adams who rejected the theory had to contend with a considerable literature that claimed to find numerous similarities between Native American customs and those of the biblical Hebrews.

For the English colonists in seventeenth- and eighteenth-century North America, the appeal of the Jewish-Indian theory was considerable. It fit into an already articulated worldview of the Old Testament as the course book of world history. Historians of the European settlement of the Americas have thoroughly documented how colonial religious leaders were convinced that they were the instruments of a divine plan. The New World was a Promised Land in which the Europeans had arrived after much wandering and travail. Their leaders were seen in the mold of Moses and Aaron—intrepid spiritual figures and able spokesmen. While most Americans understood this Promised Land model as allegorical, some saw the settlement of the New World as the actual fulfillment of biblical promise.

The indigenous inhabitants of the New World—"pagan" in their behavior —could then be viewed in a number of ways. If they were "savages untouched by God's grace," they were condemned to perdition. This view—strengthened by theories that situated the Native Americans outside the category of "the descendants of Adam and Eve"—appealed to those who advocated harsh treatment of the American Indian tribes. In sharp contrast, one Spanish defender of the Indians, the seventeenth-century cleric Bartolome de las Casas, articulated a biblical theory that elevated the Native American tribes above their European conquerors. According to las Casas, the Indians were early descendants of Adam and Eve, who had wandered to remote areas of the earth. Separated from the great majority of humankind, they had not been corrupted by the evils of cities and civilizations. This separation preserved them in an Edenic innocence for the End Time, when they would rejoin a repentant humanity. These End Time ideas did not remain in the realm of the abstract. Like many other visionaries, this Spanish dissident attempted to create a new Eden. "Las Casas and his followers, who tried to create a millennial state in Guatemala without Spanish Conquistadors, introduced a supernatural element into theories about the Indians, namely that some of them had special properties that were crucial in providential times to come."[12]

For las Casas and his followers, the Indians were not of the lost Israelite tribes, rather they were descended from an earlier offshoot of the "Adamite" family tree. But Spanish America, as we have seen with Montezinos's deposition before Rabbi Menasseh Ben Israel, was also the scene of speculation that at least some of the Indians were lost Israelites. In *The Hope of Israel*, Menasseh, after weighing Montezinos's evidence and the reports of other European explorers, concluded that the great majority of indigenous Americans arrived there from Asia. It was possible, he said, "that the group encountered by Montezinos could be part of a lost tribe. This fits with other evidence that the fulfillment of God's Promise is at hand, and that we will witness the redemption of Israel. *The Ten Tribes will emerge and return to join the other two (Judah and Benjamin) in Israel in the near future.*"[13] In the early decades of the eighteenth century, the Jewish-Indian theory was adopted by the eminent New England jurist Samuel Sewall. A colleague of his reported that Sewall would not support a war against the Indians, "not from mere humanity and compassion, but because he was inclined to think that they were part of the ancient people of God and that the tribes, by some means or other, had strolled into America."[14]

These ideas would reverberate in American culture two centuries later. For example, the Church of Jesus Christ of Latter-Day Saints, America's "new religion" of the mid-nineteenth century, would consider the Middle Eastern origins of the Native Americans a matter not of speculation, but of certainty. The Book of Mormon tells of Israelites who came to the New World thousands of years ago. Some of their descendants were the New World Indians discovered by the Europeans. The church hierarchy still deems Mormons who challenge the historicity of this form of the Jewish-Indian theory heretics.[15]

The Original Language

While they did not agree on the multiplicity of claims for linguistic evidence of the Lost Tribes of Israel, Jewish and Christian thinkers did agree on one linguistic matter. For within the Jewish and Christian traditions the assumption that there was *one* original language is the legacy of the biblical tale of the Tower of Babel. When the survivors of the flood and their descendants haughtily set out to build a city with "a tower with its top in the sky" in an effort to make a name for themselves, "The whole world had the same language and the same words" (Genesis 11:1). God, as punishment for the effort to construct this tower, said, "Let us then go down and confound their speech, so that they shall not understand one another's talk. God dispersed them from over the whole earth, and they stopped building the city."

Medieval Jewish thinkers, when they engaged the question of humanity's original language, did not all agree that it was Hebrew. Some relied on an opinion expressed in the Babylonian Talmud (Sanhedrin 38b) that Adam spoke Aramaic in the Garden of Eden. Aramaic was therefore suggested as an earlier, and more sacred, "key to creation." But Hebrew as the original language became the accepted view of most Christian thinkers. St. Jerome, the most philologically sophisticated of the early church fathers, had articulated this concept in his commentaries of the Old Testament. Many later scholars affirmed Jerome's statement, and from the fourth century onwards, the idea of Hebrew as the "primeval" or original language has a long and illustrious history.[16]

Hebrew, because of its perceived "simplicity," was thought to be the most direct and concise of languages. The poet Dante Alighieri (1265–1321), building on traditions already transmitted over a millennium, used religious ideas familiar to his readers to remind them that Hebrew was the language of Adam, and that the first human word was "El, the word for God." As to why Jesus used Hebrew, and why Hebrew words (*Hosanna*, *Sabaoth*) were retained in the text of the New Testament, the great Italian poet offered an inventive Christian theological explanation. "This form of speech was inherited by the sons of Heber, and called Hebrew after him. It remained their peculiar possession after the confusion of the Tower of Babel, so that our Savior, who was their descendant in his humanity, might use a language of grace and not of confusion. The Hebrew language, then, was formed by the lips of those who were the first to speak."[17]

Though he does not state this directly, Dante is here evoking another powerful Christological concept: Jesus is a second Adam who will restore humankind from its fallen state. How fitting it is that the *second* Adam should speak in the tongue granted by God to the *first* Adam. Furthermore, Dante refers to the conundrum of the Jew's persistence in history—and their despised state in Christendom—with his phrase, "their descendant in his humanity." Spiritually, Jesus is the beginning of a new dispensation, one rejected long ago by the very people from whom he sprang. The language of that people, Hebrew, still retains its sanctity for Dante and his readers. The people first associated with that language are yet another matter. They may be despised, but their language is still honored through its "Christian" associations.

At issue here is the ambivalence inherent in Christian study of Hebrew, an ambivalence that springs from the love-hate tension in some Christian views of the Jewish people. The Jews were, at one and the same time, the people who produced Christ, and the enemies of that same Savior. They are both "the people of the Old Dispensation" and the "Murderers of God." The study of Hebrew, the ancient language of this people, evoked for many Christian scholars the same degree of ambivalence and love-hate tension that the study of Jewish ritual and texts did. On the theological plane the resolution of that tension as it applied to the Jews as a people was well-nigh impossible. The Jews remained a mysterious presence in history. Hebrew—with its dual function as representative of the Jews and of Christian origins—offered intellectual grounds on which this incompatibility could be played out, if not resolved. For those Christian scholars and adventurers whose story is told in *God's Sacred Tongue* there was a constant tension between a powerful attraction to Hebrew and a guarded interest in Jewish practices and practitioners. We will see these forces surface again in the twentieth-century encounter between various American Christian groups and the State of Israel.

Christian Hebraism

European ideas of Hebrew as the original language were an integral part of a larger tradition of Christian Hebraism, a tradition whose roots go all the way back to the first Christian centuries. St. Jerome, who so forcefully promoted the idea that Hebrew was the *prima lingua*, or first language of the human race, can be thought of as the first Christian Hebraist. To ensure the authenticity and accuracy of his translation of the books of the Bible into Latin, Jerome journeyed to Palestine, settling near Bethlehem. There, he studied with scholars both Jewish and Christian. Women participated as well in this Christian study of Hebrew, despite strict limitations on women's education and intellectual advancement. Two Roman noblewomen, Paula and Julia, accompanied Jerome to Palestine, where their wealth helped support his scholarly work. He, in turn, included them in his scholarly and religious projects and attested to their proficiency in the "sacred tongue."[18]

From the mid-fourth century when Jerome and his companions lived in Bethlehem, until the Reformation when Hebrew studies were revived, Hebrew studies were only of interest to a very small coterie of biblical exegetes. In medieval Europe the intricacies of the Hebrew language were of little interest to scholars. The Catholic Church saw itself as the "New Israel," replacing the language and culture of the "Old Israel"; the study of the language of the "Old Israel" held little fascination. There were periodic outbursts of interest in the study of Hebrew, most significantly in twelfth- and thirteenth-century England. But it is only with the Renaissance and the Reformation that we find a resurgence of the Christian study of "the sacred language." In the sixteenth century the Church's reformers invoked the concept of *sola scriptura*: only the text of the Bible was to be used as a source of religious authority. In this view, the closer we get to the original meaning of the Bible, the closer we are to God's intentions. In the endeavor of *sola scriptura*, as in the earlier study of Hebrew in the twelfth and thirteenth centuries, England was to move to the forefront of Christian Hebraism. Scholars in Germany, Switzerland, and the Netherlands also made significant contributions to an emerging discourse of Hebrew studies. In 1540, Henry VIII established the

Regius Professorships in Hebrew at Oxford and Cambridge. Knowledge of Hebrew became, in England as on the Continent, the mark of a truly educated person, one with access to the original texts of both the classics and the Bible. In Renaissance Europe, one often finds expressions of admiration for "the trilingual scholar" who was master of the three great languages of antiquity—Greek, Latin, and Hebrew. The "trilingual scholar" was often a woman. Networks of "learned ladies" were established in seventeenth- and eighteenth-century Europe. Members of local political and religious aristocracies, these women formed an alternative to universities and academies that excluded women from higher education. Particularly in Germany, England, and the Low Countries, female Hebraists and Classicists created substitute structures in which they could study texts and engage biblical and post-biblical exegetical questions.[19]

As interest in Hebrew grew, Protestant scholars compiled dictionaries, grammars, and Hebrew chrestomathies, collections of passages from Judaic literature to aid students studying the language. In the sixteenth and early seventeenth centuries, these books were printed widely and used in colleges in Europe and in the new schools of the American colonies. Some Christian scholars in Europe availed themselves of Jewish informants. In Italy, for example, we find much Jewish-Christian scholarly cooperation. But in Germany and Poland mutual suspicion and wariness precluded any such collaborative efforts. The Jews were afraid of Christian missionary activity, while Christians who studied with Jewish scholars were likely to be accused of "Judaising tendencies."

Long before the English Crown established university chairs for the study of Hebrew and "other oriental languages," English Christianity developed a special affinity for the rhetoric of the Bible and its cadences. The notion that Hebrew was first among languages held special fascination for the English. The Venerable Bede, the eighth-century English churchman, was one of a number of early Christian writers who "evince a special fascination with the 'Veritas Hebraica': God's own chosen means of communication with the world." Thus, Bede declares, "Hebrew was the 'prima lingua'—the 'prime' or 'first language' of the human race. Later it was disrupted and dispersed at Babel as a punishment for still another sin of pride. And from that disruption there arose the current multiplicity of languages coexisting with Hebrew, Adam's original tongue."[20]

This English affinity for Hebrew texts and the Hebrew tongue helped set the stage for American Hebraist endeavors. Especially among the founders of the early American colleges, the Hebraist legacies of Oxford and Cambridge were formative influences. As we shall see in later chapters, instruction in Hebrew language and texts were at the core of the early American college curriculum.

Christian Kabbalism

Parallel to the larger traditions of Christian Hebraism, another European cultural tradition emerged: Christian Kabbalism. Many Renaissance-era Christian scholars and mystics sought the "secret doctrine" of the Jews. Jewish mystical traditions, expounded in the thirteenth-century Zohar and other esoteric texts, caught the attention of Christian seekers who eagerly sought confirmation of "the Christian truth" in the Jewish tradition. Knowledge of Hebrew and of Aramaic—the language of the Zohar—was a prerequisite for these investigations; thus, we find some overlap between the Hebraists and the Kabbalists. While many Christian Hebraists sought Hebraic knowledge to proselytize the Jews, this impulse was not dominant among the practitioners of Christian Kabbalism. Many of them looked to common themes in both religious traditions. While this commonality was often more real than imagined, it did presage the development of a less hostile, more irenic view of the Jewish tradition.

The scholars and practitioners of Christian Kabbalism were influenced by the great Renaissance scholar Pico della Mirandola, who died in 1494. Pico was interested in the scholarly aspects of the Jewish mystical tradition, not in the value of Hebrew as a tool for anti-Judaic polemics. He did not seek to convince the Jews, through the evidence of their own sacred writings, to convert to Christianity. Rather, he sought to increase the body of newly discovered knowledge by integrating "hidden" Hebrew classics with the recently discovered and translated texts of the Greco-Roman world. Among these texts were many thought to be ancient, such as those of the Hermetic corpus. Pico set out to create a synthesis of the Hermetic and the kabbalistic. If the Jewish material confirmed and validated the mystical teachings alluded to in the classical texts, so much the better. That would lend an aura of the sacred to the secrets of classical texts, the teachings of which clashed with Christian doctrine and were therefore suspected of being profane. Frances Yates, whose mid-twentieth-century works on Renaissance magic illuminated the cultural centrality of the occult, wrote: "The profound significance of Pico della Mirandola in the history of humanity can hardly be estimated. He it was who first formulated a new position for European man, man as Magus using both Magia and Kabbalah to act upon the world, to control his destiny by science."[21]

In his search for kabbalistic secrets, Pico, the wealthy, influential fifteenth-century count of Mirandola, had help from both Jews and Jewish apostates to Christianity. In his famous *Oration on the Dignity of Man* Pico summarizes his understanding of the Kabbalah and pointedly claims, "I saw in them not so much the Mosaic, as the Christian religion."[22] Pico felt that Hebrew would give students of the mystical path access to a hitherto-concealed "spiritual magic"—one that tapped the higher spiritual powers of the cosmos. This was the magic of the "practical kabbalah, which invokes angels, archangels, the ten sephiroth which are the names or powers of God, God himself, by means some of which are similar to other magical procedures but more particularly through the power of the sacred Hebrew language."[23]

Pico's "discovery" of the Kabbalah has to be viewed in the context of his application of the principles of allegorical interpretation. As the twentieth-century philosopher Ernst Cassirer put it, "Pico makes an unlimited, indeed we could say a hyperbolic, use of allegory." Cassirer, who sought in the fifteenth-century philosopher's work an affirmation of "the perennial philosophy, an enduring truth, in its main features immutable," explained Pico's fascination with the Zohar in this way: "Neither in the Bible nor in any other sacred document is there for him a sentence we can understand in its proper literal sense. There is always needed a difficult interpretation to release the genuine, the mystic and spiritual sense from the literal one. And only when we have penetrated this meaning is the religious truth disclosed to us. For this reason the Kabbalah acquires for Pico a controlling and central significance. For it is the key that first truly unlocks the secrets of the divine nature."[24]

Pico's contact with Jewish scholars and apostates was facilitated by the historical circumstances of his time and place. Late-fifteenth-century Italy was the only country in Europe that welcomed Jewish refugees from the Spanish Inquisition and expulsions. The Italian Humanists eagerly sought out the scholars among these Jews and New Christians. In this the Humanists risked the wrath of the Dominican and Franciscan orders, the members of which "preached frenzied sermons against unbelievers," particularly against the Jews.[25] But their need for authentic sources of information on Jewish matters overrode any scruples the Humanists may have had about associating with unbelievers.

Both the study of the Hebrew language and the study of Jewish mysticism had great influence in English intellectual life. The English cultural legacy, transmitted across the ocean to the American Zion, expressed itself in new ways on American shores. Throughout this examination of American Christian Hebraism, the search for the mystical truth from a Hebraic source is a constant theme. Two subjects of Part I, Harvard's Judah Monis and Yale's Ezra

Stiles, studied kabbalistic texts. Kabbalism is also a previously unnoticed element in the writings of theologian Jonathan Edwards, and it informed the worldview of Joseph Smith, the Mormon prophet.

The American Colonies as Promised Land

In the minds of early American Protestant thinkers, Ancient Israel served as both a model for structuring a covenantal society and a warning of the consequences of failure to adhere to the divine covenant. Literary critic Sacvan Bercovitch, in his studies of typology in American culture, speaks of the "Puritan mythico-historiography" in which "the emigrants had fled England as from certain destruction. Behind them, they believed, lay the failure of European Protestantism—and before them, as their refuge, what they called 'wilderness,' 'desert' . . . The New World, according to that image, was the modern counterpart of the wilderness through which Israel reached Canaan, of the desert where Christ overcame the tempter."[26] The arduous journey of those who left English shores for the New World only strengthened English affinity for the Bible's exhortations, cadences, and images. God had destined these pilgrims to pass through the wilderness to the new Promised Land so that they could create a new society based on biblical models.

America's English colonists saw themselves as a "chosen people" fleeing the pharaohs of Egypt and arriving in the Promised Land. As one colonist wrote, "What shall we say of the singular providence of God bringing so many shiploads of His people, through so many dangers, as upon eagles' wings, with so much safety from year to year?" American religious dissidents, resentful of Puritan triumphalism, were known to satirize this identification with biblical Israel and use it in gentle jibes against the Boston clerical elite. Peter Folger, Benjamin Franklin's grandfather, agreed with his Rhode Island compatriot Roger Williams that the Old Testament had too great a hold on American religious thought. In 1676 he wrote, "New England they are like the Jews, as like as like can be."[27]

And like Jews throughout the Diaspora, New England's laity and clergy established schools that would perpetuate traditions of Hebrew learning. All ten of the colleges founded on American soil before the Revolution offered instruction in "Hebrew and the shemitish languages." Harvard, the first college established in the American colonies, was founded and led by clergymen—scholars whose own academic interests were centered on Hebrew language and textual study. These clergymen endeavored to perpetuate their intellectual legacy in what Cotton Mather dubbed "New England's Beit Midrash."

While expertise in Hebrew was the province of early Harvard's intellectual leadership, the study of the Bible in English was at the core of New England's spiritual life.

For all of the early English settlers, whether they were settled in the North or the South, the Bible was the central text of religious and political discourse. Though few were familiar with "the sacred writ in its original tongue," all knew the Bible in its various English translations. These translations appeared in print from the 1530s onward and they had a profound effect on English religious and political life. The Authorized Version or King James Bible, soon to become the standard text, was completed in 1611, only nine years before the establishment of Plymouth Colony. More than twenty Christian Hebraists, many of them familiar with the classical Jewish commentaries, were among the group of scholars that produced the King James Bible. Some of these scholars had studied with Jewish informants. All of them were heirs to the recently reconsidered Christian ideas about Hebrew and the Bible, ideas that would enter the colonial American mainstream and from there help shape the self-concept of Americans during the early years of the Republic.

2

A TALE OF TWO TEACHERS

HEBREW AT HARVARD

All that are educated in this Seminary of Learning, consider the excellency
of the Holy Scriptures above all the wisdom of the world.
Samuel Langdon, president of Harvard, 1776
The Puritans of New England were obsessed by the Jewish Bible,
but they were not hospitable to Jews, or to Judaism.
Arthur Hertzberg

Harvard's College Hall was filled to capacity. The assembled crowd of students, faculty, and townspeople, was hushed. On the morning of Sunday,
March 27, 1722, they were gathered to witness the baptism of Rabbi Judah
Monis—"formerly of Leghorn, Italy and Amsterdam." The *New England Courant* of that week reported, "The solemnity was attended by a considerable
part of the Church in this town, and as numerous an Assembly as the place
would admit." A month after his baptism Monis was appointed instructor in
Hebrew at Harvard College. He taught at the college for the next forty years.

The occasion of Monis's baptism, a singular and noteworthy event in early-
eighteenth-century New England, provides a rich point of departure for an
investigation of the role of the Hebrew language in emergent colonial American culture. At the baptism the Rev. Benjamin Colman, the officiating clergyman, praised Monis's much-vaunted learning: "He is truly read and learned in
the Jewish Cabbala and Rabbins, a Master and critic in the Hebrew; he reads,
speaks, writes, and interprets it with great readiness and accuracy and is truly
didaktos, apt to teach."[1]

Colman had opened the baptism ceremony with a discourse on John 5:46
in which Jesus says, "For had ye believed Moses, ye would have believed me;
for he wrote of me." The *New England Courant* reproduced the essence of
that discourse, and made special note of Judah Monis's reply. Colman expounded on John 5:46, "from which Words he showed how exactly several
notable Passages of Moses' writings have been accomplished in our Savior
Jesus Christ. The rabbi followed this with a learned Discourse, answering

(from the holy scriptures and their own approved authors) nine of the chief arguments brought by the modern Jews to prove that the Messiah is not yet come." More scriptural citation and exegesis followed. The newspaper capped its report of the event noting that Monis "concluded with a solemn Profession of his Faith in the Messiah already come." Historian of ideas Frank Manuel has suggested that New England Puritans, Calvinist in their thinking and ritual, were apt to think of the conversion of the Jews as an act that would remove the stigma attached to that people. "Among Calvinists, it was only the failure of the Jews to accept Christ that stood in the way of a total approval of Jewish experience."[2]

For the New England clergy the baptism of a Jewish scholar was a rare and religiously significant event. Increase Mather, Harvard's president pro tempore, had confided to his diary, "I desire nothing more than the conversion of the Jews." His son, Cotton Mather, shared his progenitor's fervor for the long-awaited conversion of the Jews and eagerly awaited the opportunity to be present at the baptism of a Jew. Twenty-six years earlier Cotton Mather had written in his diary, "This day, from the dust, where I lay prostrate, before the Lord, I lifted up my cries: For the conversion of the Jewish Nation and for my own having the happiness, at some time or other, to baptize a Jew, that should be my ministry, brought home to the Lord."[3] Though the younger Mather's greater hopes concerning the Jewish nation were not to be realized, each individual conversion of a Jew to Christianity struck him as that much more significant (that there were more than a total of three such conversions in colonial New England is doubtful). This was especially true of the conversion of someone of Monis's maturity and eminence. For Monis was not a young man. He was close to forty when he converted to Christianity, and he had served as a rabbi in New York before moving to Cambridge, Massachusetts. While the elder Mather, Increase, was in fact too ill to attend the baptism, the younger members of the family were there. We may imagine that Monis's future wife Abigail Marret and her father, a respected Cambridge merchant, were in church for the occasion as well, although the *New England Courant* did not attest to their presence.

Cotton Mather and his fellow New England clergymen eagerly accepted and spread any rumor of the conversion of Jews. They firmly believed that "the millennium was near and was to be much hastened by the immediate conversion of the Jews after their complete dispersion through every country of the world." In numerous pamphlets, first among them *Faith of the Fathers* (dedicated to "The Jewish Nation"), Cotton Mather called on the Jews to "Return, O Backsliding Israel" and to recognize that Christianity was the true heir to the legacy of the Old Testament. With no more than a handful of Jews in the American colonies in the early eighteenth century, one wonders how many of "the Jewish Nation" actually read these tracts. Increase Mather, it seems, had convinced Judah Monis that baptism would ensure him a position as instructor of Hebrew at Harvard. In recognition of his scholarly accomplishments the college had awarded him an M.A. in 1720. Monis became the recipient of "the only degree conferred upon a Jew by Harvard, and actually of any college in America, prior to 1800." But he was to remain a Jew for another two years only. Whether he was able to assume a Christian identity and "lose" his Jewish identity is an issue that will concern us throughout this chapter.[4]

It was the New England clergy's veneration of Hebrew, the "primeval language," and their eschatological hopes for the conversion of the Jews that made Monis so desirable a catch for the Puritan divines. As historian Jacob Rader Marcus trenchantly observed, "Hebraic studies were most intense in Colonial New England where Jews were conspicuous by their absence . . . The original Puritans were interested in Hebrew and in ancient Hebrews . . . but not in their descendants as long as they remained Jews." Increase Mather, whose respect for Hebrew learning was considerable, had great hopes for Monis: "God grant that he, who is the first Jew that I ever knew converted in New England, may prove a blessing unto many, and especially some of his own nation." Within a year, Increase Mather, ill at the time that he wrote these words, passed away. As we know of no other cases of Jewish conversion in this period of colonial history, Monis truly fulfilled one of the aging minister's hopes.[5]

Despite the welcoming enthusiasms of the Mathers and other New England notables, an element of distrust lingered in the clergy's attitude toward Monis. His acceptance was not complete. At Monis's public baptism, Rev. Colman assured the assembled that Monis was sincere in adopting his new faith: "There is no cause to fear that Mr. Monis will Renounce his Christianity since he did embrace it voluntarily and gradually"; Monis was "a Jew in whom there is no guile." This New Testament phrase appears a number of times throughout the history of Hebrew in America. It was used to express approval of Jewish scholars who "brought treasures" to Christian exegetical and theological discourse.

A Private Life

Monis's family origins were obscure. Eisig Silberschlag noted in a 1970s essay on Monis: "An aura of mystery surrounds this enigmatic personality: was he an Italian or an Algerian Jew? Was his conversion to Christianity at the age of 39—the conversion of a man who served as rabbi in the New World and who continued to his death to observe the seventh day as the Sabbath—an act of his faith or an act of opportunism?" According to the pamphlet issued at his ceremony of baptism, Monis was "sometime rabbi of the synagogue in Jamaica, and afterwards in New York, who commenced Maskil Venabon, in the Jewish Academies of Leghorn and Amsterdam etc."[6] His contemporaries said nothing of his birthplace and childhood. Did Monis deliberately obscure his family history? He surely took no pains to inform any of his contemporaries of his origins. One of his Harvard students described him as "a Jew of Algiers," but we have no confirmation of this description. Through a bit of scholarly detective work, George Foot Moore, Harvard's early-twentieth-century scholar of early Judaism and comparative religion, concluded that the Monis family settled in Northern Italy, to which they had emigrated from Portugal. There they lived as "Marranos" until they found the opportunity to immigrate to the New World. Moore and others considered the reference to Monis as "sometime rabbi" of the synagogue in Jamaica to refer to the Caribbean island of Jamaica. "Of his residence in Jamaica, no record has hitherto been found, but in view of the commercial relations of the island, it is entirely probable."[7] More recently, however, scholars have pointed out that Monis was living in Jamaica, *Long Island*, before he moved to Massachusetts and that he may have served a small Jewish congregation in that New York town.[8]

Soon after moving from Long Island to Cambridge, Monis took a job at the local hardware store. He and the owner's daughter, Abigail Marret, met and fell in love. In order to marry, Monis had to be baptized. He hoped to find love and a profession through conversion to Christianity. After his baptism in 1722, Monis married Abigail and began a teaching career at Harvard that would last nearly four decades. Despite his adoption of the Christian faith, he remained "Rabbi" Monis to his Harvard colleagues and students, never rising above the level of instructor.

Monis's marriage to Abigail Marret seems to have been a happy one. After years of living frugally on Judah's Harvard salary and income from the hardware store, they were able to purchase pasture land which yielded some small income. In 1753 Monis petitioned the state legislature for a grant to supplement his Harvard salary. In the petition, in which he referred to himself in the third person, he mentioned that he had little income from the family hardware store, and even less from the acreage. "What he receives from his instructing is meager and he fears that he shall now in his old age, be obliged not only to expend the little that he now has left, but be reduced to want." Whether Monis's request was accepted or denied is not recorded.

Abigail Monis died in 1760. She had shared her husband's "respectable obscurity" for more than thirty-five years. Soon after Abigail's death, Judah resigned from Harvard. Now alone in Cambridge, he decided to move to Northborough, Massachusetts, where Abigail's brother, John Martyn, was a

Congregational pastor. In that small Massachusetts town Monis was an active participant in church and other communal affairs for the next four years.

In 1764 at the age of eighty-one Judah Monis died. He had led a vigorous physical and intellectual life until his last few months. "Before his death he professed his firm belief in the Christian religion and left the bulk of his estate as a permanent fund for poor widows of Christian ministers."[9] He left three unusual silver communion cups to the First Church of Northborough. These particularly valuable cups are now in museum collections in Boston and Worcester. His estate "continued to be administered by the American Unitarian Association into the twentieth century."[10] The Massachusetts Convention of Congregational Ministers currently administers the estate, and widows of ministers still benefit from it.

Judah Monis was buried in the Northborough, Massachusetts, churchyard.[11] His epitaph, still clearly visible on his elegant tombstone, reads as follows:

Here lies buried the Remains of Rabbi
JUDAH MONIS, MA. Late HEBREW
Instructor at HARVARD College in
Cambridge in which office He continued 40
years. He was by Birth and Religion a Jew but
embraced the Christian Faith & was publicly
baptised at Cambridge AD 1722 and
departed this life April 25 1764 Aged
81 years 2 months and 21 days

A native branch of Jacob see
Which, once from its olive broke
Regrafted, from the living tree   Rom. XI
Of the reviving sap partook.

From teeming Zion's fertile womb   Isai.LXVI.8
As dewy drops in early morn,   Psal.CX.3
Or rising bodies from the tomb   John V.28,29
At once be Israel's nation born.   Isai.LXVI.8

A Career at Harvard

Despite Judah Monis's dedication and evident religious sincerity, his career at Harvard was a troubled and uneasy one. His colleagues and students persisted in calling him "rabbi"—his obvious Jewish origins could not be obscured. His colleagues did not take his teaching or scholarship seriously, and his students often mocked him. Benjamin Colman noted early in Monis's career that his fellow Harvard tutors "are not so just and honourable to him as were to be desired." Toward the end of his career, both students and colleagues questioned his competence as teacher and scholar. During the first decade of his career there were twenty to thirty students in his classes. Later, only a handful attended. Remarkably, Monis was not embittered by his inability to rise in the Harvard ranks or by the stinging criticism and occasional ridicule heaped upon him over the years. He accepted his fate with humility and dignity.

According to the stipulations of his contract, Monis was required to teach Hebrew to all Harvard College students. Only the first-year students were exempt. Students attended his classes four days a week; few of them, it seems, were pleased about that requirement. From 1722 to 1734 each student had to make his own copy of Monis's Hebrew grammar. This was an arduous task—especially the reproduction of the verb paradigms and the vowel points. Monis insisted that these be copied precisely; in the debate among Christian Hebraists as to the value of the Hebrew vowels Monis sided with those who insisted that Hebrew without its "points" was incomplete and unintelligible. But this task was not assigned to single out unruly or lazy students. Copying textbooks was the norm during Harvard's first century and the study of Hebrew was no exception. When in 1734 the college underwrote the publication of Monis's grammar, one thousand copies were printed. Monis sold most of the printing to his students and to Christian clergymen in the Boston area.

With the elimination of the requirement to copy out the Hebrew grammar by hand, one might assume that student opinion of Monis's classes would improve. This does not seem to have been the case. Students took out their frustrations on their copies of Monis's Hebrew grammar. In one copy a student has defaced the book's cover, changing the words "Instruction in the Primitive tongue by their own study" to "Destruction of the Brimstone Tongue by their own Stupidity." In another copy the words "composed and accurately corrected by Judah Monis, M.A." were transformed into "Confuted and accurately corrupted by Judah Monis, M.(aker of) A.(sses)."[12]

A decade after the printing of Monis's grammar, in 1745, a Harvard student, obviously displeased with Monis, was fined for "breaking the windows of the Hebrew School." This small building, set aside for Monis, gained notoriety as a magnet for student anger and an outlet for student frustration. Toward the end of Monis's career, in the fall term of 1758, the Hebrew School was still the object of hostility. Faculty records record "an insult having been offered to Mr. Judah Monis, the Hebrew instructor by throwing bricks, sticks, ashes etc. in at the door of the Hebrew School while he was instructing his pupils there." The records go on to name five students involved and record their punishment: "That all of them be subjected to a public admonition in the chapel, some to suffer depredation and some a pecuniary punishment."

Monis's long years of service to the college were not rewarded. By the late 1740s the college curriculum was undergoing radical change and the need for the Hebrew instructor's services was diminished considerably. Monis's teaching responsibilities were reduced and he taught only one day a week. At times Monis returned to work in his in-laws' hardware store, thus supplementing his meager income. We know from the record book of Harvard president Benjamin Wadsworth that Monis's salary was always below that of the lowest-paid tutor at the college. College records show that in the 1730s Monis sold the following objects to the Harvard Corporation: nails, locks, iron, lathes, pipes, tobacco, and hinges. Because he was engaged in commerce, the corporation voted him the low teaching salary of fifty English pounds per year. His salary rose over the four decades of his career, but "although Monis's salary was increased periodically, it seems that his usefulness as teacher decreased."[13]

The German Jewish poet Heinrich Heine was to observe a century later, "The baptismal certificate is the entry ticket into European culture." The same could be said of entry into the New England culture of the early eighteenth century, and especially of entry into the ranks of one particular elite of that culture, the faculty of Harvard College. Monis entered those ranks, but never rose in them. For his close to forty years as a teacher, he remained at the level of instructor. Despite his adoption of the Christian faith, he remained "Rabbi" Monis in the eyes of his colleagues and students. It was not until after his death that Harvard appointed a Hebrew teacher of professorial rank to the faculty. This was Stephen Sewall, a former student of Judah Monis whose troubled career we will follow later in this chapter.

A Teacher of Hebrew

For New England Puritans Hebrew was a valuable tool for New Testament study. Monis stated in a letter to the Harvard overseers, "I think the more acquainted the Ministers of the Gospel are with the Hebrew tongue, and so with the Old Testament, the better able they will be to understand the New Testament and so to preach our glorious Lord Jesus Christ who was spoken of by all the Old Testament Prophets."[14] The Hebraic background and Hebrew vocabulary embedded in New Testament texts provided Monis the opportunity to demonstrate that Christianity was the natural fulfillment of Judaism. Whether or not Monis believed in the doctrines he was validating remains an open question.

Monis was not the first instructor of Hebrew at Harvard. In 1722, the year of his appointment, Hebrew language instruction already had a long history at the college. Since the founding of Harvard in 1636, the "learned languages"—Latin, Greek, and Hebrew—had been at the core of the curriculum, with Hebrew having special pride of place. According to Harvard historian Samuel Eliot Morison, the college's first two presidents, Dunster and Chauncy, were both good Hebrew scholars. In addition to Hebrew, they studied and taught Aramaic, Arabic, and Ethiopic.[15]

Harvard, though often identified as a "seminary," was much more than that. It was a college in the European sense of the word. Only one-third of its graduates were ordained as ministers; the majority served the colonies in other ways, or entered the world of commerce. As Harvard's overseers saw it, even these more worldly graduates needed some Hebrew knowledge. Hebrew and the classical heritage were hallmarks of an educated person. As Morison noted, "It cannot be emphasized too strongly that the cultivation of the Hebrew Scriptures in early New England was a continuation of an honorable humanistic European tradition."

Harvard students tended to acknowledge the justifications for the study of Greek and Latin—both sacred and secular, but they put up considerable resistance to daily engagement with the grammatical and syntactical rules of Hebrew, "that ancient tongue." Greek carried with it the nobility of the classical world and the sanctity of the earliest New Testament manuscripts. Latin remained the language of scholarship throughout the colonial period; all college *entrants* were expected to read and "converse" in Latin. The Hebrew language and the people of Israel were associated with religious piety and obscurantism, not qualities that would endear them to students. We have seen that Monis's students took out their frustrations on him directly—and when they could not do that they defaced their copies of his Hebrew grammar.

A Scholar of Hebrew

At the baptism in 1722, Rev. Colman had praised Monis's scholarship and erudition—"to crown all, his knowledge of the Old and New Testaments was very happy and extraordinary." What has survived of Monis's scholarly work does not bear out this claim. His one published work, *The Hebrew Grammar*, with its striking examples of Christian Hebraica, including the Lord's Prayer in rabbinic Hebrew, was riddled with inconsistencies and errors and burdened with a system of transliteration for English-speaking students that one twentieth-century scholar has characterized as "monstrous." During his close to forty years as teacher of Hebrew at Harvard, his students complained many times about the inadequacies of his book and his teaching methods.

Monis's unpublished manuscripts have fared no better than his grammar book in the evaluations of modern scholars. *Nomenclatura hebraica*, a small Hebrew-English dictionary compiled for the use of his students, was discovered in the Harvard College library in 1910. A contemporary Hebraist characterized this meager dictionary as "sloppy, shoddy, and deceptive," with neologisms that could be described as "grammatical monstrosities." But these inadequacies, if they were recognized in the eighteenth century, did not dampen the New England Divines' enthusiasm for the reception of Monis into the Christian fold. They recognized that "a Jew rarely comes over to us but he brings treasures with him."[16] Christian interest in extrabiblical subjects cannot be explained solely by Christian interest in Old Testament exegesis, since existing tools of scholarship could be easily deployed to satisfy that interest. This scholarship included the great number of Hebrew dictionaries and grammars circulating in the Protestant world, many of them written by practicing Hebraists in every Protestant country. All of these were a rich source of information about matters biblical and Hebraic. What someone like Monis could provide was access to "new" Hebraic material that shed light on Christian doctrine and belief; he would accomplish this by providing new insights into Jewish *and* Christian texts.

The variety of texts and genres that Monis taught and studied reflect the multifaceted interests of Christian Hebraists. In addition to the Hebrew of the Bible he taught rabbinic Hebrew; he also studied kabbalistic manuscripts. Monis's interest in kabbalistic lore and texts has been overlooked in many earlier evaluations of his life and career. In light of Gershom Scholem's reassessment of the importance of Kabbalah for both the Jewish and Christian intellectual traditions, it behooves us to investigate thoroughly Monis's interest in, and study of, Jewish mystical texts. The alternatives offered by earlier researchers—either that Monis was a Marrano who clung to Jewish ritual and some vestige of Jewish religious identity (as per G. A. Kohut), or that he fully embraced Christian doctrine and practices for reasons of convenience of belief or some mixture of pragmatism and belief (as per G. F. Moore)—need to be nuanced. Kabbalism, of both the Christian and Jewish varieties, may be one key to Monis's interior life, and it might help to explain his assertion that his affirming view of Christianity's messianic claims was based on Jewish mystical writings.

In the three discourses that Monis published on the occasion of his baptism, he made use of kabbalistic sources. These included the *Sefer Yetzirah*, the Zohar, and the writings of the Lurianic Kabbalists. These and other texts were pressed into service for the purpose of proving that the Jewish mystics had perceived the "truth" of Christian doctrine. In the distant past the Kabbalists may have deliberately obscured their conclusions about the "Christian Truth."

Now, Monis claimed, was the time to reveal a Christian understanding of the "true meaning" of the various Jewish textual traditions.[17]

Among the kabbalistic manuscripts that Monis copied into his own hand is a collection of abstracts from *Emet Le-Ya'akov*, an eighteenth-century commentary on the writings of Rabbi Isaac Luria (1533–72) ("The Ari"). Harvard's George Foot Moore, basing his conclusions on the mystical arguments advanced in Monis's *Three Discourses*, concluded that "Monis not only was acquainted with a considerable range of Cabbalistic literature, but that he attributed it to the highest authority." While Rabbi G. A. Kohut mentions the existence of this manuscript he does not confront its content or implications. Kohut, as a Reform thinker, shared Reform Judaism's embarrassment about Jewish mysticism.[18]

The question of Monis's mystical inclinations now takes on aspects of a tale of scholarly detection. Moore, finding that kabbalistic material was outside the areas of his expertise, which included early rabbinic Judaism but did not include the study of Jewish mystical texts, conferred in the 1920s with the eminent Talmudist Louis Ginzberg of New York's Jewish Theological Seminary. Moore, with Ginzberg's assistance, identified the close to four hundred pages of Monis's manuscript as a collection of Lurianic texts that included a biography of Rabbi Luria, writings of his most influential disciple, Rabbi Hayyim Vital, and texts penned by lesser kabbalistic luminaries of the Lurianic School. These teachings originated in Palestine, in the city of Safed, and among the European cities in which they took hold were Leghorn and Amsterdam, cities in which Monis, according to his certificate of ordination, was trained. Had Monis been influenced by Dutch and Italian teachers of Kabbalah? Had that influence worked to convince him that Christian claims about the Messiah were true? There is some evidence that this was so. Yes, baptism enabled him to marry into a Cambridge merchant family and to join the Harvard faculty— at however low a rank. But was convenience the only reason for his apostasy? Perhaps Monis sincerely believed that the path he was following was his destiny.

"Nothing but the Truth," the third of Monis's published discourses, "proves the Doctrine of the Trinity—both out of the Old Testament and with the Authority of the Cabalistical Rabbis, Ancient and Modern." Monis's use of "Cabalistic" sources to "prove" Christian doctrine had a venerable, if not scientifically and methodologically rigorous, lineage. "Christian Kabbalism"— the use of kabbalistic texts and symbols to validate Christian doctrine (especially Christian arguments against Jewish belief)—had its origins in the Renaissance and the Reformation. During the years between 1480 and 1650 many Christian thinkers and writers made use of kabbalistic materials in one fashion or another. In an age when European thinkers were searching for all-encompassing systems of knowledge, "the Hebrew cabala made an excellent subject for the type of treatment given by these seekers of synthesis." The Italian Renaissance figure Pico della Mirandola was the author of the first of the Christian Kabbalist grand syntheses. Pico, unwittingly, was the "mediator and introducer of Kabbalism to the Christian world." Both Jewish scholars and Jewish apostates to Christianity played a role in the dissemination of these mystical ideas. Judah Monis, born within a half-century of Christian Kabbalism's greatest flourishing and imbued with mystical teachings through his European rabbinical training, was directly in that line of influence.

A Question of Sincerity

According to the testimony of his colleagues, Monis and his wife kept the Sabbath on the biblical seventh day, Saturday, rather than on Sunday, the day designated by Christians as the Lord's Day. G. A. Kohut, early-twentieth-century Reform rabbi and scholar, saw Monis's adherence to Jewish Sabbath observance as proof of Monis's Marrano origins. "He remained loyal to Israel at heart, while apparently devoted to Christianity. Like Heine, Boerne, and others, he changed his faith in name only, in order to reach the object of his ambitions. . . . It is evident that Monis, though converted, was a Jew at heart, and a Christian in public life." [19]

The issue of seventh-day Sabbath observance is not as straightforward as Kohut suggests, since seventh-day observance is not necessarily an indicator of Jewish allegiance. For the question of when to mark the Sabbath was one that had divided the English churches since the English Revolution of the 1640s. While some English Baptists (and their New England counterparts) concluded that "Christians were required to observe, along with the synagogue, the seventh day, as the only true Sabbath," some Puritans taught that Old Testament injunctions against work on the Sabbath day "had been transferred to the New Covenant first day of the week." This understanding was based on the New Testament's teaching that Jesus was raised from the dead on the first day of the week (Matthew 28:1). The interdenominational polemics on this issue had swept through the American colonies at the end of the seventeenth century and one can imagine that Judah Monis's insistence on seventh-day Sabbath observance was understood if not easily accepted. For it touched on the question of Monis's Jewish origins as well as raising issues of sectarianism within the New England churches. As to Monis's actual responses to being identified as Jewish throughout his life, he left us no record.

Scholarly opinion is sharply divided on the sincerity of Monis's conversion to Christianity. As noted above, G. A. Kohut saw Monis as continuing the legacy of Marrano culture from which his family emerged. His conversion to Christianity then was insincere. And when possible, the former rabbi hewed to Jewish ritual practice. In contrast, George Foot Moore has no doubt of the sincerity of Monis's new religious convictions. Is this disagreement merely a reflection of those scholars' circumstances? Kohut, a Reform rabbi in Dallas at the end of the nineteenth century, was affirming the continuity of Jewish tradition. In a Jewish community not yet secure in the American religious landscape, the affirmation of continuity was all important. Yes, Kohut seems to be saying, Jewish scholars might apostatize, but in their innermost selves they remained Jews. For Moore, a Harvard historian of the development of rabbinic Judaism and its relationship to early Christianity, Monis's religious choices were clear. His Jewish beliefs and practices were subsumed into his "fulfilled" Christian identity. If his colleagues and students persisted in calling Monis "rabbi," it was out of personal or religious antagonism, not because Monis persisted in his Judaism. Yes, Monis may have observed the Sabbath on Saturday, but this could have arisen as the result of a *Christian* decision.

Perhaps we are placing too much emphasis on theology and religious orthodoxy. Even in Puritan New England in the first decades of the eighteenth century, there was more to important personal decisions than questions of creed. As Samuel Eliot Morison noted in the *The Intellectual Life of Colonial New England*, the Puritans were not as "puritanical" as their later detractors claimed. In the realm of marriage they had something in common with Jews who, like them, eschewed celibacy and sexual abstinence. "In its attitude toward love, Puritanism had more in common with Judaism than with medieval Christianity or Jesuit piety. . . . The clergy married young and often; their church offered no monastic retreat for men who were too much troubled by women. Milton's invocation 'Hail wedded love!' in *Paradise Lost* expresses the puritan ideal very neatly." Such perceived parallels to Jewish thought and practice led the Puritans' detractors to label them "Jews" or "Judaizers." Historian James T. Adams revived this idea in the early twentieth century, calling the Puritans "Jews and not Christians" and emphasizing the "Jewish" nature of the Puritan Sabbath.[20]

A number of European parallels to Monis's apostasy and subsequent teaching career suggest themselves. Some of these were contemporaneous with Monis's life. Others were close enough to his time and unusual enough to have lodged in the memories of Christian observers. In the late seventeenth century, Rabbi Johan Kemper, a Polish Jew who immigrated to Sweden and converted to Christianity, was appointed professor of Hebrew at the University of Uppsala. This appointment had implications beyond his individual case for it sparked an intense Swedish interest in the study of Hebrew, the Bible, and the Jewish textual tradition. During Kemper's long tenure at the University of Uppsala he "trained a whole generation of Swedish scholars in Oriental and Rabbinic studies."[21] Kemper remained loyal to the Swedish church throughout his life. As he had changed his name at baptism, his Jewish origins were not immediately apparent to his students, and as far as we know he did not continue to observe Jewish ritual practices. In the early seventeenth century, another rabbi, Naphtali Margolioth, apostatized and was appointed to the professorship of Hebrew at the University of Altdorf, Germany. As Colman described it in his preface to Monis's *Baptismal Discourse*, this scholar, who took the Christian name Julius Conrad Otto, "quitted his profession and returned to Judaism after decades as a practicing Christian." Even more troubling to Colman was the late-seventeenth-century story of Freidrich Albert Christiani, "a Rabbinical Professor at Vienna, who was thought to be Zealous for Christianity, so that he translated Paul's Greek Epistle to the Hebrews into the Hebrew tongue." He too "returned to his Judaism." Rabbi Judah Monis, Colman assured his readers, was not one of these backsliders. Monis would remain steadfast in his Christianity.[22]

Colman's inclusion of Judah Monis in the roster of eminent European Hebraists of Jewish origin was relevant to Christian observers of the Jews. For the baptism at College Hall was of more than local interest. News of Monis's conversion reached ministers and scholars throughout the American colonies. It also proved to be of interest to European observers of the American cultural and religious situation. Soon after officiating at Monis's baptism, Colman wrote to his friend Robert Wodrow, a Scottish Presbyterian scholar and pastor of a church near Glasgow. He and Colman had carried on a rich and varied correspondence since 1717, for Wodrow was an archivist of the Presbyterian church and a historian of development within the Protestant denominations. He was especially interested in religious change in the American colonies. Colman assured his correspondent, as he had assured the readers of Monis's *Discourse*, that the newly converted rabbi was sincere in his convictions. What pleased Colman most were not only Monis's public profession of faith, but also his declared determination to work for the conversion of "his nation." That nation, "that once beloved people" in Colman's phrase, might be brought closer to Christianity through the prayers of believers, and through the efforts of prominent converts from Judaism, such as Judah Monis.[23] Judah Monis, in a follow-up to Colman's letter, wrote to Wodrow in Hebrew. Wodrow, unable to read the letter ("my Hebrew is rusted") had to ask some Edinburgh University colleagues for assistance. With their assistance—and with the help of a Hebrew-English dictionary—he deciphered Monis's missive. That letter echoes a strange admixture of Christian and Jewish themes—all expressed in rabbinic Hebrew. The letter is dated (in Hebrew) "in the year of the Messiah of Righteousness, 1723."

Despite reservations about the sincerity of Monis's conversion, Monis's Harvard faculty later used his name to enforce New England's theological orthodoxies. In the *Dictionary of American Biography*, early-twentieth-century Harvard Jewish studies professor Harry Wolfson mentions that Monis's name appeared on letters concerning George Whitefield (1744). These letters from Monis and his Harvard colleagues condemned the religious enthusiasms of Whitefield and other New Lights preachers. Monis and all other members of the Harvard faculty joined in distancing themselves from that charismatic English preacher and his American followers.

One wonders what Judah Monis, at the end of his long life, felt about his religious and professional choices. He had lived half his life as a devout Christian. Did he regret his decision to apostatize? Did the memory of his years in European and North African Jewish communities and Talmudic academies return to haunt him? Did he yearn for a community from which he had separated himself forever? And what of the small Jewish communities to which Rabbi Monis had ministered before moving to Cambridge and the Harvard faculty? Did they know of their former rabbi's apostasy and his long teaching career? If so, they no doubt thought of him as a *meshummad*, an apostate to an alien and hostile religion, an individual with whom they should have no further contact. As Judah Monis left us no diary, no spiritual autobiography, no deathbed retraction or recanting of his apostasy, we can only conclude that he was at peace with his momentous decision to join the Christian faith.

The story of Monis at Harvard has captured the imagination of Jewish scholars for more than a century. A list of the authors of the scholarly papers on Judah Monis, the first of which appeared a century ago, in 1889, is a veritable "who's who" of Semitic and Judaic studies in American colleges and universities. It is as if on entering the academy these scholars had to confront the ghost of the first American college teacher whose career was dedicated to Hebrew. First among these authors was G. A. Kohut, Reform rabbi and educator, whose 1889 article "Judah Monis, M.A." appeared in W. R. Harper's *American Journal of Semitic Languages and Literatures* (now the University of Chicago's *Journal of Near Eastern Studies*). Twenty years later, in 1919, George Foot Moore, Harvard's first professor of comparative religion and author of the magisterial work *Judaism*, presented a detailed paper on Judah Monis to the Massachusetts Historical Society. Other lesser luminaries, among them "scholarly amateurs" who had an abiding interest in the history of Jewish life at Harvard University, produced scholarly work on Monis's life, teaching career, and writings. The commemoration of Harvard's 350th anniversary in 1986 was a cause for further inquiry into Harvard Hebraism in general and Judah Monis in particular.

Fascination with Monis is a reflection of these authors' interest in the ambivalence inherent in Christian Hebraism. This tension is evident to all modern scholars who follow the history of Hebraism. Through their study of the Hebrew language and Hebrew texts, premodern Christian scholars sought validation of the Christian idea of the superseded but still sacred Old Testament. St. Jerome offered a concise expression of this idea in his famous dictum: "In the Old Testament, the New Testament is concealed. In the New Testament, the Old Testament is revealed." A source for such validation was the sacred literature of the Jews, the very people who had rejected Jesus and the "Christian truth." Were the postbiblical Jewish texts reliable sources for scriptural interpretation and theological speculation? Or had their authors, hostile to Christological interpretations, deliberately obscured the "true" meaning of those ancient texts? These and other unsettling questions presented themselves to Christian Hebraists. They would answer these questions in a variety of provocative and engaging ways. Their solutions to the conundrum presented by Hebraism—were Jewish texts a source of truth or a source of lies?—would be varied and creative.

A Harvard Professorship in Hebrew

In 1764, the year of Monis's death, Boston businessman Thomas Hancock left a thousand pounds to establish a "professorship of the oriental languages, especially the Hebrew," at Harvard College. (The languages of the Middle East and of the Far East were at that period all deemed "oriental.") The Harvard Corporation established the Hancock Professorship of Hebrew the following year. Among the rules of the appointment was Hancock's provision that on the day before the new faculty member's induction into office "he shall publicly declare himself to be of the Protestant reformed religion, as it is now professed and practiced in the churches of New England." Were Hancock and the Harvard overseers concerned that another rabbinical figure would occupy a position so important in the life of the college? Did Judah Monis's forty-year career at Harvard leave the faculty with a bitter doctrinal taste in its mouth? Stephen Sewall, the first Hancock professor, expressed his discomfort with his predecessor's foreignness in a letter to his close friend and associate Thaddeus Mason Harris: "Monis . . . the aged incumbent, was a Jew of Algiers. Becoming a convert to the Christian religion, and publicly Baptized at Cambridge in 1722, he was appointed to teach a language, which, though he perfectly understood himself, as a grammarian and philologist, he was not happy in enabling others to understand. He retained, moreover a great fondness for rabbinical lore, and his criticisms were so abstruse, and his conversation and manners so uncourteous that he did not conciliate the respect of his pupils, and attendance on his teaching was deemed a disgusting requisition." Professor Sewall was equally harsh (though not as prolix) in his condemnation of Monis's *Hebrew Grammar*. In a letter to English Hebraist and clergyman Richard Grey (1694–1771), Sewall explained Harvard's intention to introduce a new Hebrew grammar "in room of a very bad one, which had been used before, and was then out of print."[24]

In 1765, a year after the deaths of both Judah Monis and Thomas Hancock, Stephen Sewall's appointment was marked in a public ceremony. As stipulated in the Hancock grant, Sewall had to affirm his belief in the Westminster Confession, but this was a mere formality and only a small part of the instillation ceremony. How very different this was from the widely publicized baptism of Judah Monis. In Boston, and at Harvard, the public profession of religious convictions was less important than it had been half a century earlier.

While Sewall's religious background proved perfectly acceptable to the Harvard overseers, his class background may have raised some eyebrows among the highly class conscious Boston aristocracy. Born into a poor Maine family, Sewall, the youngest of ten children, apprenticed to a local shipbuilder and worked until he was twenty-three years old to raise money for his Harvard tuition. Despite his late start at college (or, perhaps, because of it), Sewall excelled in many academic fields, including what was then dubbed "natural philosophy" or the study of scientific principles and their application. The college overseers, on the lookout for promising students who could fit the recently reconfigured idea of what a college teacher should be—an expert in a discipline, rather than a tutor who was a guide to instruction in all subjects—took note of his teaching talents while he was still an undergraduate. The science of philology, then emerging from the control of church doctrine, was the area in which the young Stephen Sewall chose to excel. He invested his considerable intellectual energies in the study of Hebrew and the wider field of "oriental languages." In his public lectures and classroom teaching his approach was methodical, consistent, and "scientific" in its presentation.

When the Harvard Corporation chose Stephen Sewall to succeed Judah Monis, Sewall was, unlike his predecessor, appointed to professorial rank. The Hancock professorship stipulated that the teaching model for the Hebrew appointment should be similar to that of the other recently established university professorships. The incumbent would (1) deliver public lectures that were open to the whole student body, (2) tutor those students who were specializing in this field, and (3) give private instruction to advanced students who wished to study beyond the requirements of the undergraduate curriculum.

While Monis's duties had been limited to language instruction and the supervision of the recitation of Hebrew texts, Sewall was charged with the additional responsibility of delivering lectures on the history and development of the Hebrew language and its religious and literary traditions. The Harvard records show that Sewall, soon after his appointment to the Hebrew professorship, embarked on an "eight-year series of seventy-two lectures which discussed the grammatical genius of Hebrew and other oriental languages— Chaldee, Syriac, Samaritan, Ethiopic, Arabic and Persic," to use the linguistic terms of the period. As historian of Harvard College Thomas Jay Siegel has remarked: "Given the range of material in Sewall's lectures, we can discern the new meaning that the study of Hebrew came to have at Harvard in the late 1760s. His goal was to teach Hebrew and its related topics scientifically—not as a language, but rather as a subject."[25] In a sharp departure from Monis's method, "Sewall attempted to establish a new modern approach more in agreement with that used in the college—particularly the lectures in the sciences by Professor John Winthrop and the readings in history and politics that the students were doing on their own."[26]

Sewall's lectures were surprisingly wide-ranging. His material encompassed intellectual issues then engaging European and American scholars. Among these was the question of the origins of the human capacity for language. A corollary to that question, and one that occupied a good deal of Sewall's attention, was the issue of "the primitive tongue." Given early man's gift of speech, what language was the first language of humanity? Hebrew was the obvious candidate for that distinction, but it was by no means the only candidate.

The shift from Monis's prosaic, routine Hebrew instruction to Sewall's more sophisticated presentation of Hebraic intellectual questions is best understood in the context of the late-eighteenth-century shift in Harvard's educational policy and philosophy. One explanation for this shift is that ideas of the European Enlightenment replaced the ideals of Puritan learning of the seventeenth century. Thomas Jay Siegel, in his work on the Harvard curriculum, notes that "this explanation is too linear and fails to take into account how the changing goals and methods used in the study of all subjects, but especially Hebrew, reflected the college's desire to balance its adherence to orthodoxy with its excitement for the new."[27]

The full answer to our questions about curriculum change would have to take into account a number of changes in English and colonial American intellectual life. The older, soon to be outdated, view of higher education was that the student, with the help of a well-trained tutor, could master the "encyclopedia of knowledge." Mastery of methods of appreciation was foremost; these included competence in logic and an understanding of divine revelation and its place in the unfolding of human knowledge. Armed with these tools and guided in their use by a tutor, the student would be "educated" in the sense practiced by the great English universities. Students would understand and apprehend the encyclopedia of "proven" knowledge, which they could then put to use in their own lives and the lives of their parishioners, clients, or trading partners.

With the advent of the Newtonian and Lockean intellectual revolutions, this harmonic view of apprehensible knowledge changed radically. Knowledge was seen as infinitely expandable, and the mastery of that body of expanding knowledge was beyond the talents of any one tutor, no matter how gifted. The university now had needs of *professors*, experts in one area of knowledge. The tutor system was soon seen as inadequate. Spurred by shifting intellectual patterns in England and the Continent, those Harvard overseers who advocated reform "pressed forward with plans to alter the college's mode of formal instruction from a tutorial system based upon generalist tutors to one based upon specialist professors."[28]

Harvard appointed three professors during this period: Edward Wigglesworth Jr., John Winthrop, and Sewall. Sewall and Wigglesworth were brothers-in-law, and both had been Judah Monis's students—and ungrateful students at that! As a late-twentieth-century observer noted, "Both men, profiting by Rabbi Monis' instruction, had obtained professorships, but seem to have disliked their teacher profoundly."[29] From the above description of Monis's troubled career, we learned that his students were ungrateful to him and mockingly critical of his methods. In Sewall's case anti-Judaism seems to have been a factor in his hostility to Monis. Some of Sewall's lectures, despite their focus on the history of the language of the Jews, are imbued with anti-Jewish sentiment. In these talks, Jewish scholars of the Bible and Hebrew grammar receive especially harsh comment. In his discussion of the history, development, and "decline" of the Hebrew alphabet "from its earlier purity and aesthetic grandeur" he wrote, "But considering that the Jews, even as early as the days of our Savior, had, through their traditions made void divine law, it is not strange, that, from a like fanciful humour of innovation, they should have equally depraved their alphabet too."[30]

As a specialist professor—the third such position created at the "new" Harvard—Stephen Sewall was given the opportunity to define the parameters of his discipline. The seventy-two lectures that Sewall delivered over an eight-year cycle constituted a history and description of oriental languages. The subject was the "Hebraic" in its widest possible sense. Questions that we would today identify as linguistic, philological, and anthropological were approached with considerable sophistication. In contrast, we know little of the actual content of Monis's lectures, though we may imagine that most of them were devoted to issues of grammar and syntax.

The Harvard University Archives have preserved a full set of Sewall's lecture notes, and a glance at their contents gives one a sense of the very wide range of subjects that they encompassed. The first five talks focused on the debates then raging in academic circles concerning the origins of human language. The title of Lecture No. 3 captures the essence of that debate: "Which of the known languages in the world bids fairest to be the original one; and whether any now extant has all its marks." Hebrew and its sister or cognate languages were thought to be prime candidates for the distinction of "original language," but Sewall (and the authorities he cites) was engaging in larger philosophical debates through the question of Hebrew. We can contextualize this engagement with the question of "the original language" by referring to Enlightenment debates on the origins and nature of human speech. Scholars debated "whether Adam innately had the knowledge of language, or gained that knowledge as he experienced life." Sewall's conclusion strikes a balance between positions that we might today describe as "nature" and "nurture." Humans were initially granted basic patterns and powers of speech "derived from the immediate impressions of the Deity." Later, "through the exercise of his own powers, he should be able to make additions to his language as circumstances required." In a subsequent lecture Sewall argued that "simplicity . . . is the most essential property of the first language."

Over the series of the following three lectures Professor Sewall led his students and other listeners to the conclusion that Hebrew was humanity's "original language." There was, of course, nothing new or astonishing in this conclusion. This was the conclusion that most of his listeners expected to hear, though it might have been a startling assertion for his young undergraduates.

After establishing that Hebrew was the "original language" Sewall went on to describe "related" languages and scripts—Egyptian, Samaritan, Phoenician—devoting a number of lectures to the little of what was then known of these dead languages. This was before (though not more than a few decades before) the decipherment of hieroglyphics at the beginning of the nineteenth century and the subsequent decipherment of the various ancient Near Eastern scripts. Sewall's lectures offer us a fascinating glimpse into premodern European understandings of the ancient world. They also reflect premodern ideas about the relationship between scientific observations and Christian views of scriptural authority. Sewall, influenced by the Enlightenment philosophers, makes the case for integrating scientific and biblical views. In this spirit, Lecture No. 42 is titled: "No reason for supposing a miracle when the phenomena can be accounted for on natural principles."

Sewall held the Hancock professorship for twenty years, from 1765 to 1785. Toward the end of his tenure, his health deteriorated, and his teaching abilities were impaired. The college records state that he retired because of illness. Some twentieth-century historians suggest that his illness was exacerbated by chronic alcoholism: "After the death of his wife and several unsuccessful attempts to deal with his problem with alcoholism, Sewall's teaching began to suffer, and in 1785 he was removed from his professorship."[31]

Though his alcoholism was a long-term and persistent problem, one sympathetic friend chose to attribute Sewall's infirmities to the rigors of "Oriental Scholarship," rather than to the effects of what we would today term "substance abuse." Sewall's Harvard friend wrote that "a person whose nerves are in perpetual tremor from a long and laborious prying into the ramifications and import of words in Latin, Greek, Hebrew, Syriac, Arabic, Chaldee, Samaritan, Ethiopic, and Persick, may to the careless observer, seem like one under the influence of inebriety."[32] This was a brave and creative defense, but not one that convinced the Hancock professor's students or colleagues.

Despite his infirmities, Sewall's influence extended beyond the confines of Harvard College. As one of three Harvard professors and an expert on matters biblical and Hebraic, his reputation throughout the American colonies was considerable. In the 1770s Sewall was befriended by Ezra Stiles, pastor of the Newport, Rhode Island, Congregational Church and future president of Yale. Stiles, who would rightfully earn the sobriquet of the "American Colonies' foremost intellectual," was deeply devoted to the study of Hebrew and the Bible.

Sewall was Stiles's guest at Newport on a number of occasions. During a visit in the 1770s Stiles took his esteemed guest to Shabbat services at the Newport synagogue. For Professor Sewall and most Christian Hebraists of pre–Civil War America, the few Jews they met were of intense interest as objects of study. When Ezra Stiles took up the ministry of Newport's Second Congregational Church in 1755, he found in Newport a small but vibrant synagogue, Congregation Yeshuat Israel. For the next twenty-five years, until he left Newport to serve as the president of Yale, Stiles was a constant and careful observer of Newport's Jewish life and citizenry.

Unfortunately, we do not have Sewall's recollections of his visits to Newport or his impressions of the Shabbat service. We do, however, have Stiles's evaluation of Sewall's scholarly capabilities. "Mr. Sewall is well acquainted with Hebrew and its Dialects as Samaritan, Ethiopic, Syriac, Arabic, Chaldee — but not with the Armeanian, Persic, and Coptic." But Sewall's reputation was also attacked in a manner reminiscent of the attacks on the reputation of his teacher Judah Monis. In a 1761 letter from Wigglesworth to Sewall, the Hollis Professor of Theology wrote to the Hancock Professor of Hebrew that he hoped that "Rabbi Monis has gone to *Abraham's Bosom*, as he used to term it." Might we detect more than a hint of anti-Semitism here, an animosity coupled with contempt for an "inadequate" instructor and his distasteful methods?[33]

As the writings of Cotton Mather and his Harvard colleagues demonstrate, many a churchman sought to convert Jews to the Christian faith. But few opportunities for preaching to Jews presented themselves. There were even fewer opportunities for Christian scholars to converse with Jewish scholars. The negative experience of Judah Monis's teaching may have discouraged some American Christian scholars and clergymen from any such meeting. There were few Jews in the American colonies at the time of the American Revolution, and among those Jews there were no rabbis or other scholars of Judaica. Thus, even if Christian Hebraists wished to consult with Jewish scholars about matters Hebraic and Judaic, there were no such scholars resident on American shores. As we shall see, Christian Hebraists eagerly sought out visiting rabbis. Yale's Ezra Stiles, the subject of the next chapter, met with a number of visiting European and Middle Eastern rabbis while serving as pastor in Newport and president of Yale.

3

AMBIVALENCE AND ERUDITION
IN NEW HAVEN
EZRA STILES, YALE COLLEGE, AND
THE JEWISH TRADITION

*Between the early American Christian and the early
American Jew there hung an awkward ambivalence.*
Peter Grose, *Israel in the Mind of America*

In 1778, two years after the beginning of the American Revolution and half a
century after Judah Monis publicly proclaimed his belief in Christian doctrine,
Ezra Stiles, recently appointed president of Yale College, wrote his presidential inaugural address in fluent Hebrew. He then translated it into English and
delivered it in that language. Three years later he spoke to the Yale community using the Hebrew original of that oration. Unlike many of his New England predecessors, who spoke Hebrew with a "divinity school" pronunciation that would have been unintelligible to Jewish listeners, Stiles endeavored
to enunciate his Hebrew text "in the rabbinic manner." Unlike his New England Christian contemporaries Stiles did not rely solely on grammar books
and college instruction for his knowledge of Hebrew syntax and composition.
In the decades preceding his assumption of the Yale presidency he had ample
opportunity to learn Hebrew from Jewish informants. When he assumed the
presidency of Yale he not only made Hebrew language instruction mandatory,
but also took on the teaching of Hebrew. Throughout his nearly twenty years
at Yale he taught Hebrew and French, and guest-lectured on many other subjects as well.[1] A child of New England's intellectual aristocracy, Stiles (1727–
95) was widely recognized as the "most learned man in New England."

Hebrew orations and the study of the Hebrew language were not Stiles's
innovation at Yale. They had been staples of the Yale curriculum since the
college's 1701 organization. The Yale insignia—an open book emblazoned
with the Hebrew words *Urim Vetumim* ("light and perfection") and the Latin
words *lux et veritas*—was adopted in 1736. Harvard's insignia—three books

College seals of Yale, Dartmouth, and Columbia

inscribed with the Latin "Veritas"—served as the model for Yale's design. Yale harkened back to Old Testament Hebraic models and used Hebrew letters in the insignia. Borrowing Luther's imagery, we might say Yale's leaders preferred to drink from the Hebraic "fountain" rather than from the Latin "pool." The *urim* and *tumim* are the precious stones set in the breastplate of Aaron. Christian Hebraists understood this symbol of light and truth as a reference to, and prefiguration of, Jesus. For them, the seal was thus a Hebrew testimony to the "Christian Truth."[2]

By the 1770s Hebrew at Yale had declined—it was no longer mandatory, and there was little enthusiasm for it among the students. Stiles was determined to change that—and many other things at a college battered and impoverished during the revolutionary struggle against the British.

Ezra Stiles's journey to the presidency of Yale was not an easy or an obvious one. Grandson of the Puritan theologian and religious poet Edward Taylor, Stiles was born in New Haven. His father, Isaac Stiles, was pastor of the local

Congregational church, and it was expected that Ezra would attend Yale College, which had been established a decade before his birth. From an early age Ezra showed great intellectual promise and a remarkable aptitude for science and mathematics. The rich traditions of learning in his family (on both his mother's and father's side) provided an atmosphere of scholarship and intellectual engagement. Stiles was particularly aware of his grandfather's eminence and accomplishments. In describing Edward Taylor, Stiles noted, "He was an excellent classic scholar, being a master of the three learned languages."[3] (Stiles's "evaluations" of colleagues, family, and friends often included a note on their knowledge of languages.) In that atmosphere—both at home and at his father's church—he was "prepared" for college. Young Ezra was ready for college at age twelve. But for procedural reasons, and because his father felt that he was too young for the rigors of Yale, he did not matriculate until 1742, when he was fifteen.

Even before his college training and clerical ordination, Stiles experienced an intellectual atmosphere that he would later identify as "rabbinic" in character and method. The idea of the Jews as preservers of sacred learning had already taken hold of the imagination of American intellectuals, as we saw in the story of "Rabbi" Judah Monis. Cotton Mather expressed it dramatically at the end of the seventeenth century when he described Harvard as New England's *Beit Midrash* (or Talmudic academy) and its teachers as its "rabbis." Stiles made this analogy himself many times. But there was an inherent ambivalence here. While Jewish traditions of learning and their methods of scholarship carried a valuable message for Christians, the Jews themselves were considered to be locked into permanent ("eternal") doctrinal error. This ambivalence produced a wide variety of results and reactions. In Ezra Stiles it led to amity, cooperation, and openness, not, as in the case of some later American intellectuals (nineteenth-century essayist John Jay Chapman, for example), to animosity and hostility.

At Yale College, Ezra Stiles "distinguished himself in all branches of learning but showed special fondness for mathematics, astronomy, and Biblical history."[4] Lest this last item strike us as belonging to another category of knowledge, we should remember that before the European Enlightenment and the challenges to biblical authority that came with mid-nineteenth-century discoveries of the age of the earth and the process of evolution, "biblical history" was the universally accepted standard of historical truth.

Despite his interest in matters biblical, Stiles did not study Hebrew during his undergraduate years at Yale. That language and its texts, which would become the center of his attention in the second half of his life, seemed of little importance to the young Stiles. It was natural philosophy or science that interested him in his youth. As in the case of his older contemporary and acquaintance Jonathan Edwards, the contemplation of the wonders of the natural world led to a greater appreciation of the "mysteries of the divine." Stiles's *Literary Diary* is replete with accounts of new scientific discoveries and experiments.[5] And in a fashion which would become unusual in the nineteenth century—when science and theology clashed mightily—these scientific observations occur alongside theological speculations.

Stiles remained in New Haven after graduation. He studied theology on his own and prepared himself for the ministry. Three years after graduation he was ordained and licensed to preach by the New Haven Association of Ministers. In that same month (May 1749), however, Stiles accepted the position of tutor at Yale. The ministry, the prospect of which presented him with intellectual doubts and emotional problems, would have to wait. The young Stiles found it difficult to accept certain Calvinist doctrines that were essential elements of New England orthodoxy. These included the doctrines of Predestination, Election, and Salvation. Stiles's reading had led him to rationalist positions. "My Deistical Turn gave a very thorough Disgust against the Authority of Councils and Decretals." This "disgust" was influenced and reinforced by his wide reading in contemporary European thought. In his typically methodical fashion, Stiles kept a record of these influences, which he titled "Review of the Authors I read and admired during the Rise, Height and Decline of my Scepticism."[6]

Unable to embrace wholeheartedly Calvinist doctrine, Stiles rejected the family tradition of serving in the ministry. Aware that he would have to earn his living in some other manner, he studied law. As in all of his intellectual endeavors, here too he excelled, and in late 1753 he was admitted to the bar. Not neglecting his theological studies, he continued reading in a variety of Christian sources and in the classics of the European philosophical tradition.

For several years Stiles retained his job as Yale tutor while practicing law and reading in the classics. What "cured" him of his skepticism was his very modern reading of Scripture, which he read in what we might call a "comparative" manner. As Rabbi Arthur Chiel notes: "Having rejected the bleak dogma of his Puritan forefathers Stiles was not satisfied to let the matter rest there. He persisted in his search for some basic religious principles to which he might remain committed as a believing Christian."[7]

The essence of these principles had a relationship to the Bible, but they were not slavishly bound to every detail of that text. Intensive study of what William James a century later would call "the varieties of religious experience," relativized, but did not destroy, Stiles's sense of the authority of Scripture. He compared his search for absolutes to the work of Sir Isaac Newton. Newton sought, in Stiles's words, a law "obtaining in the solar system and probably throughout the stellar Universe." This law the great mathematician found in the principle of gravity. Stiles found his "one principle" in the acceptance of two linked events, one in the past and one in the future. "Some one principle may be the basis upon which the whole system of Revelation may be firmly supported. Such is the fulfillment of Prophecy respecting the Jews. Such is the Fact of the Resurrection of Jesus." Every word of Scripture, then, did not have to be thought of as "inspired by God." Stiles found he could make his peace with the inconsistencies of the biblical text if he made a leap of faith. As long as he could embrace Resurrection and Redemption Stiles could remain a believing Christian and accept a ministry in the church.[8]

The manner in which he resolved his crisis of faith, and the force of his convictions, led Stiles to an intense lifelong interest in both the Old Testament and the religious lives of the Jews of his time. He may have felt that divine providence was at work when his first assignment as a minister was to the Second Congregational Church of Newport, Rhode Island. For the thriving port town had a small but influential Jewish community and was home to the second-oldest synagogue in the American colonies. To quote the late Rabbi Chiel, an astute student of Stiles's obsession with the Jews, "Stiles had in Newport an excellent laboratory in which to observe Jews and to learn at first hand about their customs and traditions."[9]

From 1755 to the outbreak of the Revolutionary War, Stiles ministered to his Newport flock. Parishioners, other townspeople, and visitors considered him the most scholarly of the town's citizens. Newport was the American port of entry for many European visitors. These travelers and immigrants often visited Stiles; if they did not call on him, he soon sought them out, thirsty for news of new ideas, inventions, and books. Stiles then carefully recorded his impressions of these European visitors and their intellectual wares in his *Literary Diary*.

Stiles as Pluralist

For most Christians in the eighteenth century the study of Hebrew and the study of the Jews as a living community were separate and often unrelated enterprises. A scholar engaged with Hebraic sources might have no relationship with Jews. In the preceding two centuries of Christian Hebraist endeavor we see, however, a wide range of engagement with and varying attitudes toward Jews. In the formative period of Christian Hebraism (mid-sixteenth to mid-seventeenth centuries), interaction between Jewish and Christian scholars was crucial not only for the development of Hebrew studies in the West, but also for wider intellectual developments in the history of ideas. From

Reuchlin and Buxtorf onward (sixteenth century), Hebraists realized that Jewish scholars, schooled in reading and interpreting Hebrew texts, were valuable "informants." This term, which evokes the language and discourse of modern anthropology, is appropriate in this context, for European Jews lived a dichotomous existence. While they lived in proximity to European Christians and shared with them elements of culture such as language and national identity, Jews were separated from Christians in other aspects such as religious ritual and belief and ethnic language (what we now call an "ethnolect"—such as Yiddish).

In Europe during the Reformation, Christian scholarly contact with rabbis and other Talmudists reached the highest levels of the Protestant and Catholic hierarchies. Historian of ideas Frank Manuel points out that Reformation-era Christian Hebraism had a personal, one-to-one aspect. "A Christian scholar possessed with a zeal to learn the language of the accursed Jews, at the risk of his soul resorted to a rabbi or rabbinic convert who would teach him the rudiments."[10] Perhaps the most famous such teacher was Rabbi Elijah Levita (1468–1549) who exchanged lessons with Cardinal Egidio de Viterbo of Rome. For more than a decade, Rabbi Levita taught the Cardinal Hebrew in exchange for lessons in classical Greek.

After the formative period, however, Christian Hebraism developed on its own, without the help of Jewish informants. Christian scholars who authored exhaustive tomes on Jewish life and ritual most often wrote those studies without visiting Jewish communities or synagogues. They relied on translations of Jewish texts and extrapolated from these texts to paint a portrait of Jewish religious behavior. For the English Reformation scholars by whom the American colonists were trained, the question of using Jewish informants was a moot one. Since their expulsion in 1290 there were no Jews resident in England (or at least none who lived publicly as Jews) until they were readmitted under Cromwell. Hebraists at Oxford and Cambridge relied on Continental Christian books and visitors for secondhand information about Jewish language, texts, and rituals.

During the second half of the seventeenth century, encouraged by England's decision to readmit Jews, a small but influential group of Jewish scholars were invited to teach at the two great English universities. These included the Abendana brothers, Isaac and Jacob. They translated the Mishna and some of Maimonides's philosophical writings from Hebrew into Latin. Thus, the precedent for acceptance of Jewish scholars of Hebrew was established. Contact with Jewish scholars was sanctioned, if such scholars could be found. In the American colonies at the time of the American Revolution there were few Jews (approximately fifteen hundred out of a population of three million) and there were no rabbis or other scholars of Judaica. Thus, even if Christian Hebraists wished to consult with Jewish scholars about matters Hebraic and Judaic there were no such scholars resident on American shores.

Ezra Stiles, working and writing at the end of the third century of post-Renaissance-era Christian Hebraism, was a pioneer of sorts, or one could say he was returning to an earlier Christian Hebraism that encouraged engagement with Jews and Jewish scholarship. While his immersion in the study of Hebrew and the Bible was total—he notes in his diary that he read the complete Old Testament eight times, including a number of times in the Hebrew original—he also sought out Jewish scholars, mystics, and synagogue leaders to learn about the beliefs and practices of Jews. His way of interpreting the data would be Christian—there was no denying the doctrinal errors of the Jews—but his method was more "authentic," based as it was on firsthand observation and study.

Stiles's interest in "exotic" religious communities was not limited to the Jews of Newport. He tried to learn as much as possible about Protestant denominations other than his own, as well as about other ethnic and religious minorities. He advocated religious and ethnic tolerance, and eventually took a strong interest in the situation of black Americans. In 1754 Stiles embarked from New Haven on a young man's "grand tour" through the Northeast. His biographer Edmund Morgan described the tour: "Characteristically he determined to make the experience as broadening as possible . . . with ostentatious catholicity he attended services of the churches of different persuasions in the towns he visited: Quaker at Newport and Philadelphia; Episcopal at New York and Boston; Dutch Calvinist at New York; Roman Catholic at Philadelphia. There were not enough Sundays to make room for others."[11]

Stiles as "Hebrician"

Stiles's 1778 Yale inaugural address, which he wrote in Hebrew, was a remarkable accomplishment, as he had begun his study of the language only a decade earlier. As a student at Yale he had "greatly neglected" the study of Hebrew. When Yale's President Clap promoted the language for the benefit of future ministers, Stiles, then senior tutor, was obligated to endorse the new program. Even so, Stiles "learned no more than the alphabet and got away with it." When he settled in Newport and deepened his study of the Bible, he initially turned to his reference books for help in explicating difficult Hebrew texts. It was at that point that his pluralistic attitudes toward other faiths came into play and enabled him to turn to "native informants" of the Hebraic tradition. As he got to know members of the Jewish community he turned to them for help. Abiel Holmes, Stiles's son-in-law and first biographer, has left us a charming account of Stiles's first steps in Hebrew studies. "Some light, indeed, he derived from the Jews at Newport, particularly from their *hazzans* or teachers, by asking them the import of those Hebrew words which stood for particular passages in the Bible. Proceeding in the study of the Scriptures and of divinity, he felt the necessity of the knowledge of Hebrew. His frequent attendance at the Jews' synagogue increased his wish to possess at least as much of it as to see a little into their books and service."[12]

Stiles's interest may have been piqued initially by a desire to "see a little" into Jewish life and texts, but with characteristic energy and determination he rapidly made the study of Hebrew and its cognate languages the focal point of his rich intellectual life. Science, with all the excitement of discovery and experimentation, now took second place. His curiosity about the "scientific" meaning of biblical Hebrew, and his growing friendships with Jewish citizens, became the central factors behind these endeavors. But the immediate catalyst for his quickly mastering the rudiments of Hebrew was much more concrete. The University of Edinburgh, Scotland, awarded Stiles an honorary Doctor of Divinity degree on the recommendation of his friend Benjamin Franklin.[13] As Abiel Holmes related, Stiles's "ambition was touched, or rather a sense of shame excited, that a Doctor of Divinity should not understand a language so important and so easily acquired."[14] In 1767, when he was forty years old, Stiles relearned the Hebrew alphabet. Determined to enter the world of Hebrew learning, he would become an "Hebrician" through his own efforts. He read the Nineteenth Psalm over the next five days and found himself greatly encouraged. It was only then, after starting the project on his own, that he turned for help in Hebrew to the *hazzan* or cantor of the Newport synagogue.

Stiles, then, was working in a tradition of Christian contact with Jewish savants, though how aware he was of the intellectual antecedents of such contacts it is hard to say. While the Italian Humanists, first and foremost among them Pico della Mirandola, focused on the "secrets" of Hebrew language and on the Aramaic text of the Zohar, Stiles cast a wider net. He was intensely interested in the communal rituals of Jewish life, and as I have noted, he had in his own town the ideal laboratory for observing synagogue practices. In a sense, Stiles became a "participant observer" in Jewish life in Newport. He attended prayer services, marched in synagogue processions, and on at least one occasion addressed the congregation. One could argue that as a participant observer he affected the communal life of the Newport synagogue, but we need to be careful here. For the Jews were one of a number of religious groups he took an interest in. Stiles also had friendly relations with a number of "Christian denominations including the local Catholic community,"[15] but he was not as deeply engaged with them as he was with the Jews. I also want to be careful to distinguish Stiles from the other clergymen and scholars of his place and time. He was unique in the intensity of his interest in Hebrew and the Jews. The Puritan Hebraism he was evoking and embracing had already waned. Stiles had adopted and transformed that Hebraism and forged something new, and out of that new synthesis he formulated his plans for the strengthening and transformation of Yale College. Like the other leaders of the ten colleges founded before the American Revolution, Stiles saw the college's function as a religious and spiritual one, and a function biblically inspired. The early American colleges understood themselves to have been inspired by the "schools of the prophets" of the Old Testament.

But by Stiles's time these biblically inspired educational models were on the wane. Thomas Jay Siegel has made the point that Stiles was exceptional; his interests were not generally the interests of his society. His attitudes toward the study of Hebrew and toward the Jews of his time were unusual and not the rule in colonial and early republican New England. "Though a descendant of an Old Light Calvinist, he had more than a touch of the mystic about him."[16] In conjunction with his intense intellectual curiosity about Judaic texts, it was his mystical bent that led him to the study of the Hebrew of the Bible and the Aramaic of the Zohar.

Stiles delighted in the Hebraist endeavors of his contemporaries. He valued his friendship with Stephen Sewall, Judah Monis's successor at Harvard. Sewall's students displayed their linguistic achievements at the Harvard commencement exercises of July 1770, which Stiles attended. (Note the small numbers of Harvard students in the eighteenth century: that year thirty-four students received the Bachelor's degree and forty-three the Master's.) In his diary Stiles notes with approval that "among other exercises was a Dialogue in Chaldee held between three Bachelors—taken out of Daniel: at the close of this the President [the recently appointed President Locke] subjoined a short speech in Chaldee: but he did not make any Latin Oration" (July 16, 1770).[17] Stiles's own Aramaic study had by that time progressed quite far, and he was no doubt pleased to hear Aramaic recitations by both the students and president of America's Cambridge. That *Aramaic* was chosen and that Latin was not must have pleased him too. While the biblical Aramaic of the Book of Daniel was quite familiar to him, the Aramaic of the Zohar, mixed as it was with rabbinic Hebrew and Talmudic Aramaic, was a much greater philological and intellectual challenge. To what extent Stiles met that challenge we shall soon see.

Ezra Stiles spent twenty-two years in the Newport Congregationalist ministry, from 1755 to 1777. Among other events, he witnessed the excitement and upheaval of the colonial struggle against the British, which he described in his diary and in his sermons with biblical imagery and language. Along with the majority of Newport's citizens, Stiles fled the city in October 1775, fearing the British would occupy the town. He was one of the last of Newport's prominent citizens to leave. On the eve of his departure he noted in his diary: "How does this town sit solitary that was once full of people! I am not yet removed, although three quarters of my beloved church and congregation are broken up and dispersed" (Oct. 10, 1775). This diary entry opens with the opening verse of the Old Testament book of Lamentations. In comparing the plight of threatened Newport to the plight of the fallen city of Jerusalem, Stiles is writing within the New England "biblicist" tradition. In Stiles's writings, that tradition, so rich in typological thought and biblical imagery, had a period of efflorescence, before it waned at the beginning of the nineteenth century.

The constant stream of foreign and American visitors who passed through Newport during his tenure there enabled Stiles to keep abreast of developments in the sciences and the humanities. Americans overseas, including his friend and correspondent Benjamin Franklin, kept Stiles well informed of European developments and well supplied with English books and pamphlets. He was as well informed concerning European and English events as anyone in the American colonies.

For Stiles, the most unusual of these Newport cultural and religious opportunities was the presence of the Newport synagogue. I have described Stiles relearning the Hebrew alphabet decades after he had studied it at Yale. Isaac Touro, hazzan of the synagogue, taught Stiles the correct pronunciation of the consonants and vowels. "During pleasant weather, Stiles, with a Hebrew Psalter open in hand, and Touro at his side, walked the Newport Parade, Stiles enunciating slowly the text for his instructor. As the colder weather set in, the two clergy met at Stiles's or Touros's home for study sessions."[18] Even at this most rudimentary stage of Hebrew study Stiles set high goals for himself. He wrote that, "If God should spare my life I would like to move on to the study of the Mishna, The Gemara, and perhaps even the Cabala."[19] His diligence in Hebrew and other "oriental" study was remarkable. Once he set his mind to the task he began each day with the study of Hebrew.

In 1769, two years after he commenced his studies with Isaac Touro, Stiles added Arabic to his studies. He read a chapter of the Bible in Hebrew each morning and followed it with a chapter of an Arabic historical text. Only then would he allow himself to eat breakfast. On Sundays he omitted the Arabic reading, which, unlike the Hebrew reading was a secular pursuit. This daily text study represented study as a devotional act, a concept in Jewish law that appealed to Stiles and many other Christian Hebraists. In his enthusiasm for his new intellectual and spiritual endeavor he taught Hebrew to his wife and children. On many mornings they joined him for Hebrew recitation, as G. A. Kohut has pointed out: "His wife and children all took upon themselves the yoke of the torah, philologically speaking."[20] In May of 1771 Stiles reports that his twelve-year-old son Ezra, "having spelt and read to the 52nd Psalm in the Hebrew Psalter, this day began to translate the first Psalm. I propose he shall translate only a verse or two a day before breakfast" (May 14, 1771). The elder Stiles was tougher on himself. He would master more than a verse or two. A complete chapter of the Bible was his morning's fare. He applied himself diligently to his morning Hebrew study and within three years of learning the Hebrew alphabet he records that he had finished reading the Old Testament in the "Original Hebrew."

His many overseas correspondents and friends were aware of Stiles's growing interest in Hebraica and Judaica. Benjamin Franklin, whose nomination of Stiles as a candidate for an honorary doctorate from Edinburgh was the catalyst for the Newport minister's engagement with the Hebrew language, sent from London Reland's *Introduction to the Rabbinical Literature*. This book, together with the English scholar John Selden's many works on Jewish law, was Stiles's opening to the "Sea of the Talmud." Though he did not delve into the Talmud as deeply as he studied the Zohar, it seems he was familiar with its structure and method.

During his first decade in Newport Stiles made an occasional visit to the synagogue, but was not a regular visitor and observer. It was his study of Hebrew, embarked upon in his second decade in Newport, and his growing interest in Jewish ritual, that made him a regular at Sabbath and holiday services. In order to follow the liturgy closely Stiles worked his way through the Jewish prayer book in much the same manner as he had methodically read through the Hebrew text of the Bible. Not content with his mastery of the standard daily and Sabbath prayer book, Stiles began working on the High Holiday Mahzor, which he described as "a collection of Jewish Prayers and Service for the *Beginning of the Year*, and the great *Fast or Day of Atonement*. . . . Among other things this Book contains descriptions of the Workshop of the Angelic Hierarchies, i.e. the grand Divisions under which they worship God. Also the Keter Malkut" (March 2, 1762). From 1767 until the British occupation of Newport forced him and his flock into exile from their beloved town, Stiles was a regular visitor to the synagogue. His friendship with the leaders of the congregation led to encounters and friendships with a succession of visiting European and Middle Eastern rabbis.

In his 1778 inaugural address, and in the Hebrew-language version of that address, delivered at the 1781 Yale commencement, Stiles thanked those visiting rabbis from whom he had learned so much about Jewish practices and texts. "I have been taught personally at the mouth of the Masters of Wisdom, at mouths of five Rabbis, Hochams of name and Eminence." He names and identifies these scholars, praising each individually for their accomplishments.

"In all of them I took great delight, for I know them to be men of *light* as well to be men of name 'anshe shem.'"[21]

The first of these rabbinical emissaries to Newport's wealthy Jewish community was Rabbi Moses Malchi. A native of Safed in the land of Israel, Malchi held special fascination for Stiles. When, in 1759, Malchi came to Newport, Stiles was engaged in the study of the question of Israel's place in the drama of Christian salvation. He had become convinced that the Jews of his time had a pivotal role to play in that drama and that any sign of the return of the Jews to the Holy Land would presage the Second Coming. The issue of the restoration of the Jews to their land, a question which had occupied some of the great Puritan writers of the seventeenth century, most notably Henry Finch, now occupied the mind of Stiles, the "Gentle Puritan." Stiles relates: "I asked Rabbi Malchi, whether if the Grand Sultan would give public proclamation inviting the Jews to come and settle the Holy Land, they would not at once readily return? He replied, he believed the sultan would not give out such an invitation."[22]

In Stiles's brief conversation with Rabbi Malchi are encapsulated major themes in the emerging American Christian idea of the salvific function of the Jews, and the place of the "Return to Zion" in that model of the End Time. Unlike their Catholic counterparts, who had rejected the idea of a living Israel in favor of the Catholic Church as the "True Israel" and supplanter of the people of Israel, Protestant thinkers of the various denominations had to struggle with the "problem" of the Jews. If the Jews were not condemned to eternal exile, and were understood to have a larger part to play in the drama of the Second Coming, how was their role in history to be understood? Various answers would suggest themselves. One powerful answer was to place the Jews at the center of the End Time drama.

One contact that influenced Stiles's growing interest in the Jews was his remarkable extended friendship with Rabbi Hayyim Carigal. Carigal, who came from Hebron in Ottoman Palestine, which Stiles and other Protestant intellectuals knew as the Holy Land that would play so central a part in the drama of salvation, represented a "divine messenger" of sorts. Also, the personal chemistry was there. These two scholarly clerics liked each other immediately. Unlike the other rabbis who visited Newport and made Pastor Stiles's brief acquaintance, Carigal forged a lasting friendship with Stiles—one which persisted until the rabbi's death in Barbados five years later. Carigal's visits and friendship were the culmination and fulfillment of Stiles's fascination with Hebraica and Judaica. Rabbi Carigal, the most knowledgeable and accomplished of the five rabbinical emissaries who visited Newport, provided answers to questions Stiles had wanted to ask for years. Chief among them were questions about the Zohar and Kabbalism.

Rabbi Hayyim Isaac
Carigal of Hebron, 1773
(Yale University Library)

Stiles made Rabbi Carigal's acquaintance in the spring of 1773. Two young American visitors to Newport told Stiles that "a Hebrew Rabbi from Machpelah in the Holy Land" had accompanied them on their travels from Philadelphia. Stiles's curiosity was piqued and he took the earliest opportunity to visit the synagogue and observe the new visitor. He knew that the Jewish holiday of Purim was only four days away. On the eve of the holiday, Ezra Stiles walked to the synagogue and listened to the reading of the Purim Scroll, the Megillah. There he saw "a large man, neat and well dressed in the Turkish habit. . . . He has the appearance of an ingenious and sensible man" (March 8, 1773).

Rabbi Carigal, this "sensible man," was to stay in Newport for the sequence of Jewish holidays that runs from Purim through Passover to Shavuot (or Pentecost), a period of close to ten weeks. (That year, March 8 to May 28, 1773.) Soon after Purim, Stiles sought out the rabbi and they had the first of a series of long, intense conversations. The dialogue between the New England pastor and the Sephardic *hakham* resulted in an intense amor intellectualis. This was surely so from Stiles's side; possibly the affection was reciprocated by Carigal. (Because the rabbi's writing style is so flowery that it borders on the hyperbolic, it is difficult to evaluate the sincerity of the encomia he heaped on Ezra Stiles.)

Stiles noted the content of these conversations in his diary. Some of Carigal's reactions are recorded in his letters to Stiles.[23] Questioning Carigal about his travels Stiles learned that the rabbi, then forty years old, had been travel-

[*Zion on American Shores*]

ing throughout the "Jewish world" for twenty years. Born and educated in the Hebron Jewish community, where he received rabbinic ordination, Carigal first traveled to Middle Eastern *kehillot* (communities) before turning westward to Italy, Germany, Holland, and England. He then made his way to the Americas. The 1760s saw Carigal serving as rabbi and teacher in various farflung American places, among them the Caribbean island of Curaçao. At the time the two scholars met, Stiles had been studying Hebrew for six years. Eager to display his knowledge—and to learn the "true" pronunciation of the sacred tongue—Stiles conversed with Carigal in halting Hebrew, which soon became more fluent. Stiles wrote in his diary, "We conversed much freely, he is learned and truly modest, far more so than I ever saw a Jew" (April 16, 1773). Conversation with Carigal also provided an opportunity to hear Arabic spoken, a first for Stiles: "I suppose I then for the first time heard the true pronunciation of Arabic." For the next two months the two new friends met for a few hours of conversation every few days. When Carigal preached the Shavuot sermon at the synagogue, Stiles was there. Although the rabbi's "Spanish" (actually Ladino, the Jewish ethnolect based on late-Medieval Spanish) was somewhat difficult for Stiles to follow, "the Affinity of the Spanish and Latin enabled me to understand something of the Discourse." In addition to the content of the sermon, Stiles recorded in his diary his impressions of the synagogue and worshippers on that holiday, noting that "the synagogue was decorated with flowers" (the tradition for the Shavuot celebrations) and that the Haftarah was changed by a youngster, "Mr. Rivera's little son, eight or nine years old, read the first chapter of Ezekiel" (May 28, June 8, 1773). The participation of the young in Jewish ritual made a deep impression on Stiles, and no doubt influenced his determination to give all of his children a thorough education in Hebrew scripture.

But it is Stiles's record of the content of the sermon, transcribed without comment or reservation, that is most remarkable in the context of a prolonged dialogue between a Calvinist preacher and a traditional Sephardic rabbi. For in the sermon Carigal directly and deliberately engages and refutes a set of arguments often used by Christians against Jewish interpretations of history.

After describing Carigal's oratorical skills as "fine and oriental" and "very animated," Stiles moves to the essence of the talk. "He expiated upon the Miseries and Calamities of their Nation in their present Captivity and Dispersion and comforted them under their Tribulations by the assured Prospect of the Messiah's Kingdom—he exhorted them not to be discouraged but to persevere. The Jews hold this belief—that their Messiah will redeem them and free them from their 'Captivity.' He showed that Calamities and sufferings were not evidence of their being forsaken by God—that Adversity and Judgements were the common lot of all nations and countries" (May 28, 1773).

Here Carigal challenged the Christian view that Jerusalem was destroyed, and the Jews exiled, dispersed, and persecuted because of their rejection of Christ. Carigal cited other examples of historical calamity, in particular the eruption of Mt. Vesuvius near Naples, which he had witnessed. "It was a deluge of liquid matter flowing and carrying all before it . . . yet Christian's did not consider this as an evidence against their religion. Neither was the destruction of the Temple and the city of Jerusalem by the Romans any arguments against the truth of the Jewish religion" (May 28, 1773).

Rabbi Carigal left Newport and sailed for Surinam in late July 1773. When he arrived he wrote to Stiles, beginning a correspondence that continued until the rabbi's death in May of 1777. Some of these letters are in Hebrew; still extant is a twenty-four-page letter written in 1774 in Hebrew from Stiles to Carigal. In memory of his friend "the illustrious Hebrew," Stiles had Carigal's portrait painted from a sketch drawn during the rabbi's stay in Newport. That portrait still hangs in the Yale University library.

Stiles and Kabbalism

In contrast to most Christian Hebraists, Ezra Stiles did not limit his Hebrew studies to the Hebrew Bible and Jewish commentaries. He took a lively interest in Jewish mysticism and its texts. In his correspondence and diary he made frequent reference to the Christian Hebraist notion that Christian doctrine is alluded to in (and can be demonstrated from) Jewish texts. For example, he wrote a letter to Francis Alison of Philadelphia in which he expounded "on the Plurality of Elohim in Jehovah, and the Rabbinical Trinity in the Zohar" (April 1, 1769). Here Stiles is referring to the essence of Christian Hebraist and Kabbalist thinking, that the Trinitarian idea is alluded to in the Hebrew Bible and the Zohar, the central text of the Jewish mystical tradition. For Christian Kabbalists these allusions are found in God's divine names, including the *Elohim* name of the creation account in Genesis. It is in the grammatical plural because it refers to the three persons of the Trinity. According to Stiles the Zohar affirms this interpretation. He also suggests that Jesus's name and story are alluded to in the Old Testament text. Kabbalistic methods of exegesis can help the Christian reader "discover" these hidden allusions to Jesus. Johann Reuchlin, the sixteenth-century father of Christian Hebraism, wrote a long monograph on this subject and titled it *De Verbo Mirifico* ("the wonder-working word"). Stiles had these ideas second hand, from, among other places, Judah Monis's baptismal discourse of 1722. He was now eager to study the primary sources of the Jewish mystical tradition firsthand. In 1772 he purchased from a London bookseller a full set of the Zohar. "This day I received from London the Zohar, a Hebrew Folio volume of 800 or 770 pages, Sultzbach edition, 1684, and published at Nuremberg. It is a mystic or Cabbalistic commentary upon the Pentateuch by Rabbi Simeon ben Jochai" (October 29, 1772). Stiles's diary entry on the Zohar he received from London closes with this note on the book's language: "The whole is in rabbinical Dialect, or the Language of the Jews in our Saviour's Day, being much the same as the Syriac New Testament—and nearly as different from the Mosaic Hebrew, as the present Italian from the Latin of the Augustan Age."[24]

Harvard professor G. F. Moore, in a 1918 report to the Massachusetts Historical Society, noted Stiles's acquisition of the Zohar and his lively interest in that text. In assessing Stiles's knowledge of the Kabbalah, Moore asks an obvious and infrequently posed question about Christian Hebraism. "The book is written in a mixture of Hebrew and a peculiar Aramaic, which would be laborious reading even were it all about matters apprehensible by the unsophisticated intelligence. . . . It does not seem reasonable that any ordinary Christian could make anything out of it . . . without an exponent of the living tradition at his elbow. . . . The question therefore was, Did Stiles really read it and if he did, how?"[25] A close examination of Stiles's diary, and perusal of Stiles's copy of the Zohar, which Moore found in the Harvard library, convinced him that Stiles read through the complete text. As to how much he understood it is difficult to judge.

In portraying Stiles as a Kabbalist, Moore is tying Stiles's studies to earlier stages of Christian Hebraism. It is somewhat artificial to separate the "disciplines" of Christian Hebraism and Christian Kabbalism one from the other. From its Renaissance and Reformation beginnings European Christian Hebraism was engaged with the study of Jewish mystical texts. Stiles's Hebrew endeavors began with the study of the Bible and the languages cognate to Hebrew—Arabic and Ethiopic. He bypassed the study of classical rabbinic literature—Mishna and Talmud. But he did not neglect rabbinic commentary on the Hebrew Bible. In 1774, after he had the opportunity to meet and converse with the "learned rabbis" who visited Newport during the 1760s and early 1770s, Stiles received a box of Hebrew books from a bookseller in New Haven. He noted that the box contained "six folio volumes entirely Hebrew, not having a single letter of another tongue or character. It is a complete edition of the Bible, with the most eminent rabbinical authorities. . . . I have now a feast of Hebrew, as I can at pleasure turn to any text and examine the criticism of these commentators."[26] That "feast of Hebrew"—a copy of the multivolume rabbinic Bible—once digested, would, he was sure, enable him to read mystical texts.

Many Jewish scholars have questioned the antiquity of the Zohar; some have found its teachings of questionable provenance, even heretical or worthless. Stiles's acceptance of the Zohar as ancient and "authentic" might be contrasted with the idea put forward by the eighteenth-century Talmudist Rabbi Hayyim Joseph David Azulai, that studying the Zohar is good for the soul, even if it is wrong and its text full of mistakes. Rabbi Azulai acknowledged that the Zohar might not be the "ancient" rabbinic text that many claim it is. But for Azulai and other rabbinic authorities, its overall spiritual value was greater than questions of historical veracity.

Ambivalence and Erudition

Our description of the Newport clergyman and Yale president's relationship with Jewish texts, scholars, and community reflects Stiles's affection for Jewish tradition; Stiles's philo-Judaism seems remarkable for its time and place. But two aspects of his endeavors strike the modern Jewish observer as problematic. Through his "very long affair" with Hebraica and Judaica the Christian-Jewish polemical edge remains. The constant referent of his search is the "Christian truth" and the relevance of Hebrew to the uncovering of that truth. His professional and personal relationships to Jews in Newport and elsewhere in the colonies are at times tinged with prejudice. Arthur Chiel has noted that "the evidence adduced from his extensive writings reveals an anti-Jewish bias at times, certainly during his early years at Newport, somewhat less so in his later years there, and a growing Jewish sympathy in the post-Revolutionary War period, during his presidency of Yale. Perhaps Stiles's attitude toward the Jews might be best characterized as one of ambivalence."[27] At issue here is Stiles's diary entry of reports of a Jewish "secret intelligence office" in London which was coordinating efforts against the American revolutionaries. Stiles writes of these reports in a manner which renders them plausible. While the Jews of Newport might be trustworthy, he implies that foreign Jews were conspiring against American revolutionary ambitions.

Even in his correspondence with Rabbi Carigal Stiles cannot divest himself of his polemical edge. His long Hebrew-language letters to Carigal include references to what Stiles understands to be allusions to Jesus in the Zohar. How Carigal responded to these Christological claims we do not know. Most of his side of the correspondence is not extant. We might imagine that he deflected the claim, rather than challenged it.

An important question at this juncture is how important a figure in American intellectual life was Ezra Stiles? Do his researches and attitudes deserve as much attention as we are granting them? Do those attitudes reflect tendencies among a class of clergymen and scholars, or are they limited to Stiles? Late-twentieth-century scholars of the revolutionary period concur in their high estimation of Stiles's accomplishments. As Yale historian Edmund Morgan concluded in his 1967 book *The Gentle Puritan: A Life of Ezra Stiles, 1727–1795,* "He was not an original thinker. But his intellectual curiosity was omnivorous, and precisely because his mind was more receptive than creative. . . . The Stiles papers, furnish, I believe, a unique access to the intellectual life of eighteenth-century New England." Stiles's diary provides an extensive, unique, and highly personal view of his times. Jewish and Hebraic issues occupy a considerable amount of space in that diary, and Stiles's account of them offers the modern student a rare window into early American Christian-Jewish encounters. One cannot call Stiles representative of his time; he was too scholarly and intellectually ambitious for that designation. But he was influential, both as pastor and as college president. His views were well known throughout the colonies, and upon independence, throughout the churches and colleges of the early Republic. Thus, it might be claimed that Stiles's ambivalence about the Jews of his time represents a general American tendency.

Stiles as Educator

In 1778 Ezra Stiles accepted appointment to the Yale presidency with considerable trepidation. He had few illusions about the burdens of a college presidency. "An hundred and fifty or 180 young gentleman students, is a Bundle of Wild Fire not easily controlled and governed—and at best the Diadem of a President is a Crown of Thorns" (Sept. 19, 1777).

The revolutionary struggle against the British had left Yale battered and depleted. Stiles understood that great efforts were needed to restore the college and move it forward into the era of American independence. Stiles "rebuilt a college demoralized by the Revolution, its students few in number, and its finances at loose ends, to make it an important factor in American education."[28]

The decision to accept the Yale presidency was a difficult one; it required much soul-searching on Stiles's part. His Newport congregation was reluctant to let him go—it had grown and prospered under his direction. Friends to whom Stiles wrote, however, encouraged him to accept the Yale job. For "many men are qualified to serve God as pastors, but few as presidents."[29] For Stiles and his fellow clergymen, to lead a college, which prepared young men for the ministry and for other pivotal positions in New England life, was both a religious obligation and an unparalleled professional opportunity. Thus, Stiles resigned himself to wearing Yale's "crown of thorns."

Evoking the "School of the Prophets" model that had inspired the founders of Harvard and Yale, Stiles, as Yale's new president, made that biblical allusion more concrete by tying his own given name to that of the biblical Ezra. In the September 12, 1781 Hebrew Oration at Yale Commencement and the English-language version of which he delivered as his inaugural address, Stiles spoke eloquently and forcefully of the biblical figure Ezra the scribe and his work as educator of the Jews and restorer of the Jewish Commonwealth. As restorer of the glory of Yale after the turbulent years of the struggle against the British, this contemporary Ezra would fulfill a similar function. "There was a Restoration of the School of the prophets, and Ezra became the first President or Head of the College at Jerusalem, after the return from Babylon" (Jan. 8, 1778).[30]

While overburdened by the official and ceremonial duties of a college president, Stiles still had the consolation of serving as college teacher of the "sacred tongue." "From my first accession to the Presidency (1777–1790) I have obliged all the Freshmen to study Hebrew. This has proved very disagreeable to a number of the students. This year I have determined to instruct only those who offer themselves voluntarily. . . . Of 39 Freshman 22 have asked for instruction in Hebrew and these accordingly I teach at 4 p.m. Mondays, Wednesdays and Fridays" (June 30, 1790). Stiles then made Hebrew an elective course, leaving the choice of studying with the president up to the incoming students.

It seems that even those students who chose Hebrew bridled against the strict regimen of language study that Stiles wished to impose. As the Yale curriculum, and the Yale student body, adopted a more scientific and secular approach to learning, faculty demands that students memorize selected biblical texts, word lists, verb tables, and other linguistic paradigms were met with open rebellion. According to Yale graduate Jeremiah Mason (Class of 1788), Stiles's response to student reluctance to commit a number of the Hebrew Psalms to memory was to say that those Psalms "would be the first we should hear sung in heaven, and that he would be ashamed that any one of his pupils should be entirely ignorant of that holy language."[31]

In addition to teaching Hebrew, Stiles delivered an annual lecture series "which attempted to give coherence to the whole undergraduate program." In an educational program influenced by seventeenth-century *Technologia*, which presented a unified theory of human knowledge, Stiles's lectures, organized into the *Encyclopedia of Literature* and the *Encyclopedia of Science*, were designed to give the students an over-all perspective of human learning.[32] Because of these efforts Stiles was often called "the one-man university faculty."

Respectful Communication with All

Five years before his death at age sixty-eight, Stiles wrote a "self-evaluation" in which he addressed the issue of religious pluralism. In that statement he noted: "It has been a principle with me for thirty-five years past, to work and live in a decent, civil, and respectful communication with all; although in some of our sentiments in philosophy, religion, and politics, of diametrically opposite opinions. Hence, I can freely live, and converse in civil friendship, with Jews, Romanists, and all the sects of Protestants, and even with Deists."[33]

We could call Stiles an early American proponent of civil and religious rights. His last official act before leaving Newport for Yale was to free the Stiles family slave, christened "Newport," who was in 1778 close to thirty years old. "Before climbing into the carriage for New Haven, Stiles liberated him."[34] Newport had a large slave population and Stiles in his diary often expressed concern about the physical and spiritual welfare of African Americans. He often invited African Americans to pray at his house: "In the evening a very full and serious Meeting of Negroes at my House, perhaps eighty or ninety: discoursed to them on Luke 14:16–18. They sang well. They appeared attentive and much affected" (Feb. 24, 1772). Over the coming years, Stiles would become acutely aware of the inhumanity of slavery, and a decade later he declared himself an activist in the antislavery cause. In 1790 he was appointed the first president of Connecticut's Society for the Abolition of Slavery.[35]

In his *Literary Diary* Stiles noted the accomplishments of educated women he had known or read of. His special interest was women who knew the Hebrew language. He was familiar with the scholarly accomplishments of "Learned Ladies" of antiquity and sought parallels in the accomplishments of women of his own time. Stiles "had always been fascinated by brilliant women . . . and he liked to encourage erudition in young ladies."[36]

Several of Stiles's daughters became proficient in Hebrew, as well as in French and Latin. But Yale College was not open to women. This was problematic to Stiles; he was acutely aware of the unfairness of their exclusion. At Yale debates he had the students raise the issue of women's education. I am not suggesting that he would have changed the rules that prevented women from entering the college, or even contemplated doing so. But he knew that an injustice was being committed. In 1783, six years after assuming the presidency of Yale, he conducted an interview with Lucinda Foot, the adolescent daughter of a fellow pastor. At the end of the interview he handed her a solemn parchment certificate in Latin, testifying that her gender alone prevented her from entering the Yale freshman class. It would be close to two hundred years before women were admitted to Yale and other elite universities.

Stiles's interest in Jewish life and the study of Hebrew and the Bible clearly influenced his pluralism, his sympathy for other peoples and cultures. Among the most persistent of Stiles's Hebraic and Judaic interests was the fate of the Ten Lost Tribes of Israel. He was fascinated by—but did not endorse—what historian of ideas Richard Popkin has called "the Jewish-Indian theory." As I described in Chapter 1, this set of ideas theorized that the indigenous peoples of the Americas were the descendants of those Hebrew tribes exiled by the Assyrians in the eighth century B.C. Stiles also wanted to make connections between the Lost Tribes and the indigenous peoples of South Asia. All of this is within the framework of a much larger concern, the attempt to use biblical ideas to explain the diversity of human settlement and culture. Stiles's interest in the Lost Tribes of Israel predated his study of Hebrew by almost a decade. His view of the aboriginal peoples of the Americas was biblical. He wrote, "The American Indians, I suppose sprang from the Canaanites or the Phoenicians."[37] If they were not Israelite, they nevertheless had a relationship to ancient Israel. That was the only context in which an eighteenth-century intellectual could understand American origins. The choices were limited. A believing Christian could not see beyond the confines of the biblical narrative.

I am not claiming that Jewish observers and scholars were any more scientific or open-minded about this question. Some Hebrew-language Jewish accounts of the New World and its startling variety of inhabitants are as fanciful and fabulous as any penned by Christian savants. I focus on Stiles and other Christian writers on the origins of the indigenous Americans because these writers were deeply influential in their wider societies, and their views had repercussions in religious and social policy areas. Only a small, though attentive, audience of readers of Hebrew read the few Jewish authors who referred to this issue. For the most part this was an audience without power or influence; whatever communal influence it did have did not extend to the halls of the New England colleges, churches, and meetinghouses.

The biblical prophecies concerning the return of the Jews to the land of Israel were taken quite literally by Stiles. His Lost Tribes interests were intimately linked to the idea of the return to Zion. The early-twentieth-century Jewish scholar George Alexander Kohut called Stiles an "early American Zionist." According to Kohut, Stiles "desired that a more thorough and effectual search should be made after the Lost Tribes; as from the prophecies he always had in mind, he had no doubt of their future re-gathering and of the re-establishment of the Twelve Tribes in Palestine."[38]

Earlier, we mentioned Ezra Stiles's tendency in his diary to evaluate the accomplishments and reputations of scholars with whom he came into contact. It is clear from several of these entries that he greatly respected his older contemporary, Jonathan Edwards of Massachusetts. Upon Edwards's early death in 1758, Stiles took specific note of Edwards's linguistic achievements, especially of his knowledge of Hebrew. In the history of American thought, Edwards has been read and remembered for other reasons, and his reputation as an original thinker has eclipsed Stiles's fame as an educator and a chronicler of American life. But Stiles recognized in Edwards a Hebraist dimension, a dimension which, despite Edwards's deserved fame, has yet to be fully explored.

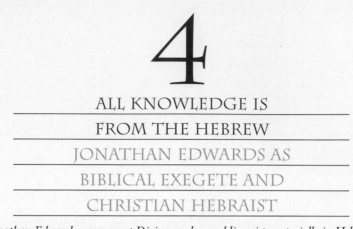

4

ALL KNOWLEDGE IS FROM THE HEBREW
JONATHAN EDWARDS AS BIBLICAL EXEGETE AND CHRISTIAN HEBRAIST

Jonathan Edwards was a great Divine, and a good linguist—especially in Hebrew.
Ezra Stiles

On October 19, 1757, five months before his death, New England theologian Jonathan Edwards replied to a letter from the trustees of the College of New Jersey offering him the presidency of the college. The first part of Edwards's well-known response, in which he sets out the conditions of employment, is often quoted. Less familiar is Edwards's agreement that, besides the "work of a president," he would "added to all, be willing to do the whole work of a professor of divinity in public and private lectures, proposing questions to be answered, and some to be discussed in writing and free conversation, in meeting of graduates and others appointed in proper seasons, for these ends." More specifically, he expresses an interest in teaching a language: "It would now be out of my way to spend time in constant teaching of the languages, unless it be the Hebrew tongue, which I should be willing to improve myself in by instructing others."[1] There is more here than the expression of a need to learn through teaching.

Edwards, at this late point in his life, still felt the need for further immersion in Hebrew studies, though this is not to imply that he neglected Hebrew at earlier stages of his life. Two grand projects that he had embarked upon, a work on typology and a "great work on the harmony of the relationship between the Old and New Testaments," necessitated a deepening of his knowledge of "the sacred tongue." It was this he set out to accomplish in the early 1750s.

The Puritan understanding of typology was predicated on St. Jerome's formulation: "In the Old Testament the New Testament is concealed; in the New

Testament the Old Testament is revealed." The method followed a basic pattern: search for a type in the Old Testament (a person, place, or event) and then link it to an antitype in the New Testament. As Edwards scholar Mason Lowance Jr. has put it, "The basis of this assumption is that the Old Testament is not a complete document in itself, but contains a series of prophetic adumbrations of Christ, the 'anti-type.'" Such foreshadowing of Christ might include Adam, the first man, or Moses, the first prophet. These identifications were familiar to readers of the Church Fathers. What set seventeenth- and eighteenth-century American typology apart was the specificity and concreteness of its development in the American Zion. In Lowance's concise description, "The peculiar circumstances of the New England experiment—the New Exodus, the journey through the wilderness, the establishment of a New Israel—provided the Puritans with a continuous analogy to the great biblical dramas."[2]

One of Edwards's grand projects was a "harmony" of the Old and New Testaments. For an American scholar who wanted to explore the relationship between the two Testaments—"the two breasts of Solomon's beloved," in one highly allegorical reading of the Song of Songs—and the extended unfolding of biblical typology in American history, knowledge of Hebrew was a necessity. Jonathan Edwards, eager to improve his knowledge of Hebrew, offered to teach the language in addition to his other responsibilities at the New Jersey college. A more thorough knowledge of Hebrew would provide Edwards with one of the central building blocks of his two grand projects—an explication of biblical typology and a comprehensive work that would harmonize the two testaments.

In his letter to the college trustees, Edwards writes of his "method of study: it is very much by writing, applying myself in this way to improve every important hint . . . thus penning what appeared to me my best thoughts, on innumerable subjects, for my own benefit." In the 1877 *History of the College of New Jersey*, Princeton president John Maclean asserted that Edwards's request to teach Hebrew, as well as his statement in the same letter that he was deficient in the Greek classics ("my Greek learning having been chiefly in the New Testament"), refuted the claims of Edwards's early biographers that the young Jonathan Edwards had "thorough knowledge of the Latin, Greek, and Hebrew."[3] Edwards, as Maclean saw it, was *deficient* in the learned languages, and toward the end of his life wished to improve his skills by teaching. A half-century later, Thomas Johnson, in his influential 1931 essay "Jonathan Edwards's Background of Reading," agreed with Maclean's assessment and had this to say of Jonathan Edwards's knowledge of languages: "Though Edwards seems later to have read Latin with ease, he always preferred English translations whenever he could secure them; he seldom made reference to a

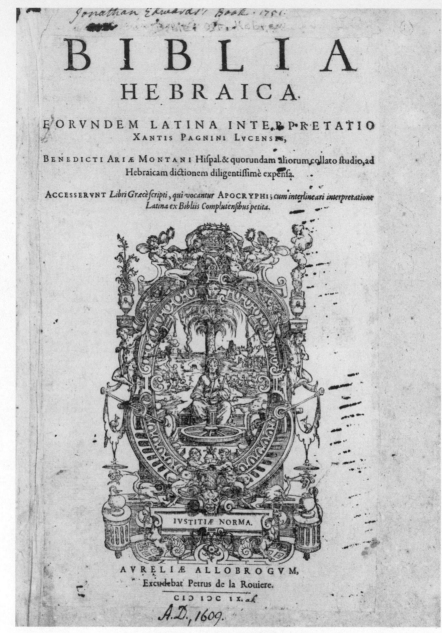

Jonathan Edwards's copy of Biblia Hebraica,
1609 (Princeton University Library)

Greek text, and *all that remains of his Hebrew is a negligible amount of marginalia and a few Hebrew idioms that he jotted on old envelopes.*[4] Today, some seventy years after Johnson's essay was published, it is clear to scholars that Edwards's Hebrew marginalia are *not* negligible, that the Hebrew idioms he discusses are numerous and significant, and that the references to Hebrew words, concepts, and texts in his writings reveal a growing familiarity with the Hebraic and Judaic traditions.

It is also clear at the beginning of the twenty-first century that Edwards's importance in American intellectual history has not diminished but increased remarkably. Once dismissed as a darkly puritanical preacher, Edwards is now viewed as a great American philosopher and literary stylist. Historians of ideas and literary critics alike have worked to restore Edwards's reputation. Today, no American theologian is as widely read and written about in the American academy, and no theological construct is as widely studied as typology. In 1972, Thomas M. Davis could argue that, in the work of Edwards and others, "when noticed at all, typology has been generally viewed as an aspect of the regrettable Puritan flirtation with allegory." Today, however, most scholars of American religion and American literature would agree that "an understanding of typology is central to reading Puritan texts and to identifying the references of Puritan imagery."[5]

As a young man Jonathan Edwards resolved "to study the Scriptures so steadily, constantly and frequently, as that I may find, and plainly perceive myself to grow in the knowledge of the same." Edwards spent a lifetime in pursuit of a full understanding of the Bible, and, as scholar Stephen Stein has noted, "Despite the quantity of his writings on the Bible, there is an amazing paucity of serious scholarship dealing with it."[6] This chapter is an attempt to fill that gap in the study of Edwards's spiritual and intellectual development. If, as Wilson Kimnach noted, "the biblical text is the ultimate point of reference in the Edwards manuscript canon," it behooves students of that canon to approach Edwards's understanding of the biblical text through the prism of Christian Hebraism and its study of biblical and rabbinic Hebrew.[7]

Edwards, as a Christian Hebraist, was working in the tradition of the Hebraists who were heirs to what Jonathan Elukin has dubbed "the enthusiasm for Hebrew that became one obsession of the scholarly world of the Renaissance and the Reformation."[8] But he never mastered the intricacies of Hebrew grammar and syntax. Nor did his study of Hebrew take precedence over his other multifarious intellectual pursuits. Despite the interest in Hebrew that Edwards displayed throughout his life, it is difficult to agree, as of yet, with one contemporary scholar's assertion that "Edwards had command of Latin, Greek, and Hebrew, and that he was well equipped to deal with the subtleties of Hebrew syntax."[9] Nevertheless, Edwards's Hebrew knowledge has been underestimated, and the importance of Hebrew studies to his work has yet to be fully explored. Throughout his life, in each of his many roles—young scientist, philosopher, exegete, author of sermons, polemicist—Jonathan Edwards made use of his Hebrew knowledge and constantly endeavored to enlarge that body of knowledge.

Ezra Stiles, a contemporary of Edwards, praised Edwards's Hebrew learning. In his *Literary Diary*, he eulogized Edwards as "a great Divine, a good linguist—especially in Hebrew."[10] This was quite a compliment from Stiles, who, as we saw in Chapter 3, had a lifelong obsession with matters Hebraic and Judaic and often styled himself a "Hebrician." In the spirit of Edwards's request to teach Hebrew at the College of New Jersey in Princeton, Stiles himself taught Hebrew to first-year students during the first ten of his sixteen years as president of Yale College (1788–95).

A Father's Only Son

Timothy Edwards and his wife Esther Stoddard raised eleven children. Jonathan was the fifth child and the only boy; four girls were born before him and six more followed. The Edwards home served as a school for the children, with their father as schoolmaster and teacher. It was in Timothy Edwards's parlor school that Jonathan, age six, began the study of languages. The elder Edwards had a fine reputation as a scholar and educator. Though listed as a Harvard graduate, class of 1694, he does not seem to have attended classes. "It is an old Connecticut tradition that Timothy never studied at college but simply appeared on commencement day, 1694, and by his brilliant scholarship qualified for his two degrees at the same time. . . . He was a thorough scholar in Latin, Greek, and Hebrew, and annually prepared a number of students for Harvard and Yale."[11] This old tradition has proved to be something of a fiction. The records reveal that Timothy Edwards did attend Harvard classes for two years, from 1686 to 1688. He received his degree some six years later.

The emphasis in the Edwards schoolroom was on precision in grammatical analysis, a lesson that young Jonathan learned well. In a letter dated August 7, 1711, Timothy Edwards, away in Albany, requested that his wife make sure Jonathan's sisters practiced his Latin with him. "I desire thee to take care Jonathan don't loose what he hath learned. . . . I would also have the girls keep what they have learnt of Grammar and get by heart as far as Jonathan hath learnt." Specific Latin texts are mentioned in the letter, which closes with the request, "Tell my children I would have them to pray daily for their father, and for their souls." Similar exhortations must have been forthcoming for the study of Greek and Hebrew. "By his tireless persistence, which brooked no indolence and no half-knowledge, Timothy Edwards fortified his son for life against textual errors, major and minor, and made thoroughness one of the Ten Commandments."[12]

When he arrived at the Collegiate School, which developed into Yale College, Edwards was well prepared for the rigors of the college curriculum. He mentions that his father gave him "the little Buxtorf"—the famous Hebrew grammar on which generations of Christian Hebraists were trained—as a gift.[13] Edwards studied it and other Hebrew grammars and lexicons—such as Leigh's *Critica Sacra* (1650)—assiduously.[14] As an undergraduate, he also acquired a number of Hebrew Bibles, in which he màde copious notations. David Brainerd, the evangelist to the Indians about whom Edwards wrote a short biography, later bound Edwards's well used copy of the Buxtorf. It is now in the Princeton University Library.

During his first year at Yale, Edwards devoted considerable time and energy to Hebrew. The Collegiate School had three rival branches. The Wethersfield branch, under the leadership of tutor Elisha Williams, was where Edwards began his Hebrew studies. In theory, Latin was the language of all instruction, and conversations between tutors and students were to be carried on in Latin. But a bit of skepticism is in order here. Latin conversations, recitations, and orations were a feature of college life that persisted until the beginning of the nineteenth century, but for the most part they were a formal, almost ritualistic, display of familiarity with the classical tradition. Orations in Latin, Greek, and Hebrew adorned the commencement ceremonies of the New England colleges. While the speaker and his teacher understood these orations, others merely listened politely. In the New England classroom the use of Latin as the language of instruction was quite limited.

As to Edwards's early Hebrew studies, we have eighteen pages of Hebrew exercises from his *College Notebook*. These are preserved in the Yale Edwards Collection. Most of the words are transliterated from the Hebrew and the transliteration system is cumbersome and inaccurate. These are Edwards's analyses of the first five verses of the First Psalm. All of the Hebrew words of these verses are transliterated, though Edwards does copy individual Hebrew letters into the righthand side of the page when he wants to make a point about the use of certain letters. These exercises were probably written during Edwards's second year at Yale; it was a standard of the curriculum that students embarked on the study of the Psalms in Hebrew during the sophomore year.[15] Samuel Johnson complained that the college tutor was inadequately prepared in Hebrew and that the students were given "a very superficial knowledge of part of the Hebrew Psalter."[16] Though Edwards and his tutor studied only a small portion of the Psalms—the first section of the First Psalm—one would not call Edwards's notes on that text superficial. The grammatical analysis is an in-depth one and owes much to Buxtorf's grammar and lexicon. As in many of his intellectual pursuits, Edwards pressed far beyond the lessons provided by his college tutor. Other students at Yale may have gained "a very superficial knowledge" of Hebrew, but Jonathan Edwards clearly surpassed them. In the early years of the college the organization situation was quite chaotic, even after the three schools coalesced in 1718. Other students may have shirked their responsibilities; Edwards did not.

Soon after leaving Yale, Edwards began preaching. When composing his early sermons, he often made reference to translations from Greek and Hebrew. In 1723, he wrote of his dedication to "reading the scriptures, in writing on types of the Scripture, and other things, in studying the language."

From the summer of 1722 to the spring of 1723, Edwards ministered to a small Presbyterian congregation in New York City. In New York he first encountered members of non-Christian faiths, and confronted the possibility that other beliefs were devoutly held. "I once lived for many months next to a Jew (the houses adjoining one to another) and had much opportunity daily to observe him; who appeared to me the devoutest person that ever I saw in my life; great part of his time being spent in acts of devotion, at his eastern window, which opened next to mine, seeming to be most earnestly engaged, not only in the daytime, but sometimes whole nights." [17]

In 1724, Edwards was appointed senior tutor at Yale, where Hebrew instruction was one of his responsibilities, and he remained tutor until 1726. During that period, "practically the entire responsibility (of the college) rested upon his shoulders alone." [18] This responsibility would have included the teaching of the "Learned Languages," Greek, Latin, and Hebrew.

All Knowledge Is from the Hebrew

At some point in the late 1730s or early 1740s, Edwards read Theophilus Gale's two-volume work *The Court of the Gentiles*, a book that influenced him deeply. It is a massive exposition of neoplatonist ideas about the origins of language and language's relationship to "the mysteries of creation." Previously unmentioned in reference to Jonathan Edwards's intense interest in Hebrew is that language's importance in the idea of *prisca theologia*, "ancient theology," an idea central to *The Court of the Gentiles*. First articulated by the Church Fathers, this Christian appropriation of the classical tradition asserted that the message of the Greek philosophers was biblical in origin. In the words of Edwards scholar Gerald McDermott, "The *prisca theologia* was developed . . . to show that the greatest philosophers had stolen from the Chosen People." Gale asserts in his book's preface that "all knowledge is from the Hebrew." As John

Smith has noted, "Gale's scholarly life was devoted to a single idea of showing that all ancient languages and learning—particularly philosophical thought—was derived from the Hebrew scriptures."[19]

Theophilus Gale's massive tome (both volumes come to almost a thousand pages) is an erudite elaboration of one basic idea: all ancient learning is derived from the Hebrew language and the text of Scripture. This idea, first articulated by the Church Fathers, had been advanced earlier in English letters and was expanded upon in the Renaissance writings of Pico della Mirandola. What sets *The Court of the Gentiles* apart is the elegant exposition of the central theme. For the subsequent two centuries Gale's book was "applauded as a model of erudition" by English stylists.[20] The volume opens with this declaration: "Argument; namely that the wisest of the Heathens stole their choicest Notions and Contemplations, both Philologic and Philosophic, as well as Natural and Moral and Divine, from the Sacred Oracles." Anticipating the opposition of exponents of the venerable traditions of English Greek and Roman classicism, Gale endeavored to portray the Hellenic traditions as Hebraic in their origins. The proof of this lies in the relationship between Hebrew and the "later" languages: "Now the matter of this Discourse is not Logic, but Philologic, touching the springhead and Derivations of human Arts and Sciences."[21]

According to Gale's understanding of history, the function of the Christian church was to transmit the totality of Hebraic culture to the nations. This function expands the Christian role of transmitting Scripture to a point at which all human learning is subsumed under the rubric of the biblical. "That the poor Temple of Jerusalem should have a Court for the Gentiles, to which they must be beholding for their choicest Wisdom! How great an honor is this for Mount Zion, the Church of God?"[22]

For Gale and other exponents of the Hebraic origins doctrine, the Hebrew language represents a perfect form of expression from which humanity fell because of its sins. (A kind of linguistic "original sin.") As Gale writes in *Court of the Gentiles*: "This Holy Language was for Nature's Empire Fit / But Sin and Babel ruined it."[23] For Gale and his circle, Hebrew was the "language of Eden." It could reveal both the Edenic origins of humanity and its future redemption in the restored Eden of the end of time.

Edwards had encountered similar ideas before he read Gale. In his "Miscellanies" (no. 350) we find his meditations on an idea he later found elaborated upon in Gale: "The philosophers had the foundations of most of their truth from the ancients or from the Phoenicians, and what they picked up here and there of the relics of revelation." In his Blank Bible, "a large Bible with wide margins in which he commented on the biblical text, Edwards noted that heathen stories about gods and goddesses were actually distortions of Hebrew counterparts. Saturn, for example, is a transmutation of Adam, Noah, and Abraham."[24] As a result of this close reading of Gale, Edwards undertook to make "a dictionary showing the force of terms and phrases of the Scripture both in English and in Hebrew."[25] Wilson Kimnach notes that the dictionary was begun in 1747. Earlier, in 1743, Edwards had begun his list of *Hebrew Idioms*. Far from being a mere list of Hebrew words, the items culled by Edwards from the text of Genesis are terms he later put to literary and theological use. The importance of these idioms to our understanding of Edwards's work lies in their value for a project in which he would compile explicit typological readings of the Bible. For these readings to be correct they had to be based on the text's original language.

In *Hebrew Idioms* Edwards retains the cumbersome transliteration system that he had used in his college exercises at Yale. The first entry, from Genesis 16:2, is written in Hebrew characters—*ibaneh*—"It may be that I shall be built up, i.e. I shall obtain children." After the first entry, he switchs to transliteration. Subsequent entries are transliterated, with occasional use of individual Hebrew letters. A number of times throughout the list Edwards corrects his transliteration; it is clear that he is working from the original Hebrew. This may seem an obvious point, until one realizes that some Christian Hebraists were working from already transliterated texts. Transliteration, in contrast to using the Hebrew writing system, represented one strain of English Hebraism, a strain associated with innovations in liturgical practice. For example, volumes of the Psalms, such as those published in London in the early eighteenth century, provided the Christian reader with a fully transliterated English text of all 150 Psalms. The power of the Hebrew word, even in its transliterated form, was considerable and necessary.

Typology, Hebrew, and the Natural World

Edwards became fascinated with the theological and literary uses of typology while still in his twenties. He tended to see beyond the typological links between the two Testaments to a new understanding of a method that embraced a biblical understanding of the natural world. For Edwards, the Bible, properly interpreted, provides the faithful reader with the keys to unlock the secrets of the natural world.

An encounter with Andrew Wilson's 1750 work, *The Creation the Ground-Work of Revelation and Revelation the Language of Nature (A Brief Attempt to Demonstrate that the Hebrew Language is Founded on Natural Ideas)*, led Jonathan Edwards to focus on the "philosophical meaning" of Hebrew and its "secret mysteries." Andrew Wilson reminds his readers of the importance of

Hebrew Idioms

Gen. 16. 2. It may be I shall be **built up** by her. אִבָּנֶה i.e. I shall obtain children

Gen. 16. 11. The Lord hath **HEARD** thine affliction i.e. hath regarded thine affliction.

Gen. 16. 12. and He shall be a **WILD ASS** man. i.e. a wild man.

Gen. 18 He hastened to **make it** Laagnassoth. i.e. to dress it. also v. 8.

Gen. 18. 11. old & ~~come~~ **coming to days** i.e. well stricken in ~~years~~ age

Gen. 19. 4. mikkātzeh. ~~from~~ ab extremo ~~from every quarter~~ from the **EXTREME** the **LIMITS** or **utmost** part. i.e. ~~from every quarter~~.

Gen. 19. Korāthi. ~~Rafters~~ **Rafter BEAM** or **TIMBER** i.e. ~~the~~ have roof.

Gen. 19. 21. I have **ACCEPTED thy FACE** for I have accepted thee

Gen. 19. 28 ~~towards~~ To the **FACE** of Sodom. i.e. towards Sodom. So to the Face of all the Place v. 29.

Gen. 20. 9. ~~was~~ deeds which **SHALL not** be done i.e. which ought not to be done

Gen. 20. 11. **ONLY** the Fear of God is not in this Place. i.e. surely the Fear &c —

Gen. 20. 13. Say to O me he is my Brother i.e. of me.

Gen. 21. ~~God ~~ Beno for the ~~Course~~ of his Son. i.e. because of his Son or on the account of his Son.

Jonathan Edwards, "Hebrew Idioms"
(Beinecke Library, Yale University)

Hebrew studies for *both* Old Testament and New Testament studies, but this reminder by itself is not unusual in an eighteenth-century tract. What distinguishes Wilson's Hebraism is his insistence that typology cannot be understood without a knowledge of Hebrew. Edwards's unique understanding of typology, which extends typological analysis to the phenomena of the natural world, may owe something to the influence of Wilson. Andrew Wilson writes, "So much does the Hebrew language agree with the figurative nature of the Old Testament dispensation, that it is impossible to explain the meaning of most of the types, without the assistance of the language, because the names for those things which are assumed as types express their natures or these qualities in them or relating unto them."[26]

Wilson's tract presents Hebrew as both the key to a proper understanding of typology and the key to a "scientific" understanding of the natural world. The Hebrew name of a being or object was understood to express its "nature" or "quality." Wilson decries the fact that in considering "that structure of the languages in its necessary connexion with, and relation unto things and operations of nature . . . the learned have so universally agreed to neglect that language . . . which is the most complete of any, and which is the most perfect example of adhering to nature in all its branches that can be imagined."[27] The convergence of nature and Scripture was central to Edwards's system of thought. Two decades before he responded to Andrew Wilson's work, Edwards delineated his understanding of the relationship between the biblical text and the natural world. In *Images* he expressed the inextricable linkage of Scripture and nature in this manner: "The Book of Scripture is the interpreter of the book of nature in two ways: viz. by declaring to us those spiritual mysteries that are indeed signified or typified in the constitution of the nature world; and secondly, in actually making application of the signs and types in the book of nature as representations of those spiritual mysteries in many instances."[28]

Another area of theological inquiry in which Hebrew struck Edwards as relevant was the area of sin and repentance. He discussed the Hebrew vocabulary of sin and repentance in his essay "Types of the Messiah," written between 1744 and 1749. Edwards analyzes the oft-quoted passage in Daniel 9 that speaks of the "seventy weeks which will seal up the vision and prophecy." Unlike many of his contemporaries and predecessors, Edwards was not interested in using this passage to calculate the precise date of the "end of days." Rather, he wished to demonstrate that the temple sacrifices were "types of the Messiah" and, as such, referred directly to Jesus. To do so he analyzed the Hebrew text, addressing complex questions of grammar and syntax. Hebrew words translated by earlier Christian translators as "sin," "transgression," and "iniquity" are discussed at length. The biblical vocabulary of sin will again concern Edwards when he writes his own treatise on original sin.

Original Sin

Edwards's expressed wish to improve his Hebrew knowledge may have been influenced by the fact that some of his theological conversation partners and adversaries were Hebraists by training. Among them was John Taylor, author of *The Scripture-Doctrine of Original Sin Proposed to Free and Candid Examination* (1750). Edwards's argument with Taylor takes us to the end of Jonathan Edwards's career and the composition of his *The Great Christian Doctrine of Original Sin Defended*.

Edwards, in the preface to that work, argues with Taylor's book and states that "no one book has done so much toward rooting out of these western parts of England the principles and scheme of religion maintained by our pious and excellent forefathers." Clyde Holbrook has noted that "Taylor's best work from the standpoint of pure scholarship, probably lay in his linguistic studies, but his *Scripture-Doctrine of Original Sin* was destined to attract more attention from friends and foes." Taylor produced a great deal of Hebraica, including a Hebrew grammar and a Hebrew concordance. His use of Hebrew words and grammatical terms "undoubtedly prompted Edwards to labor doggedly over alternative senses of key biblical terms, often sending him to Buxtorf for aid in ferreting out these alternative Hebrew meanings."[29]

During the period in which he was writing *Original Sin*, Edwards displayed renewed interest in language study, and this may have been a factor in his decision to offer to teach Hebrew at the College of New Jersey. In the final footnote to *Original Sin*, Edwards endeavors strongly to make the case that the Jewish tradition believed in the doctrine of original sin. This would refute Wilson's contention that the concept of original sin is a late-Christian idea. Here Edwards quotes the Jewish sources from the Latin or English translations. The many quotes from rabbinic authorities, both Talmudic and medieval, are derived from the work of the English Christian Hebraist Henry Ainsworth. (Gale's *Court of the Gentiles* is cited as Edwards's authority for the view of the Greek philosophers.) The frontispiece of Edwards's *Original Sin* is adorned with ancient quotes on the topic, including quotes from Jarchi (the erroneous name that Christian Hebraists used for the twelfth-century exegete Rashi) and from Ibn Ezra. These quotes are culled from Latin translations and do not accurately reflect the sense of the Hebrew original.

In utilizing Christian Hebraist translations of rabbinic texts, Edwards is well within the tradition of eighteenth-century Christian Hebraism, which relied on the work of those seventeenth-century Christian scholars, Ainsworth most prominent among them, who translated sections of the Talmud and Zohar into English. But, when referring to biblical words and phrases, Edwards cites the Hebrew original. Edwards's personal copy of the Pagninus/Montanus 1609 *Biblia Hebraica*, which presents an interlinear Latin translation of the Hebrew text, is replete with his notations on Hebrew words and phrases. He later referred to these notations in sermons and other writings. For Edwards the Old Testament was cited with reference to the original Hebrew text; postbiblical Jewish texts could be quoted in translation.

Edwards's death in 1758, just a few weeks after his assumption of the presidency of the College of New Jersey, deprived colonial America of its greatest theologian and exegete. His early interest in Hebrew had recently reasserted itself and his plans for future study and teaching of the sacred tongue were in place. To proceed with both of the major projects to which he intended to devote himself, a complete and thorough "History of the Work of the Redemption" and what Edwards called "another great work," "The Harmony of the Old and New Testaments," he would have to rededicate himself to the study of the original text of the Hebrew Bible.[30]

An Edwards Dynasty

Just as Timothy Edwards bequeathed to his son Jonathan a legacy of dedication to the study of languages, Jonathan Edwards bequeathed to Jonathan Edwards Jr. a similar legacy. I mentioned that Timothy taught young Jonathan the "learned languages" and gave Jonathan his copy of Buxtorf's grammar; Jonathan Edwards passed on this Hebraist legacy to his son. We know that the younger Edwards evinced a lifelong interest in language study, especially in the study of Hebrew. Educated at the College of New Jersey, Jonathan Edwards Jr. studied Hebrew grammar in his third year and the text of the Hebrew Bible in his fourth. His 1788 book *Observations on the Language of the Muhhekaneew Indians* was based on his study of the dialect of the Indians of Stockbridge, a dialect which he had acquired as a child in that Western Massachusetts outpost in which his parents settled. In his book, Jonathan Edwards Jr. makes reference to the theory that the Native American languages are related to the "Asiatick" languages. The book's subtitle is "In which the extent of the language of North America is shown; its genius is grammatically traced; some of its peculiarities and some instances of analogy between that and the Hebrew are pointed out." This reference is an allusion to "the Jewish-Indian theory," a discussion of which, as I noted earlier, engaged John

Adams and Thomas Jefferson in an exchange of letters. While they rejected the idea as fanciful, many of their contemporaries in fact took it seriously. Jonathan Edwards Jr. did not fully endorse this theory, but he did allude to it a number of times, and seems to have done so approvingly. When in 1802 Jonathan Edwards Jr. assumed the presidency of Union College in New York, he encouraged the study of Hebrew there, establishing a tradition of Hebrew scholarship at Union that persisted throughout the nineteenth century. Today, visitors to Union's upstate New York campus can still see the Hebrew inscription that graces the library dome.

Throughout his life Jonathan Edwards evinced an interest in Hebrew studies, and this interest deepened in the last years of his life. I am not making the case that this interest led to great expertise in Hebrew. While Jonathan Edwards translated comfortably from the Latin, and less comfortably from the Greek, when citing Hebrew texts he always acknowledged the authority of the canonical Christian Hebraists and often quoted directly from their translations. In the final footnote to *Original Sin* there are extensive quotations from the rabbinic authorities, but these are all from secondary sources; Edwards did not translate these citations directly from the original. In dealing with questions of biblical interpretation rather than matters of theological speculation, Edwards was more apt to refer to the Hebrew original.

Jonathan Edwards's interest in Hebrew bears some relation to what Wilson Kimnach has identified as Edwards's "pursuit of reality." According to Kimnach there are two aspects to this pursuit: "a sustained evaluation of the nature of human experience; and a method of preaching." Study of the language of Scripture both enabled Edwards's pursuit of the religious meaning of "reality" and validated it. Edwards sought to "unify the words of the Bible and those of life."[31] In pursuit of unifying structures Edwards turned to the Hebrew language and to the style and techniques of scripture. Kimnach points out that "the most pervasive of Edwards's literary devices, repetition . . . was sanctioned in his eyes by Hebrew poetry." In the discussion of typology, I have alluded to the perceived relationship between nature and language. These modes of thought would have led Edwards to the writings of the Kabbalists, but I cannot emphasize too strongly that his references to Kabbalism are to Christian Kabbalism, a doctrine with some Jewish roots, but one that had developed its own identity by the eighteenth century. Though the kabbalistic strains may seem strong in some of Edwards's speculations, we should be cautious of overemphasizing Kabbalism's influence on Edwards's thought.[32]

We have seen that mystical Jewish ideas and their expression in kabbalistic writings helped shape the lives and ideas of other Hebraists. Judah Monis, a Jewish convert to Christianity, referred to the Zohar in his baptism discourse and studied Lurianic texts. Ezra Stiles studied the Zohar, the primary text of

Kabbalism, and sought "Christian truths" in that Jewish text. In a later chapter we will investigate claims that kabbalistic ideas influenced the doctrines of a new American religion. The writings of the Mormon prophet Joseph Smith provide us with a case of Christian engagement with Jewish mystical ideas.

In his introduction to Edwards's *Images or Shadows of Divine Things*, Perry Miller notes that for Edwards and his Puritan predecessors, typology, as a system of interpreting the rhetoric of the Bible, held the "promise of delivering a unified meaning for history. Furthermore, history was enacted in nature. . . . By an unavoidable compulsion typology was forced to seek for a unity greater than that of the Bible, a unity of history, nature and theology."[33] Edwards expressed this search for unity in a pivotal section of *Images*: "Wherever we are, and whatever we are about, we may see divine things excellently represented and held forth. And it will abundantly tend to confirm the scripture, for there is an excellent agreement between these things and the Holy Scripture."[34] For Jonathan Edwards, the Hebrew language was a key to comprehending that agreement, and it was toward a more thorough knowledge and understanding of that language that Edwards was working at the end of his remarkable life.

5

EVANGELIZING THE JEWS

CHRISTIAN MISSIONS &

JEWISH RESPONSES

*I really wish the Jews again in Judea an independent nation. Once
restored to an independent government and no longer persecuted they would
soon wear away some of the asperities and peculiarities of their character, possibly
in time become liberal Unitarian Christians.*
John Adams

The Mission to the Jews

Remote and fanciful as "the Jewish-Indian theory" might seem to early-
twenty-first-century observers, this powerful idea and the enthusiastic
support that it attracted had an indirect but significant effect on American
Jewish history, and on Christian-Jewish relations in the early years of the
American Republic. When combined and conflated with Christian missionary
aims, the theory had an unintended effect on the then quite small American
Jewish community. This effect is best examined through the life stories of two
early-nineteenth-century American public figures, Elias Boudinot, director of
the U.S. Mint, and J. S. C. F. Frey, prominent churchman and missionary to
the Jews. Both men were affiliated with the American Society for Meliorating the Condition of the Jews (ASMCJ), a mid-nineteenth-century society
with a name that, in the elegant phrase of historian Hyman Grinstein, was
"another long title from the leisurely past."

Some modern historians of American Jewry have noted the powerful effect of Christian missionary activity on nineteenth-century American Jews
and their communities.[1] The effect, however, was not what the missionaries
had anticipated. Very few Jews apostatized, and the organized Jewish community was spurred into action by the perception of an outside threat. The
first American Jewish newspapers and journals were published in response to
missionary activity. Among them was Isaac Leeser's *Occident and American*

Jewish Advocate. The name of this important journal was a direct response to Frey's journal, *Israel's Advocate*, which called for the Jews of the United States to convert to Christianity.

What is striking about this intense missionary effort to convert the Jews is that there were so few Jews in the United States at the time. In 1820, the year of the formation of the "Jews Society" (as the ASMCJ was known), there were two to three thousand Jews in the Republic, out of a total U.S. population of ten million. Jews represented only one-tenth of 1 percent of the American population, but their small numbers did not lessen the enthusiasm of Christian missionaries, who, like Cotton Mather in the early eighteenth century, aspired to bring Jews into the Christian fold.

"Meliorating the condition of Jews," an odd locution for Jewish apostasy, was a cause taken up with vigor by thousands of prominent Americans at midcentury. In the decades before the Civil War, "Christian causes"—social work, refugee care, and general social gospel work—were at the forefront of Protestant philanthropic enterprise. Many wealthy and publicly minded Americans devoted their monies and their energies to missionary activities within the United States. While some of their social peers supported Protestant missionary activities abroad (particularly in Asia and Africa), many felt that encouraging the "conversion of the Jews" in the United States would hasten the Second Coming and highlight America's destined role in the events of the End Time. Jews were only one of the groups targeted by American missionaries. Catholics and Muslims were equally important targets. Those who supported foreign missionary work (some wealthy Americans supported *both* foreign and "home" missions) were exhorted to their efforts by this 1811 missionizing pronouncement made by the American Board of Commissioners for Foreign Missions: "Prophecy, history, and the present state of the world seem to unite in declaring that the great pillars of the Papal and Mohametan impostures are now tottering to their fall. . . . Now is the time for the followers of Christ to come forward boldly, and to engage mankind in the great work of enlightening and reforming mankind."[2]

By the 1840s the United States had more than two hundred chapters of the Society for Meliorating the Condition of the Jews. (Roughly one chapter for every ten Jews!) At its founding in 1816, John Quincy Adams, then secretary of state, was on its governing board—as were many other prominent public figures. Wives often joined the Society as well, and in some cities they formed "Female Societies for the Conversion of the Jews." The first half of the nineteenth century saw increased opportunities for women to participate in the burgeoning support for Christian social causes. Women were often in the forefront of these societies for "good works." Hannah Adams, a prominent New England intellectual, convened the Boston women's ASMCJ. Later she would write the first American *History of the Jews*.[3] Like her distant kinsman John Quincy Adams, she called for respect for the Jews and their history, and for all good Christians to work toward their conversion.

The ASMCJ failed in its stated purpose, as very few Jews apostatized, and of those who did, many were driven by economic needs. The missionary society promised and provided financial assistance, employment, and schooling for the young. When they became better established, many converts returned to Judaism. Over time, missionary activity had an effect that was the opposite of what John Quincy Adams and his associates intended. Rather than weaken the Jewish community, missionary pressures cemented ties; Jews saw a common need to respond to attacks on their religious and communal integrity. In the 1820s and 1830s Jewish authors published a number of books countering Christian missionary claims. Magazines and journals defending Judaism and Jews against their detractors were widely disseminated and found a readership among Americans of many religious denominations. Christian missions to American Jews helped define the contours and concerns of the emerging, and until then internally divided, Jewish community. Jewish identity was strengthened, not weakened, by missionary efforts. As historian Lee M. Friedman noted in his description of early-nineteenth-century American Jewry, "To most persons in America the Jews were then still a mysterious biblical nation which had survived to modern days to demonstrate the strange truth of prophecy."[4] The prophecy of mass Jewish conversion to Christianity was not to be fulfilled in the United States.

In New York in 1820 an anonymous author published *Israel Vindicated: Being a Refutation of the Calumnies Propagated respecting the Jewish Nation; in which the objects and views of the American Society for Ameliorating the Condition of the Jews, are investigated*. Despite this bold and, one might say, inflammatory title, the clerk of the Southern District of New York, who had authority to censor all books published in that state, did not exercise that authority. One might expect him to have done so. In the early nineteenth century an attack on Christian missions was understood as an attack on the Republic itself. The author of this tract therefore chose to remain anonymous. Although the book was published, the clerk did censor the conclusion of its already extended subtitle—"and Reasons Assigned for Rejecting the Christian Religion." For the author's main concern seems to have been a refutation of Christian doctrine, not a defense of Judaism. While refutations of Christian doctrine were "seditious," attacks on the mission to the Jews were merely unusual, not punishable by law. The secularization of American society was only in its beginning stages. From the early colonial period onward, the multiplicity of denominations in the America Colonies had mitigated against the rule of one dominant religious ideology. Still, the nation's self-concept was that it was a "Christian nation." Only later in the nineteenth century was this idea challenged and weakened.

Elias Boudinot (1740–1821)

Elias Boudinot, president of the Continental Congress and one of the signers of the Constitution, served as the first president of the ASMCJ. Born into a wealthy Philadelphia colonial family, Boudinot trained as a lawyer and quickly rose to the top of the legal profession. Sympathetic to the revolutionary cause, he was appointed to high military and diplomatic positions within the emerging American government. A deeply religious man, he found great significance in having been baptized by evangelist George Whitefield. Boudinot abhorred war but supported the cause of freedom. Appointed commissary-general of all prisoners taken in the war, he wrote to his wife that he was being drawn into "the boisterous noisy, fatiguing unnatural and disrelishing state of war and slaughter" (July 22, 1777).[5] In 1782 he was one of the drafters of the peace treaty with England, as well as one of its signers. For his services to the nation, George Washington appointed Boudinot first director of the U.S. Mint.

Boudinot bridges the gap between colonial speculation about Native American origins and the missionary fervor that gripped the American Republic in the first decades of the nineteenth century. He believed that the Native Americans were the descendants of the Ten Lost Tribes. As an independent nation, the United States now had the opportunity to unite these "lost" tribes with their Jewish brethren. Both groups could then be gathered under the wide Christian tent of American Protestant faith. The stage would thus be set for the "salvation of all mankind." Following the "returned" Lost Tribes, Americans would lead the way into the millennium. The final act of the drama would be the entry of the Lost Tribes, the Native Americans among them, into a rebuilt Jerusalem. For one reading of the Jewish-Indian theory considered missions to the Indians attempts to return them to the Israelite fold from which they had sprung.

In his strange book *A Star in the West; or, A Humble Attempt to Discover the Long Lost Ten Tribes of Israel, Preparatory to Their Return to Their Beloved City, Jerusalem*, Boudinot presented and defended the notion that the Native Americans were descended from the Israelites. The book was published in New Jersey in 1816. Boudinot's "Star" was the American equivalent of the Star of Bethlehem. Just as that star spread "the glad tidings of salvation among the distant nations of the earth," the message that the American Indian tribes were of the lost seed of Jacob would "become a guide to the long suffering and despised descendants of that eminent patriarch, to find the once humble babe of Bethlehem." That is to say, the Jews, when presented with the evidence that the Native Americans were the Lost Tribes of Israel, would turn to Christianity and fulfill their destiny.[6]

Boudinot's tract, recounting a long series of historical injustices, attempts to create sympathy for both the American Indians and the Jews. It opens with a rather sympathetic call to recognize the unique role of the Jews in history: "However despised the nation of the Hebrews were among the Greeks, Romans, and others of their neighbors . . . and by all the nations of the earth ever since, there can be no doubt now, that they have been and still are the most remarkable people that have existed since the first century after the flood" (p. 23). The "strange blindness" of the Jews may have prevented them from seeing the Christian truth, but that does not exonerate Christians for the cruel treatment meted out to them. In the end, Boudinot asserts, "God will call their oppressors to a severe account for the unchristian manner in which they carried the divine judgments into execution. Little of it has been done for the glory of God" (p. 202).

Boudinot concludes his survey of biblical and postbiblical history with the assertion that the Ten Lost Tribes persist in his own day. "Every serious reader, who takes the divine scriptures for his rule of conduct, must believe that the people of God are yet in being in our world, however unknown at present to the nations" (p. 49). The Ten Lost Tribes, according to Boudinot, were superior to the Jews. They had been exiled long before the Jews rejected Jesus and, as Christians understood it, suffered the fate of losing their land for that rejection. "From this awful and tremendous fate, the ten tribes, by their previous captivity and banishment, have been happily delivered, having no hand in this impious transaction" (p. 75). Thus, American Indians were ideal agents of redemption. While descendants of the Ten Lost Tribes and thereby of the chosen people, they were not tainted by the rejection of the Christ. Boudinot uses the Jewish-Indian theory to solve one of the great Christian conundrums—what is to be the fate of a "chosen people" who are also a rejected people? The Lost Tribes, now in the form of the American Indians, are exempt from the curse placed on the Jews of history, and thus are able to play a central role in the redemption.

Some historians of American religion consider Boudinot one of the most important figures in the beginning of American fundamentalism. He saw the American Revolution as a pre-millennial event. The French Revolution, thirteen years later, only confirmed this worldview. Working to bring the Native Americans to Christianity, Boudinot thought that these new converts would serve as leaders of an American revival of the Christian faith. To this end, he founded a school to train Native Americans as Christian ministers.

A young Indian orphan of the Cherokee tribe attended the school and became a Christian minister. Upon entering the school, he was given the name "Elias Boudinot." But contrary to the elder Boudinot's expectations, this young man did not become a Christian leader of his people. At the Connecticut mission school for Native Americans, the younger Boudinot met a young Anglo-American woman. They fell in love and married, which led both his mentors and the Cherokees to ostracize him. He left the tribe and the Christian clergy. Later he rose to prominence, not as an Indian leader of a Christian revival, but as a negotiator who gave away the Cherokee territories and rights. For his part in what many perceived as treachery to his tribe, the younger Boudinot was murdered in 1839, but not before serving as a missionary and working as a newspaper editor—the first to publish in the newly developed written Cherokee language. Closer to our theme of explicating American understandings of the relationship of the Old World to the New, he collaborated on a translation of the New Testament into Cherokee.

For Elias Boudinot and other American proponents of what we today call the Jewish-Indian theory, there was no inconsistency in the idea of converting the Indians from "paganism" to Protestant Christianity. In the chiliastic imagination the return of the Lost Tribes would be a return to Christianity ("fulfilled Judaism"), bypassing, as it were, the Jewish stage of religious development. By the time Boudinot wrote *Star in the West* this notion had a long and venerable history. In a 1649 pamphlet titled "The Glorious Progress of the Gospel Among the Indians in New England," the English Puritan writer Edward Winslow found it "wondrous that God has opened the hearts of the Indians to the gospel just when so many eminent divines expect the conversion of the Jews."[7] In this scenario the Jews would abandon their "stubborn faith" and embrace "the Christian truth." The Indians of New England would then join them in embracing Christianity as the process of redemption was unveiled.

Toward the end of his life Boudinot helped found the American Bible Society. This was one of Jacksonian America's most successful and enduring religious voluntary organizations. As historian Peter Wosh has noted: "Boudinot and his A.B.S. colleagues shared his pessimism concerning the impact of Jeffersonian dissent on American social and religious values. Placing the Good Book in every household, in the minds of many, might lay the foundation for a common Christian social consensus."[8] The remarkable successes of the American Bible Society led to a deepening of American familiarity with biblical names and places, a familiarity which enabled and encouraged the nineteenth-century American fascination with the Holy Land.

[*Zion on American Shores*]

Boudinot's unlikely interlocutor in the unfolding American speculation about the Jews' role in the "process of redemption" was the founder and promoter of the American Society for Meliorating the Condition of the Jews, the Rev. J. S. C. F. Frey. Both Boudinot and Frey earned a place in the early-twentieth-century *Dictionary of American Biography*. The American Council of Learned Societies organized the project, designed to emulate the British *Dictionary of National Biography*, and the Ochs family of the New York Times Company financed it. Covering the colonial period and the first 125 years of the Republic, it was, for its time, remarkably inclusive. Entries were not limited to Anglo-Saxon Protestants with trinomial names (John Quincy Adams). There was a conscious attempt, no doubt motivated by the Ochs family's Jewish origins, to include members of religious minorities, some women, and a number of African American and Native American personalities. Frey is sandwiched between Jefferson's associate, poet Philip Freneau, and American industrialist Henry Clay Frick.

Despite Frey's inclusion in this biographical dictionary, which served as an early American "Who's Who," the details of his life are nevertheless sketchy. Not that we do not have enough data on him. Rather, there is too much, and all of it written by Frey. The child of a traditional rabbinic family of Eastern Europe, he became a Christian in his mid-twenties. He wrote many books, pamphlets, and broadsides about his life, but for many of the events of his early life there is no corroborating evidence. We have only his word for many of the stories he relates. His *Narrative* appeared in nineteen different editions over a period of half a century and was read by many Americans.

Frey knew that the conversion of the Jews was seen by millenarian thinkers as the crucial penultimate event before the commencement of the thousand-year Reign of Christ on earth. Speculation about these questions in early-nineteenth-century England and the United States ensured Frey an audience for his detailed retelling of his journey from European Jewish orthodoxy to various forms of Christian religious practice. For Frey, as a Christian, remained unsettled and restless in his religious choices. He was to switch Christian denominations many times.

As Frey's books are conversionist narratives—their stated purpose is to bring Christianity to his "Jewish brethren" through a narration of his life story—they are problematic as biographical sources. Joseph Samuel Christian Frederick Frey's story begins with his curious string of given names. His opponents used this long name against him, frequently mocking him for his pretentiousness. Isaac Leeser, spokesman for traditional Judaism in mid-nineteenth-century America, referred to Frey as "this curious being, equally famous for length of name as the number of creeds he has professed."[9]

His parents gave him the name Joseph Samuel Levi. They were a poor Jewish couple living in Bavaria. His father served as the town *melamed* (Hebrew school teacher), while his mother was a shopkeeper. Born in 1771 in Lower Franconia, the third of ten children, Joseph Samuel received a traditional Jewish education. He began studying the Hebrew Bible at the age of three. At age seven he embarked on the study of the Talmud. At eighteen he had completed his study of the Talmud and was certified soon after as a teacher and synagogue officiant. He seemed destined to follow in his father's professional footsteps and become a *melamed*. He acquired the skills of a *shochet*, the ritual slaughterer who prepares kosher meat. He also became a cantor and Torah reader.

But the presence of many brothers and sisters and the poverty in which they lived served as catalysts for the young Samuel Joseph to leave his small town in Germany and travel in search of work as a Hebrew and rabbinics tutor. As Frey explained in his often-published *Narrative*, it was on one of these trips in his mid-twenties that he met a "Christian gentleman" who spoke to him about Jesus and his message. After mulling over this conversation for several months, Frey "decided to contact the local minister about his feelings and with many conversations and some study he became more and more convinced of the truth of Christianity."[10] When he was baptized in 1798, Frey took two additional names, Christian and Frederick, and adopted the family name of Frey. He explained in his *Narrative*, "My surname, to remind me of the text from which the presiding Lutheran Minister preached on this occasion, 'And ye shall know the truth and the truth shall set you free.'" He was now free of the rule of rabbinic law—or so he understood the Christian reading of the "Mosaic past."

Frey's *Narrative* makes much of alleged Jewish hostility to Christians and to Christian doctrine. When telling the story of his childhood and of his schooling in the classical Jewish texts he claims, "Our tutor took every opportunity to impress us with prejudices and hatred against the Christian religion. . . . The person himself who believes the Christian religion, becomes the object of their utmost abhorrence. One of the names by which such a person is called, is *meshummad*, from the root *shamad*, which signifies to destroy; and to this name they generally add *yemach shemo vesichro*; i.e. let his name and memory be blotted out."[11]

After his apostasy at age twenty-seven, Frey spent a year enrolled in a Lutheran seminary in Berlin. Then, determined to embark on missionary endeavors, he set out for London. His ambition to preach to Jews, whom he called his "brethren and kinsmen according to the flesh," soon found fulfillment in the activities of the London Missionary Society, whose seminary Frey attended for a number of years. Upon graduation he began preaching to the Jews. In 1809 after a falling-out with his superiors, he organized his own missionary society, the London Society for the Promotion of Christianity among the Jews.

Mel Scult noted in his 1978 study of Frey's activities in London that, while Frey brought few Jewish converts to the church, the amount of money and time spent in attempts to convert them was staggering. "In the period between 1809 and 1816 the approximate number of (Jewish) converts was one hundred and they cost about five hundred pounds sterling a piece. . . . Converting the Jews was thus a major concern in the minds of many people. It was also a fantastic exercise in futility and we cannot help but wonder how the missionaries persisted with such vehemence in the face of so little success."[12]

The low rate of return on an investment of time and money was of course not the point. Frey's Christian supporters, among them prominent clergymen, politicians, academicians, and society women, saw his society's activities as acts of Christian charity. The resistance of individual Jews to conversion did not disappoint or discourage the London Society's supporters. As they saw it the very resistance of the Jews to conversion was a divine trial that they, the Society's supporters, had to endure. The difficulty of the task was deemed proof of its importance. The title of a society lecture of 1813 provides a context for this understanding of missionary activities: "Christian Love, the Most Powerful Motive to Attempt the Conversion of the Jews."

As often happens, love of another kind intruded on and disrupted the "good works" of the London Jews Society. Though married to Hannah Cohen, who had also converted to Christianity, Rev. Frey was nevertheless rumored to be overly attentive to some of his female charges. These rumors reached scandalous proportions with regard to Frey's conduct at a country estate used by the Society. Frey was using the estate to train converted Jews to become missionaries among their former coreligionists. Among his students was a young couple, the Josephsons. Mrs. Josephson had been a prostitute in London and was "saved" by the Society, of which Mr. Josephson was a member. As one trenchant observer noted, "Mr. Frey constantly attended on Mrs. Josephson . . . and so very desirous was he to improve her understanding that as early as six o'clock in the morning, was the divine seen coming from her house after having performed his 'religious functions.'"[13] Other rumors soon surfaced: "It was learned from Frey's housemaids, from the girls in a house of ill fame in Ipswich, and from other sources, that Mrs. Josephson had not been the only recipient of Frey's amorous attentions."[14]

Frey was summarily fired by the Society and within a few months he embarked on a voyage to New York. Upon arrival he established a new missionary organization, the ASMCJ. Protestant America was ripe for his efforts, and as we have seen he quickly gained support for his organization. As often happens in these cases, Frey was quick to condemn others for sexual license. His condemnation of Judaism and its practitioners included the accusation that "fornication was common among them."[15]

Before we leave the London Society that Frey founded, we should note that it entered literary history through an unexpected Irish connection. Leopold Bloom, in James Joyce's *Ulysses*, notes that his Hungarian Jewish father, Rudolph Virag, was converted to Protestant Christianity through the offices of the London Society for the Promotion of Christianity among the Jews. Bloom's Jewishness is a persistent theme in Joyce's novel. Bloom is sensitive to Irish Catholic attacks on Jews and the Jewish tradition, but says of himself that he is not really a Jew—as his mother was Catholic. There is more at issue here than ethnic identification. In the novel the Hellenic and the Hebraic merge and separate. Shem and Sean, the Hebraic and Gaelic "ancestors," inhabit both the waking world of *Ulysses* and the dream world of *Finnegan's Wake*. The penultimate chapter of *Ulysses*, "Ithaca," dwells at length on perceived or imagined similarities between the Hebrew and Gaelic languages and between Jewish and Irish culture.

Hebraism and the Mission to the Jews

Central to Frey's missionary activities among the Jews was his use of the Hebrew language as a tool of conversion. He seemed convinced that appealing to Jews in their sacred language would bring them to Christianity. The London Society for the Promotion of Christianity among the Jews spent a great deal of money and effort translating, publishing, and disseminating Hebrew-language missionary tracts. These included translations of the New Testament into biblical Hebrew, Hebrew-language editions of Christian prayer books and hymnals, and Hebrew-language sermons on Christianity. For Christian scholars and clergymen who wished to work among the Jews and to understand their languages and texts, Frey published a series of grammar books and dictionaries. In the preface to his *A Hebrew, Latin, and English Dictionary* of 1815, Frey wrote of the "excellence of Hebrew learning. . . . Almost ever since the author has enjoyed the happiness of being a member of the Christian church, and particularly since he has had the privilege of living in this highly favoured land, he has felt an ardent desire to call the attention of his fellow Christians to this important study, and to assist them in the pursuit of it."[16]

Frey's *Hebrew Grammar* (1811) included prose examples from Jewish and Christian materials. We find at the book's end a passage from the Gospel of Matthew translated into biblical Hebrew, complete with the cantillation marks of the Old Testament text. It is preceded by the first chapter of Genesis, thereby creating the impression of a seamless link between the languages and contents of the "Two Testaments."

Frey warned his Christian readers that both correct pronunciation of Hebrew and a thorough knowledge of the vowel points were essential for carrying on missionary activities among Jews. "At the present enlightened period of the world, and in the happy country in which we live, where zealous endeavours are being made to promote the conversion of the Jews, it might be urged that the Hebrew language, if well understood, rightly pronounced and brought into use, for that purpose, might be most efficacious to prove, from Moses and the Prophets, that Jesus is the Christ." But this is not the only reason for Christian scholars to study Hebrew. After recounting recent European advances in the study of "Arabic, Persian, and other Eastern Tongues," Frey makes a special case for the intensive study of Hebrew: "But to the scholar, to the Christian, and more especially to the Minister of the Gospel, the acquirement of the Hebrew language, it being that in which the Old Testament was originally written, presents itself with peculiar force and propriety, as an object very greatly to be desired."[17]

Like Judah Monis a century earlier, Frey believed that Hebrew knowledge was the most potent weapon in the missionary's arsenal. Without it no Jewish scholar or layperson would take the Christian message seriously; with a knowledge of Hebrew the Christian evangelist could counter Jewish claims based on scriptural references. Just as Judah Monis addressed his baptismal speech to "My Brethren According to the Flesh," Frey used similar language in speaking to the Jews of London and New York. Frey arrived in New York almost a century after Monis's baptism. The Jewish community of the northeastern states was still small and disunited, but his activities would spur them to action. Frey's Hebrew tracts did not persuade American Jews to convert. Rather, in reaction against his and other missionary activity, American Jews began to pursue their own Hebrew studies, establishing synagogue schools in which the rudiments of the Hebrew language were taught to their children. We shall study this development in the next chapter.

Another scholarly byproduct of Frey's missionary efforts was an improvement in Hebrew printing in England and the United States. One of the stated aims of Frey's London Society for the Promotion of Christianity among the Jews was to provide Jewish converts with the skills to earn a living in their new Christian environment. At the "Jews Chapel," a former French Protestant church in London, the Society established a printing office staffed by recent converts from Judaism. The total number of congregants at the Jews Chapel's Congregation Beni Abraham was fifty. Many of them were employed at the printing office. It was this press that issued missionary tracts, promotional material, Hebrew Bibles, and the Society's Hebrew New Testament.

David A. Borrenstein, a young student of Frey's who converted to Christianity under the missionary's supervision, excelled in the printing trade. When Frey left for America, Borrenstein left the Society. In the early 1820s in London he published a series of teaching charts for students of Hebrew, Arabic, and Syriac. By 1823 he had moved to New York City where he had some success in publishing "Oriental Language" textbooks. His *Elements of the Chaldee Language*, by Rev. William Harris, introduced the study of Aramaic to an audience of American theology students eager to learn the rudiments of that ancient biblical language. In the style of the nineteenth century, the book included commendations by experts in the field, among them Clement C. Moore, professor of Hebrew at the Episcopal Theological Seminary, and the Rev. J. S. C. F. Frey—now resident in New York.

In 1824 Borrenstein established a printing press in Princeton, New Jersey. Working with the faculty of the Princeton Seminary he issued the *Biblical Repertory*, "a quarterly containing a series of treatises and dissertations, principally in biblical literature." This would later become the famous *Princeton Review*, a journal which reflected and shaped the theological debates that buffeted Protestant America during the mid-nineteenth century. The issues of slavery and abolition, the implications of new scientific discoveries for established religion, and the question of the limits of religious dissent, were all hotly debated within the pages of the *Biblical Repertory* and the *Princeton Review*. The *Biblical Repertory* also became a forum for the ideas of Edward Robinson, the biblical scholar and Hebrew instructor who assumed the journal's editorship in 1830. Robinson, whose story is told in Chapter 7 of this book, became the father of modern Holy Land studies. He traveled to Palestine in 1838 and 1852, and reported his findings first in the journal and later in his multivolume book *Biblical Researches in Palestine*.

In a sense, Frey and his disciple Borrenstein paved the way for Robinson's stewardship of the *Biblical Repertory* and the *Princeton Review*. Here we have one of a series of ties among Christian missionary activity, Jewish converts, and Palestine exploration. This set of relationships came to full development in mid- and late-nineteenth-century Palestine. We explore this connection in Part III of this book.

Missionary Societies

Even before Frey arrived on American shores his London tract *The Converted Jew* spurred the formation of The Female Society of Boston and the Vicinity for Promoting Christianity among the Jews. This first American Protestant mission to the Jews collected contributions for the foreign Jewish mission centered in London.[18] The "First Directress" of the Female Society was Elizabeth Winthrop of the famed colonial family. Within a few years the Female Society would boast a membership of more than four hundred prominent American women.

The Female Society's founder, Hannah Adams of Boston, was a distant relative of President Adams and a remarkable woman. Historians of the early Republic have dubbed her the "first American female litterateur." A sickly child, she was educated at home by her father, an omnivorous reader who taught her Greek and Latin. "She became interested in religion at an early age and read widely and deeply in religious lore."[19] An abridged version of her book *A Summary History of New England* (Boston, 1799) became the standard history text used in New England schools of the early nineteenth century. Her *History of the Jews* was the first American book on that topic.

In his *Narrative* Frey noted that in America, "though inhabited comparatively by few of my Jewish brethren, yet the harvest is truly great, and the labourers comparatively few, and there is a much brighter prospect for the comfortable support of a growing family." Though Frey was ousted from the London Society for sexual misconduct, his *Narrative* puts a different spin on the events. Frey says he journeyed to the United States in 1816 with his wife and four children—three daughters and a son—in search of a "brighter prospect." Naturally, support of his family was a major concern. This explains his eagerness to serve as pastor of an American church immediately upon arrival. In New York City he attempted to organize a new mission to the Jews. Failing that he joined the recently formed American Society for Evangelizing the Jews, but this group, attracting no Jews to its lectures or prayer services, ended its activities after only a year of operation. Left without a ministry, Frey joined the Presbyterian Church, in which he was ordained a minister in 1818. He served as a Presbyterian minister for two years before boredom and restlessness set in. "The desire to be in the limelight and to preach to great crowds was very strong within him."[20] He would later switch Christian denominations yet again.

It was at this point that Frey was introduced to Elias Boudinot, who had retired from the directorship of the U.S. Mint and was now the president of the American Bible Society. Frey knew of Boudinot's wide influence and of his intense interest in the origins and present conditions of the American Indians. Frey described their meeting in this way: "Having submitted to him the proposed object and plan, together with various documents on the subject, and conversed much about the state of the dispersed in Judah and the long-lost tribes of Israel, he communicated to me his opinion in the following letter."[21]

In the letter, Boudinot, still vigorous at the age of eighty, reiterates the details of a proposal for a new mission to the Jews and offers Frey his unconditional support.

Frey planned to form a new mission to "colonize and evangelize" the Jews. The former was the means to accomplish the latter. The Jews were to be gathered into a colony, that there they might have an opportunity of earning their bread by their own industry. Approaching Boudinot for support was a brilliant move. Boudinot was a devout Christian, a biblical scholar, an eminent American hero, and a very wealthy old man. He was also a firm believer in the Jewish-Indian theory and a strong supporter of missionary activity.

Boudinot agreed to serve as president of the new organization, which was to be called the American Society for Colonizing and Evangelizing the Jews. Armed with Boudinot's name and leadership, Frey applied to the New York legislature for a charter. When some legislators objected to the blatant words "colonizing" and "evangelizing" in the title, Frey substituted "Meliorating" for the offending verbs and the charter was granted. The Society's stated purpose was *not* to convert Jews already resident in the United States. Rather, it proposed that Jews who became Christians in Europe would be provided with agricultural settlement and vocational training in the United States.

In 1821, only a year after the ASMCJ's establishment, Elias Boudinot died at age eighty-one. Boudinot's will contained a special provision for the settlement of Jews under the ASMCJ's care. "I would aid and assist in promoting the settlement of a body of Jews, who have been represented to me as desirous of removing from the Continent of Europe to some asylum of safety, if any should offer, where they may be able to examine and judge for themselves, into the great things of our divine religion, without fear or terror." He left the Society a large parcel of land in Pennsylvania, but this property proved too distant from New York to be of use. During the first two decades of its existence the Society did, however, purchase two New York State properties—one in Harrison and one in New Paltz—with plans to establish "Jewish farms" on them. Both properties were eventually sold, however, due to lack of applicants and residents. Frey and his associates had a far-reaching and transformative vision of the Jewish future, a vision that extended beyond conversion to include within its evangelical worldview a vision of the Jews as a people "returned to the land." In Frey's words Jews would again "delight in pastoral occupations."

These ideas resonated with other calls—both Jewish and Christian—to "normalize" the situation of Europe's Jews by having them engage in productive agricultural pursuits. For example, English politicians, churchmen, and intellectuals were promoting similar ideas. Seventy years later the "return to the land" would become the bedrock of political Zionism. If we compare

Christian Zionist and Jewish Zionist ideas, it is possible to make a case that the former not only preceded, but also influenced the latter. In an 1823 report the ASMCJ argued for Jewish engagement with agriculture in a manner reminiscent of later Zionist arguments:

It is a matter of undisputed scriptural history, that no nation was ever more attached to agriculture than the Jews in Palestine . . . and though it must be conceded that since their dispersion, no people was ever so averse from agriculture . . . it is because they have almost everywhere been denied the privilege of acquiring and cultivating land. . . . They have only to be restored to the privilege of acquiring real estate, a privilege which is secured to them in this free and happy country in order to revive all that love of cultivating the soil, and all that delight in pastoral occupations, which characterized them on the mountains of Gilboa, and the vales of Bethlehem.[22]

In this missionary plan Jewish agriculture would be revived in the United States—an idea that would find many supporters in the late nineteenth century. The return to Zion was left for the distant future. Jews would become agriculturalists in the United States, and in a sense this would be their Zion. In the End Time the Jewish people would be gathered from exile and returned to their land. Again we have the conflation of two distinct ideas: "the American Zion" and the Zion of the Holy Land.

Along with many other nineteenth-century English and American millenarians, Frey considered the Jewish return to Zion a prerequisite for the beginning of the millennium. "While the millenarian belief in the restoration of the Jews to Palestine was certainly not original with Frey, nevertheless his espousal of it lent it added weight since he was an educated Jew with great familiarity with the Bible."[23] This idea had prominent American supporters like John Adams: "I really wish the Jews again in Judea an independent nation. Once restored to an independent government and no longer persecuted they would soon wear away some of the asperities and peculiarities of their character, possibly in time become liberal Unitarian Christians."[24]

From 1823 to 1826, the ASMCJ published a monthly journal, *Israel's Advocate: The Restoration of the Jews Contemplated and Urged*. This journal and Frey's frequent speaking engagements galvanized the American Jewish community. To answer Frey's antirabbinic polemics, Jewish leaders published broadsides, pamphlets, and a regularly appearing magazine. This reaction, which began in the 1820s, continued until the Civil War. The threat of this common enemy—the Christian missionary—cemented the relationships between Jews of Sephardic, Germanic, and Eastern European origins. Denominational lines were crossed and erased. Orthodox and Reform leaders could agree on the danger of missionary activities. In response to the missionary claim that Judaism was a religion of superstition, Frey's critics wrote: "Is the Jewish religion then the only religion which can be accused of superstition? How stands the Christian religion in this particular? Does not the Protestant accuse the Catholic of superstition—while the Catholic accuses the Protestant of impiety? Does not one sect of the Protestant church accuse the other of idle ceremonies and mockeries, while it retorts in return upon its accuser for a want of proper decorum and respect?"[25]

Curiously, Frey himself crossed Christian denominational lines many times. Baptized in the German Lutheran Church, he remained in that tradition when he moved to England. But when he arrived in the United States in 1816, Frey used his missionary ties to acquire ordination in the Presbyterian Church. Several years later, he converted again, this time to the Baptist faith. Although Frey's enemies saw these changes as the product of expedience, the evidence is to the contrary. Jewish sources often spoke of Jewish apostasy as motivated by greed, cynicism, or expedience. Certainly the power relationship between Christians and Jews was one-sided, but these material explanations overlooked the possibility of "true belief," religious crisis and its resolution, and the convert's sincere belief that Christianity is the "fulfillment" of Judaism. Frey was vilified, condemned: both his apostasy and his moves from one Protestant church to another were seen as motivated by a search for power and money. The evidence, however, supports his claims of sincerity. In his writings Frey grappled with the doctrinal issues that motivated his various denominational allegiances. His thinking may have been muddled and confused, but he seems sincere in his convictions. Certainly none of his many religious conversions brought him financial security.

In 1827 Frey joined the Baptist Church. He explained this choice in terms of his search for the appropriate form of baptism for his children. He and his wife Hannah had four children prior to their arrival in the United States, five more afterwards. Each time Frey baptized one of his children, he questioned the origin and meaning of this ritual. He wrote his *Lectures on Baptism* (1834) not only to address these issues, but also to justify his joining the Baptist Church. "At the christening of one of my children, the minister exhorted us to bring up our children in the nature and admonition of the Lord. He said, 'These children are now members of the church, adopted into the family of God.' The declarations were forcibly impressed upon my mind, as if I had never heard them before. I resolved, therefore, not to present another child of my own, nor to baptize the children of any others, before I had thoroughly investigated the subject."[26]

Frey's two-hundred-page exploration of baptism was neither comprehensive nor original. Like much of his work it quoted extensively from both the

Church Fathers and Protestant divines past and present. In the volume's preface Frey defended his motives for adopting the Baptist view. No doubt his adversaries, both Jewish and Christian, had questioned these motives. "I was aware that the subject would excite much attention; that many of my best friends would be displeased, and others would not hesitate to ascribe my conduct to improper motives, especially to that of 'filthy lucre.' But surely, if such had been my motives, I not only acted most basely, but also most foolishly in leaving the large, rich, and respectable body of Presbyterians."[27]

As harsh as his Christian critics were, his Jewish critics were harsher and more confrontational. As we have noted, there were a number of American Jewish newspapers and journals born in reaction to Frey's mission. This reaction began in the 1820s and it continued until the Civil War. The attacks on Frey were united; every Jewish denomination participated. For example, in its first issue, published in April of 1843, Isaac Leeser's *Occident and American Jewish Advocate* ("a monthly periodical devoted to the diffusion of knowledge on Jewish literature and religion") responded directly to the ASMCJ and its journal, the *Jewish Chronicle*. Leeser opened his article on Frey with an apology to the public: "We would have been much pleased could our first number have appeared without a complaint against any portion of the American people. . . . Prejudice in its worst form, a dislike for our religion, is still the characteristic of a vast multitude, and the effect of this prejudice is seen in the revival of the ASMCJ and the revival too of its organ, Israel's Advocate, under the humbler title of Jewish Chronicle."

These Jewish responses did inform and influence their readership, but they seem to have had no effect on Frey and his confederates. Though his Jewish opponents derided him and some Christian associates questioned his behavior, there are nevertheless many reasons to take Frey seriously. Perhaps he was an opportunist in financial and sexual matters, but that is not a reason to dismiss his intellectual and religious project. (Though in the nineteenth- and twentieth-century American Protestant world, it seemed to many as adequate grounds for dismissing his whole project.) A dispassionate look at his career might yield a more nuanced and balanced picture of his publishing and other activities. Frey's accomplishments included the publications of the London Jews Society Library, as well as an edited version of Van Der Hought's Hebrew Bible, the first Hebrew Bible published in United States. He not only commissioned translations of Hebrew texts, but also organized a translation of the New Testament into Hebrew. Frey was the author of many editions of *A Hebrew Grammar in the English Language*. He claimed that Sidney Willard's *A Hebrew Grammar*, published at Harvard College in 1817, was plagiarized from his 1811 *Grammar*. Willard was Hancock Professor of Hebrew at Harvard from 1806 to 1830; his father was president of the university. He also served for a time as mayor of Cambridge, Massachusetts. Perhaps he was "too busy" to write his own grammar and used Frey's as his main source?

Frey insisted on the careful, precise presentation of Hebrew grammar and syntax. This insistence on precision and accuracy was related to his conversionist project. "If Christian Preachers were sensible of the good or bad effort produced upon the minds of the Jews, according as they pronounce the Hebrew language correctly, they would think no time too long and no pains too great to acquire the correct and accurate pronunciation."[28]

Frey's presentation of Hebrew to the Christian public was also related to his understanding of the millenarian aspect of Hebrew studies. Pointing to the increased interest in and study of Hebrew in the first quarter of the nineteenth century, Frey asks: "May it not be considered an encouraging sign, that the salvation of Israel is at hand? . . . Judah hath been scattered amongst all nations and become a hissing and a proverb amongst the people; but of late both the Hebrew Nation and the Hebrew Language have been remembered for good, and it is hoped that the Christian world will never cease to promote their true honor and glory till that happy day shall arrive when the Lord shall turn to the people a pure language, and all shall speak the language of Canaan."[29]

Frey and his ideas about the Jews and the millennium fit well into the religious life of early-nineteenth-century Protestant America. Many Americans believed that they and their country had a special role to play in bringing about the millennium. The conversion and restoration of the Jews was an important step in the commonly accepted millennial scheme. "Frey, the converted Jew who optimistically preached that the Jews should and could be converted, and that free and liberal minded America should be especially interested in this cause, strengthened the belief of Americans that they could play a significant role in the unfolding of God's plan for history."[30]

Frey addresses the question of the Jewish part in the events of the End Time in his book *Judah and Benjamin*. In this tract we see an engagement with some of the concepts that informed Boudinot's writings. Boudinot, as we have seen, was not only a benefactor and official of the ASMCJ; he was the author of the historical-theological treatise *The Star in the West*, a book that validated and authenticated the rationale for an American mission to the Jews. For both of these writers, God had chosen the New World and its inhabitants as the catalyst of the redemptive process.

As Frey relates his story, he delights in telling the reader how far he traveled, how many people he preached to, and how much money he collected for the Society. "In 1822–3 I engaged as agent to the society. In my first tour to the South, during six months I traveled 2,305 miles by land, preached 196 times, collected about $4,600 and formed 51 auxiliary societies. This I continued traveling as agent for several years, collecting many thousand of dollars, and formed more than four hundred auxiliary societies." In 1834 he claimed that "since my arrival in this country in 1816, I have been enabled to preach four thousand four hundred and seventeen times; and I have reason to hope my labors have not been in vain in the Lord."[31]

The *Dictionary of American Biography* described his activities in this way: "He traveled up and down the country, preaching some three hundred sermons a year and telling the story of his life. Jews were still objects of curiosity in the United States, and wherever Frey went crowds flocked to gape at him and hear him preach. As in England he succeeded in creating much interest in the cause and raising considerable sums of money, but he does not appear to have made a single convert."[32]

In one sense, his labors were in vain, for no Jews converted to Christianity because of his exhortations. In other ways, he achieved success and left a legacy. One of those ways was in his contributions to the study of Hebrew in the United States.

Frey and Hebraism

Though Frey's Hebrew scholarship was undistinguished and unoriginal, his missionary efforts spurred the scholarly activities of more competent and creative Christian Hebraists. During his years at the London Society for the Promotion of Christianity among the Jews (1809–16), Frey coordinated the work of a group of scholars who translated the New Testament into Hebrew. There had been earlier attempts to produce a New Testament that would appeal to Jewish readers. The language and formatting of the translations emulated Jewish texts familiar to Jews from the synagogue ritual. Few Jews were persuaded by these translations. Nevertheless, enthusiasm for such translations remained high among English churchmen. Curiously, earlier Jewish scholars had translated the Gospels in order to provide their coreligionists with arguments against Christian doctrinal claims to Old Testament roots and authenticity. But these translations were accompanied by caveats. A 1750 Hebrew translation, titled "The Book of the Gospel Belonging to the Followers of Jesus," ends with this note: "Heaven is my witness that I have not translated this, God forbid, to believe it, but to understand it and know how to answer the heretics." The Hebraist Richard Simon (1638–1721) took a lively interest in these Jewish translations. He tells of one manuscript of Matthew whose title page warned the reader: "This is the book of Jesus. It is called the Evangel which Matthew wrote about Jesus of Nazareth. It should not be trusted because it is a worthless fraud and falsehood."[33]

The majority of the translation efforts, however, flowed in the other direction, from Christians to Jews. Frey's London Society was stimulated to embark on a New Testament translation by the reports of an Anglican missionary recently returned from India. Rev. Claudius Buchanan returned from India in 1810, where he had spent many years as a Christian missionary on the Malabar Coast. In Travancore he purchased a large collection of Hebrew manuscripts that included both a chronicle of the Jews of Cochin and a Hebrew New Testament. Buchanan identified the translator of the New Testament as one Rabbi Ezekiel, who had carried on disputations with the Syrian Mar Thoma Christians of Malabar. Here was yet another New Testament translation produced by Jewish scholars for the purpose of refuting the claims of proselytizing Christians. Buchanan approached Frey's society with the suggestion that this manuscript serve as the basis for a printed Hebrew edition of the Gospels. The Indian translation in fact proved too Jewish in tone—"too full of rabbinisms" in the words of the review committee—so a decision was made to embark on a completely new translation using a "more Christian" Hebrew. To achieve this the translators worked directly from the Greek. Between 1813 and 1816 all four Gospels were published, with the complete New Testament issued in a uniform edition in 1818. In a later edition this Hebrew New Testament would play a significant role in Christian missionary efforts in Jerusalem. Frey's efforts bore fruit in this unexpected quarter, among English and German Protestant missionaries in mid-nineteenth-century Palestine. But here too, Frey himself and his work proved less important than his role as catalyst.

In an attempt to influence events in the Holy Land, missionaries and diplomats made use of the Hebrew tracts that Frey and his associates had developed. For it was in the 1830s and 1840s, after the decade-long Egyptian campaign to take Syria from the Ottomans, that Palestine was opened to the West. Protestant missionaries, some of whom were American, journeyed to the Holy Land to convert Jews, Muslims, and Eastern Christians. Explorers and "biblical researchers" joined these missionary expeditions. As cultural historian Naomi Shepherd remarked, "From this time forward, Palestine was to be ransacked for 'evidence' of the accuracy of the Bible, not simply revered as the site of the Holy places."[34] These explorers and adventurers who flocked to the shore of the eastern Mediterranean considered knowledge of Hebrew, Arabic, and other recently deciphered ancient Near Eastern languages as the tool that would enable them to understand the past. In the late nineteenth and early twentieth centuries the material cultures of the ancient world were unearthed and interpreted, but before that could happen the techniques of archaeology—excavation, stratigraphy, and decipherment—had to be developed.

Frey's Final Years

Until the mid-1830s Frey traveled throughout the United States speaking to receptive, enthusiastic Christian audiences. He spoke at hundreds of churches, and "wherever he went, large audiences gathered to see and hear this religious oddity. The novelty finally wore off and Frey was compelled to find some other means of earning a livelihood."[35] Frey convinced the ASMCJ to send him to England, where he hoped to raise funds for further conversion efforts. At age sixty-five, he embarked on a tour of England and Ireland with remarkable energy. While there he completed and published a German-language translation of his messianic tract *Judah and Benjamin*, but the rest of the tour was a failure. Frey raised very little money, fell out with the board of the ASMCJ, and returned to the United States without any means of support.

In 1840 Frey was elected pastor of a Baptist church on Long Island. Reenergized by his contact with Baptist churchmen, he left his Long Island pulpit after only two years and embarked on a missionary lecture tour among American Baptist congregations. He spent two years on the road. "He preached over nine hundred times in more than eight hundred churches and traveled over ten thousand miles." In 1845 he persuaded the Baptist Church of New York to found a mission to the Jews. During a seven-month period in 1845 Frey made his first speaking tour of the American South. He visited Tennessee, Alabama, Georgia, Louisiana, and Mississippi. He made a point of including African Baptist churches as speaking venues, and he recorded in his reports information on the Black churches and spoke of the money these churches were willing to donate to the cause of converting the Jews to Christianity.

Frey's American Baptist Society for Evangelizing the Jews was short lived. By early 1847 it ran out of funds. Frey, then in his mid-seventies, sought a job that would support him and his family. He settled in Pontiac, Michigan, where he taught Hebrew at the recently established University of Michigan. Frey died in June 1850. An obituary published in a Michigan newspaper noted that "during the three years of Mr. Frey's residence in the West he occupied himself in preaching and giving instruction in the Hebrew language of which he was a most enthusiastic admirer and a popular and distinguished teacher." The obituary goes on to describe Frey's last few months, during which he was in considerable pain. "During the two weeks preceding his death his sufferings were exceedingly severe, but the more his afflictions abounded, the more the consolations of God toward him seemed to abound. . . . More than once he said 'My Jewish brethren have often said that I was a hypocrite, and that I would never die a Christian, but I wish them to know that they were mistaken.'"[36]

Both Boudinot and Frey were key figures in American religious life. Boudinot, American aristocrat and revered figure of the Revolution, lent his name and prestige to Frey's missionary endeavors. A few years after Boudinot's death in 1821 the American Bible Society embarked on what historian Paul C. Gutjahr has called "the most ambitious scheme in the history of American publishing," namely, to provide every American household with a copy of the Holy Scriptures. By 1830 the Bible Society was on its way to distributing over half a million Bibles throughout the United States. In the subsequent thirty years the annual production of Bibles increased greatly, and by 1860 the American Bible Society was printing a million Bibles a year. Many of these editions were illustrated with scenes from the Holy Land. Throughout the country families were familiarizing themselves with the landscapes of the Galilee and the domed structures of Jerusalem. All of this would interest American readers in the history of Palestine and influence American ideas on the fate of the Holy Land. Boudinot's enduring legacy, the American Bible Society, from its headquarters in New York, today still publishes and distributes Christian Bibles in all of the world's written languages—including Hebrew and Yiddish.

Frey's legacy is more problematic. Frey, who built on Boudinot's prestige, wealth, and influence, quoted liberally from Boudinot's *Star in the West*, using it to argue for his own missionary efforts. He did achieve a measure of fame. His sermons were heard by tens of thousands of churchgoers; his books were printed in many editions. But the emerging Jewish community of the United States vilified him. Because he was an apostate Jew he was the focus of their anger at Christian missionary efforts. His Hebraist endeavors met with limited success; his role as catalyst to other Hebraists proved more important.

While Frey attracted considerable public attention he was a failure as a missionary to American Jews. In fact, American Jewish life grew and became better organized partly in response to the activities of Frey and other missionaries. Synagogue growth paralleled his popularity. In 1825 there were but six synagogues in the United States. (Here I am speaking of congregations with buildings and an organization.) By the 1840s there were forty synagogues nationwide. In New York City, which in the early years of the Republic became the center of American Jewish life, the number of synagogues grew from three—Shearith Israel, Bnai Jeshurun, and Ohavey Zedek—in 1825, to over a dozen in the 1840s.

It is to these synagogues and their congregants that we might turn in search of another type of Hebrew learning in America. For while Christian Hebraist scholars were teaching and studying Hebrew in seminaries and colleges, Jewish worshippers were using Hebrew in their daily and Sabbath prayers. Can we then speak of a "Jewish Hebraism" in the nineteenth-century United States? If we can—if there was a parallel American Jewish endeavor to study and teach Hebrew—were there contacts between these distinct endeavors, the Jewish and the Christian? Or did each exist in splendid isolation?

6

THE AMERICAN
JEWISH COMMUNITY AND
ITS ENCOUNTER WITH
CHRISTIAN HEBRAISM

While we have been busy converting the Jews in other lands, they have outflanked
us here, and effected a footing in the very center of our fortress.
New Haven Register, 1843

The American Jewish community of today, in all of its diversity, differences of opinion, and remarkable accomplishments, is the product of two waves of immigration. The first wave, from the 1820s to the late 1840s, brought 200,000 German and Central European Jews to the United States. Many Bavarian Jews, excluded from economic opportunities in that German province, came to the United States in the 1830s. Then with the unrest that followed the failed revolutions of 1848, a great number of displaced Europeans immigrated to the United States—among them many Jews. The second wave of immigration occurred between 1880 and 1924, when some two to three million Eastern European and Russian Jews arrived in the New World. They were part of the roughly forty million Europeans who entered the United States from 1880 until America shut its doors in 1924 with the implementation of restrictive immigration acts.

The Russian and Polish Jews of the second wave of immigration fled Europe for two reasons: poverty and persecution. They had lived at the margins of the economy for centuries. With the establishment of the Pale of Settlement at the beginning of the nineteenth century the Jews were forced into deeper poverty by laws that limited their residence to the Pale. Active persecution, as distinct from "low-level" endemic anti-Semitism, marked the end of the nineteenth century. Russia's Jews were beset by discriminatory legislation (including the May Laws of 1881) and pogroms. From 1881, hundreds of thousands of Russian Jews entered the United States.

The organizational structures, educational institutions, and religious denominations of contemporary American Jewry stem from these two waves of settlement, the "German" and the "Russian." The conflicts between the already established German Jews and the upstart greenhorns of Eastern Europe and Russia have been the subject of many a novel, drama, and social history. But in the mid-nineteenth century, while the first great Jewish migration to the United States was still taking place, all of this lay in the distant future. For both the German and Russian immigrations had been preceded by the arrival of small groups of Sephardic Jews, the earliest of whom had arrived in New York in 1654. The American Jewish community, dominated by some Sephardic aristocrats and German Jewish businessmen, was small, poorly organized, and had very few scholars or centers of learning. This community understood its encounters with predominantly Protestant America as engagements between competing religious traditions, of which Christianity was the more powerful. Jews had little to gain from such encounters.[1]

Jews may have had little to gain, but not so their Christian counterparts. The enlarged Jewish presence in North America brought many first-time encounters between Christians interested in the Bible and Hebrew, and Jewish scholars and Jewish laymen. For example, the Christian missionary community took an active interest in the Jewish immigrants. Though most missionary efforts had focused on work overseas, the presence of "the as yet unconverted Hebrew people" on American soil now added a new dimension to the work of evangelization. In addition, Christian scholars with no missionizing agenda were eager to learn more of Jewish synagogue ritual. They were especially eager to learn the Torah cantillation system. In the mid-1820s, for example, Moses Stuart, dean of Andover Theological Seminary, invited Joshua Seixas of New York to chant the Torah for his theology students. The Jewish scholar was honored to perform the task.

The Early American Synagogue

During the late colonial period and the first decades of the Republic the Jewish population grew from fewer than two thousand people at the time of the Revolution to fifteen thousand in 1840. Those Jews who arrived in small numbers in the eighteenth century founded several congregations. The first Jewish settlers, those of New York and Philadelphia, were Sephardic refugees from the Portuguese areas of South America. Jews from Holland, Germany, England, and elsewhere on the Continent arrived later. Until the 1820s hegemony in matters of ritual and congregational authority rested with the Sephardim. Then from the 1820s onward German immigrant communities began to found their own synagogues. By 1825 there were six synagogues in the United States—only one of which was in New York City.[2]

Prior to the mid-nineteenth century it is difficult to speak of organized Jewish life in the United States, especially in the realm of education. There were a few synagogues of both the Sephardic and Ashkenazic traditions. But unlike the synagogues of the late nineteenth and early twentieth centuries, these synagogues served solely as prayer houses; there were few schools or social welfare organizations attached to them. The model of the synagogue as "Jewish Center" (what would later be known as "the shul with the pool") developed a full century later.

In the early synagogues of New York, Philadelphia, Charleston, and Newport, prayers were conducted in Hebrew, but formal study of the language was sorely neglected. There were, however, some attempts to teach Hebrew to children of synagogue families. At New York's Shearith Israel congregation, for example, there was a Hebrew school as early as the 1730s. The congregation, established in the late seventeenth century, constructed its first permanent structure in 1729. Its founders and ritual were Sephardic, but by the 1730s many Ashkenazic members had joined the congregation. Marriages between Sephardic and Ashkenazic congregants followed, and these marriages, especially those among the leading families of the community, facilitated a rare integration of two very different Jewish ritual communities. But despite this mixing of Sephardic and Ashkenazic elements the culture of the congregation was still dominated by the Sephardim. As many of the founders had come to New York from Brazil and other former Portuguese possessions, the congregational records were kept in Portuguese, and some prayers were recited in that language. The congregation's charter stipulated that the *hazzan* (cantor) must "chant according to the Sephardic rite." These rules persisted into the early nineteenth century, even though the majority of congregants by that time were of Ashkenazi lineage, since few Sephardim arrived in New York after the American Revolution.[3]

Teaching Hebrew

The Shearith Israel Hebrew School of New York City was unusual because its stated purpose was to teach the Hebrew language. By the first decades of the twentieth century, Hebrew school had become more focused on maintaining Jewish identity in America, and less concerned with teaching the Hebrew language and Jewish texts. Intended as afternoon schools that would reinforce an endangered sense of community, the emphasis in the classroom was on the teaching of folkways and folktales, not on the study of language and texts. The teachers were underpaid and overworked, the students resentful that they were inside studying while their non-Jewish friends were outside playing. Mutual frustration often flared up into violence both verbal and physical. American Jewish fiction of the mid-twentieth century abounds with descriptions of such eruptions.

In contrast, at Shearith Israel in the late eighteenth and early nineteenth centuries, the approach was scholarly, the teaching method systematic. The instructors taught the rudiments of Hebrew syntax and grammar. This was more than a century before the much-vaunted "revival" of the Hebrew language by Eliezer ben Yehuda of Jerusalem.

With the stated "purpose of teaching the Hebrew language three hours each day," the Shearith Israel School enrolled both boys and girls, which was quite unusual for eighteenth-century America.[4] From the school records it seems that about 20 percent of the students were girls. Within the synagogue community many women were literate. They could read, if not understand, the Hebrew prayers. That some girls got the benefit of a Hebrew education was the result of America's distance from European centers of Jewish life. In Europe, Jewish girls might be educated at home but not in a formal school.

Among American synagogues Shearith Israel was the exception; it provided a Judaic education for the next generation. In general, ignorance of Hebrew and incompetence in matters of Judaic scholarship were the norm throughout the new United States. As historian Jacob Rader Marcus reminds us: "The cultural level of American Jews in the early national period was not high. . . . Of the 15,000 Jews—men, women, and children—in this country in 1840, a *few* were at home in the Hebrew Bible, the Talmud, the codes, and Jewish history."[5] There were as yet no ordained rabbis in the United States. In the older congregations such as New York's Shearith Israel and Philadelphia's Mikve Israel, congregational leadership was vested in the hands of a *hazzan*. While the narrow definition of the term is "cantor," the wider meaning was "ritual expert" and representative to the government and the Christian public. Protestant observers understood the *hazzan*'s role as parallel to the role of a minister. During the American Revolution and the early years of the Republic, individual *hazzanim* made representation to the government, participated in public ceremonies, and welcomed national and local leaders into their synagogues. New York's Gershom Mendes Seixas, *hazzan* of Shearith Israel congregation, was a familiar figure at public events. On many occasions he attended public ceremonies held in the city's Protestant churches. Influential in the city's academic life, he was appointed to the governing board of Columbia University in 1785. These *hazzanim* were self-taught in matters of Judaic leaning; they did not have the benefits, or the doctrinal baggage, of a traditional yeshiva education. (The first American yeshivot would not be established until the early twentieth century.)

Christian visitors took a lively interest in Jewish study of, and proficiency in, the Hebrew language and liturgy. We saw in Chapter 3 that Ezra Stiles made frequent visits to services at the Newport synagogue. Emulating Jewish educational practices and traditions, Stiles taught his wife and children Hebrew and made daily recitation of a biblical passage in Hebrew part of his household ritual. Among other Christian Hebraists who taught their children Hebrew was Kings (later Columbia) College president Samuel Johnson of Connecticut. He claimed that both of his sons were fluent in spoken Hebrew by the age of ten.

Establishing a Foothold

During the first decades of the nineteenth century, American Christian Hebraism was at its height. American colleges, which had neglected Hebrew studies in the period after the Revolution, returned to the subject with renewed vigor. Two factors contributed to this renewed interest in Hebrew: the professionalization of college teaching, in which "subject experts" emerged rather than tutors who would teach all subjects, and the reexamination and subsequent revival of seminary education. Under German Protestant influence, text and language study achieved a new centrality and importance. In a sense colleges were "shamed" into Hebrew study by the rise of Protestant theological institutions, foremost among them Andover Theological Seminary of Andover, Massachusetts. In the theologically conservative and intellectually ambitious atmosphere of Andover, Hebrew had a central place. Under the leadership of Rev. Moses Stuart, professor of biblical exegesis, Andover exerted enormous influence on American cultural and religious life. Hundreds of Andover Seminary graduates achieved prominence in the churches of various Protestant denominations. Training more than fifteen hundred Protestant missionaries for foreign work, Moses Stuart extended his influence internationally. Stuart's star pupil, Edward Robinson, would explore Palestine in the 1830s and 1850s, pioneering biblical archaeology and the study of the Holy Land as the "fifth gospel." I will tell his story in a later chapter.

While American Protestant missions overseas were endeavoring to bring Jews, Muslims, and "heathens" into the church, American Jewish religious life established a foothold in New England, the cradle of U.S. missionary activities. Some Christians took this as an affront; America was to "shine with the light of the gospel," not serve as a refuge for those who denied its truth. When Congregation Mishkan Israel was established in New Haven, Connecticut, in

[Zion on American Shores]

1843, the *New Haven Register* fulminated against the "invasion": "While we have been busy converting the Jews in other lands, they have outflanked us here, and effected a footing in the very center of our fortress. Strange as it may sound it is nevertheless true that a Jewish synagogue has been established in this city."[6]

The irony of the situation was that, while American Christians—clergymen, intellectuals, and educated laymen—were studying Hebrew and the Bible, American Jews, as they struggled to establish themselves in the United States, were neglecting the study of their sacred language and texts. But perhaps this dichotomy is too harsh; there were also class issues at work here. Long-established Christian elites had a system of higher education that was some two centuries old; American Jews, as a group, would not organize school systems for another century. Many American Protestant intellectuals saw themselves as stewards of the Hebraic tradition. Thus, the conflict here was over ownership of the ultimate intellectual property, the Bible in its original language. As we have seen, Christian Hebraism was very strong in colonial and Revolutionary America, but its appeal had diminished somewhat by the beginning of the nineteenth century. With the secularization of American education the Bible and the learned languages became less important. But America's role as an emergent "missionary power," linked to the religious revivals of the 1820s and 1830s, gave impetus to a revived Hebraism, a rekindled interest in Hebrew and the Bible. Protestant scholars published many Hebrew textbooks, Bibles, and commentaries. In contrast, for the Jewish community "it took fully two hundred years from the arrival of the Jews in North America before the pangs of Hebraic culture produced a Hebrew book in the full sense of the term." This was the 1860 book *Avnei Yehoshua* by Rabbi Joshua Falk.[7] Rabbi Falk's book is a commentary on the Mishnaic tractate Avot, commonly called "The Ethics of the Fathers." On its frontispiece he identifies the book as "the first sacred text to be composed in the Nation of America."

This is not to say that there were no Jewish students of Judaica in the early years of the American Republic. Manuel Josephson, a prominent layman in New York's Congregation Shearith Israel, owned the best library of rabbinic texts in colonial times and was well versed in rabbinic Hebrew. Josephson was one of the three *dayanim*, or judges, on the Shearith Israel *bet din*, or rabbinical court. But as historian Arthur Hertzberg notes, Josephson, who died in 1796, "did not believe that there was a future in America for knowledge of the rabbinic texts. He specified that his volumes in Western languages be sold at auction, but that his books in Hebrew be packed up and sent to Europe."[8]

Exemplifying a model of cultural action and responsibility that would typify American Jewish intellectuals of the following two centuries, Manuel Josephson took a strong interest in emergent American literature, collecting editions of novels and poems by American writers and befriending and supporting young poets.[9] Though later Jewish supporters of the arts evinced little or no interest in Jewish literature and learning, Josephson displayed interest in both areas. But he had little hope for Jewish learning in America. It was best to send his Judaica collection to Europe, where he was sure it would be utilized.

Throughout the history of the American encounter between Christians and Jews, scholarly Christians have bemoaned the decline of Jewish learning in Jewish communities and individuals. This complaint would become a constant theme in the memoirs of twentieth-century literary critic Edmund Wilson. Wilson was known to chastise his young American Jewish acolytes in the 1950s and 1960s for neglecting the study of Hebrew and the Bible.

Jewish Learning in America

In the writings of Jewish observers, diatribes, jeremiads, and lamentations for the state of Jewish learning in America became a common genre by the end of the nineteenth century. For example, *Vehu Shaul*, a book-length jeremiad written in Hebrew and Yiddish, asserts that a fully Jewish religious and cultural life is not possible in the United States. European Jewish visitors to American shores often expressed this opinion. For this reason many prominent rabbis discouraged their followers and students from emigrating to America—a land which later earned the unappetizing sobriquet "the *treyf* (non-Kosher) country."[10]

One eminent visitor, Arnold Ehrlich, who earned fame in Europe for his Hebrew and German commentaries on the Bible, noted in the Hebrew-language newspaper *Hamagid* that American Jews have "forsaken the wisdom of our ancient sources. . . . Just as the air of the Land of Israel makes one wise, so does the air of our country make one clever; and if the wise man is said to have his eyes in his head, the clever one is guided by practical aims. He will therefore not turn to knowledge that can only support him frugally, but will engage in business or any trade that can bring him financial gain. . . . Because of their wealth they consider themselves wiser than those who came before them, so what need is there for Jewish learning?"[11]

Was there really no hope for Jewish learning in America? Diminishing Hebrew knowledge led some Jewish recipients of Hebrew correspondence to turn to Christian scholars for assistance in translating the Hebrew. Yale president Ezra Stiles tells of a number of such consultations. But we can assume that these cases were exceptional and speculate that Stiles delighted in recording them. Jews seeking Hebrew knowledge from a Christian scholar validated Stiles's self-image as an "Hebrician." As an expert in Hebrew and the Bible and heir to ancient traditions of learning, Stiles saw himself as more competent to read Hebrew than most Jewish readers. He did, however, recognize the superior accomplishments of the European rabbis he met in Newport. In his letters to Rabbi Hayyim Carigal, for example, he praised Carigal's mastery of Hebrew.

The use of Hebrew in letter writing provides one sign of continued Hebrew learning among Jews. For centuries Hebrew served as an international language of correspondence between members of far-flung Jewish communities. The great collection of letters found in the Cairo *Geniza* at the end of the nineteenth century attests to the use of Hebrew as a mode of communication between remote areas of the Mediterranean World. In colonial and early republican America this tradition continued. Solomon Simson, a Jewish merchant of New York, had extensive commercial relations with the Orient. "In 1787, he received a Hebrew letter from the leaders of the Jewish community in Cochin, India and was in communication with them. In 1794 he endeavored to contact the Jews of China, writing to them in Hebrew."[12] No response from the Jews of China (the small Kaifeng community) is recorded, but this did not discourage Simson. He persisted in attempts to establish contact with remote Jewish communities. The Cochin Jews had sent him a chronicle of their community's origins; perhaps other lost and exotic Jewish communities would do the same. Simson also hoped that these communal ties would enhance his commercial contacts in the East.

The Simson family saga provides us with a rare example of the persistence and continuity of Hebrew learning within one early American Jewish family. Their preservation of Hebrew as a living language led to scholarly interactions between family members and American Christian Hebraists. In most European states, where Jews were a disdained religious minority, these kinds of interactions were unheard of, but the multiplicity of religious traditions represented among the English and European settlers in America created an atmosphere in which tolerance and some degree of mutual respect developed. In later chapters we will examine encounters between Jewish scholars—such as Isaac Nordheimer of New York University and Joshua Seixas of Western Reserve College—and their Christian Hebraist colleagues. These interactions between Jewish and Christian scholars of "Hebrew and the oriental languages" yielded some fascinating results, and served as a formative influence on emerging forms of American Christianity. The Mormons, in particular, influenced by the Hebraist interests of their prophet, Joseph Smith, began a "romance" with Hebrew and the Jews that continues to this day. This romance extended to the idea of the restoration of the Jews to Palestine, and led to Mormon support of the State of Israel.[13]

The Simsons of Congregation Shearith Israel

Joseph Simson, Solomon Simson's father, was an English Jew who came to the colonies in 1718. He established himself as a merchant in New York and participated in the building of the Shearith Israel Synagogue. J. R. Marcus, dean of American Jewish historians, noted that the elder Simson was "an excellent Hebraist, and his own generation referred to him as Rabbi."[14] Yale University's Ezra Stiles corresponded with Joseph Simson in Hebrew and on one occasion visited the elder Simson at his home in Wilton, Connecticut. J. R. Marcus suggests that Governor Jonathan Trumbull of Revolutionary War Connecticut consulted with Joseph Simson on "some knotty problems of Hebrew grammar."

But it is Sampson Simson, Joseph Simson's grandson, who has left us the most solid evidence of American Hebraic learning at the turn of the nineteenth century. Sampson attended Columbia College (the first Jew to do so) and graduated in 1800 in a class of fifteen students. At the graduation ceremonies that year, he delivered a Hebrew oration titled, "Historical Traits of the Jews, from Their First Settlement in North America." Gershon Mendes Seixas, *hazzan* of the Shearith Israel congregation and a trustee of Columbia College, had composed the oration. The manuscript opens with this note: "One of the professors of Columbia College has requested me to write something for master Sampson to speak in public in the holy tongue on commencement day, should you not object to his request." J. R. Marcus has called this oration "the first evidence of a communal self-consciousness among American Jews." One doubts that more than one or two of the attendees understood the oration. As with college orations in Greek and Latin, no translation was provided. To have done so would have destroyed the charming illusion that the assembled listeners knew the "learned languages"—Latin, Greek, and Hebrew.

Sampson Simson's reading of Seixas's oration followed the salutary address in Latin and three short speeches in English. The Republican Watch-Tower of New York City noted in its report on the commencement festivities, "The friends of classical learning witnessed, with more than usual pleasure, the display of Grecian, Roman, and Hebrew literature on this occasion."[15] The Hebrew speech placed the Jewish experience in America within the context of American history. It surveyed the recent and distant past, affirmed Jewish support for the American Revolution, and looked forward to Jewish participation in the future of the Republic. The text of Simson's Hebrew oration, translated from the Hebrew, follows:

Although not accustomed to speak in public, I rise with perfect confidence that you will kindly consent to listen to me and I earnestly crave your indulgence for any error I may commit in the course of my address. And if I have found grace in your eyes I shall speak concerning my brethren residing in this land. It is now more than one hundred and fifty years, since Israelites first came to this country, at the time when this province was under the dominion of Holland, but until now no one of them or their children has on a similar occasion been permitted thus to address a word in public, and I am a descendant of one of those who were among the first settlers here. It is known to you, that at the time when this province, then called New Amsterdam, was exchanged for the colony of Surinam, all the inhabitants remaining here came under the dominion of England. Among them were the Jews who until then could only congregate for worship in private rooms in their own dwellings until the year 5490 (1730) (according as we reckon in this city of New York). It was then that our regular Synagogue was built, where we have been serving Almighty God unmolested for upwards of seventy years. During this long period the Jews have not been as numerous as the other sects, for only few in number they came hither; but now, behold the Lord has enlarged and increased in this and in all the other provinces of these United States the descendants of those few families that came from Holland in the year 5420 (1660), one hundred and forty years ago. Among these was one man with his wife, one son and four daughters. The father and son died soon after they had reached this place, leaving the wife with her four daughters and behold they have exalted themselves in this city, and from them sprang fourth many of the Congregation now known as "Shearith Israel." Afterwards, in the year 1696, there came from France some families by the way of England, who brought with them letters of denization from the king, constituting them freemen throughout all the provinces under this dominion. And in the year 1776 at the time when the people of this country stood up like one man in the cause of liberty and independence every Israelite that was among them rose up likewise and united in their efforts to promote the country's peace and prosperity. And even now we endeavor to sustain the government of these provinces, free of any allegiance to any other whatsoever, monarchical or republican, and we exclaim in the language of King David, "Rid us, O Lord! From the hand of the children of the stranger, whose mouth speaketh vanity and whose right hand is the right hand of falsehood."[16]

The choice to make this statement of the American Jewish experience in Hebrew was a significant one. In 1800 Hebrew had academic and religious significance for American Christians, but Jews had no public forum in which they could lay claim to their own intellectual traditions. At Columbia College ("King's College" before the American Revolution), students were encouraged to study Hebrew and the Bible. The president of the college, Samuel Johnson of Connecticut, was an ardent and committed Hebraist. He published a Hebrew grammar and was said to have taught his two sons to "converse in the sacred tongue." Hebrew, then, served the Jewish community not only as a medium of cultural preservation, but also as a medium in which to present itself to Christians.

Sampson Simson, on completing his studies at Columbia, studied law with Aaron Burr and became a prominent attorney in New York City. He maintained an apartment on Bleecker Street and an estate in Yonkers. He managed the considerable wealth he inherited from his father very well. He carried on the philanthropic traditions of his father and grandfather, focusing his donations on then emergent Jewish educational institutions. He also contributed to his alma mater, Columbia College, and was, in fact, the first Columbia alumnus to bequeath a large sum to the college. Toward the end of his life he took a lively interest in the first Jewish agricultural colonization attempts in Ottoman Palestine. On his death in 1857 Sampson Simson left a cash legacy to "teach the Jews of Eretz Israel artisan skills, and mechanical and agricultural trades." The North American Relief Society for Indigent Jews in Jerusalem, Palestine, was established to fulfill this bequest.[17]

But Sampson Simson's support for Jewish settlement in the Land of Israel came at the end of his life. Most of his earlier philanthropic activities were centered on assistance to New York City's poor. Simson donated the land for "the Jews Hospital in New York" (later renamed Mount Sinai) and laid the cornerstone in November 1853. He is considered the founder of Mount Sinai Hospital, today one of New York City's premier healthcare institutions. That he also left money for Jewish settlement in Palestine was, in retrospect, quite significant. For it presaged the dual nature of later Jewish philanthropy in the United States. While supporting charities at home, American Jews would contribute heavily to the restoration of the Jewish homeland.

Hebrew and the Jewish Community

Sampson Simson's 1800 oration was an unusual secular use of Hebrew. There were also American Jewish expressions of Hebrew scholarship in the religious and liturgical realms, and though these were limited, they too shed light on

Jewish communal life. Officials of the synagogues in the port cities of New York, Newport, and Charleston edited and printed prayer books, broadsides, and sermons in Hebrew. Early in this process a decision was made to provide American English translations of the Hebrew texts. A 1766 publication of the Sephardic ritual "Prayers for Sabbath, Rosh-Hashanah, and Kippur" presents both the Hebrew texts and the English translations. Today such translations are a familiar sight in all American synagogues, but two centuries ago there seems to have been resistance to the idea. The translator, Isaac Pinto of Congregation Shearith Israel, felt it necessary to explain why he provided an English translation:

> A Veneration for the Language sacred by being that in which it pleased Almighty God to reveal himself to our Ancestors, and a desire to preserve it, in firm Persuasion that it will again be re-established in Israel; are probably leading Reasons for our performing divine Service in Hebrew: But that, being imperfectly understood by many, by some, not at all; it has been necessary to translate our Prayers, in the Language of the Country wherein it hath pleased the divine Providence to appoint our Lot. In Europe, the Spanish and Portuguese Jews have a Translation in Spanish, which as they generally understand, may be sufficient; but that not being the Case in the British Dominions in America, has induced me to attempt a Translation in English, not without Hope that it will tend to the Improvement of many of my Brethren in their Devotion; and if it answer that Good Intention, it will afford me the Satisfaction of having contributed toward it.

Why did Pinto feel the need to offer an explanation for translating the prayer book? The justification for an English translation was evident to many. Sephardic Jews elsewhere had Spanish translations—Pinto mentions Isaac Nieto's Spanish prayer book. According to George Kohut, the Sephardic authorities of London would not allow an English translation to be published in England. This would compromise the Sephardic tradition. To publish one in the American colonies was an audacious move.[18]

Gershom Mendes Seixas wrote Sampson Simson's Columbia oration in fluid rabbinic Hebrew. Other examples of Seixas's Hebrew prose include communal prayers and addresses for American public commemorations. His skills, however, did not extend to the composition of Hebrew poetry, a task requiring more training and erudition. I have found only one such early American Hebrew poem, written by a colleague of Seixas to commemorate the 1784 peace treaty between England and the United States. Fifteen years before the Columbia oration, an official of Seixas's congregation composed an elaborate prayer in the classical mode of Hebrew liturgical poetry. Seixas at the time was serving as the *hazzan* of Congregation Mikve Israel of Philadelphia. The poem praises both Governor Clinton of New York and General George Washington in rabbinic Hebrew style.

Most Christian Hebraists ignored these Jewish uses of Hebrew. Ezra Stiles, pastor of Newport's Congregational church and later president of Yale College, was the exception. But with Stiles's death in 1795, Christian Hebraist interest in Jewish ritual and literary uses of Hebrew ceased until the revival of Hebrew studies at colleges and seminaries in the 1820s and 1830s. In the mid-1830s Joseph Smith, the Mormon prophet, invited a Jewish teacher to establish a Hebrew school for his new church and community. The teacher was Joshua Seixas, son of New York's Gershom Mendes Seixas. The younger Seixas was to have considerable influence on the founder and elders of the early Church of Latter Day Saints. I will tell his story in a later chapter. Two other early-nineteenth-century Christian Hebraists, Moses Stuart and Edward Robinson, also eagerly engaged Jewish informants who could provide them with "authentic" insights into Jewish texts and practices.

The central Jewish use of Hebrew was in prayer. To participate in prayer a congregant must possess the ability to recite Hebrew, but understanding the language is not necessary. That English translations of the liturgy were provided indicates that many Jewish worshippers had the skill of recitation, but not that of comprehension. There were, however, a few examples of American Jewish Hebraica that indicated a facility with the language and the ability to compose and respond in it. Religious ceremonies that require Hebrew facility would include officiating at weddings, divorces, and the decisions or actions of rabbinic courts. "There are also some ceremonies or religious practices, for example tombstone inscription, which, while not *requiring* the use of Hebrew, often employ it nonetheless, and these can help reveal how much Hebrew the colonial Jew actually possessed."[19]

Despite the absence of both trained rabbis and laymen with a formal Judaic education, American Jews used Hebrew for both secular and religious purposes. The categories of legal and ceremonial use encompass the greater part of this American Hebraic legacy. Rites of passage—births, circumcisions, naming ceremonies, marriages, divorces, death, and burial—all necessitated some use of Hebrew. A small number of Hebrew *ketubot* (marriage contracts) from the early years of the American Republic are extant, including the *ketubah* of Revolutionary War hero Haym Salomon and his bride Rachel Franks. (Salomon's signature on his *ketubah* is the only extant Hebrew version of his name.) Divorce documents (*gittin*), by their very nature, are harder to find. For the *get*, written by a scribe and delivered by the husband to his estranged wife, is torn by the scribe and filed in the rabbinic court "to avoid any later suspicion that it was not absolutely legal."[20] Thus, unlike *ketubot*, which were kept and treasured by the married couple, divorce documents were filed away and not seen again. As Nathan Kaganoff has noted, this is unfortunate, for "it would be fascinating to see one, since the laws involving divorce are much more complex than those pertaining to marriage, and the preparation of a get requires both a rabbinic court and a broader knowledge of Jewish law."[21]

One astute observer of American Jewish life noted that "the question of gittin has always been one of the most intricate and troublesome of American Jewish life." In 1861 a Polish rabbi, Joseph Moses Aaronson, was invited to New York City for the express purpose of "introducing order and dignity into the matter of American gittin." His senior rabbinical colleagues in Poland encouraged him to make the arduous journey to America because many European Jewish men, who had emigrated to the United States for work, later sent bills of divorcement to their wives in Europe. "Therefore," said Rabbi Aaronson, "I took upon myself this difficult journey."[22]

The changes in American divorce documents that Aaronson insisted upon were minute—or might seem so to the outside observer. For example, one long legal response deals with the proper Hebrew spelling of the name New York. Should it be one word or two? Should the spelling reflect the Yiddish pronunciation or the American? As the *get* must identify precisely the city or town in which the divorce is granted, an identification achieved in Talmudic times by naming the nearest body of water, Aaronson wondered whether the Hudson River or the Atlantic Ocean should serve as the marker designated in New York *gittin*. He decided in favor of the Hudson, as the ocean is "so far away." From his letters to his European colleagues one learns little or nothing of the social situation of American Jews, or of the marital problems that many immigrant couples experienced. His concerns, and those of his European rabbinical colleagues, were solely with the proper form and content of the divorce document, not with the social or psychological aspects of divorce.

Different Approaches, Some Commonalities

We might contrast this rabbinic use of Hebrew with Christian Hebraist interest in Hebrew. For Hebraists, Hebrew was the key to biblical exegesis and, by extension, to the resolution of theological questions. It played no part in the legal or ritual life of Christians. One might say that while Christian Hebraists were studying Hebrew, Jewish ritual experts were utilizing it in as precise a manner as possible. If Hebraists had known of these Jewish investigations into Hebrew usage they would have condemned them as examples of "Jewish excessive legalism." Their use of Hebrew was more "pure." With their knowledge of the language the Hebraists sought to unlock the secrets of the biblical text.

A shared use of Hebrew was on tombstones. Many colonial Jewish tombstones are still identifiable; most, if not all, had Hebrew inscriptions. As these inscriptions are for the most part formulaic they do not testify to creativity on the part of their authors, but they do testify to the persistence of Jewish tradition in the New World, and to the ability of Jewish community leaders to carry on those traditions even without the benefit of formal training in Hebrew language and rabbinic tradition. Hebrew inscriptions also appear on the tombstones of some New England Protestant scholars. Though Christian Hebraists and Jewish legal scholars had markedly different approaches and attitudes toward the use of Hebrew, we find some commonalties of usage in the commemoration of the dead. For example, the grave of William Bradford, leader of the Pilgrims at Plymouth, was adorned with three Hebrew words: *adonai maoz hayay* ("God is the strength of my life").

Bradford's dedication to Hebrew learning is well known. His Mayflower colleague William Brewster also devoted himself to the study of the sacred tongue. Both men's understanding of the Pilgrim experience in the New World was firmly anchored in an Hebraic worldview. The three-centuries-long persistence of the New England Christian Hebraist tradition is well attested to in the deathbed request of Edmund Wilson, eminent American literary critic, who died in 1973. His simple gravestone in the Wellfleet, Massachusetts, Protestant cemetery is inscribed with the Hebrew phrase *hazak hazak venithazek*. This is the rabbinic phrase chanted after the completion of the public reading of each of the five books of Moses. Wilson was deeply moved by the spirit of this injunction and its frequent recitation at junctures of reading and rereading.

Wilson, after studying Hebrew and the Bible for a decade, complained during the 1960s that his young Jewish interlocutors were woefully ignorant of Hebrew traditions and Jewish literature. Christian Hebraists of the American colonies had made similar complaints. The Jews were categorized and romanticized as "a religious people," and Christians expected them to know their own language, scripture, and history. Ezra Stiles sought "Hebraic knowledge" from Jewish interlocutors and at times he found that knowledge—namely, in his intense rounds of correspondence and conversation with Rabbi Isaac Carigal of Hebron. At the same time Stiles and his Hebraist counterparts in Europe felt that even the most educated and knowledgeable of Jewish scholars was denying "the Christian truth," a truth demonstrable through the very Hebrew sources that the Jews themselves had preserved and transmitted within their own communities. The ambivalence built in to this situation, an ambivalence that echoed Christian ambivalence toward the Jews as both the source of Christianity and the deniers of the "truth," was to influence the enterprise of Christian Hebraism in startling ways.

For the few Jews in early America, where they were but one-tenth of 1 percent of the population, these theological issues were abstract and distant. As individuals they were struggling to make their way in a new country. As a loosely organized religious community their concerns were the establishment of houses of worship and schools for religious instruction. As Jacob Kabakoff has noted, these American Jews "clung to Hebrew language as the language of prayer and religious instruction, demonstrating thereby that the Hebrew language was a necessary instrument for maintaining their identity."[23] For the vast majority of these American Jews the notion that American Protestant scholars were devoting their scholarly efforts to Hebrew and the Bible would have seemed strange at best. To some, it might have seemed sinister. For they knew that some Christian Hebraists, and some recently converted Jews, were employing Hebrew as a missionary tool with which to bring American Jews into the church.

II

SCHOLARS, PROPHETS, MYSTICS

NINETEENTH CENTURY

The preceding chapters have shown that from an early period of American history we can discern a curious pattern emerging: the founders of the early American colleges were almost without exception Christian Hebraists. This pattern would replicate itself, with decreasing intensity and frequency, through the history of American higher education. Let us review, before proceeding, some salient scenes from Part I.

Harvard's first two presidents were "primarily Hebraists," as was King's College (later Columbia) founder Samuel Johnson. Johnson's commitment to Hebrew was so serious that he taught his two young sons to "converse in Hebrew." Yale, founded in 1701 by Harvard men unhappy with the older college's doctrinal drift toward what would become Unitarian Christianity, emphasized Hebrew study as a bulwark against unwanted theological change and innovation. Ezra Stiles, president of Yale in the last decades of the eighteenth century, described himself as a "Hebrician." He taught Yale's freshman Hebrew class throughout his tenure as president. His *Literary Diary*, a classic of American letters, is replete with references to Hebrew and the Bible.

As we shall see, Hebraist engagement with American higher education persisted into the nineteenth and twentieth centuries. Many of the founders of nineteenth-century "frontier institutions" were Hebraists. The opening of the Western frontier led to the establishment of institutions of higher learning on that frontier. For example, the 1830s and 1840s saw the establishment of Oberlin College and Case Western Reserve. Hebrew was taught in the early years of both institutions. Seminary education flourished in the nineteenth century, with the "sacred tongues" at the core of the curriculum. Moses Stuart, whose story is told in Chapter 7, was the dean of seminary education in the United States in the first half of the nineteenth century, and he trained hundreds of future clergymen and educators in the basics of Hebrew grammar and syntax. Another pioneer of American education, William Rainey Harper, was professor of Hebrew at Yale before he was appointed president of the University of Chicago.

In early American cultural life "Hebraism" referred to the study of Hebrew. In the second half of the nineteenth century a new use of the term "Hebraism" entered Western cultural discourse through the writings of Matthew Arnold. In *Culture and Anarchy* Arnold posited that Western culture rested on two forces, "a sense of duty, self-control, and work," and "the intelligence driving at those ideas which are the basis for right practice—the ardent sense for all the new and changing combinations of them which man's development brings with it." The first force Arnold dubbed Hebraism, the second Hellenism—"between these two points of influence moves our world." Attributing these two forces to historical peoples—"Hellenism is of Indo-European growth, Hebraism is of Semitic growth"—Arnold saw England and its culture—as well as "our American descendants across the Atlantic"—as possessing an affinity for "the genius and history of the Hebrew people."[1]

As Lionel Trilling noted in the 1950s, Arnold's essay emerged from a cultural and biological reification of racial essentialism that is no longer acceptable. "Arnold's untenable theory of race, however, differs in one important respect from many others—in that it was not intended to separate peoples but to draw them together." Arnold's Hebraism was both a philosophical construct and a concept with which to evaluate the elements of a unified culture, and as such it still retains its relevance. Though the term in his usage does not refer directly to the study of Hebrew language and texts, it does emphasize the English and American affinity for the biblical tradition, an affinity that lies at the heart of our discussion.[2]

The Protestant romance with Hebrew and the Bible was expressed in other ways. In earlier centuries, as they discovered and settled the Americas, European Christians had relied on an Hebraic model to interpret their experiences in the New World. By the nineteenth century we find the heirs to this tradition using their knowledge of Hebrew and the Bible to understand a new terrain, the rediscovered ancient world, particularly the world of ancient Israel and its neighbors. Their explorations of the America–Promised Land continuum inform the biographical portraits of Part II of this book. While their Hebraist predecessors were engaged in the scholarly and spiritual aspects of Hebrew study, nineteenth- and twentieth-century American Hebraists were influenced by their Hebrew studies to explore the physical remains of the biblical world. This endeavor, in turn, led some of these scholars to take a stand on political issues both national and international. American attitudes toward the nations and peoples of the Middle East were shaped during this period.

American scholars, among them Hebraists, archaeologists, and New Testament experts, flocked to the Holy Land in the mid-nineteenth century. Before the establishment of American graduate education, aspiring "biblical research-ers" went to Europe to study the fledgling sciences of archaeology and biblical criticism, sciences first developed in Germany and England. Using the knowledge of Hebrew and the Bible that they had gained in European universities and seminaries, these scholars went on to explore and uncover the world of biblical antiquity. To them we owe the development of biblical archaeology. Their efforts focused on the great centers of ancient Near Eastern civilization, Egypt and Mesopotamia, though Palestine, lying between these two centers, had pride of place. Egyptian and Mesopotamian sites and artifacts were interpreted in a context that placed the Bible at the center. Early archaeologists were "biblical researchers." As scientific exploration moved away from this biblical orientation to the ancient Near East, the term biblical archaeology was replaced by the more neutral term Near Eastern archaeology.

Many of these "biblical researchers" were, in fact, Protestant missionaries to the peoples of the Near East. Pliny Fisk, an Andover Seminary graduate and member of the first American Palestine Mission (1819), noted in his "Sermon Preached Just Before the Departure of the Palestine Mission" that "there are now a considerable number of Jews at Jerusalem, and in the vicinity. Notwithstanding all that this people have suffered; notwithstanding all their dispersions; they will continue a distinct people, and retain their ancient language, customs and religion."[3] It was the culture of this still "distinct people" that fascinated American travelers and scholars. Christian missionaries viewed the Jews of their time as "the long descendants of the Israelite." The subtext here is a familiar one. Knowledge of the "ancient language, customs and religion" of the Jews would make American missionaries all the more effective in their efforts to convert the Jews at Jerusalem, "the scene of almost all that is interesting in sacred history." When, in the 1840s, English missionaries opened a hospital for the Jews of Jerusalem, they placed a Hebrew translation of the New Testament in every room. With the establishment of the English-Prussian church in Jerusalem, under the leadership of Bishop Solomon Alexander (a Jewish apostate), daily prayers in Hebrew were instituted. Today, at the beginning of the twenty-first century, these Hebrew Christian prayers are still recited every Sunday at the same church in Jerusalem's Old City.

The career of Edward Robinson, whose story is told in Chapter 7 of this book, illustrates the change from "Hebrew in America" to "Hebrew in Palestine," from a Hebraic understanding of the American experience to the American use of Hebrew as a key with which to unlock the secrets of the recently "rediscovered" Holy Land. Trained by Moses Stuart at Andover Theological Seminary, Robinson was to become Stuart's successor as Protestant America's most respected scholar of the Bible. Robinson argued that to understand the Bible one had to go to Palestine and identify its lost holy sites. He

and his followers considered the Holy Land to be "the Third Testament." The five volumes of Robinson's *Biblical Researches in Palestine* (published in 1841 and 1852) became an American classic.

So great was the American interest in the Holy Land and in the physical evidence of the biblical truth, that books like Robinson's accounts of his travels and one by his friend William Thompson, *The Land and the Book* (a travelogue and guide to Palestine), became best sellers in the United States. These books, and others like them, fired the public imagination and sold hundreds of thousands of copies in the mid-nineteenth century. The only book in pre–Civil War America that outsold the Palestine exploration accounts was Harriet Beecher Stowe's *Uncle Tom's Cabin*. Stowe's work also has its Hebraist connections. Her earliest novels are imbued with Puritan Hebraism, a Hebraism absorbed in the home of her father, Lyman Beecher, prominent theologian, preacher, and biblical scholar. In 1850, her husband, Calvin Stowe (whom she dubbed "my little Rabbi"), was appointed professor of Greek and Hebrew at Maine's Bowdoin College. As Harriet Beecher Stowe wrote to a friend, Professor Stowe could from then on always be found "with his nose in the Hebrew books." Elaborating on the story of her marriage to Professor Stowe, Harriet commented that "I was married when I was twenty-five years old to a man rich in Greek and Hebrew, Latin and Arabic, and alas! rich in nothing else!"[4]

It was upon their arrival in Maine that Harriet Beecher Stowe became engaged in the great moral and political issue of the day, the question of slavery. Friends exhorted her to use her talents to expose and publicize the cruelty and inhumanity of the southern slaveholders. *Uncle Tom's Cabin*, published in 1852, was the result of her efforts. The novel is replete with biblical allusion and metaphor. When Tom and his companions are taken to Simon Legree's plantation, Tom leads them in a Methodist hymn: "Jerusalem my happy home / Name ever dear to me! / When shall my sorrows have an end / Thy joys when shall be."[5]

But Jerusalem was not the dominant biblical metaphor of the slave experience. Rather, it was the story of the Exodus from Egypt that gave African slaves hope for their eventual liberation. In earlier chapters of this book, we saw how the Exodus and entry into the Promised Land served the American colonists as a dominant metaphor. As late as 1783 Ezra Stiles had characterized the new American republic as "God's American Israel." But as scholar Albert Raboteau has written about the mid-nineteenth century, "Slaves and free blacks . . . located themselves in a different part of the Exodus story than white Christians. From their perspective America was Egypt, and as long as it continued to enslave and oppress black Israel, America's destiny was in jeopardy."[6]

Calvin Stowe, Edward Robinson, and other American Protestant biblical scholars were among the first Americans to grapple with the theological and social implications of German Higher Criticism. Moses Stuart and his students were practitioners of the "lower criticism," which sought to uncover the authentic meaning of the text. The "higher criticism" looked for possible "sources" of the text. By the mid-nineteenth century this school of interpretation, which subjected the biblical text to the same rigorous historical analysis as it did the texts of the classical world, was seen as a challenge to the belief that Scripture was divinely inspired. Churchmen and theologians feared that this subversion of biblical authority would lead to the spread of "unbelief." Many considered exploration and discovery in Palestine to be an "antidote to the poison of unbelief."

From their vantage point as outsiders to the debates that raged within Christian scholarly communities, Jewish scholars saw in German biblical criticism a challenge to both biblical authority and traditional Jewish methods of interpretation. Solomon Schechter, reader in Hebrew at Cambridge University, and one of the great Jewish scholars of the late nineteenth century, termed this criticism, "the Higher anti-Semitism." Schechter was referring to Wellhausen's two-pronged attack on the Judaic tradition. The first prong was to invoke the well-known idea that the text of the Hebrew Bible was neither as old nor as coherently unified as the Jewish tradition claimed. The second prong, which expanded on Paul's polemic against the Law, sought to refute the rabbinic idea that the Law was at the core of biblical religion. In Wellhausen's words, "It is well known that there never have been more impudent inventors of history than the rabbis."[7] Schechter's lecture was the first counterattack in a sustained Jewish critique of the Documentary Hypothesis, the theory that claimed that the text of the Old Testament was composed of distinct documents redacted at the end of the biblical period.

The tensions between Christian and Jewish understandings of the Bible are evident in the lives and careers of three associates of Edward Robinson—Isaac Nordheimer (Chapter 8), Joshua/James Seixas (Chapter 9), and George Bush (Chapter 10). Each of their stories reflects the complexity and potential creativity inherent in Jewish-Christian arguments about the Hebrew Bible and its commentarial traditions. Isaac Nordheimer's encounter with American Protestant biblical scholarship highlights the ambivalence some Christian scholars felt toward a Jewish colleague. Seixas's life story shows us the effects of scholarly endeavor on personal religious belief. In Professor George Bush's academic career, his own religious deliberations were played out within the arena of Christian mysticism's struggle with Protestant rationalism.

Part II concludes with the story of Selah Merrill, U.S. consul in Jerusalem during most of the last two decades of the nineteenth century. Merrill was a New England churchman who had served as chaplain of a black regiment during the Civil War. He was an avid student of biblical history and a pioneering archaeologist. His appointment to the U.S. consular post in Jerusalem came at a time of increased Jewish emigration to Palestine. He opposed this *"aliyah"* vigorously, stating in his 1891 annual report to the U.S. State Department that "Palestine is not ready for the Jews, and the Jews are not ready for Palestine."[8] The report emphasized the unsuitability of Palestine as a place for colonization as well as the unsuitability of European Jews as colonizers. Merrill's story problematizes the popular understanding of the relationship between Hebraism and the call for the restoration of the Jews to Palestine. While some Christian scholars and church leaders did support an early form of the Zionist idea, many others, both in England and New England, opposed the idea.[9] Forty years earlier Edward Robinson had encountered a group of American Christians in Palestine who hoped to bring the Jews back to agricultural pursuits. He wrote, "It is hardly necessary to remark, that the idea of speedily converting the Jews, living as strangers in Palestine, into an agricultural people, is altogether visionary."[10]

One American alternative to support for Jewish immigration to Palestine was to support the territorial claims of the indigenous Arab population. The

Arabs of Palestine were also viewed through a biblical prism; they were described as living exemplars of the ancient biblical world. In many an illustrated American book Abraham and the other Patriarchs were depicted as Bedouin, and the denizens of the Israelite Kingdoms as *qufiyah*-clad Arab men and traditionally dressed Arab women. The Arabs of Palestine were thus seen as the authentic inheritors of the biblical past, a past that had to be kept in its "unchanging purity." Rejecting Jewish claims to Palestine, some American thinkers couched their opposition to Zionism in biblical terms. For these opponents of political Zionism, the Holy Land, holy to Christians, belonged to its Arab inhabitants, as their culture demonstrated the continuity between past and present, in an area of the world thought to be "unchanging." Thus both opponents and proponents of the restoration of the Jews to Palestine framed their arguments within the context of biblical belief.

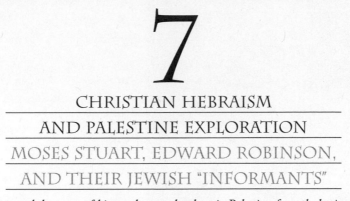

7

CHRISTIAN HEBRAISM
AND PALESTINE EXPLORATION
MOSES STUART, EDWARD ROBINSON,
AND THEIR JEWISH "INFORMANTS"

*Nature and the course of history show us that here in Palestine, from the beginnings
onwards, there cannot be any talk of chance.*
Karl Ritter

A Young Scholar Adventurer

Of the nineteenth-century scholars discussed here, the one whose books had
the greatest influence on American perceptions of the meaning of the Holy
Land in the American national experience was Edward Robinson of Palestine exploration fame. Edward Robinson was our first "Indiana Jones"—explorer, archaeologist, biblical scholar, intrepid traveler, and raconteur. His
life and activities paved the way for other scholar-adventurers. Robinson's accounts of his Middle Eastern adventures and his reports of archaeological discoveries had a wide readership, and subsequent generations of travelers and
writers acknowledged their debt to him. Furthermore, his influence extended
far beyond American shores. Late-nineteenth- and early-twentieth-century
German scholars, then at the forefront of the study of geography and eth-
nology, acknowledged their great debt to his work. As a young man Robinson had studied with German savants; later they deferred to his encyclopedic
knowledge of Palestine and the adjacent areas of the Near East.[1]

Robinson was at the forefront of the new American methods of research
and publication, which later gained European acceptance. Until the end of the
nineteenth century there was no graduate education in the United States. Germany was the country where aspiring American academicians went to study.
Armed with their German doctorates they returned to the United States and
built a system of graduate education. Robinson's intellectual heirs were instru-

mental in shaping that system. Johns Hopkins, in the late 1880s, was the first American graduate school, and the study of Semitic languages was one of the first fields of graduate study. The University of Chicago, where graduate education flourished in the early decades of the twentieth century, also focused its energies on the study of the Middle East. Its founding president, William Rainey Harper, was a Hebraist of renown, and Chicago's Oriental Institute, under the leadership of Harper student James Henry Breasted, made great contributions to the study of ancient Egypt and Mesopotamia.

Robinson's years of study and travel, in Germany and elsewhere in Europe, broadened his intellectual and spiritual horizons. These expanded intellectual horizons would later influence Robinson's students at Andover and Union Theological Seminaries. Most significant for our later discussion of Christians and Zionism, his biblical researches in Palestine had a profound effect on American perceptions of Palestine. For the outcome and implications of his research would influence not only American understandings of Palestine history, but also emergent Jewish understandings of the relationship between the land of Israel and modern Jewish history. Spurred by reports of Christian exploration and settlement in Palestine, European Jews were inspired to launch their own settlement plans.

Born into a New England Congregationalist family that had immigrated to the colonies in the 1630s, Robinson was imbued with a strong sense of spiritual and intellectual mission, and with the still powerful sense of biblical urgency and imagery that accompanied the early British migrations to the American colonies. Of his childhood, Robinson wrote:

As in the case of most of my countrymen, especially in New England, the scenes of the Bible had made a deep impression upon my mind from the earliest childhood; and afterwards in riper years this feeling had grown into a strong desire to visit in person the places so remarkable in the history of the human race. Indeed in no country of the world, perhaps, is such a feeling more widely diffused than in New England; in no country are the Scriptures better known, or more highly prized. From his earliest years the child is there accustomed not only to read the Bible for himself; but he also reads or listens to it in the morning and evening devotions of the family, in the daily village-school, in the Sunday-school and Bible-class, and in the weekly ministrations of the sanctuary. Hence, as he grows up, the names of Sinai, Jerusalem, Bethlehem, the Promised Land, become associated with his earliest recollections and holiest feelings. With all this, in my own case, there had subsequently become connected a scientific motive. I had long meditated the preparation of a work on Biblical Geography; and wished to satisfy myself by personal observation, as to many points on which I could find no information in the books of travelers. This indeed grew to be the main object of our journey, the nucleus around which all our inquiries and observations clustered.[2]

Here we see biblical Palestine as a source of childhood imagery and the Promised Land concept as a way of understanding America's destiny. As Robinson's biographer noted, "Although he traveled to New York for his education and to Palestine for his most important research, Robinson remained to the end a thoroughly Connecticut Yankee." One could argue that for Robinson, the two most significant "American" spaces were Connecticut and Palestine. Ezra Stiles had termed the United States "God's American Israel." For Robinson's readers, Palestine—a reciprocal model of America as Holy Land— was imagined as sharing a special relationship with the United States. As Hilton Obenzinger has argued: "The religious influences carrying the images of Palestine were, of course, deeply ingrained and pervasive from the first moments of North American colonization."[3]

The New England educational system, with its focus on the Greco-Roman classics and the New Testament, was still in place in 1794, the year of Edward Robinson's birth in Southington, Connecticut. But challenges to classical educational models were in the air; Benjamin Franklin's emphasis on practical rather than scholastic knowledge was one significant challenge. Robinson's father William was the Congregational pastor of the small town between Hartford and New Haven. In Connecticut there was one official state church —Congregational—and the law stipulated that the church and its schools be supported by taxes. This would change after 1818, but in Robinson's youth the system was still very much in place. His father was both church and school authority, and, of course, a leading citizen of the town. Educated and ordained at Yale, William Robinson was an admirer of both Ezra Stiles and Jonathan Edwards.

Benjamin Franklin's educational reforms had yet to make inroads into small town life. Franklin advocated physical education and excursions to "real life" places of work and edification; this too was long in reaching the conservative burghers of Connecticut. In rural Southington there was no formal Latin school, but Robinson, beginning at age fourteen, managed to receive a classical education through group study with a local minister. In this small private academy the curriculum included "a rich dose of Latin grammar and a taste of the Latin classics in the original tongue. Grammar schools were, indeed, just that: grammar, grammar, grammar. Robinson was one of those who took to the subject with great enthusiasm and ability."[4]

Robinson studied Latin, but as yet no Greek. That language he would master at the recently established Hamilton College in New York State. To be accepted to Hamilton one had to know some Greek, and to that language Robinson devoted himself during his eighteenth summer. The future professor of Hebrew and Greek, however, was not "all work and no play." He loved the outdoors and the rigors of physical labor and he traveled as much as he could throughout the wilderness areas of Connecticut and New York. From an early age he recorded his thoughts on the people and places he visited. In his diaries and letters he developed great powers of observation, powers that he would use to great effect in his biblical researches in Palestine.

While Robinson's future fame was to rest on his accomplishments in biblical interpretation and Holy Land exploration, his preparatory and college education did not address these subjects. The Hebraism of liberal Harvard and of more conservative Yale had waned by the first decade of the nineteenth century. Classicism thrived; Hebraism declined. Even at Yale, where President Stiles had until 1795 championed "Hebraic education," Hebrew study had declined and was no longer mandatory. In a sense, Hebrew was the first elective course. The founders and faculty of Hamilton College, who had been trained at Yale, did not view Hebrew as central to their mission and they neglected it in the early years of the college.

What then did the one hundred students at this early-nineteenth-century college study? "Latin, Greek, basic mathematics, moral and natural philosophy all flavored with a strong dash of congregational piety."[5] The same could be said for all American colleges—though piety was not as strong an element at all of them. Harvard's detractors called it impious and after the outbreak of the Unitarian Controversy condemned its values as too "modern." Hebraism was often associated with the inculcation of piety.

Edward Robinson would revive that Hebraist stratum in American intellectual life and, in a sense, take it from the latent to the manifest. He would transform it from a purely academic subject—Hebrew as an aid to understanding the Bible—to a practical one—Hebrew as key to unlocking the physical, actual remains of ancient Israel. A related shift accompanied this transformation in the study of Hebrew—a shift from the metaphorical view of America as the Promised Land to a rediscovery of Palestine as the true Promised Land. This rediscovery would be pioneered by American researchers imbued with a biblical understanding of history, both of their own American history, and of the history of ancient Israel and its neighbors.

Edward Robinson was the star pupil at the small New York State college, and in storybook fashion married Eliza Kirkland, the youngest daughter of the college president. Upon graduation Robinson was appointed instructor in Greek at Hamilton. Eliza was close to forty; he was twenty-four. Within the year she was dead, possibly from the complications of childbirth. Edward Robinson fell into a deep depression that lasted several years. He emerged from this depression by immersion in hard work, and it was philology that cured him. Working tirelessly, Robinson translated several books of the *Iliad* and prepared critical selections of the Greek text that college students could use to study Greek and prepare their own translations. At some point he decided to turn this project into a textbook. The very notion of a "textbook" with graduated exercises was an innovation in American higher education. Up to that point language instruction had been for the most part recitation—reading assigned passages aloud in the classroom. Often the students had been called upon to copy the contents of a collection of texts, with some grammatical information included, but a textbook written with the students' needs in mind was an innovation.

An Emerging Hebraist

In 1822 Robinson traveled to Andover Theological Seminary to work on the proofs of his Greek textbook and consult with professors there. Having made his contribution to the study and teaching of the Greek classics, he turned his attention to the study of Hebrew. As of yet he had not articulated a connection between the study of that ancient tongue and the investigation of peoples or places related to the biblical narrative. But what was at first a purely philological exercise would later turn into a spiritual and geographic quest. So central did Holy Land exploration become in Robinson's worldview that he was later to dub the study of Palestine exploration "the fifth Gospel" or "the Third Testament."

In 1824, two years after the twenty-eight-year-old Robinson began to study Hebrew, the scholarly world was abuzz with the great scholarly breakthrough of the previous year: the decipherment of Egyptian hieroglyphs by the young French savant Champollion. In early-nineteenth-century Europe and America there was a fascination with the rediscovery of the East and the decipherment of the "mysterious ancient languages." This rediscovery was linked to the expansion of European colonialism and the development of scholarly guilds devoted to understanding and controlling the East. In the language of the postmodern critique of European orientalism, by becoming expert in the ancient, one could control the modern. In the 1820s Champollion deciphered Egyptian hieroglyphs; in the 1830s German scholars made advancements in the decipherment of the cuneiform writing systems of ancient Mesopotamia. Simultaneously, British entrenchment in Egypt intensified and general European interest in colonizing the Muslim East grew.

At Andover Theological Seminary, which had been founded to counter the "liberal tendencies" of Harvard, Robinson fell under the influence of Moses Stuart, "the father of biblical philology." Stuart was the most prominent American scholar schooled in the techniques and ideologies of German Protestant study of the Bible. For the first thirty years of the nineteenth century Moses Stuart was the preeminent Protestant biblical scholar in the United States. Robinson, in many senses, became his successor. In Moses Stuart Robinson found a devoted teacher and kindred spirit. Both teacher and student were theological conservatives with an unusual openness to innovations in scholarly approaches to Scripture, and they shared a remarkable ability to learn languages both ancient and modern.

Robinson initially went to Andover to check the proofs of his book on the *Iliad*. He was to stay for fourteen years. A year after Robinson arrived Moses Stuart appointed him his assistant for Hebrew and biblical studies. Before assuming his professional duties, however, he had to pass one final stage of initiation. Robinson had to be licensed to preach in the church. He chose as the subject of his first sermon "the fulfillment of prophecy." He called his listeners' attention to the spate of recent discoveries in the East; these, he pointed out, validated the biblical depiction of the Fall of Babylon. "Babylon . . . has been recently explored by an English traveler, Mr. Rich, and the description which he has given would almost support the assertion that the prophesy had been accomplished." This theme, that the most recent discoveries in the ruins of the ancient near East could help moderns understand and confirm the teachings of the Bible, would become the cornerstone of biblical archaeology. Many consider Edward Robinson the founder of the field.

Robinson's Continental Education

In 1826, twelve years before he set out for Palestine, Edward Robinson embarked on a long course of study in France and Germany. He spent a total of four years at some of the great European universities, including Göttingen and Berlin. Now that he was licensed to preach and well established as a teacher and scholar at Andover Theological Seminary, he aspired to achieve a European style graduate education. Armed with letters of introduction from Moses Stuart and other New England luminaries, Robinson met and studied with a remarkable array of European intellectuals, among them the great French savant Silverstre de Sacy, the brothers Alexander and Wilhelm von Humboldt, the theologian Schleiermacher, and the preeminent church historian August Neander. At the University of Berlin he heard Hegel and Schopenhauer lecture; this was heady stuff indeed for a young American scholar of the 1820s.

Robinson's observations on these intellectual luminaries, preserved in letters to his sister, are delightful. Of Hegel he says, "He is nearsighted and bends his head down quite to the table, while he speaks low and thick and muttering like an old woman, repeating his words twice and over and often three times." Robinson is respectful of these towering figures, but he also enjoys puncturing their pomposity a bit; and his literary instincts, later so useful in the construction of his travels in Palestine, tend toward the detailed and the irreverent. Robinson on a dinner party with Schleiermacher: "He stands very high as a man of talent, tho' his personal appearance is bad. . . . I was amused in looking at him. He is the most distinguished preacher in Germany and also very eminent as a philosopher and as a man of uncommon talents. He sat between two young ladies and seemed to be the happiest man in the room."[6]

During his sojourn in Berlin Robinson studied Arabic and Syriac and attended lectures by Wilhelm von Humboldt and August Neander. Neander, a church historian, made a profound impression on Robinson and his recorded observations on their encounter speak to many of the issues confronted in this book. "The man who interests me most, however, as a literary man and as a Christian, is Neander. He is by birth a Jew and has all the characteristical national features in his outer man; but his inner man is truly Christian, kindness, meekness and love."[7] Robinson's fascination with Jews, and especially with Jews who "became Christian," had developed before he set out for Europe. He and Moses Stuart had engaged several "native informants" on Jewish rituals and texts. In Europe, Robinson would find other, and more complex, permutations of Jewish and Christian identity. August Neander was, to Robinson, the most interesting and compelling of these ethnic-religious hybrids.

Neander, born into an Orthodox Jewish family as David Mendel, was a child prodigy who was baptized into the church soon after his graduation, with highest honors, from Hamburg's Johanneum Gymnasium. He took the name "Neander," Greek for "new man." By 1812 in his mid-twenties, he was considered the most promising young church historian in Germany. At age twenty-five he was appointed professor at the University of Berlin. For Robinson, as for many other observers, Neander would in some sense remain a Jew, though his "inner man" was Christian. A decade after Robinson heard Neander lecture, the still young church historian would help to confirm this somewhat ambivalent view of his Christian identity. He was Germany's preeminent church historian, yet he retained loyalties to the Jewish community. The 1840 Damascus Affair, in which the Jews of that city were accused of murdering a Christian child for "ritual purposes," generated opposition and protest worldwide. Neander, in Berlin, made his view known that "the whole ritual murder charge was a falsehood."[8] Neander's views had a salutary effect on many of his German readers. Along with the words of scholars throughout Western Europe and the United States, his condemnation of the Damascus "Blood Libel" brought pressure to free the imprisoned Jews of Damascus.

Moses Stuart, Robinson's teacher, was prescient about his student's abilities. Robinson's four-year sojourn in Europe bore remarkable fruit. The German philological approach was a natural fit for his remarkable gift for mastering the ancient languages. On his return in 1830 to Andover Seminary Robinson was appointed professor of sacred literature. But however great Robinson's accomplishments, his success was predicated on a broad base of American and European scholarly support. Foremost among his supporters was his teacher and mentor Moses Stuart. With his interest in native informants, Stuart had prepared the way for renewed scholarly conversation between Jews and Christians, a conversation which Robinson continued and built upon. Furthermore, it was Stuart's academic and administrative work that would make Robinson's Palestine endeavor possible.

Moses Stuart, Robinson's Mentor

Moses Stuart, born at Wilton, Connecticut, in 1780, entered Yale in 1797 and graduated at the head of his class in 1799. At Yale he excelled at mathematics and Greek, but he did not study Hebrew. The influence of Ezra Stiles,

Moses Stuart

who died two years before Stuart entered Yale, was on the wane. Hebrew was offered, but very few students availed themselves of the opportunity to study it. Stuart went into law after his graduation but soon returned to Yale, where, under President Timothy Dwight's influence, he studied divinity. As tutor he taught Latin and New Testament Greek but again did not study biblical Hebrew.[9]

When, in 1808, the trustees of the newly founded Andover Theological Seminary invited Stuart to fill the post of professor of sacred literature, his duties were described as being, in part, "to aid the students in the acquisition of a radical and adequate knowledge of the sacred scriptures in their original languages." Stuart accepted the post in 1810, but he was faced with one serious problem—he knew little Hebrew. According to Stuart's biographer, John Giltner, his deficiency in Hebrew was a painful embarrassment. To further complicate the matter, he could not find a competent teacher to help him learn the language quickly.

Left with little choice, Stuart embarked on a rigorous program of self-instruction and taught himself the rudiments of biblical Hebrew. Within a few months he had mastered the first twenty chapters of Genesis. He used Charles Wilson's *Elements of Hebrew Grammar* (3rd edition, 1802) as his grammar book. Wilson viewed the Hebrew vowel points as an impediment to the swift acquisition of the language, and he advocated ignoring them completely. Because his readers would know that the Jews taught Hebrew with the vowel points, Wilson felt it necessary to add an explanatory note in which he attacked both the "points" and the Masoretic apparatus as a whole. "But, as many bibles are printed on the Masoretic plan; as this plan has been patronized by respectable names, and much time and labor has been spent in the improvement of it; as it is a mode of reading invented by *Jews*, who it is presumed, should best know the language and traditions of their forefathers, a work of this kind might be thought imperfect, if an explanation of *doctrine* of vowel-points were altogether neglected." He then went on to criticize both the antiquity and necessity of the vowel points.[10]

The rabbinic Masorah, the technical apparatus that dictated how biblical Hebrew was pronounced, had long presented a challenge to Christian Hebraists. Wilson's anti-Masoretic comments were in the same spirit as the remarks of Professor Stephen Sewall in one of his public lectures at Harvard. Sewall had considered the vowel points "a very great clog and hindrance" and claimed that because of them "the Hebrew language is considerably maimed and deformed."[11]

In the spirit of Wilson and Sewall, Moses Stuart published his own *Hebrew Grammar without Points* in 1812. When he used this book in the Andover classroom he quickly realized that in discarding the vowel points he had perhaps chosen the most difficult way of teaching Hebrew. In December 1813, Stuart wrote to a colleague, "The more I study Hebrew, the more misgivings I have about studying without the points." But he did not rush to change his pedagogical methods. This was not an issue to be decided lightly. He wrote that "whether students can in fact become acquainted with the Hebrew sooner with the points or without them is a question that can be settled only by experience. In an institution like ours, it is of great consequence that the question should be settled and rightly settled."[12]

Despite the difficulties of studying Hebrew in so artificial a manner (that is, without vowel points), the students did make remarkable progress in their studies. In a year they read twenty chapters of Genesis, sixty psalms, and the first ten chapters of the Book of Job. This was a remarkable achievement, and would certainly be considered so in today's colleges and universities. Still, Moses Stuart doubted that he had "rightly settled" the question.

By 1817 Stuart's "conversion experience" with regard to the importance of the vowel points was complete. During the 1816–17 year he began for the first time to teach with the vowel points, and he addressed the issue in his 1817 report to the Andover Board of Visitors. "The class has read nearly one third more of Hebrew than any preceding class. I am persuaded that were they to pursue Hebrew study another year, they would at the end of it have acquired double what they could have learned without the use of points. I have been misled on this subject by Parkhurst and Kennicott, and am very sorry for it, for

I have not only lost much time myself but have been the occasion of much loss to others. . . . I am beyond all question in favor of the points."[13] His decision about the vowel points seems to have been influenced by the new German philology. The works of the German Hebraist Gesenius were becoming known in New England, and the German advocacy of, and reliance upon, the Jewish Masoretic apparatus most likely influenced Stuart in his decision to teach Hebrew with the vowel points, in the "mode of reading invented by Jews."

Stuart, Robinson, and Their Jewish Sources

When the young Moses Stuart arrived at Andover Theological Seminary in 1808, the Puritan Hebraism of colonial America had declined to the point of near disappearance. The elites of the new Republic valued and practiced classical models of education, with Latin and some Greek serving as the mainstays of the college curriculum. Hebrew's place of honor had diminished considerably, but within two decades Moses Stuart, working with Edward Robinson and a few others, would reverse this trend.

By the mid-1820s Hebrew and its cognate languages (Aramaic, Syriac, and Arabic) had become a critical dimension of the Andover curriculum. As the study of Hebrew assumed greater importance at the seminary, Stuart petitioned the board to institute a "Hebrew rule"; all entering students would be required to have a reading knowledge of the language. From 1827 to 1837 this rule was in force, and it was during this period, when Stuart's position as "Dean of Biblical Science in America" was assured, that he met scholarly informants who were to help him greatly. It seemed that in his gradual acceptance of the authenticity and relevance of the Jewish system of the Masorah, and in his widening knowledge of the classical Jewish commentaries on the Bible, Stuart was led to entertain the notion that Jewish experts on matters biblical and Hebraic would be helpful to his scholarly project. Three scholars would be particularly helpful to Stuart and his student Robinson in their scholarly investigations of the Jewish tradition.

The first of Stuart and Robinson's "informants" was a non-Jew, William Gottlieb Schauffler. In Germany, as a child, Schauffler had displayed a flair for the learned languages, including Hebrew, Greek, and Latin. A few years after he completed his secondary education he immigrated to the United States and enrolled in Stuart's seminary. In five years at Andover he mastered the seminary curriculum and embarked on an independent study of "exotic" languages. The *Dictionary of American Biography*, in recounting his startling linguistic talents, cites his study of "Chaldaic, Syriac, Arabic, Persian, Turkish, Rabbinic, Coptic and Ethiopic." The singling out of "Rabbinic"—postbiblical

Hebrew—as a distinct language is worthy of note. While at Andover Schauffler served as Stuart's informant on the exotic Near Eastern languages and on
Rabbinics, the language and content of rabbinic texts. In Stuart's 1829 *Hebrew
Chrestomathy*, a textbook that included selected biblical passages, a glossary,
and grammatical notes, he thanked William Schauffler for "his revisions and
corrections of the text." The chrestomathy system, in which texts and a glossary were arranged in a systematic fashion for the beginning student's convenience, was used in the study of Greek and Latin. Stuart adapted the form for
Hebrew studies.

Upon his graduation in 1831, Schauffler was ordained as a minister and appointed "missionary to the Jews of Turkey." ("Turkey" here refers to all of the
Ottoman Empire.) In November of that year, at Boston's Park Street Church,
Stuart delivered a "Sermon at the Ordination of the Rev. William G. Schauffler, Missionary to the Jews." In this long sermon, which was later published in
a number of editions, Stuart called for renewed efforts to convert the Jews and
reminded his listeners (and readers) that, "Israel has been blind to the excellence and glory of the gospel." He claimed that "the Jews enmity to Christians
has been decidedly greater than toward Pagans." The Jewish convert to Christianity was to be encouraged and admired, for "the Jews regard with universal
horror the man who has deserted their ranks and gone over to Christianity.
They will not hear him. They name him a derogatory acronym 'meshummad,'
i.e., one who is accursed, or ought to be devoted to utter destruction." In the
published text of the sermon, the word *meshummad* is printed in Hebrew characters. For Stuart the study of Hebrew gave Christians the ability to dispute
Jews in matters of faith. With Hebrew, Christian scholars would be able to
"turn their own weapons against them."[14]

Stuart's cosponsor in the appointment of Schauffler as missionary was
the American Society for Meliorating the Condition of the Jews, which, as
described in Chapter 5, played a major role in shaping and, paradoxically,
strengthening the American Jewish community. Among Schauffler's accomplishments as a missionary-scholar was his translation of the New Testament
into Ladino (or Judaeo-Spanish). It was hoped that a Ladino New Testament
would be a useful tool to convert those Jews whose Spanish origins were reflected in the family use of Judeo-Spanish. Schauffler's translation was inspired
by Moses Stuart's exhortations to Andover graduates to bring the Bible into
the languages of the world.[15]

As Moses Stuart's Hebrew studies broadened to include rabbinic Hebrew,
and the missionary value of mastering Hebrew became more apparent, Stuart
turned to his second informant, a Jewish acquaintance named Joshua Seixas,
for information about Jewish texts and practices. Son of New York Congre-

gation Shearith Israel's leader Gershom Mendes Seixas, Joshua, who would later refer to himself as James, was a self-styled "Professor of Hebrew" and something of an adventurer and "freelance scholar."

During the early 1830s Seixas taught Hebrew as an adjunct professor at colleges and seminaries in the Northeast, among them Andover Theological Seminary. While advising Stuart on Hebrew sources, rabbinic texts, and the authenticity of rabbinic manuscripts, Seixas also served as an informant in Jewish liturgy and ritual. In a September 1832 letter to Seixas, Stuart remarked, "I should be exceedingly glad to have you come up and spend a day with me, were we not at the very close of our term. . . . The students have a strong desire to hear you cantillate."[16] Joshua Seixas would, however, soon drift away from Stuart's orbit. In Ohio in the mid-1830s, teaching at the recently founded Oberlin College, he met the founders of the Mormon Church. They invited Seixas to teach Hebrew at the "Hebrew School" in their Kirtland, Ohio, temple, and it is there that Seixas entered Mormon history as "Professor of Hebrew" and a "devout Jew." We will explore his story in detail in Chapter 9.

With Seixas's departure for the western states, Stuart did not remain long without a Jewish informant. Isaac Nordheimer, who Stuart met in 1828, served as the third of his informants, the most knowledgeable in Hebraica and Judaica. Born into a family of Hungarian Orthodox rabbis in 1809, Nordheimer was a child prodigy, an *iluy*. As a teenager, he attended the famed Yeshiva of the Chasam Sofer at Pressburg and later studied at German universities under some of the great scholars of philosophy and what we would now term linguistics. A year after receiving his doctoral degree, he immigrated to New York. Through meetings with Christian clergymen and academicians he met the founders of New York University, who appointed him professor of Arabic and other oriental languages.

Within three years of his arrival in the United States, Nordheimer published his *Critical Hebrew Grammar*, a work in two volumes. This grammar, which relied on both modern philological method and rabbinic sources, impressed Stuart, Robinson, and their students. In 1839 Nordheimer published a thirty-five-page essay on the history and methodology of Hebrew lexicography that further impressed and influenced his Christian colleagues. Nordheimer's underlying assumption in this article was that the technical apparatus of the Masorah—the vowel points, the cantillation marks, the "scribal correction"—was all authentic and reliable. Using numerous examples he demonstrated to his Christian audience that "the Masorah in fact is a most important and useful collection of ancient critical remarks."[17] The shift from Stuart's earlier condemnation of the Jewish Masorah system was influenced by Nordheimer's teachings on the centrality and dependability of the Masoretic tradition. Through Nordheimer, Stuart and Robinson became ardent students of the Masoretic apparatus.

Stuart was to incorporate Nordheimer's insights into later editions of his Hebrew textbooks, but he remained acutely aware of his own limitations in rabbinic areas of knowledge. Further collaboration between Moses Stuart and Isaac Nordheimer was prevented by Nordheimer's tragic early death at age thirty-three in 1841. Mourned by Christian and Jewish friends and colleagues alike, Nordheimer was, as far as I am aware, the last of Robinson and Stuart's Jewish informants. I examine the life of Isaac Nordheimer in the next chapter.

In 1852, while Robinson was en route to Palestine, his teacher Moses Stuart died at his home at Andover Seminary. During his final illness, weakened by typhoid, Stuart insisted on working on the proofs of his current project, a commentary on the Book of Proverbs. At his funeral, his student Calvin Stowe, husband of Harriet Beecher Stowe, gave the eulogy. Stuart had passed the biblical age of seventy; from the time of his retirement four years earlier he had worked tirelessly on his biblical commentaries and articles addressing issues of the day, foremost among them the slavery question. In his slavery pamphlet he distanced himself from the "proslavery biblicists" who used Scripture to justify the institution. He also distanced himself from the radical abolitionists, claiming that the Bible supported neither radical abolitionism nor the institution of slavery.

A local New England newspaper sent a reporter to Moses Stuart's funeral. The January 1852 paper reproduced some of the eulogies delivered and closed with this vignette, in which the reporter counts himself among the mourners. "It was a sad and silent farewell that we gave as we passed one by one through piles of snow and frozen clods, and looked down upon the lowly bed of the Father of Biblical Philology."[18]

Hebraism and Palestine Exploration

By the middle of the nineteenth century, European Christian study of Hebrew, now widespread in seminaries and colleges, was codified and restored to a position of respectability in the academy. German Protestant scholar Wilhelm Gesenius (1799–1842) and his students standardized the grammatical rules and historical periods of Hebrew. A professor at the University of Halle, Gesenius was known in Germany as "the father of modern Hebrew lexicography." On his long study tour of Germany, Robinson became fast friends with Gesenius. Robinson then introduced Gensenius's methods to the United States.

In both Europe and the United States Gesenius's scientific approach was almost universally accepted and there was no longer a need for the Jewish informant to serve as an expert in the "sacred language." With the German-Jewish immigration of the 1840s and 1850s, the number of synagogues in America grew, and the opportunity for Christians to observe Jewish liturgy and ritual was no longer rare. The American Jewish community also was beginning to produce its own Hebraic scholarship. Lexicons, biblical translations, grammars, and study guides written by Jews were being published, among them H. A. Henry's "Imrai Shaipher"—a small dictionary—and Isaac Leeser's Bible translations. In the second half of the nineteenth century Jews would produce Hebrew materials for Jews, and Christians would produce Hebrew materials for Christians. Crossover was rare. With the emergence of Semitic studies at early-twentieth-century American universities, a great deal of teaching and research was in the hands of Protestant scholars. By the middle of the twentieth century another shift would occur and Christians and Jews would find in the academy a space for mutual conversation about Hebrew and the Bible. But arenas of competition remained.

Robinson's teacher, Moses Stuart, had done much to restore Hebrew studies to a place of honor in American academic culture. Robinson would complete the task. One way in which Robinson emphasized the centrality of Hebrew studies was by linking them to the exploration of Palestine. As an extension of the theme articulated in his ordination sermon of 1822—that discoveries in the East indicated the fulfillment of biblical prophecy—he embarked in the late-1830s on his own expedition to Palestine. As he and his theologically conservative colleagues saw it, the publication of his "biblical researches" would shore up religious authority against the "forces of unbelief."

This was a fascinating shift. Before the 1830s, when Muhammad Ali broke away from Ottoman control and opened Palestine to the West, Christian interest in the Holy Land had centered on the events described in the New Testament. Pilgrims wanted to walk in the footsteps of Jesus; saints, scholars, and adventurers identified "authentic" relics of Christian history. During the mid-nineteenth century, however, the search for proofs of biblical accuracy—Old Testament narratives, places, and personages—assumed a prominent role in the new discourse. The borders of biblical inquiry widened beyond the geographical confines of Jerusalem, Judea, and the Galilee. Scholars and pilgrims now wanted to trace the travels of the Israelites in the Sinai wilderness, and visit the lands east of the Jordan where Moses gathered the Israelites before bidding farewell to them at Mount Nebo. An early-nineteenth-century term, "the Fifth Gospel," made reference to the New Testament aspects of contemporary Palestine, but it excluded the then burgeoning interest in Old Testament narratives. To include that interest, Palestine exploration became known as "the Third Testament," a physical landscape that filled out and authenticated the narratives of both the Old and New Testaments.

Robinson's two journeys to Palestine, in 1838 and 1852, laid the scientific and philological foundation on which later biblical researchers would build. A full articulation of the relationship between Holy Land exploration and scriptural authority would, however, only come later, in the last quarter of the nineteenth century, in the work of English scholar George Adam Smith, author of *The Historical Geography of the Holy Land*. In Smith's 1872 master-work he expounded a theory of Holy Land exploration that drew on then current European ideas about Jewish history. Central here was E. Renan's idea that the Jews were a "people of religion." Intellectuals in nineteenth-century Europe were attracted to Renan's notion that by studying minority groups one could find vestiges of the ancient past in their contemporary behaviors. In the case of Jews and Christians, a curious appropriation took place. For Christian scholars, the study of the Jews, and of their ancient ancestral land, could reveal much about the Christian past. As Smith put it: "In the economy of human progress every race has its office to fulfill, and the Bible has claimed for Israel the specialism of religion. . . . There is no land which is at once so much a sanctuary and an observatory as Palestine; no land which, till its office was fulfilled, was so swept by the great forces of history, and yet was so capable of preserving one tribe in national continuity and growth." Smith presented a picture of Palestine's significance that squared nicely with the emerging Western conception of that "rediscovered" land's centrality in Christian history. Smith also articulated and reaffirmed a classical Christian view of the function of the people of Israel: they were "one tribe in national continuity and growth until their office was fulfilled"—that is, until Jesus.[19]

The nineteenth century witnessed the clash of centuries-old religious worldviews confronting the implications of nineteenth-century scientific discoveries. The first challenge was geology, which demonstrated that the earth was far older than the few millennia of the Bible's account. Not long after came Darwin's ideas on the origin of species, which challenged the Genesis narrative of creation. For Smith and others, the Jews and their land were no longer actors on the stage of history; but exploration of these Jewish traces could lend moderns insight into the biblical narratives. These insights could then be used to counter scientific claims that challenged the authority of the Bible.

Challenges to religious belief could be countered by facts about biblical events. For Robinson, Smith, and many of their readers in the late nineteenth century, there were religious and philosophical conclusions to be drawn from the "facts" uncovered by recent discoveries, which, for these readers, validated and authenticated the narratives of the Old and New Testaments. "If a man can

[*Scholars, Prophets, Mystics*]

believe that there is no directing hand behind our universe and the history of our race, he will say that all this is the result of chance. But for most of us only another conclusion is possible." For George Adam Smith, Edward Robinson, and other Christian thinkers determined to buttress the foundations of Christian belief, the response was clear. The science of exploration and discovery could prove that the Bible was historically accurate. For Smith the most explicit expression of this idea was from the pen of the great early-nineteenth-century German geographer Karl Ritter, one of Edward Robinson's mentors. "Nature and the course of history show us that here in Palestine, from the beginning onwards, there cannot be any talk of chance."[20]

Ritter had developed the idea of "geopiety"—geography as influenced by religious beliefs. Under this idea Ritter included two categories: the way faith communities related to sacred landscapes, and the way individual geographers were influenced by their religious convictions. In the cases of Robinson and his companion Eli Smith, it was clear that their exploration of Palestine, "scientific" as it was, was inspired by religious conviction.[21]

For Americans the study of their own geography had religious implications and overtones. American geography was an area of study that attracted the attention of many churchmen. Mapping the contours of the American landscape was seen as God's work. In the decades before the 1859 publication of Darwin's *The Origin of the Species*, American clergymen did not see science as a threat to established religion, though some were alerted to advancements in geological science, which posed a challenge to the Genesis account of the age of the earth. Research, teaching, and study of American and Middle Eastern geography provided scholars with tools with which they could examine and compare the American landscape with America's geographic and ideological counterpart in the Middle East—Palestine. In the thirty years between the mid-1830s and the mid-1860s, from Edward Robinson's first visit to Palestine to the end of the Civil War, American travel to Palestine grew exponentially. America's engagement with the past, present, and future of the Holy Land took root in that period. Charles Warren, head of the British Palestine Exploration Fund, noted the phenomenon: "I must admit that the manner in which many of the Americans were well grounded in Palestine topography surprised me; they accounted for it by telling me that their clergy make a point of explaining and describing it from the pulpit frequently."[22]

Biblical Researches in Palestine, 1838

In the German philological tradition Edward Robinson found an intellectual template in which to fit his linguistic abilities. He engaged in comparative analysis of the languages of the Bible, but unlike many others in the German Protestant scholarly tradition, he did not endorse the use of philology as a critical method that might bring the divine origins of Scripture into question. Rather, Robinson used his linguistic talents and his powers of observation—powers developed as a traveler in the United States and Europe—to strengthen Christian belief through his "biblical researches." We have seen these ideas expressed by the geographers Karl Ritter and George Adam Smith. For these scholars the scientific challenges to belief in the Genesis narratives could be met by a counteroffensive of scientific data that would "prove" the historicity of the Bible. Research in the lands that had been the settings of the biblical narratives would confirm those stories and counter the "destructive" evidence of geology and the theory of evolution.

Robinson was to make the latent power of Holy Land "rediscovery" manifest. In 1832 Eli Smith, an American missionary in the Middle East and onetime Andover student, visited Robinson at Andover, where he was professor of sacred literature. Together the two generated the idea of a shared journey to explore the Holy Land. Smith had mastered Arabic during his years in the East and would later use that knowledge to produce a new translation of the Bible into Arabic. He suggested to Robinson that the combination of Robinson's deep knowledge of the ancient biblical world and his—Smith's—familiarity with the contemporary Arab Middle East would yield a new American portrait of Palestine, one that would integrate geographical studies into the science of biblical studies. For had not Robinson's work of the early 1830s—in which he produced American biblical reference works (many of them translated and adapted from the German)—established the study of the Bible on a firm academic basis? Now, American scholars had to study the land of the Bible firsthand. The "basic facts" were hard to gather, for many of them were in dispute. "All that was left for Robinson to do was to provide the basic facts about the land and its people—with maps—so that scholars could not only read the Bible accurately, but visualize the scenes which its text depicts."[23]

Robinson, about to embark on a teaching career at New York's Union Theological Seminary (UTS), asked for an extended leave to travel with Smith to the Holy Land. During Robinson's four-year leave from UTS his colleague Isaac Nordheimer, Jewish scholar of biblical and Semitic studies, taught some of Robinson's classes. Despite Nordheimer's excellent academic qualifications, a special arrangement had to be made to accommodate a Jewish scholar. Union was a liberal seminary, but it was liberal within a Protestant worldview; the UTS faculty had to vote to allow Nordheimer to join the faculty on a temporary basis. No doubt his association with Moses Stuart, "father of biblical philology" and Robinson's mentor, eased his path. Sadly, Nordheimer died in 1841, the year that Robinson returned to teaching.

Although Robinson's companion Eli Smith knew well the culture and language of early-nineteenth-century Palestine, very little material on that subject got into the final draft of *Biblical Researches in Palestine*. The local inhabitants and their lives and customs were of little interest to Robinson's readers. They wanted to read of the ancient denizens—the Hebrews. Smith used his knowledge of modern Palestine to smooth the way with local rulers and inhabitants. Using his Arabic, Smith could find the precise Arabic place name and spelling of sites they visited. He and Robinson would then seek to identify these places with their cognate biblical place names. Traveling through the hill country of Judea, near the Palestinian town of Ain Shems, he ventured that this might be the site of the biblical Beth Shemesh. The village of Shuweikah they identified with the biblical Socoh, a way station on the route of the Exodus. These were but two of hundreds of such identifications made by the two travelers. A century later Israeli archaeologists would utilize many of their identifications to create the map of modern Israel.

Smith and Robinson began their two-and-a-half-month journey in Cairo in mid-March 1838. Egypt too was part of the biblical landscape they wished to explore and describe. The Exodus from Egypt and the sojourn in the Sinai Desert are described in elaborate geographical detail in the Bible. Like many researchers before them, Smith and Robinson aspired to match the modern Egyptian landscape with the terrain described in the Bible, but unlike those researchers they were determined to trace the route themselves, rather than rely on earlier legends that they dismissed as fanciful. By identifying the eastern Nile delta with the biblical Land of Goshen, Robinson invoked a popular nineteenth-century conception of the relationship between the Bible and the contemporary Middle East: the current Middle East, both the landscape and the people, were accurate representations of the biblical narrative. "The immediate descendants of Jacob were doubtless nomadic shepherds like their forefathers, dwelling in tents; and probably drove their flocks for pasture far up in the Wadys of the desert, like the present inhabitants of the same region."[24]

Nineteenth-century photography would reify Robinson and Smith's understanding of the landscape of the Middle East. For a picture of what Palestine looked like in biblical times—and of what its people looked like—one could visit and photograph contemporary Palestine. Photography could bring the Bible to life. Illustrated Bibles published throughout the United States affirmed this connection between the Bible and the contemporary Middle East.

As Smith and Robinson traveled by camel through the Middle Eastern countryside they asked the local people to tell them all of the old and new names of the surrounding sites. While they knew that throughout the history of the Holy Land Christian monks had identified the "exact locations" in which the biblical narratives had transpired, these two Protestant explorers were deeply skeptical about "monkish" Catholic traditions, and they made it their custom to visit monasteries only after they had formed their own opinions about the local topography. As historian P. J. King remarked, Robinson had a deep disdain for the fanciful stories circulated by the monks of the Holy Land. Despite this disdain for monks and monasteries, Robinson knew that he had to visit the great monastery of St. Catherine's in the Sinai Desert. Ten days after setting out from Cairo and stopping at Suez (this was thirty years before the Suez Canal was built), Robinson and Smith arrived at St. Catherine's. This monastery, founded in the fifth century, was peopled with monks of the Greek Orthodox Church. Robinson made no definitive identification of the site of "Mount Sinai," but his account of his sojourn to St. Catherine's is imbued with a passion and emotionalism missing from his other travel writings. Reaching the monastery and finally alone after weeks of travel, Robinson reports, "I was affected by the strangeness and overpowering grandeur of the scenes around us; and it was sometimes difficult to realize, that we were now actually within the very precincts of that Sinai, of which from the earliest childhood I had thought and read with so much wonder. Yet, when at length the impression came with its full force upon my mind, although not given to the melting mood, I could not refrain from bursting into tears."[25]

From the Sinai, Robinson and Smith traveled to Aqaba and then north through the Jordan River valley. On this leg of the journey they correctly identified the desert fortress of Masada, a site that would accrue great symbolic significance a century after their 1838 visit. When the Americans visited nearby Ein Gedi in the company of local Bedouin tribesmen, they surveyed the nearby cliffs with their telescope and correctly surmised that the massive flattop rock with steep sides was Masada, the site described by the historian Josephus in *The Jewish War*. Though they did not explore the site of the ancient fortress, their report still generated excitement among American and European explorers. In 1842 the American missionary S. W. Wolcott would be the first to explore the site. Thus, American Protestant geographers in search of the roots of biblical and postbiblical history discovered the ancient site of Masada, a site later adopted by the Zionist movement as a sign of reborn Jewish nationalism and resistance to foreign rule.

The travelers soon reached Hebron and then headed toward Jerusalem and its environs, the exploration of which they devoted much of their time in Palestine. Then, moving to the coastal plain they journeyed north, by way of Nazareth and Tiberias, to Beirut. For these American explorers the Holy Land included Egypt and all of the lands of the Eastern Mediterranean. For the locations of both the Old and New Testament narratives extended beyond the land mass of ancient Israel. With the borders of Middle East states ill defined in the mid-nineteenth century, the definitions of both the "Holy Land" and the "biblical lands" were quite fluid.

After ten weeks in Egypt, Palestine, and Syria, Robinson went to Germany, where he finished writing up his researches and preparing them for publication in both German and English. Smith, his translator and guide, stayed in the Middle East and continued his missionary work. The result of their dual efforts, *Biblical Researches in Palestine*, published in 1841 in German, English, and American editions, opens with Robinson's declaration: "The following work contains the description of a journey, which had been the object of my ardent wishes, and had entered into all plans of my life for more than fifteen years."

Earlier descriptions of the landscape of the Holy Land and its biblical history had relied on the travel accounts of pilgrims. Robinson rejected most of these earlier pietistic accounts and insisted on seeing each site on its own merits, stripped of its "monkish legends." As Albrecht Alt, mid-twentieth-century German biblical scholar, put it, "In Robinson's footnotes are forever buried the errors of many generations."[26] Robinson's methodology called for direct observation of the topography and ancient remains, and description of current sites and their inhabitants. Robinson and Smith, equipped with simple surveying equipment, a telescope, and a bag of books—including Bibles and works of ancient history—approached their task with a freshness that struck their readers as characteristically American. Practical, precise, and enthusiastic, their travel account caught the attention of a wide English, German, and American readership.

The subsequent century and a half of archaeology in Palestine validated the great majority of Robinson and Smith's site identifications. The accuracy of their findings was remarkable, for they were not doing what we would today call "archaeology," in the sense of excavating sites and recovering buried artifacts. Techniques of excavation, discovery, and decipherment that were refined in the latter decades of the nineteenth century were unknown to Robinson and Smith. They saw many ruins, but could do no more than examine the surface of these ruins. Perseverance and intuition, knowledge of Arabic and local culture, and a profound insight into the Bible and its languages enabled Robinson and Smith to map the biblical history of Palestine. They undoubtedly missed important sites. For instance, Jericho and Lachish were buried under tells, "those truncated cones dotting the landscape of Syria-Palestine, composed of successive occupation layers containing the stratified remains of ancient cities."[27] Western researchers in Mesopotamia would soon articulate the idea that a tell was the remains of an ancient inhabited site, but Robinson and Smith were not aware of this development. Despite their limitations, they identified hundreds of biblical sites whose accuracy was later confirmed by archaeological excavation and decipherment. Among these sites were Capernaum in the Galilee, Herodium in the Judean Desert, the fortress of Masada, and the Siloam tunnel in Jerusalem. Today these are among the most frequently visited sites in the Holy Land.

Robinson and Smith explored the Siloam tunnel on the eastern edge of the walled City of Jerusalem at great personal risk. Their torches were extinguished in mid-journey and they had to slither through that long water passage in the wet darkness. They could see neither the walls of the tunnel nor the ancient Hebrew inscription that identified Hezekiah as the Judean King who had ordered the tunnel constructed in the eighth century B.C. This inscription was not found until 1880. Yet, in 1838 Robinson, integrating his knowledge of the Bible with his reading of the contours of the landscape of Silwan, the village to the east of the Ottoman walls of Jerusalem, correctly identified this conduit as Hezekiah's tunnel. Robinson and Smith realized that the Arabic name of the village, Silwan, was cognate to Shiloah, the Hebrew name of the waters of the spring.

In the Hebrew Bible, 2 Kings 20 tells of Hezekiah's plan to bring water into Jerusalem in anticipation of the Assyrian siege. The king dug a conduit to bring the waters of the spring to a reservoir within the city. The Bible does not tell us how the tunnel was excavated, but the inscription found in 1880 provides the missing story. The Hebrew-language inscription, written by the officials who presided over the building of the tunnel, is a dramatic retelling of this engineering feat. "And this was how the tunneling was completed: as the stonecutters wielded their picks, each crew toward the other, and while there were still three cubits to go, the voices of the men calling each other could be heard, since there was an increase in sound on the right and left. The day the breach was made, the stonecutters hacked toward each other, pick against pick, and the water flowed from the source to the pool twelve hundred cubits, even though the height of the rock above the heads of the stonecutters was a hundred cubits."[28]

Siloam was also associated with the life of Jesus, making its identification doubly important to Christian explorers. In a New Testament story told in chapter 9 of the Gospel of John, Jesus cures a man who was blind from birth. He restores the man's sight after a prayer and ritual that culminate in Jesus's telling the blind man to "wash in the Pool of Siloam."

Robinson's book on his travels became an American best seller, an indication both of the popularity of Holy Land narratives and of Robinson's felicitous and accessible style. Sometime in the mid-1840s Robinson envisioned writing his magnum opus, a systemic historical geography of Palestine. While his *Biblical Researches* was a narrative of discovery in which much information was embedded, it was not a comprehensive guide to the Holy Land and its history. Here the methodical approach of Robinson's German teachers stood before him. To write this book he would have to see and explore Palestine a second time.

The Second Journey to the Holy Land, 1852

When Robinson embarked on his second Palestine journey in 1852, Eli Smith's Arabic Bible translation was just being printed. Genesis was printed first, followed by the remaining four books of the Pentateuch. Elias Boudinot's American Bible Society facilitated the printing of these volumes, demonstrating the growing relationship between Palestine exploration and missionary work. Robinson had asserted that the purpose of American Christian missions to the Middle East was "not to draw off members of the oriental churches to Protestantism; but to awaken them to a knowledge and belief of the gospel truth in the purity and simplicity of its original scriptural form."[29] It was hoped that the publication of an Arabic translation of the Bible would accomplish that purpose.

Robinson began his second survey in Beirut, where he had completed his researches of 1838. His intentions were to fill in the gaps in the earlier researches and to publish the results as quickly as he had fourteen years earlier. Eli Smith accompanied Robinson for part of the journey; other American missionaries took over when he had to leave. Robinson traveled south from Beirut to Sidon and entered Palestine through the northern Galilee. Acco and Haifa were his next destinations. Via the hills of Samaria he reached Jerusalem, and again the Holy City occupied his attentions for several weeks. Turning north, Robinson and his companions then traveled back to Beirut through the Jordan Valley and southern Lebanon.

Like the 1838 journey through Egypt, Syria, and Palestine, this second excursion took ten weeks. Robinson was fifty-eight years old and not as hardy as he had been fifteen years earlier. Near the Huleh Swamp he contracted malarial fever, which weakened him considerably. Normally quite robust, he would never fully recover from these attacks of fever. Some biographers have concluded that this illness led to his final weakness and early death.

Near Jerusalem, Robinson met a group of remarkable and eccentric Americans with whom he disagreed profoundly. Mrs. Clorinda Minor and her "Hope Colony" had come from Philadelphia in 1850 to teach agriculture to the impoverished Jews of Palestine. Viewed with suspicion by Jews wary of Christian missionaries, Minor assured Jewish visitors to her agricultural colony that her work was charitable and ameliorative, not missionary. She and her dozen or so American coworkers hoped to teach "industrial and agricultural trades" to the Jews. In her 1849 pamphlet "Meshullam," Minor expresses the hope that an eventual restoration of the Jews would be a harbinger of the Redemption, but she makes clear that she is not embarking on a direct mission to the Jews.[30] Robinson was interested in the ancient village of Artas, in which the Minor group was then living and farming, but he was deeply skeptical about the prospects of his fellow Americans. He was a Hebraist, but not a proto-Zionist. He wrote, "It is hardly necessary to remark, that the idea of speedily converting the Jews, living as strangers in Palestine, into an agricultural people, is altogether visionary."[31] Robinson, along with most American and European visitors to Palestine, was convinced of the "visionary" nature and practical impossibility of Jewish settlement and agricultural engagement. Yet, a minority of American Christian observers differed. They would be the first American Christian Zionists. By the 1880s their voice in American politics would be heard, and by the end of the twentieth century they would wield considerable political influence.

In October of 1852 Robinson returned to the United States from his second journey through Palestine. With his teacher Moses Stuart now dead, Robinson assumed the mantle of senior American scholar of biblical studies. Four years later he published his account of the 1852 voyage to the Holy Land as *Later Biblical Researches in Palestine, and in the Adjacent Regions.*

American Painting and the Holy Land

Robinson's Palestine travel accounts had an unexpected and perhaps surprising effect on American art, and more specifically on American traditions of landscape painting. His writings coincided with an expansion in the subject matter of American painting in the first half of the nineteenth century. We see a move from portraying and evoking the American landscape to portraying Mediterranean and Middle Eastern scenes. Art historian John Davis noted that Robinson's "attention to the actual landscape of Palestine led the way to the nineteenth century obsession with looking to natural history to authenticate the narrative of the Bible. . . . In this light, Robinson's importance to American artists is seminal. His complete trust in the Bible on one hand, and the evidence of the land on the other, formed the basis for the main justification of American landscape painting in the Holy Land."[32]

Frederic Church was the best known of the American artists drawn to the Holy Land. Already a celebrated American landscape painter when he embarked on his 1868 journey to Syria and Palestine, he found when he arrived in Beirut that "there are Americans innumerable in Syria. All landlords look to them for their profits. The few Englishmen here stand with their hands in

[Scholars, Prophets, Mystics]

their pockets and exclaim 'most extraordinary—these Americans!'"[33] Steamship travel was in its first stage of transatlantic use and many wealthy Americans availed themselves of the opportunity to travel to the eastern Mediterranean and see the sites of biblical history. The year before Frederic Church's journey, Mark Twain had traveled to Europe and the eastern Mediterranean with a group of wealthy American tourists. His hilarious send-up of their adventures and misadventures, which was first published in a San Francisco newspaper, was later collected in Twain's first book, *The Innocents Abroad*.

Frederic Church and his wife were based in Beirut, a city then in a period of great growth. Curiously, Church never painted that city, despite its picturesque mountain setting and the rich human variety of its inhabitants. One modern historian of the period speculates that Beirut would not have been a proper subject for Church, as the city had no mention in the Bible. Damascus, though, with its Old and New Testament associations, drew many American visitors, Church among them. Middle Eastern folklore reinforced the image of Damascus as a place of great antiquity. That the green oasis on which the ancient city was centered had been the Garden of Eden, and that after the expulsion from Eden, a city was established on the site, was often related in local histories of Damascus. For some American travelers the modern city was an evocation of the Edenic past. As Mark Twain writes in *The Innocents Abroad*: "Damascus is beautiful from the mountain. It is beautiful even to foreigners accustomed to luxuriant vegetation, and I can easily understand how unspeakably beautiful it must be to eyes that are only used to the God-forsaken barrenness and desolation of Syria." Twain relates the oft-repeated legend that this luxuriant vegetation was the location of the Garden of Eden. But this American observer of the East is skeptical of biblical claims: "It may be so, but it is not paradise now, and one would be as happy outside of it as he would be likely to be within. It is so crooked and cramped and dirty that one cannot realize that he is in the splendid city he saw from the hilltop."[34]

When Edward Robinson began his study of the Bible he was confronted with a vast literature on its languages, historical settings, and history of interpretations; "he recognized with his sober vision that this endless literature in general rather obscured biblical reality than illumined it."[35] To create a clear, unobstructed view of both the biblical text and the landscape of Palestine became Robinson's life project. The text—obscured by problems of translation and layers of misinterpretation—demanded clarity. Holy Land exploration was enslaved by "the monkish legends of the Catholic Church" and the fanciful accounts of centuries of European pilgrims and travelers. Only a fresh, contemporary look (might we say, only an "American" look) could see the biblical texts and the biblical landscape without preconceptions. This view is what Robinson attempted to provide. And for many Americans the attempt was successful. From the 1840s onward thousands of American travelers followed the routes mapped by Robinson and Smith. As the result of Robinson's influence, scores of these travelers published accounts of their journeys, and hundreds of thousands of Americans read these accounts. William Thomson, who guided Robinson on part of his 1852 journey, published *The Land and the Book* in the late 1850s; it too became an American best seller. In the period before the Civil War only *Uncle Tom's Cabin* outsold the Palestinian travel narratives.

Edward Robinson's fresh interpretations of Holy Land exploration and discovery influenced emerging American views of the place of Palestine in world history and world affairs. Robinson was also instrumental in shaping American academic attitudes toward Jewish scholars of Hebrew and the Bible, as we shall see in the following chapters.

8

AN ISRAELITE TRULY IN
WHOM THERE WAS NO GUILE
ISAAC NORDHEIMER

Here sleeps alone, amid sepulchral night, the long descendant of the Israelite.
Semi Weekly Courier and New York Enquirer, 1842

Remembering the early years of New York University, which was founded in 1832, Tayler Lewis, the university's first professor of Greek, wrote glowingly of the feelings of collegiality among the founding faculty of that institution. "Never shall I forget the beautiful harmony of our faculty meetings as they were weekly held for nearly eleven years. We were of various denominations in religion. There was Professor Draper, of European celebrity and Nordheimer, the distinguished Orientalist, and an Israelite truly in whom there was no guile."[1] Christian colleagues of Nordheimer mourned the early death of the gentle and promising scholar. Edward Robinson of Union Theological Seminary eulogized Nordheimer as "standing at the head of the scholars of the new world, in an exact and familiar acquaintance with the whole range of the Hebrew language and its philology." For Robinson, Nordheimer's accomplishments were all the more remarkable in that the Jewish scholar had "to break away from the trammels and fetters of rabbinic education, from that nightmare of Talmudic absurdity."[2] These encomia, offered by two nineteenth-century clergymen-scholars, reflect their ambivalent attitude toward what was to them a new and startling phenomenon in America: a Jewish scholar, schooled in rabbinic tradition, who was also conversant with the German philological tradition and the scientific study of the Hebrew language and the Bible.

Though Nordheimer died too young to realize his full scholarly potential—at the age of thirty-three he succumbed to the tuberculosis that had weakened him since his adolescence—his life and writings had considerable influence on the leading American Protestant Hebraists of the first half of the nineteenth century: Moses Stuart of Andover Theological Seminary, George Bush of New York University, and Edward Robinson of Union Theological Seminary. Both the Christian and Jewish communities of New York City mourned his demise and an elegy was composed in his honor and printed in the local press.

Nordheimer has not been completely forgotten by historians of Jewish learning in America. David de Sola Pool, writing in the *Dictionary of American Biography*, stated that Nordheimer's death "destroyed the promise of the most brilliant grammarian of nineteenth-century America."[3] William Chomsky, in his survey of Hebrew scholarship in the United States, described Nordheimer's *Critical Hebrew Grammar* as "the most scientific grammar of that period and perhaps of the century."[4] Jacob Rader Marcus has described Nordheimer as "the first scientifically trained Jewish scholar in the United States."

Isaac Nordheimer's importance extends beyond the considerable accomplishments of his own short life and truncated career. For, as Marcus reminds us: "Nordheimer is significant not only on the basis of what he wrote, but because he himself was an intimation of changes to come. In little more than a decade, America would become home for a number of scholars combining religious liberalism with a modern critical approach to biblical and rabbinical literature."[5]

Isaac Nordheimer was born in the Bavarian town of Memelsdorf in 1809.[6] Considered an *iluy*, or prodigy, in his youth, at age thirteen he was sent to study at the yeshiva of Pressburg in Hungary. This academy was headed by the eminent Talmudist Rabbi Moses Schreiber, "the Chasam Sofer." Schreiber was the leader of Hungarian Orthodox Jewry at the time. The rabbi, recognizing the young student's talents, took a personal interest in Nordheimer's development. In his five years at Pressburg, the young *iluy* mastered the text of the Babylonian Talmud. But this erudition was at the expense of his health. For it was in the yeshiva that he contracted tuberculosis. In 1828, at age eighteen, ill and discouraged, he returned home. During his yearlong recuperation he became interested in "secular knowledge" and he taught himself to read German. We thus have in Nordheimer the prototype of a figure who will become increasingly common in late-nineteenth-century Europe—the yeshiva student who becomes a *maskil*, or "enlightened one," through pursuit of the secular.

Enrolling in the gymnasium in Wurzburg, Nordheimer studied philosophy and languages and within two years he was judged competent to enter the local university. From 1830 to 1832 he continued his studies at that university where he became interested in the philosophy of language, a subject then in fashion in the German academy. In late 1832 we find Isaac at the University of Munich, where he studied philology with a concentration in Sanskrit, Greek,

Latin, and the "Shemitish languages." Comparative philology was flourishing as a new discipline in Germany and the University of Munich was a center for these studies. In 1834 Nordheimer was awarded the Ph.D. and in the same year he successfully sat for the "public exam for Jewish theologians," the state certification that would make him eligible for a rabbinic position. While a graduate student he often taught Hebrew to private students. In his capacity as Hebrew tutor he met two Americans who were also enrolled at the German university. They invited Nordheimer to teach in Charleston, South Carolina, where they assured him that the father of one of the students, a Mr. Thomas Grimké, would assist him. Embarking for America only a few months after he received his doctorate, Nordheimer expected to meet his American benefactors in New York.

Thomas Grimké, the gentleman who had so generously promised to help Nordheimer, was a member of a wealthy and distinguished Charleston family. His father, John Faucherand Grimké, was a member of the South Carolina legislature, and at the same time, senior associate ("virtually chief justice") of the state court.[7] The younger Grimké, a Yale graduate, entered the legal profession but soon found himself drawn to issues of religious and educational reform. Lecturing widely, he espoused "his conviction that the Bible should be basic in every scheme of education, from the primary school to the university."[8] In his 1829 *Address on the Expediency and Duty of Adopting the Bible as the Text Book of Duty and Usefulness in Every Scheme of Education*, Grimké called for the replacement of an educational system based on the "heathen classics" of Greece and Rome with a system based on the teaching of the Bible, the "classic, the best the world has ever seen, the noblest, that has ever honored and dignified the language of mortals."[9] He bemoaned the paucity of Hebrew knowledge among the educated, and in an 1830 address to the Phi Beta Kappa Society of Connecticut, called for the introduction of Hebrew into the American school curriculum. In his address to the Society, Grimké asserted the following:

We believe that a better and more general knowledge of Hebrew, among the clergy themselves, will be a prominent result of the general cultivation of Sacred Literature. Among the educated Laity, we should also find many acquainted with this tongue, who would otherwise never have known even the letters. And is it no object to establish this most venerable and noble language on a basis, so durable and extensive, so honorable and gratifying? The commendation bestowed upon the ancient dialect of the chosen people of God, the language of Moses and David, of Isaiah, Jeremiah and Daniel, entitles it in a philological and literary point of view, to the attention of every scholar. And no doubt if this sacred tongue is ever to become the common property of scholars, it will be indebted for such a triumph to the general cultivation of Sacred Literature.[10]

Grimké further spelled out the anticipated results of his proposed reforms in an address delivered in New York. "Unquestionably, a prominent result of the contemplated change must be that Hebrew will become peculiarly, THE CLASSIC LANGUAGE; and the Hebrew Testament, emphatically the classic, and that no one will be regarded as a man of liberal education, much less as a scholar, unless he can read the scriptures of the Old Testament in Hebrew." Grimké's younger sisters, Sarah Moore and Angelina Emily, also had considerable effect on American education and social reform. Antislavery crusaders and advocates of women's rights, their activities "had a profound impact on social reform generally in the United States, as well as on social reform among American women."[11]

Thomas Grimké must have eagerly awaited the arrival in the United States of a distinguished scholar of Hebrew, but what he thought of Nordheimer's Jewish origins we do not know. Alas, the meeting was not to take place, for in October of 1834 Thomas Grimké died at the age of thirty-eight. His ideas were to have influence in the following decade, when zealous Protestant educational reformers were to adopt his call for Bible-centered education. In their zeal to root out "pagan" influence, these reformers would surpass him in their efforts. Grimké had tempered his call for reform, saying, "I would not, indeed, have the architecture of Antiquity defaced, nor the Classics burned as is said to have been the fate of both, at the hands of Gregory the Great; but I would dethrone the latter from their despotic control in our schools and colleges, over the hearts, the consciences and the understandings of the young. I would degrade them from the rank of masters, to the condition of servants, in the education of Christian children."[12] Education reformers of the 1840s and 1850s would not show such restraint. Many condemned the study of the classics and called for their replacement with the Bible.

With Thomas Grimké's death, Nordheimer, newly arrived in New York, was left without a benefactor. On the ocean voyage he had formulated a plan for an American Hebrew grammar. It would draw on both the classical Jewish sources and the new theories of scientific philology. "While I was on the vessel's deck, the night so grand, so still, my grammar did come down upon my soul; I could not eat, I could not sleep. For three long weeks I could not sleep; but I did pray to God, if he would spare my life, till I could write my book, that I would gladly die. And God did spare my life, and I did write my book."[13]

Though inspiration came to him on board the ship, his plans for a new home and a teaching career in the United States did not work out as he had anticipated. The biblical scholar Edward Robinson, who two years later be-friended and assisted Nordheimer, described the new immigrant's first year in America:

> He arrived at New York in the summer of 1835, with the intention of pro-ceeding to Charleston, where he anticipated the efficient aid of Mr. Grimké in the arrangement of his further plans. But the intelligence which first met him on landing, was the death of that gentleman; and as he therefore could no longer hope for any specific advantages in Charleston, he concluded to remain in New York. He became acquainted with several Hebrew families; and his friends interested themselves to obtain for him opportunities for giving instruction in Hebrew. As he became gradually known to the clergy and scholars of the city, the gentleness of his character and his acknowl-edged learning were highly appreciated, and procured for him universal respect.[14]

This "universal respect" led to Nordheimer's appointment, in 1836, as pro-fessor of Arabic and other oriental languages at the recently founded New York University (NYU). Though the appointment entitled Nordheimer to rooms in the stately University Building on Washington Square Park, it was an unsalaried position. He was dependent on outside sources for his own liveli-hood—and for the support of the sister and three brothers who followed him to America. In an 1838 letter to the trustees of New York University, Nord-heimer described his first years in the city, outlined his efforts on behalf of the school, and asked for their regular financial support. This account is so revealing of Nordheimer's struggles it is worth quoting at length.

> From the period of entering upon my duties in the New York University when I had to struggle with all the difficulties and embarrassments of a foreigner newly arrived in a strange land, until the present time, I have en-joyed the satisfaction of affording my assistance to some of the most emi-nent professors of this city in the prosecution of their Oriental Studies; in addition to which I have constantly had under my instruction classes of students from other institutions of from twenty to thirty each. I have also succeeded in the formation of a class in the University, the report of whose examination has probably already been laid before you.
>
> My desire for extensive usefulness however has not been limited in its operation to the narrow circle of my pupils and personal acquaintance. This has been shown by the issuing near two years ago of the Prospectus of a Grammar of the Arabic Language, whose publication has been postponed by circumstances beyond my control; and furthermore by the recent pub-lication of the first volume of a Critical Hebrew Grammar, which some of

the first periodicals of the country have concurred in pronouncing superior to any work that has heretofore appeared on the subject.

All these facts, which agree in showing that my labours have not been and are not now unappreciated by the community among whom I have fixed my abode, are necessarily sources to me of the most lively satisfaction. Yet so far is this partial success from making me content with what I have performed, that it only leaves as an incitement to renewed and still more strenuous exertion. But in proportion as the wide extended field of useful labour opens upon my view, so does my regret increase at the necessity I am at present under of depending for the support of myself and family on the precarious proceeds of private tuition.[15]

In addition to teaching at NYU and tutoring private students, Nordheimer spent the summers of 1836 and 1837 at the New Haven Theological Seminary, where he conducted a class in Hebrew and the Bible. Having already written much of the Hebrew grammar the plan of which he had formulated on his passage to America, and having found an able assistant and editor in William Turner, a New York printer, Nordheimer was determined to find a publisher for his work. Approaching B. L. Hamlen of New Haven, he presented for consideration the complete manuscript of the first volume of his *A Critical Grammar of the Hebrew Language*. David de Sola Pool tells the story as follows:

> Hamlen, pointing to shelves filled with copies of Hebrew grammars by Gesenius, Stuart, and Bush, for which there was virtually no demand, would not even take a look at it. To Nordheimer's plea that the original discoveries on every page of his volume would make it live, Hamlen replied coldly, "your book will also die." Whereupon Nordheimer, pale with emotion, threw his manuscript on the counter, and said, "Den I will die wid my book." Touched by the depth of feeling of the gentle, curly-headed scholar, Hamlen relented, accepted the manuscript for examination, and on a favorable report, printed the book.[16]

The volume was very well received and, according to the *New Englander Magazine* (July 1874), the grammar "brought fame and revenue to its author." The author's reputation as a teacher and as an exponent of the new German philology brought Nordheimer to the attention of Edward Robinson, who had recently joined the faculty of Union Theological Seminary from the seminary at Andover, Massachusetts. At Andover, Robinson had served as professor of Hebrew. His teacher and mentor, the Hebraist Moses Stuart, was influenced by the new critical and philological studies being produced in German universities, and he transmitted his enthusiasm for this new approach to Robinson. After four years (1822–26) as instructor in Hebrew, Robinson went to Germany to study.[17] Returning to the United States in the early 1830s, Robinson introduced American scholars to the German critical approach in his lectures, books, and such journals as the *American Biblical Repository* and *Bibliotheca Sacra*. When Nordheimer, schooled in the same tradition, arrived in New York a few years later, Robinson was pleased to have an ally in his campaign to promote a "critical" approach to the study of Hebrew and the Bible. In a moving memoir published the year after Nordheimer's death, Robinson described his first meeting with the young Jewish professor. "It was in March of 1837 that the writer first had the pleasure of making Nordheimer's acquaintance. I was struck at once with the frankness and simplicity of his manners, the gentleness and sincerity of his character, and his perfect familiarity with the Hebrew, coupled with an enthusiasm regulated by sound principles."[18]

Robinson was soon to make the first of his two historic visits to Palestine. Accompanied by the missionary Eli Smith, who was fluent in the Arabic of Palestine, Robinson embarked on the travels that were to form the basis of his *Biblical Researches in Palestine*, volumes which were to have enormous impact on the nascent field of biblical archaeology and, by extension, on American attitudes toward the Holy Land.[19] Robinson recommended that Nordheimer take over his Hebrew classes at Union Theological Seminary. As Robinson himself later told it: "In the autumn of 1838, in consequence of the writer's prolonged absence from his station in the Union Theological Seminary in New York, the charge of the elementary Hebrew department in that Seminary, was committed to Dr. Nordheimer, and from that time forward until almost the last day of his life, he continued to give regular instruction in Hebrew to the classes, in such a manner as to secure the entire confidence of the Directors and Faculty, and the unwavering respect and affection of the students."[20]

The founders of Union Theological Seminary, "ecumenical Presbyterians"[21] though they might have been, did not readily agree to the appointment of a Jew to the faculty. Robinson does not mention this detail in his memoir of Nordheimer, but it was an issue that the seminary board had to confront. As the *Dictionary of American Biography* put it: "His mastery of Hebrew obtained for him in 1838, Jew though he was and remained, the position of instructor in sacred literature at Union Theological Seminary, where all the other members of the faculty had to profess the Westminster Confession. Attempts were made to draw him into religious controversy, but when his interpretations were challenged, he studiously limited himself to grammatical issues and was able to avoid all theological questions."[22] The seminary board would not appoint a Jewish scholar to the faculty again until the early 1960s, when Abraham Joshua Heschel of the Jewish Theological Seminary was invited to fill the Fosdick Visiting Professorship.[23]

Moses Stuart of Andover and George Bush of NYU, both of whom had published Hebrew textbooks before making Nordheimer's acquaintance, recognized that Nordheimer's grammar was in many ways superior to their own works. In the introduction to the second edition of his *A Grammar of the Hebrew Language* (1837), Stuart remarked:

> As the closing sheets of this work were about to be struck off, I received a copy of the first portion of Professor Nordheimer's new *Critical Hebrew Grammar*, now in a course of publication. It was too late to avail myself some of the ingenious suggestions, which this foreigner, at present a Professor of the Oriental Languages in the University of New York, has made in respect to the orthography, of the Hebrew. His design is, to give a copious treatise on the subject of Hebrew Grammar. While I thank him for his kindness in favoring me with a copy of this learned work, I regret that I could not earlier avail myself of its use.[24]

Nordheimer's work had a direct effect on the scholarship of his American colleagues. The second edition of George Bush's *A Grammar of the Hebrew Language* (1839) reflected the new influence of the German School of "scientific philology." Explaining the reasons for his revisions, Bush wrote:

> It struck me, as I proceeded, that in the present state of Hebrew learning in our country, the attempt might be made to incorporate in my work some of the results of the recent labors of German philologists in this department. . . . To the very valuable grammar of my friend and official associate, Professor Nordheimer, I have made occasional references, and they would probably have been still more numerous but for the fact, that the body of my work was entirely written before I became aware of his intention to publish. Had I known it at an earlier date I might have questioned the expedience of going on with my own undertaking. Perhaps it had been wiser to have waved it, as it was; but one is slow to come to a decision that would require him to throw away the labor of many months; and as I perceived that our several plans were in many respects different, I determined on the whole to cast my bread also upon the waters.[25]

Some of Nordheimer's Christian associates portrayed him as a man who was moving away from Judaism during his years in America. The implication was that Nordheimer, had he not died young, would have converted to Christianity. For example, the July 1874 issue of the *New Englander* published "Reminiscences of Nordheimer" by one H. Neill. This article made much of Nordheimer's attraction to Christianity. Referring to Nordheimer's stay at Andover Theological Seminary, Neill said of Nordheimer that "his mind's history was not unlike that of Neander." This is a reference to the celebrated story of August Neander, born David Mendel in 1789. His conversion to Christianity was much publicized. In his mid-twenties Neander had been appointed to a professorship at the University of Berlin and later became a prominent church historian.[26] As mentioned earlier, during Edward Robinson's sojourns in Germany, he and Neander had become friends.

Neill moves to support his assertion that Nordheimer was drawing close to Christianity, and he too invokes the New Testament quote about "the Israelite without guile."

> He studied Christianity; he revered it. With great pain he alluded to a sermon he heard at Andover, in which the students, as he thought, had not grasped or properly arranged, and pointed, the facts confirmatory of the Redeemer's resurrection. Truly his was an inquiring, a veracious, and receptive soul. And as he treaded his way along the aisles of the Christian churches, meekly bending his form, as he would, in meditation, and absorbed supplication, one could not help thinking of the words, "Other sheep I have which are not of this fold." If to the Israelite in whom is no guile great things are revealed, things making the Son of God their center, and radiating from Him, as from the head of a kingdom, and moving, as did angels, to and fro on the ladder's rounds, can it be supposed that the conscientious, inquiring, broad, reflective, devout, faithful Nordheimer was left without such a portion of the knowledge of Jesus as the Holy Ghost taken and sheweth unto men? Judaism had fallen from him.[27]

Despite these assertions, there is no evidence that Isaac Nordheimer contemplated conversion to Christianity. His friend Edward Robinson realized that Nordheimer, while rejecting "the strictures of rabbinic law," had no intention of giving up his religion. Explaining Nordheimer's reluctance to enter the rabbinate after completing his studies in Hungary and Germany, Robinson wrote, "His own religious feelings also, on the one hand, were too deep to permit him to assent to the issue of minute and often absurd ceremonial observances, which impose upon the rabbi a life of wearisome constraint; and on the other hand, he was too conscientious and high-minded to profess a faith in these observances, for which he had no feel."[28]

We know that the work of Abraham Geiger and other thinkers of early Reform Judaism influenced Nordheimer, and that his rejection of some aspects of rabbinic law was based on Geiger's ideas.[29] Robinson, who read German and who had spent a number of years studying in Germany, seems to have been aware of the stirrings of the Reform movement, and of the influence these ideas may have had on Nordheimer.

But Nordheimer did not consider apostasy. Rather, his association with the organized Jewish community of New York was strengthened over the period of his six years in the city. We have seen that when he first arrived he was employed as a tutor by a number of Jewish families. In 1841 we find him on the staff of the "Hebrew Literary and Religious Library Association," the adult school started by several members of Shearith Israel synagogue. Nordheimer's involvement with the affairs of the Jewish community, however, was not limited to educational endeavors. In the wake of the Damascus Affair of 1840 he joined a committee of thirteen prominent Jewish citizens who organized to influence American public opinion with regard to the persecution of Syria's Jewish community. The city's Jewish community was galvanized by the affair. As Hyman Grinstein has pointed out, "not until 1840 . . . with the famous Damascus Affair, were the Jews of New York really aroused to an interest in the needs and problems of Jews in other parts of the world."[30] In Chapter 7, we saw that the Jewish-born church historian August Neander spoke publicly against the calumny of the Damascus "Blood Libel."

The project that Nordheimer was working on at the time of his death in 1842 was *A Complete Hebrew and Chaldee Concordance to the Old Testament*. Only the first volume, covering the letters *aleph* and *bet*, was issued. This work was described by Edward Robinson in glowing terms: "It may be pronounced, without hesitation, as to type, paper, and arrangement, one of the most beautiful works every printed."[31] Just as Nordheimer had sketched out his grammar on board a ship long before he set out to write it, he prepared for the composition of his concordance by mentally constructing the ideal concordance of the Hebrew Bible. The form that his theorizing took was that of an extended essay on the history of Hebrew lexicography. Appearing in the *Biblical Repertory and Princeton Review* of July 1839 under the rubric of an unsigned review of J. Furst's *Concordantie Librorum Veteris Testament*, the thirty-five-page essay made a strong impression on American Bible scholars. A charming story later appeared, describing Nordheimer's essay.

An article which so absorbed Prof. Stuart of Andover, who commenced reading it in the early part of the afternoon, and who finished it only as the sun went down, to the neglect of an engagement made with Dr. Nordheimer for six o'clock, that, when he met its author at the door of the seminary, too late to rectify the omission, he exclaimed, as he caught Dr. Nordheimer's hands in his, "I ask your pardon a thousand times: I should have been at my house, but I strolled into the reading room, long before the time appointed to see you, and there I found in the *Repertory* an article on Fürst, written by whom I cannot imagine, for who in the world has knowledge so to analyze grammars, and undergird lexicons, and light up the haunts where language has been hiding?" And as Prof. Stuart poured out in this way his soul of praise in sentence after sentence, "I did forgive him every thing he ever did I could not like, and every thing he forgot to

.do about me, or my Grammar," said the grateful and childlike Nordheimer, as he described the scene.[32]

The article that Stuart had found so illuminating was, in part, a presentation of the Masoretic technical apparatus and a defense of its reliability. As noted earlier, Christian Hebraists had long impugned the antiquity and authenticity of the Masoretic apparatus. It was Harvard professor George Foot Moore's trenchant observation that "The bigger the ignorance of these gentlemen, the more they looked down their noses at anything Masoretic."[33] In the previous chapter, we read of Moses Stuart's struggle with the question of whether Hebrew should be taught with the vowel points or without them. That is, should the vowels presented by the Masoretic apparatus be considered an integral part of the Hebrew language?

Nordheimer was quite emphatic as to the Masorah's reliability. He informed his predominantly Christian audience that "the Masorah in fact is a most important and useful collection of ancient critical remarks, the constant consultation of which is indispensably necessary to every editor of a Hebrew Bible who is inspired with the laudable ambition of improving upon the labours of those who have gone before him; for the mind gifted with the highest critical powers will not refuse assent to the truth of the Talmudic axiom: the older the tradition, the greater its authenticity."[34]

In addition to beginning his concordance and explicating the history of the genre in his Fürst article, Nordheimer, ever industrious, also wrote four long articles on subjects biblical and rabbinic. For the *American Biblical Repository* he wrote two excellent articles on the Talmud, the rabbis, their schools, and their literature. In these surveys, he carried the story of rabbinic literature as far as the Golden Age in Spain. His work is probably the first objective study of rabbinic literature published in the United States. His two other journal articles were on biblical and grammatical issues. In 1838 he published "The Philosophy of Ecclesiastes," and in 1841, "On the Use and Omission of the Hebrew Article in Reply to Inquiries by Prof. Stuart."[35]

A poignant description of Nordheimer's failing health and untimely death is found in Edward Robinson's final tribute to his friend and colleague. Robinson noted that Nordheimer had been ill for many years and that lately his condition had worsened.

A cough and hectic fever were already upon him; and although he was cheerful and hoped for the best, yet his physicians gave no encouragement to his friends. He entered upon his duties in the Seminary in October with his usual zeal, but with the weakness of an expiring lamp. He last met his class on Friday, Oct. 28th; and died on the Thursday morning following, Nov. 3d. His funeral took place the next day; and the corpse was accompanied to the grave by a long line of mourning friends, comprising the Professors and Students of the Seminary, the Chancellor and some of the Professors of the University, and many of the Hebrew Community.[36]

Nordheimer was buried in the "Bet Haim Shelishi" of Congregation Shearith Israel. This graveyard, on West Twenty-First Street, west of Sixth Avenue, served the congregation from 1829 to 1851.[37] As David de Sola Pool described it in *Portraits Etched in Stone*: "The cemetery on Twenty-First Street remains to this day undisturbed. No other Jewish cemetery has withstood the city's implacable growth."[38] In 2002, Nordheimer's tombstone could still be seen from the fence on Twenty-First Street.

As Edward Robinson pointed out, Isaac Nordheimer "never spared himself in his labours and duties."[39] Four years before his death, Nordheimer, in his appeal to the board of New York University, noted that without their financial assistance he would have to "continue to make exertions greater than I can sustain, and thus be in imminent danger of ruining myself in health as well as in purse at the very outset of my career, for my works will bear witness for me that it is utterly impossible to support for any length of time the amount of intellectual toil to which I have lately been subject."[40] Many of those who mourned his untimely passing saw Nordheimer as a martyr to the rigors of the life of the mind.

For some of Nordheimer's Christian colleagues, admiration for his accomplishments was linked to the idea that he was leaning toward Christianity, but he did not apostasize. As Robinson noted: "He was buried according to the Hebrew rites; and the same touching custom was exhibited here, which is related to have taken place at the burial of Gesenius. After the corpse was lowered into the grave, the nearest relatives first threw earth upon the coffin, and then the rabbi and other near acquaintances. After the usual ablutions, the burial service in Hebrew was read in the adjacent chapel."

On his death the poem "The Tomb of Nordheimer" was published in the New York City newspaper, the *Semi Weekly Courier and New York Enquirer*.[41]

Here lies the dust, all festering and low,
That tempted greatness but an hour ago;
Here sleeps alone, amid sepulchral night,
The long descendant of the Israelite;
Here rests, by God's inscrutable command,
The adopted son and scholar of our land,
The star that rose to such a wonderous height,
So sudden vanished from its path of light,
That, as we looked, and loved, and praised aloud
It shot through ether and was lost in cloud.

Oh noble spirit, couldst not thou allay
The altar-fire which waste thee away!
Too much entranced with science' radiant face
Her rapturous beauty lured thee on thy race
And when she smiled, that very smile to thee
Like some glad angel, roused fresh energy;
Awaked each effort of thine ardent mind,
With all mighty elements combined—Alas, too fiercely!—for, thy feeble
    clay
Could not endure the soul's more potent sway,
We saw thy form so trembling, pale and strange,
And whispered sadly of the mournful change.
Ah! How prophetic were those whispers spoken
How soon to share thy weeping kindreds' gloom,
And bow in sorrow by thy lowly tomb.
And oh! The blank, the desolate, weary blank,
In that high place from which thy star beams sank
What orb shall rise, relume that vacant spot,
And fill the arduous duties of thy lot?
And what to thee, cut short amid thy toil,
And called away from this poor earthly soil,
Is now the worth, at which thy works are prized,
Thy name esteemed—Oh thou, self-sacrificed!
Yet they who ranged with thee, the classic field,
And tried what pleasure books and learning yield,
Shall never cease to mourn thy early fall,
As one, "the best and foremost of them all"
And grief shall be their broken ranks among,
Illustrious student of the Orient tongue!
For thou art gone!—thine energies are spent,
Gone to thy Humboldt, whom thou didst lament—Gone to the palace of
    the mighty dead—Gone where the marble thy last pillow marks;
Where sleep thy fathers, Judah's Patriarchs;
Where deep affection wastes its vain perfume,
And Science weeps around Nordheimer's tomb.
    New York, Nov. 6th, 1842 B.S.

9

JEWS, MORMONS, AND
CHRISTIAN HEBRAISM IN
EARLY-NINETEENTH-CENTURY
AMERICA

JOSHUA/JAMES SEIXAS

Mormonism is the Jewish-Christian tradition in an American key.
W. D. Davis
My soul delights in reading the words of God in the original, and I am determined
to pursue the study of languages until I shall become master of them.
Joseph Smith

A Mormon Legacy

The narratives of the Old and New Testaments were thoroughly alive for the members of the early Mormon Church. In the 1830s and 1840s, the formative years of the church, Joseph Smith and his followers saw themselves as living simultaneously in both a recapitulation and a continuation of biblical history. The Hebrew Bible/Old Testament held a particular resonance for these believers in a new dispensation. For Smith, the Jews of history—and the Jews of his time—were sources of inspiration and doctrine. In the early years of his prophetic ministry, Smith's fascination with Jews and Hebrew learning focused on the scholar Joshua/James Seixas, teacher of Hebrew to many prominent Christian reformers.

In the roster of prominent American Jewish Hebraists of the early nineteenth century, Joshua/James Seixas (1802–74) remains something of an enigma. His contemporaries, both Jewish and Christian, differed widely in their descriptions of his religious convictions and affiliations. We find him described by Jews as a convert to Christianity and by some Christians as a "devout Jew." Evaluations of his ability as a teacher of Hebrew and a scholar vary widely, and the researcher in search of the biographical details of Seixas's life is confronted with conflicting and confusing data. For his life was a restless one. Seixas moved around the United States in search of employment and professional satisfaction, and one is struck by the feeling that the subject of our investigations deliberately obscured the details of his personal life.[1]

Joshua (later James) Seixas's biography raises important questions about the nature of Jewish identity in the early years of the Republic, and it can serve to illustrate how the Protestant majority viewed the small Jewish minority of the period. It seems that some of Seixas's Protestant interlocutors "needed" him to be Jewish. For other Protestant scholars it was important that he be considered Christian. For Seixas himself the question of his Jewish identity and its cultural expression was complex. His books and pamphlets give us few hints about his needs and intentions.

Today, Seixas is all but forgotten. The area in which Seixas did leave his mark on American cultural and religious history is in the development of Mormon thought, and it is among students of early Mormon history that his memory has been kept alive. This is quite ironic. What was for J. Seixas a passing episode of a few short months—the encounter with Joseph Smith Jr., the Mormon Prophet—was for the nascent Mormon Church an encounter fraught with greater significance. For Joseph Smith's work of biblical translation and elaboration was to some extent predicated on material he studied with Seixas. Recently, scholars of Mormon history have focused on Joseph Smith's interest in kabbalistic ideas, ideas he may have discussed with his Jewish associates, foremost among them J. Seixas.

But this is only one of many ironies in the story of Seixas's life. Son of Revolutionary War America's most prominent Jewish leader, Gershom Mendes Seixas of New York's Shearith Israel Congregation, Joshua spent a good deal of his career teaching Hebrew to the Protestant clergy and laity. As a young man, he left New York and went west in pursuit of a career. In midlife he returned to the city that he had abandoned and there, cut off from the community in which he grew up, he lapsed into relative obscurity.

Seixas's Formative Years

Joshua Seixas, second child of Gershom Seixas's marriage to his second wife, Hannah Manuel, was born in New York City on June 4, 1802.[2] Little is known about his early life. He was only fourteen when his father died. It is not known where Joshua was educated; some have speculated that he attended Columbia College, where his father was a trustee from 1785 to 1815, but Joshua's name does not appear in the college records.

In the mid-1820s Seixas taught at the Polonies Talmud Torah School of

Shearith Israel congregation. According to Captain N. Taylor Phillips, president of the congregation in the early twentieth century and a relative of Seixas ("he was a first cousin of my father's mother"):[3] "He was for many years the congregation's chief Hebrew instructor and in fact taught my own father, the late Isaac Phillips, the portion of the law which he read at his Bar Mitzvah in 1825. He was possessed of considerable musical talent. He founded the first organized choir of that congregation at the beginning of the nineteenth century."[4]

As Hebrew teacher at Shearith Israel, Seixas followed in the steps of his father, who, as Jacob Marcus has informed us, "taught not only Hebrew, but also secular subjects, reading, writing, and cyphering." In an 1803 sermon, the elder Seixas, encouraging his congregants to study Hebrew and to teach it to their children, argued that "the Hebrew language was the only true means for ascertaining God's will."[5]

Education at Shearith Israel had changed since the early years of Gershom Seixas's tenure. During the late years of Gershom Seixas's leadership (he died in 1816) there was still "an all-day school giving both Hebrew and secular instruction," but in 1821 it became a supplementary school in which Hebrew studies were emphasized and which the children attended only on some weekday afternoons.[6] It is difficult for us to gauge the quality of Hebrew instruction in the school. While Gershom Seixas was a competent student of Hebrew by the standards of late-eighteenth-century America, he had no formal training in philology or composition. His well-known Columbia oration of 1800, delivered by Sampson Simson, was "not without errors in grammar and vocalization."[7] His son Joshua seems to have applied himself more directly to a scientific approach to Hebrew, mastering the paradigms that appeared in the standard Hebrew grammars of the day (all of them written by Protestant Hebraists) and learning the rules of syntax. There is, however, no indication that Joshua applied this scientific approach to language teaching during his years at the synagogue school. Rather, the classes seem to have been based primarily on memorizing portions of the liturgy and learning to cantillate the Torah portion of the week.

While employed at Shearith Israel, Joshua married Henrietta Raphael of Richmond, Virginia. Two years younger than Joshua, Henrietta was the daughter of a wealthy and socially prominent Jewish family. We know little of her life in Richmond; it seems that Joshua made her acquaintance through Isaac B. Seixas, Gershom Seixas's nephew and Joshua's cousin, who was the leader of the Richmond synagogue Beth Shalome.[8] At the time of their marriage Joshua was twenty years old and Henrietta was eighteen. Their first four children, Julia Anne, Esther, Myrtilla, and Virginia, were all born in New York City.[9]

[*Scholars, Prophets, Mystics*]

During the late 1820s and early 1830s Seixas taught himself Hebrew and Aramaic grammar in a systematic fashion. He prepared himself for a career in Hebrew instruction. The method that Seixas adapted for teaching was the classical one of having students memorize the paradigms of verb conjugations and noun declensions and then apply this knowledge of "the forms" to a close reading of biblical texts. Because this method could prove arduous and tedious for those with no previous training in the classical languages, Seixas decided to streamline the number of paradigms that the student had to commit to memory. By the early 1830s, when he moved to Charlestown, Massachusetts, and advertised himself as a "Professor of Hebrew," he was able to offer instruction in an enterprising system of his own devising. As he put it in a circular that advertised his method: "The time required in a course of Hebrew instruction as given by me, is six weeks, one lesson of about an hour being given each day. . . . With proper attention to the following rules under my instruction (or the instruction of any of my pupils), anyone desirous to become acquainted with this language may be enabled in a short time and with little trouble, to read with much pleasure and satisfaction."[10]

Two more daughters, Theodora and Henrietta Franca, were born in Charlestown in 1831 and 1833.[11] Seixas may have converted to Christianity during this time, though the evidence as to the date of his conversion is not conclusive. We do know that while in Charlestown he tutored students who were enrolled at Harvard and that during this period he began to refer to himself as James Seixas.

In 1833, two years after settling in Charlestown, he published the first edition of his book *Manual Hebrew Grammar for the Use of Beginners*. That same year saw the publication of a short (twelve-page) Aramaic grammar, *A Key to the Chaldee Lanugage*, a pamphlet issued for Seixas's Hebrew students. The *Grammar* was presented as a workbook for his own students. As Seixas stated in the preface:

> The following pages are intended for those only who have read or may hereafter read Hebrew with the author. The lessons and rules, though comparatively few and brief, are, I know, sufficient to give an easy and rapid insight into the general formation of the language. Some years' experience in teaching, and the favorable opinions of those whom I have had the pleasure of teaching, convince me that (with proper attention to the following rules *under my instruction or the instruction of any of my pupils*), any one desirous to become acquainted with this language may be enabled in a short time and with little trouble, to read with much pleasure and satisfaction; and to use advantageously a larger work on Hebrew Grammar.[12]

A

MANUAL

HEBREW GRAMMAR

FOR THE USE OF BEGINNERS.

BY J. SEIXAS.

Second edition enlarged and improved.

ANDOVER:
PRINTED BY GOULD AND NEWMAN.
1834.

J. Seixas, Manual Hebrew Grammar, *1834*

The first editions of *Hebrew Grammar* and the *Key to the Chaldee* were followed in 1834 by a second edition of the *Hebrew Grammar*, "enlarged and improved." In the preface to the first edition, Seixas's tone is apologetic and self-effacing. Although this is somewhat typical of scholarly modesty in nineteenth-century America, in Seixas's case it also seems to be indicative of a tendency to self-deprecation. "As trifling as these lessons may appear to many, it has cost me several years' labor to collect and arrange them. By a careful and frequent reading of the Bible, with all the necessary help before me, I have obtained what these sheets will set forth."

The preface closes with this note: "I humbly hope, through divine favor, that the time devoted to preparing this manual will not prove to have been spent in vain. A desire to benefit others and promote the best of all studies — the study of the Bible — has been my strongest inducement to undertake it."

A note to the preface in the first edition adds, "The best Grammar ever published in English is that of Professor Stuart, published at Andover, which has gone through four editions." Had he been less circumspect, Seixas might have added that his *Manual Grammar* was, in effect, a condensation of Stuart's larger and more comprehensive work.

Seixas and American Christian Hebraism, 1830–1852

As we saw in Chapter 1, the tradition of Puritan Hebraism, so strong in colonial New England and to a lesser extent in the southern colonies, had exhausted itself by the end of the eighteenth century. This tradition had provided the impetus for the teaching of Hebrew in the early American colleges; by the 1780s, with the changes in college curriculum, biblical Hebrew classes were no longer mandatory. Classes in the "sacred tongue" had become the first electives. Ezra Stiles, president of Yale from 1778 to 1795, revived, for a time, Hebrew teaching at Yale.[13] It is to Yale graduates of the early nineteenth century, most prominent among them Moses Stuart, that we owe the revival of Hebrew learning in the period between 1820 and 1845.[14]

While the Puritan Hebraic tradition, influenced as it was by the Christian Hebraism of the Renaissance and Reformation, demanded that college teachers of Hebrew be professing Christians, this new, nineteenth-century American tradition of Hebrew study was able to accommodate a small number of Jews. In fact, for some Protestants, a Jewish teacher of Hebrew was considered a more reliable source of information. As Nahum and Jonathan Sarna have noted: "Especially in America, many Protestants saw Jews as lineal descendants of the biblical figures they read and heard about. . . . Protestants who adhered to this view naturally assumed that Jews preserved special knowledge of the biblical world that others did not share. Acting on that basis, they often turned to Jews when Hebrew or Old Testament questions arose."[15]

Among the Hebraists to whom they turned was Joshua Seixas. Hebrew study was experiencing a burst of popularity. The twenty-five-year period between 1820 and 1845 saw the appearance of Hebrew grammars by a number of American scholars, most of them Protestant clergymen. These included Moses Stuart of Andover Theological Seminary, Rev. George Bush of New York University, and Stuart's protégé Edward Robinson, later professor at Union Theological Seminary. Isaac Nordheimer, also of New York University, and Joshua/James Seixas were Jewish scholars on the periphery of this group.[16] Some of the Hebrew textbooks produced by these scholars went into multiple editions; Stuart's saw six editions, one of them reprinted for use at Oxford University. The philological learning that had emerged in Germany, most notably the work of H. Ewald, influenced this new American group of Hebraists. The young Edward Robinson, in fact, translated the Hebrew grammar of the dean of German Hebraists, Heinrich Gesenius, for the English-speaking public.

In a memoir that Moses Stuart wrote in 1847 he remarked that "when [he] began to teach the Hebrew language at this Seminary [Andover] there was only one other institution where it was taught." W. F. Albright later described Stuart's situation in 1810, the year of his appointment at Andover: "At that time there was probably no native-born American who knew enough Hebrew to teach it properly. Biblical studies were entirely neglected, and the minister who showed too much interest in European biblical studies was suspected of heterodoxy."[17] Stuart, in a remarkable burst of intellectual activity and language acquisition, mastered Hebrew and its "cognate languages"—Syriac and Arabic—within a three-year period. In 1810 he "had little more than a knowledge of the Hebrew alphabet, and the power of making out, after a poor fashion too, the bare translation of some chapters in Genesis and a few Psalms," but by 1813 he had "mastered the language sufficiently to prepare a grammar for the use of his classes."[18] During his long tenure at Andover (1810–48), Stuart devoted much of his scholarly energy to matters Hebraic and biblical. The forum for publication of his articles on "Sacred Literature" was a series of journals edited by Stuart's student Edward Robinson, *Biblical Repository* and *Biblia Sacra*.

It was to Stuart and his circle that the young Joshua Seixas was drawn in the late 1820s. A decade later, Isaac Nordheimer, a Jewish emigré from Germany who had been educated in the great European Yeshivot, would become associated with the group around Stuart. Seixas and Nordheimer were the only Jewish scholars in the group.

By the time J. Seixas made Stuart's acquaintance in the late 1820s, Stuart was considered the "dean of biblical studies in America."[19] It is difficult to pinpoint their first meeting or trace their earliest correspondence, but by the early 1830s it is clear that they knew each other well. A letter from Stuart (dated Andover, September 6, 1832) to Seixas at Charlestown, Massachusetts, signed "your sincere friend," is most definitely a letter between friends and colleagues of long acquaintance. It seems that Seixas had sent Stuart an old Hebrew manuscript for perusal; Stuart apologizes for not doing much to decipher it, "but my time does not permit me . . . to delve out all the obscurities of the handwriting, as well as of the language. If I get an opportunity to sit down with you two or three hours upon it, I think we may make some progress together." The letter indicates that their collegial relationship extended to matters beyond manuscript decipherment. Stuart thanks Seixas for his help in preparing the manuscript of a new edition of his *Hebrew Chrestomathy*. "I shall send you a copy the first opportunity; also I wish to make you remuneration for looking over the sheets sent you. You will see that I have acknowledged your kind aid in the Preface to the *Chrestomathy*." We also learn that Seixas was a welcome guest at Andover: "I should be exceedingly glad to have you come up and spend a day with me, were we not at the very close of our term. . . . The students have a strong desire to hear you read and cantillate; but this cannot be done until the next term."[20]

Seixas served as one of Stuart's "native informants" on matters Hebraic. For Protestant seminarians studying the Hebrew texts, the opportunities to hear the Bible read as it was read in the synagogue were quite limited. A half century earlier, New England's most prominent intellectual, Ezra Stiles, as we saw in Chapter 3, regularly attended services at the Newport, Rhode Island, synagogue. There, Stiles was able to follow the liturgy and the Torah reading, thereby improving his skills as an "Hebrician," as he so quaintly styled himself.[21]

Stuart first consulted with Seixas some time in 1830 or early 1831. The extensive errata section in Stuart's 1831 *Grammar of the Hebrew Language* (4th edition) contained some 150 corrections made by Joshua Seixas and gratefully acknowledged by Stuart. The 1835 fifth edition, into which Seixas's additional corrections were incorporated, also acknowledged Seixas's contribution: "I have availed myself, in the present edition, of the corrections and of some additions, which my friend Mr. JH. Seixas, in a very obliging manner, has suggested to me. For his attention bestowed on this subject, and the labour which he has performed in making the suggestions just noticed, I return him my most sincere thanks and acknowledgments. A fuller catalogue still of irregular forms, according to a desire which he has expressed, would have been made out, had the limits of my work permitted."[22]

We have seen that Seixas, in the first edition of his grammar (1833), described Stuart's work as "the best Grammar ever published in English." As indicated by this exchange of compliments, the two authors were not in direct competition with each other. Seixas's book, only fifty-four pages long, was considerably shorter than Stuart's. It was conceived as an aid to instruction, not as a comprehensive guide to the language. Stuart's *Grammar* was more comprehensive and its author decried any use of shortcuts to Hebrew knowledge.[23] Each edition of Stuart's grammar (the sixth edition was published in 1838) grew thicker and more comprehensive; he had no intention of abridging the course of Hebrew study. Stuart explained:

> The author has often been asked, whether he intended to publish an *abridged* form of this Grammar. As a friend to the radical study of the Hebrew, he must answer in the *negative*. The phenomena of the Hebrew language he is not able to state in a shorter compass than he has done, and make them explicit and intelligible to learners. Any Grammar that professes to do so, must either be obscure, or leave many of the phenomena of the language untouched. Of what ultimate and solid use can the study of Hebrew be, when one half, or any considerable proportion, of forms and idioms are left unexplained and unnoticed? Those who wish a "royal road" to the Hebrew, may publish such grammars or study them, if they are content to acquire the name of Hebrew scholars without the reality.[24]

We can safely assume that Stuart played a role in the publication of Seixas's *Grammar*. The first two editions (1833 and 1834) were printed at Andover by Flagg, Gould and Newman. "This printing establishment was closely identified with the Seminary" of which Stuart was the head, and it was the firm that published Stuart's own Hebrew textbooks in their many editions. Soon after the publication of the first edition of Seixas's *Grammar*, favorable notices appeared in the scholarly and literary press. The editor of the *New England Magazine* noted: "I have lately seen a manual *Hebrew Grammar* by J. Seixas, on a new plan, viz. That of admitting *light* into the students mind, instead of *darkness*. Now I think that is the proper way, and therefore give my sincere commendation to this gentleman, whose admirable method of instructing (so far as I can learn it from his pupils), is likely entirely to refit the old, rusty, creaking door to oriental learning."[25]

In the Stuart-Seixas correspondence, Stuart, the elder and more established academician, offers his younger colleague advice on decidedly nonacademic matters. "I am sorry to hear of your ill health. But I suppose that you have not yet learned the 'art of exercise,' without which high intellectual pressure cannot possibly be borne. You may have the very best of health, if you take care of your exercise and diet."[26] But it is in the realm of the spiritual, rather than in the realm of the physical, that the Stuart-Seixas correspondence is most re-

משה אמת ונ/אטנה תירתו
ויהושוע היה משרתו
יש מרם ישוע לעתיר לבוא

J. Seixas, inscription to Moses Stuart
(American Jewish Archives)

vealing, for it is there that we see Seixas grappling with the conflict between Jewish and Christian beliefs. It is this correspondence which provides us with the earliest evidence of Seixas's conversion to Christianity. As David de Sola Pool noted in a 1914 presentation to the American Jewish Historical Society on "Joshua Seixas, Hebraist": "Little doubt is left as to his defection from the Jewish faith by the following Hebrew verses on the outside of one of his notes to Moses Stuart: 'Moses was true, his Torah was true, / And Joshua was his servant / May Jesus guard them in the future world.'"[27]

Secret Apostasy

In Chapter 2 we read of Judah Monis's apostasy. He was baptized in a ceremony at Harvard's College Hall, at which he read his "proofs of Christian doctrine." Seixas made no such clear public declaration of his beliefs. Seixas's conversion to Christianity was private. His interest in Christian doctrine is confirmed in his correspondence with James Walker (1794–1874), Unitarian clergyman and later (1853–60) president of Harvard University. In an 1832 letter to Seixas, Walker, then a Unitarian clergyman in Boston, reports enthusiastically on a recent visit to "The West," where "we found the people more civil, more moral, and more religious than is commonly supposed." Walker regrets that in the West there is not more support for "our view of Christianity; but generally speaking, there is more liberality at the West, than at the North or East." The letter closes with Walker's hope that he will see Seixas soon, and that then they can discuss "the subjects that most interest us; the power, the satisfactions and the prospects of pure Christianity."[28]

De Sola Pool reported, from an unattributed source, that Seixas "was baptized by Theodore Parker in Boston, but for a long time he kept quiet about his conversion." If Seixas did convert to Christianity with Parker's help—an assertion not supported in any other source that I am aware of—it may have been because of an earlier association of these two gentlemen, an association that has not been remarked on by earlier investigators. For Parker had been Joshua Seixas's student in Boston. Theodore Parker (1810–60), prominent Unitarian theologian and social reformer, was from a very poor Boston family. As one of his biographers put it: "Although Parker passed the entrance examinations for Harvard College in 1830, he had no funds to attend. He was allowed, however, to take the examinations for his course of study without enrolling and was granted an honorary degree. He then attended Harvard Divinity School, from which he graduated in 1836."[29]

As an independent student at Harvard, Parker lived in Watertown. During this period he is said to have mastered over twenty languages—among them Hebrew, Arabic, and Aramaic. His biographer tells us that "the two years in Watertown were eventful years both of joy and labor. The achievements in scholarship were amazing. . . . He wrote for his Sunday school class a history of the Jews, which still exists in manuscript. He began the study of Hebrew, walking to Charlestown to meet Mr. Seixas, a Jew, and entered on the study of the theology."[30] Parker's knowledge of Hebrew was so thorough that years later, when he was a student at Harvard Divinity School, he took over for a time the teaching responsibilities of Professor Palfrey, the professor of divinity and the resident Hebraist.[31]

Seixas's ties to Parker may have facilitated Seixas's conversion. As Parker was a liberal Unitarian, it may have made the move from Judaism to Christianity less radical in Seixas's eyes. Some Jews considered conversion to Unitarianism, in contrast to conversion to Catholicism or mainstream Protestantism, as not being "apostasy." In this view it was the trinitarian idea that made Christianity an anathema for Jews; Unitarianism was thus more acceptable. Prominent Christians were known to espouse the conversion of the Jews to Unitarianism. John Adams, advocating the return of the Jews to Palestine, hoped that their restoration "would soon wear away some of the asperities and peculiarities of their character, possibly in time to become Unitarian Christians."[32]

Parker's enthusiasm for the study of the "oriental languages" and Jewish texts did not, however, mitigate his hostility toward Jews as a religious community. In his widely read work *Views of Religion*, he attacked Judaism as part of his assault on all "obsolete" religious institutions. "Thus the Hebrew cleaves to his ancient religious creed, refusing to share the religious science which mankind has brought to light since Moses and Samuel went home to their God."[33]

Both Parker and James Walker, founders of Unitarianism and colleagues of Seixas, expressed in sermons and articles a consistent antipathy to the Hebrew Bible/Old Testament. "What shall we do with the Old Testament?" asked James Walker in 1838. "That question is of such frequent recurrence among laymen as well as clergymen, that any well-considered attempt to answer it, or supply the means of answering it, is almost sure of hearty welcome." A year earlier, Theodore Parker had called for a reassessment of the veracity of the Old Testament narratives. "I wish some wise man would now write a book . . . and show up the absurdity of certain things commonly believed, on the authority of the old Jews. To be plain, I mean the Old Testament miracles, prophecies, dreams, miraculous births, etc."[34]

In the early years of the American Republic—before the German-Jewish emigrations of the 1840s and 1850s—some Jews seemed to have attached less of a social stigma to conversion to Christianity. They thought that there was a possibility that the apostate would be accepted back into the Jewish community at a later time. This fluidity of religious identity was possible in a Jewish society that did not yet have an established rabbinate or religious organizational life. This is not to say that converts to Christianity were fully accepted in American Protestant society. Much as they were in European society, Jews who apostatized were acceptable in neither Jewish nor Christian circles. Writing in 1897 and describing the religious situation of American Jews in the first half of the eighteenth century, N. Taylor Phillips remarked, "At that time among the Jewish community in New York, though a man were even to publicly renounce Judaism, nevertheless he could not become a Christian in the full sense of the term so far as society was concerned; for he was notwithstanding always regarded as a Jew, and was, perforce the attitude of his Christian associates, something in the nature of a 'dead-wall between church and synagogue, or like the blank leaves between the Old and the New Testament,' being to the Jews always a Christian, and to the Christians always a Jew."[35]

The Jewish convert to Christianity labored under a considerable stigma, as we saw in Chapter 5. Organized Christian attempts to convert Jews, such as the American Society for Meliorating the Condition of the Jews (ASMCJ), a missionary society founded in 1820, were bitterly opposed by the small Jewish community of the time. At one point the ASMCJ had over two hundred chapters and thousands of Protestant members. It brought about the conversion of a handful of Jews, but more important, by posing a missionary threat, it united the small Jewish community. As Jonathan Sarna has pointed out, strong resentment against such missionary activities served as a catalyst for the founding of the first Jewish newspaper and the establishment of communal self-help organizations. Had news of J. Seixas's apostasy been made public during the stormy decade of the 1820s, it would have been greeted with dismay by his coreligionists.

Seixas's friends in the Protestant clergy, foremost among them Moses Stuart, were well aware of the strong feelings that the *meshummad*, or Jewish apostate, engendered among many Jews. In his 1831 "Sermon on the Ordination of Rev. Schauffler," delivered to mark the occasion of the graduation from Andover Theological Seminary of his student William Schauffler, Moses Stuart remarked that "the Jews regard with universal horror the man who has deserted their ranks and gone over to Christianity."[36] David de Sola Pool's remark that Seixas "for a long time kept quite about his conversion" should be seen in the context of Stuart's sermon. For despite what I have called the "fluidity" of the religious situation, Seixas felt uncomfortable publicizing his conversion. He not only hid it from Jews, but there is also some evidence that he hid it from Christians as well. For we shall see that in his encounter with the Mormons, a new American Christian group then emerging onto the national scene, he is spoken of as a Jew, even as a "devout Jew." The Mormons never referred to Seixas as a Christian.[37]

Seixas's motives for apostatizing seem to have been twofold. The first set of motives was professionally inspired. In order for him to succeed in an academic world dominated by American Protestants he had to become a member of one of the Protestant churches. Though American Jews—both emigrants from Europe and native born—benefited from the relative social fluidity and professed religious toleration of the American Republic, they still found that there were areas of endeavor closed to them as to other non-Protestants. The academy was one such bastion of privilege. In the first half of the nineteenth century the number of colleges was small and the administrations and faculties of the elite colleges were identified with the Protestant establishment. Protestant clergymen often held professorships. The field of study in which this was almost universally true was that of theology, which subsumed Hebrew instruction. That an "outsider" would teach the "sacred tongue" was unthinkable; that a Jewish scholar might apostatize in order to teach Hebrew in the academy was not. European Jewry had provided a number of illustrious examples of this phenomenon. We have noted the conversion of Judah Monis at Harvard College in early-eighteenth-century America. A month after his conversion he was appointed instructor in Hebrew, a position that he held for almost forty years.

A century after Monis's conversion, in early-nineteenth-century America, the world of academic Hebraism was still closed to Jews. Though J. Seixas sustained friendships with prominent Protestant intellectuals of his day, among them university presidents, church leaders, and professors of theology, and though their letters and papers indicate that Seixas was held in high regard by the educational and religious leaders of his time, he was never granted a full-time teaching appointment at an American college.

These professional motives do not necessarily indicate that Seixas was in-

[Scholars, Prophets, Mystics]

sincere in his espousal of Christian beliefs. For his other set of motives seem to have been religious in character. His correspondence with a number of churchmen indicates that he had adopted the basic tenets of Unitarian belief. While he may have gained professionally from his conversion, this cannot be the whole story. For, like the great poet Heine, he quickly found that he was not fully acceptable and was now thought of as a "former Jew." Excluded from the ranks of the professoriate, he spent his midlife on the fringes of Protestant society. In his last years, however, he seems to have reconciled with the Jewish community.

With the Mormons

In the autumn of 1835 we find Seixas and his growing family (his eighth child, and only son, Gershom Arnold, was born during this year) in Hudson, Ohio. There he offered his Hebrew courses to the students at Oberlin College. A historian of Oberlin tells how "the learned Hebraist brought with him all the Hebrew Bibles he could find in New York and a large supply of his own grammars, twelve of which are still in the Oberlin Library." Later that year he organized a class at Western Reserve College.[38] Both schools, recently founded, emphasized instruction in the classics and put little emphasis on science or mathematics. Theology and Bible study were at the core of their curricula.

Seixas's professional situation at the Ohio colleges was similar to his situation on the East Coast. He was never a full faculty member at either Ohio institution. According to the *History of Western Reserve University*, "He gave a private elementary course lasting two months, open to teachers and students at Western Reserve College."[39] His classes at Oberlin and Western Reserve were well attended. A note in the Oberlin catalogue of 1835 mentions that the school was "happy to state also that very special attention has been paid to the Hebrew language, under the able instruction of Professor J. Seixas. One hundred and twenty-seven pupils have pursued this course with animated zeal and decided success."[40] Seixas seems to have been a very effective classroom teacher. John Buss, a Western Reserve freshman, left a detailed journal of his experiences at the new school. He was greatly impressed with Seixas as teacher and scholar, and wrote, "I never saw any man talk and have so much to say as Mr. Seixas in recitation in my life. . . . I am well satisfied that he is a man of great learning."[41]

It was at these schools, where the spirit of revivalism and religious enthusiasm ran high, that Seixas met the future leaders of the Mormon Church. Through them he met their prophet, Joseph Smith. The Mormons were living at this time in their settlement at Kirtland, Ohio. Throughout his life the Mormon prophet kept an extensive journal, as did many of his followers. Hence this short period of Seixas's life, from the autumn of 1835 to the spring of 1836, is the most fully documented one that we have. From these journals, and from contemporary newspapers and broadsides, historians of the church have preserved every facet of the early years of the Mormon Church. Joshua Seixas is often mentioned in these accounts. As Seixas himself left no record of these meetings with the founders of America's most successful new religion, one suspects that the encounter was much more significant for the Mormons than it was for Seixas.

Lorenzo Snow, the brother of one of the first of Joseph Smith's many wives, Eliza R. Snow, was a student at Oberlin College in the autumn of 1835. Snow wrote to his sister of Professor Seixas and his "reputation as an able Hebraist," setting the stage for his employment by the Mormons in January of 1836.[42] In the developing theology of the new church, the ancient languages of the Near East played a significant role. Joseph Smith's translation of the "golden plates," which were written in what he variously described as either "reformed Egyptian" or Hebrew, encouraged the prophet and his followers to pursue "Hebrew learning."

Like the New England Puritans and their English antecedents, Mormons and other nineteenth-century "new religions" saw the Hebrew language as the original language of mankind. Knowledge of Hebrew could lead the student of the Old Testament to a clearer, unmediated understanding of that central text. This was but the first level of Hebrew's importance. For those groups influenced by mystical ideas, Hebrew offered an example of a pure, uncorrupted language, of the language of Eden in the period before the "confusion of tongues" at the Tower of Babel. New religious groups found in the Hebrew word and the Hebraic concept a source of strength and inspiration.

Some historians of early Mormon thought detect an esoteric aspect in Smith's search for knowledge of Hebrew and its cognate languages. In the 1990s two Mormon journals debated the question of the Mormon prophet's interest in Kabbalah. Asserting that Smith's "prophetic translations" of Scripture were "in nature Kabbalistic," Lance Owens posited direct Jewish kabbalistic influence on Smith, influence exerted through Alexander Niebaur, the first Jewish convert to the young church. Owens's critics argued that Smith's sources are more properly described as "American occultist" and "Hermetic," and that classical Zoharic Kabbalism does not appear in Smith's prophetic translations or discourses.[43] What does appear in Smith's writings is an evocation of a concept we have encountered in the writings of Jewish Kabbalists, earlier Hebraists, and Christian Kabbalists—the mystical power inherent in the Hebrew alphabet and language.

[*Scholars, Prophets, Mystics*]

When, in the mid 1830s, Smith founded a "School for the Elders" in Kirtland, he included within it a "Hebrew School." The School for the Elders (also called the School of the Prophets) was a church institution that taught English grammar, writing, geography, and history; the Hebrew School was dedicated to mastering the art of biblical translation through knowledge of Hebrew and Aramaic. Before Seixas arrived in Kirtland, Smith began teaching a class in Hebrew to a small group of followers.

The Mormons wanted to learn Hebrew, but they wanted to learn Hebrew from a Jew, not from a member of a Protestant denomination. "A Jew was exceedingly rare in northeastern Ohio in those days," a Jew who knew Hebrew even rarer. As Rudolph Glanz put it, "A teacher of Hebrew who was a Jew was what the Mormons came to want . . . even if they had to send, over 600 miles, to New York for one." Glanz explained the practical value of this requirement in this way: "This immediate need led to the first meeting between Jews and Mormons within the framework of American life rather than in the imaginary biblical or historic situations of the Jewish past. In the course of efforts to find a qualified Hebrew teacher, the Mormons made contact with two Jews."[44] These two Jews were J. Seixas and Daniel Peixotto.

We know from Smith's diary entry of November 20, 1835, that he was eager to acquire Hebrew texts. "In the evening President Oliver Cowdery returned from New York, bringing with him a quantity of Hebrew books, for the benefit of the school. He presented me with a Hebrew lexicon, Bible and Grammar."[45] It seems that the Mormons were encouraged to acquire Hebrew books by their encounter with the Jewish physician and academician Daniel Peixotto, who had recently moved to Ohio.

In the wake of the founding of Western Reserve and Oberlin, a third Ohio educational institution, Willoughby Medical College, opened its doors. To teach medicine the school employed Daniel Levy Maduro Peixotto, a New York Jewish physician and former head of the New York Medical Society. Peixotto, scion of a distinguished Sephardic family, was also well versed in Hebrew.[46] His presence in the area attracted the attention of Smith's followers.

A group of Mormon elders traveled to the new medical school, which was only four miles from Kirtland. There they met Peixotto and "learned that he could and would teach them Hebrew."[47] Peixotto, however, disappointed them. He was not able to fulfill his promise to teach them, but it is not clear why. Joseph Smith's diary of January 4, 1836, reads as follows: "Met and organized Hebrew School. Had engaged Dr. Peixotto to teach, but he did not keep his appointment, so Wm. E. McClellin and Orson Hyde were sent to Hudson Seminary to hire a teacher."[48] According to a historian of medical education, the Mormons were displeased with the doctor and "the relationship did not last long before they dismissed Peixotto for habitual drunkenness."[49] The church leaders then engaged Joshua Seixas and he began teaching in January of 1836.

Strangely enough, the Mormons did not know that Seixas and Peixotto were relatives who had been closely associated in their youth. Both were brought up in New York's Shearith Israel congregation, where Seixas's father was the sexton and cantor from 1784 to 1816. Peixotto's father took over these functions from 1816 to 1828. The elder Seixas and the elder Peixotto were close personal friends. As their sons were almost of the same age (D. M. Peixotto was born a year before J. Seixas), we can imagine that they knew each other well. Rachel, daughter of Gershom Seixas's brother Benjamin, married Daniel Peixotto in 1823. Through marriage to Joshua's first cousin, Daniel Peixotto became a member of the Seixas family.[50]

Did Peixotto suggest that the Mormons seek out Seixas? Were the cousins in touch with each other in Ohio, or had Seixas's conversion come between them? I have been unable to find a record of any contact between J. Seixas and D. Peixotto. Suffice it to say that Seixas was well received in the Mormon's Hebrew School, and the Mormon elders did not express any regret that they had hired him. His intensive method, in which he met with his students twice a day during a period of seven weeks, and in which the students were expected to prepare assigned biblical texts for each recitation, bore some fruit. Enthusiasm for Hebrew studies ran high, as described by a modern historian of the Kirtland settlement:

> Soon after Professor Seixas commenced teaching the forty enrolled class members, others expressed an interest in attending his classes. Consequently, three other classes were formed, each with from thirty to forty students, so that this young Hebrew scholar taught about 120 persons. Since the enrollment in the Hebrew School was much larger than anticipated, there were not sufficient textbooks for everyone. Therefore, some of the Hebrew Bibles were divided into sections, and students studied different portions of the Old Testament. . . . While classes were held daily from 10:00 to 11:00 A.M. and from 2:00 to 3:00 P.M., members often gathered before and after class to read to one another.[51]

Seixas certified at least one of his students, Orson Pratt, as a teacher of Hebrew. Pratt wrote in his journal, "After a course of about eight weeks in Hebrew I received a certificate from Professor Seixas, testifying to my proficiency in the language, and certifying to my capabilities to teach the same."[52] Seixas presented a similar letter to Joseph Smith at the end of the intensive course. This document, while not certifying Smith as a Hebrew teacher, does say that Smith "in acquiring the principles of the sacred language of the Old

Testament Scriptures in their original tongue . . . has so far accomplished a knowledge of it, that he is able to translate to my entire satisfaction."[53]

This validation of his ability to translate from the Hebrew text was very gratifying to Smith, who expressed his delight in his diary. "It seems as if the Lord opened our minds in a marvelous manner, to understand His word in the original language; and my prayer is that God will speedily endow us with a knowledge of all languages and all tongues." Later, a few months after concluding his classes with Seixas, he wrote, "My soul delights in reading the word of God in the original, and I am determined to pursue the study of languages until I shall become master of them."[54]

Not content with the initial seven weeks of instruction, Smith requested that Seixas stay on for another three weeks, which he did, "after having a vacation of two weeks." During his sojourn with the Mormons Seixas was considered by his hosts to be a Jew. Whether Seixas's reluctance to make public his conversion to Christianity, or the Mormons' refusal to see him as anything but a *Jewish* scholar, prevented the issue of his religious affiliation from coming to the fore is unclear. For the Mormons of the early church, and for Mormon historians in the future, Seixas would remain a Jew. This validated him as a source of Hebraic information. As a native informant, a Jew converted to Christianity would not do. This is not to say that Smith did not try to bring Seixas into the Mormon fold, though from Smith's diary it is difficult to tell how serious the attempt was. "Fri. Feb. 19—I conversed with Mr. Seixas on religion. He listened with attention and appeared interested. I believe the Lord is striving with Him, by his Holy Spirit, that he will eventually embrace the new and everlasting covenant, for he is a chosen vessel unto the Lord to do His people good; but I forebear lest I get to prophesying upon his head."[55]

Joseph Smith returned to Hebrew studies, though in a less intensive manner, when he met Alexander Neibaur, the first Jewish convert to the Mormon faith. In Smith's diary of May 1844 (the year of his death and eight years after studying with Seixas) he notes, "Read Hebrew with Neibaur." Here we have again the recurrent theme of attaining Hebrew knowledge from a Jewish source. Neibaur, a Jewish immigrant from Germany, had a traditional European Jewish education, though exactly what information he imparted to Smith we do not know. Recent claims that Neibaur taught Smith kabbalistic texts and doctrines do not hold up under close scrutiny.

A more significant question is, what effect did Seixas, Smith's primary Jewish informant, have on the Mormons? Despite possible Jewish influences in the realm of folklore and mysticism, which Smith probably developed through reading or through meetings with other informants, we must conclude that Seixas's influence on the Mormons was primarily philological. Throughout the remaining eight years of his life, Joseph Smith, when in search of a Hebrew term for a place or person, would use the information he had gathered from Seixas, often turning to his personal copies of Seixas's Hebrew and Aramaic grammars. Perhaps the best known of these Hebraisms is Nauvoo, the name Smith gave to the Mormon settlement in Illinois. "In April 1839, Joseph Smith, surveying from a hill the wild prospect around Commerce (Illinois), imagining what he could do with it, thought 'It is a beautiful site, and shall be called Nauvoo, which means in Hebrew a beautiful plantation.' Many have scoffed at the assertion that the name is Hebrew, but it is in Seixas's *Manual Grammar* (1834, p. 111) in a 'List of Peculiar and Anomalous Forms Found in the Hebrew Bible,' the first words under the letter Nun are na-avauh and nauvoo . . . the word nauvoo is rendered 'are beautiful' (Isaiah 52:7), 'are comely' (Song of Solomon 1:10)."[56]

This is one of a number of Mormon Hebraisms that can be traced directly to Seixas's books. Hebrew also served as a code for private communication within the church hierarchy. "Sometime between 1841 and 1843, Smith directed that the identities of some early church leaders, including himself, should be disguised by code words in the revelations which were being prepared for publication. . . . The published revelation specified that "my servant *Baurak Ale* (Joseph Smith Jr.) is the man." Apostle Orson Pratt later said, "Joseph was called Baurak Ale, which was a Hebrew word meaning 'God Bless you.'"[57]

Some historians of Mormon thought also consider the development of the "plural god" idea as related to Smith's Hebrew studies. For in Smith's reworking of the creation story in *The Book of Abraham*, "instead of saying 'God created the earth,' he wrote: '*The Gods* organized the earth.'" As Joseph Smith's biographer Fawn Brodie saw it, "This change, which represented a significant step in Joseph's slowly evolving metaphysical system, had its roots in his new learning. The idea of the plurality of God he had picked up from his classes in Hebrew, where he had learned that *Elohim*, one of the Hebrew words for God, is plural, and had therefore concluded that the Bible had been carelessly translated."[58]

Though the assertion that Smith saw earlier translations of *Elohim* as being in error seems accurate (it was confirmed by the Mormon apostle Parley Pratt, brother of Orson Pratt), the notion that *Elohim* referred to a plurality of gods did not stem from Seixas's writings or teachings. For Seixas emphasized, in keeping with traditional Jewish explanations of *Elohim*, that the plural form here is "a plural in *excellentiae*, used by way of eminence." As Michael Walton put it in a 1981 article on Seixas: "Only in the case of the key word *Elohim* is Seixas impact unclear . . . it may be that Joseph discovered it in his Hebrew studies before Seixas arrived."[59]

Whether echoes of the ancient philological debate about the word *Elohim*, a debate echoed in the Talmud, reached Smith it is difficult to know. But it is highly doubtful that Seixas would have advanced a pantheistic or trinitarian interpretation of Genesis 1. For if he had been influenced by, and baptized by Theodore Parker, there would have been no room in his Christianity for trinitarian ideas. Such notions would have been far from the "pure Christianity" of Parker and James Walker, the prominent Unitarian associates of Seixas.

In his use of Hebrew, Joseph Smith has been rightfully deemed an "artist" for his creative, if unscientific, approach to the language. Whether he was appealing to the occult powers or the theological meaning of Hebrew, we can agree with Zucker that Smith "used the Hebrew as he chose, as an artist inside his frame of reference, in accordance with his taste, according to the effect that he wanted to produce, as a foundation for theological innovations."[60]

Joseph Smith's Hebraism also informed and influenced his unique form of Christian Zionism. Smith wrote that "one of the most important points of faith is the gathering of Israel when it shall be said that the Lord lives that brought up the children of Israel from the land of the north, and from all the lands wither he has driven them. That day is one, all important to all men."[61] Mormon engagement with the idea of Jewish Restoration did not remain abstract. In 1841, Orson Hyde, one of Smith's disciples, arrived in Jerusalem and performed a ceremony in which he recited a prayer for the ingathering of the exiles and the peace of the city. Thoughout the subsequent century and a half, the Mormon commitment to the idea of a Jewish state has remained steadfast.

Into Obscurity

After his short sojourn with the Mormon elders, Seixas left Ohio, and the Mormons, in the spring of 1836. The next indication of the family's whereabouts is the record of his daughter Selina's birth in Staten Island, New York, in 1838. Back in New York after a six-year absence, Seixas made the acquaintance of the few professional teachers of Hebrew then working in the city. He acted as a consultant to Christian Hebraists who were eager to publish their grammars, much as he had served as consultant to Moses Stuart in the early 1830s. Among these scholars was George Bush, professor of Hebrew at New York University from 1832 to 1841 and the subject of the next chapter. In the preface to his *Grammar of the Hebrew Language* (second edition, 1839), Bush, who was both a professor and an ordained minister in the Presbyterian Church, thanked Seixas for "the aid very kindly tendered in correcting the proof-sheets of the latter half of the volume. . . . My only regret is that circumstances did not permit him to afford to my pages from the outset the benefit of his accurate revisals."[62]

Now living again in proximity to his father's family, Seixas found that his conversion to Christianity was a source of embarrassment to some of his relatives, as it would be to some of his descendants. They therefore tended to obscure, if not hide, this fact and J. Seixas himself was quite circumspect about it.

Seraphine, the Seixas family's ninth child, was born in New York in 1840. I find no other trace of James Seixas's activities until 1852 when the third edition of his *Manual Hebrew Grammar* was published in Philadelphia. The reasons for his lack of scholarly productivity and his prolonged silence are outlined in the preface to this last edition of the grammar: "Ill health, and the causes growing out of it, have, until the present time, prevented me from complying with the repeated and earnest solicitations of very many and valued friends, among the clergy and laity, to publish another edition of my Grammar."[63] As early as 1832, when Seixas was thirty years old, his ill health was a matter of concern to his friend and colleague Moses Stuart. We may assume that he was plagued by illness for a good part of his life.

At some point after their return to New York City, Seixas and his wife Henrietta lived apart. Her death and burial are recorded in the Shearith Israel records; his death is not. According to David de Sola Pool, "A number of James Seixas descendants remained in the Jewish community." Malcolm Stern has noted in his researches into the Shearith Israel records that, "of their children, the eldest, Julia Anne, married first a Jew, then a Christian; Esther and Selina married Jews; the others Christians."[64]

According to Seixas's granddaughter Blanche Moses, who wrote her memoirs at the end of the nineteenth century, "After his return to New York City he founded the first organized choir of the Spanish and Portuguese Synagogue where he also served for many years as chief instructor in Hebrew. He died in New York sometime in the seventies." It seems that Mrs. Moses, in her old age, confused the chronology of events. As N. Taylor Phillips noted, it was in the early 1820s that Seixas organized the synagogue choir and taught Hebrew. There is no direct evidence that he resumed his duties in the synagogue after his return from Ohio.[65]

Though some modern scholars have considered it possible that Seixas renewed his association with Shearith Israel congregation, others have expressed skepticism on this issue. Rabbi Nathan Kaganoff wrote, "Personally, I find it quite surprising, considering how strict the synagogue was, and its attitude toward Jews who were lax in their religious observance or married outside the faith. I find it very hard to believe that the synagogue would have hired him again after he converted unless he recanted and became a Jew before he died."[66]

James/Joshua Seixas's widow Henrietta Seixas survived her husband by some thirteen years. There is conflicting evidence as to whether she too had converted to Christianity. But as her death and burial are recorded in the Shearith Israel records, while her husband's are not, it seems that she remained in the Jewish community.

Other than what is revealed in the preface to the 1852 edition of Seixas's *Grammar*, we know little of his activities in the second half of his life. As mentioned above, at some point in the mid-1830s he began to use the name James instead of Joshua. The three editions of his *Manual Hebrew Grammar* were published with "J. Seixas" on the title page. The Mormon elders knew him as Joshua, but other Christian acquaintances and correspondents refer to him as James. For the Mormons, Seixas, their first informant on matters Judaic and Hebraic, had to be a Jew. For the Protestant clergymen who befriended and encouraged him, Seixas was a Jew who converted to Christianity because of his religious convictions. As they saw it, if Seixas, on the path to "true Christianity," brought some Hebraic "treasures" with him, all the better.

Scion of a large and influential colonial Jewish family, raised among the elite of New York City's oldest and most prestigious synagogue, Joshua Seixas chose to associate with scholars, writers, and clergymen of various Protestant denominations. His devotion to the scientific study of the Hebrew language, and his thorough knowledge of biblical Hebrew and Aramaic, were his entry ticket into Protestant society. As his contemporary Heinrich Heine observed, the baptismal certificate was the billet-doux into the world of European culture. But in the words of a modern observer of the consequences of Heine's apostasy: "Though he paid the price, the ticket never gave him the entry that he expected."[67] Seixas, excluded from full membership in the Protestant-dominated academy, lived on the periphery of the world of "oriental" scholarship. He taught classes or tutored students at a number of institutions: Andover Theological Seminary, Harvard College, Oberlin College, and Western Reserve College, but he never attained the status of a full member of the faculty.

Through his short-lived contact with the early Mormons and their prophet, Seixas was assured a degree of renown. If, as his granddaughter claimed, he did, in later years, rejoin the Jewish community, then it provides us with an unusual glimpse into the Jewish experience in mid-nineteenth-century America. In a community where the social order had not yet rigidified, crossing religious borders was relatively easy. Moreover, the anonymity conferred upon an individual by moving from city to city was considerable, and news of conversion may not have reached other communities. Yet despite these mitigating factors, most scholarly opinion is against the idea that Seixas was again accepted at Shearith Israel.

J. Seixas's academic career and family life are emblematic of one part of the early Jewish experience in America. Jewish teachers of Hebrew, limited as they were to working in synagogue schools, were not welcome in the wider academic world. A century before Seixas, Judah Monis, an immigrant from North Africa, converted to Christianity before becoming instructor in Hebrew at Harvard. The distinguished European Jewish scholar Isaac Nordheimer, a contemporary of Seixas, was denied the chair of Hebrew Studies at New York University; it was held by George Bush, an ordained Presbyterian minister. These are American manifestations of a pattern familiar from European cultural history: Hebraists and their living Jewish sources found themselves in relationships that had overtones of ambivalence and competition.[68]

Seixas hovered on the border between Jewish identity and conversion to Christianity, benefiting from the social fluidity of the times. In his later years he was plagued by ill health and family discord, and he did not make a major contribution to scholarship. But as teacher of Hebrew and mentor of Hebraists among Presbyterians, Unitarians, and Mormons, he left his mark on American religious and intellectual life in the mid-nineteenth century.

10

AMERICAN HEBRAIST
AND PROTO-ZIONIST

His mind was omnivorous and devoured everything that it came in contact with.
Gifted with a retentive memory, and ready on any subject, all the stores of literature and
science seemed open to him. . . . His conversational powers were remarkable, while his
amiable disposition and simplicity of manners rendered him accessible to all.
William Hayden

George Bush (1796–1859), professor of Hebrew and oriental literature at New York University (NYU) from 1832 to 1846, was, according to the *Dictionary of American Biography*, "prominent in his day as scholar, writer, and controversialist."[1] Though now well-nigh forgotten, he was once considered "one of the most profound and ingenious scholars" of the mid-nineteenth century, and his more than thirty volumes of polemic, biblical commentary, and interpretive history of religion enjoyed great popularity.[2] His views on the Hebrew language, the Jews, and their place in Christian society, and his statements about the possibility of a restoration of the Jews to the Holy Land, had considerable influence. Thus his life and work have to be taken into account in any evaluation of the early study of Hebrew and Judaism in America. They are equally important in tracing the roots of "Christian Zionism" in American Protestant circles.[3]

Education and Early Life

The scion of an old colonial family, George Bush was born in Norwich, Vermont, in 1796. At age eighteen he enrolled in nearby Dartmouth College, having gained, in his high school years, considerable proficiency in Greek and Latin, and having then read widely in the classics. Since childhood Bush had been a bookworm, and it was difficult for his family to interest him in a trade. "Put into a printing shop that he might not injure his health by too much study, he was tolerated by them but a short time because he would become so interested in reading the manuscripts that he forgot to set the type."[4]

At Dartmouth, Bush found in the study of religion a focus for his intellectual energies. Upon graduation he entered the Princeton Theological Seminary, where he was ordained to the Presbyterian ministry and later became a tutor. The seminary stressed a thorough grounding in the study of the Bible in its original languages and early translations, and in this area Bush showed great promise. In addition to Hebrew, he mastered Aramaic and Syriac, later using his knowledge of these languages in his multivolume *Notes on the Old Testament*, published in the 1840s. But he did not lead the life of a sequestered scholar, for throughout this period his teachers were grooming him to become one of Presbyterianism's denominational leaders. As a result, he preached regularly at the church in Morristown, New Jersey. It was there that he met the young woman he was later to marry, a certain Miss Condict.

In 1824 Bush was ordained and installed as pastor of the Presbyterian Church in Indianapolis, Indiana. His wife came out from New Jersey to join him. In his new post his independent and inquiring spirit asserted itself. He was soon making statements from the pulpit to the effect that there was no scriptural authority for the Presbyterian form of church government. The ensuing controversy led to Bush's removal from the pulpit. In later years he would again be embroiled in religious and academic controversy. Removal from the pulpit coincided with his wife's death from a sudden illness, so Bush decided to move back East.

For some time Bush had been interested in Islam, a subject then little known in the United States. In 1830 he published *The Life of Mohammed*, which was issued in the popular Harper Family Library series. It was the first American book about Islam. While the book's tone was inimical to Islam and its founder—the preface describes the work as "a selection and arrangement of leading particulars of the Impostor's history"—it served as a guide to, and summary of, the small body of scholarly literature in English about Islam and Moslems.[5]

Islam is presented as an "invention" by a former merchant "constitutionally addicted to religious contemplation." Bush offers various explanations for Mohammed's motives in "palming a new religion upon the world." Was the prophet sincere in his beliefs or not? Perhaps, but whether sincere or not, he soon convinced others of the divine origins of his mission. "The pretended prophet, having at length, after years of deliberation, ripened all his plans and proceeded in the most gradual and cautious manner to put them in execu-

George Bush

tion."[6] All in all, *The Life of Mohammed* was an anti-Islamic polemic typical of its time.

During his years at Princeton, and later in Indiana, Bush had gained a reputation as a preacher and a scholar. The success of *The Life of Mohammed* now added a popular book to the roster of his achievements. He was offered a number of different professorships, and is said to have turned down his alma mater, Dartmouth, where he was offered a dual appointment as professor of theology at the college and pastor of the Hanover, New Hampshire, church.[7]

Aside from his many and varied intellectual accomplishments, Bush was in demand because competent Hebraists were a rare commodity in early-nineteenth-century America. The tradition of Puritan biblical scholarship had declined considerably and the study of the Greco-Roman classics had to some extent taken is place. American higher education had undergone significant changes in the first decades of the nineteenth century. As the "inflexible curricula" of the early American colleges became more flexible, training in the learned languages of antiquity was no longer the main focus of higher education. Latin and Greek were still offered, but Hebrew had lost its luster.[8] Although Hebrew had been taught in most of the colleges founded before the Revolution, it had never been a popular subject, and students often complained about its inclusion in the curriculum—a legacy of the Puritan emphasis on understanding Scripture in its original languages. In the 1820s and 30s, under the influence of Moses Stuart, Edward Robinson, Isaac Nordheimer, and James Seixas, Hebrew studies forged a place for itself in the American academic world.

At New York University

When New York University was founded in the early 1830s, it was intended to be forward looking and scientifically oriented, a school that would break with the classical past, and more specifically, "an English college, one in which a knowledge of Latin and Greek should not be required."[9] Unlike many American colleges, NYU was a secular institution with no denominational ties. While it did not have a theological school, it did have a professorship of Hebrew and oriental literature, and in 1831 the board of the new university invited George Bush to become the position's first incumbent.[10]

Bush accepted the job and remained at NYU for fourteen years (1832–46). He did not remarry during this period; he was, in the words of a contemporary, "one thoroughly delivered up to the student life more than any person I ever met." After several years he moved his effects, including one of the largest personal libraries in New York City, to a large loft on Nassau Street in lower Manhattan. "Thither he transferred his library, collected his books and manuscripts about him, and sat himself down to literature about as completely as any man of our day. His sanctum was a perfect den of learning. And there the professor might be found almost at any time of the day or night, as the presiding genius of the place: walled in by books, thoroughly fortified within ramparts of literature."[11]

According to one of his colleagues at NYU, Bush's home became an intellectual salon. "In those days the room was the resort of enquiring and ingenious minds from most parts of the country, as well as, frequently, of visitors from abroad. . . . I think he had a wider range of intellectual sympathy, and enjoyed a larger intercourse with literary and professional men in consequence, than any other I have ever known."[12]

Ensconced in this comfortable situation Bush began to produce a steady stream of pamphlets and books. His initial success with *The Life of Mohammed* was followed by *A Treatise on the Millennium* (1833), in which he questioned the notion, then popular in some Protestant circles, that the Second Coming was imminent. This would later place Bush in direct opposition to William Miller, leader of the Adventists. As Bush saw it, there was no scriptural basis for Adventist belief. "The theory of the second personal and visible advent of the Saviour at the opening of the grand sabbatical period of the world, whether this be termed the millennium or the New Jerusalem, is in my opinion one of the most baseless of all the extravaganzas of prophetic hallucination."[13]

The year 1835 saw the publication of Bush's *A Grammar of the Hebrew Language*. A second edition of this work, "corrected and enlarged," was published in 1839. In this edition Bush acknowledged the help of his colleague the Jewish scholar Isaac Nordheimer, professor of Arabic and other oriental languages at New York University.

Nordheimer, whose story was told in an earlier chapter, had been a student at the renowned European Yeshiva of Pressburg, where he studied with the head of the academy, Rabbi Moses Schreiber. He went on to train in Semitic philology at the University of Munich, where he received a Ph.D. in 1834. Arriving in America in 1835, he was invited to teach "Arabic and other oriental languages" at NYU.[14]

Though Edward Robinson, dean of American biblical studies, judged Nordheimer to be the finest Hebrew scholar of his generation, he was not asked to teach Hebrew. Hebrew was still considered to be the province of Protestant clergymen like Bush, and was to remain so until the end of the nineteenth century, for Christian Hebraists, while thoroughly immersed in "Hebrew learning," were still deeply ambivalent about Jewish participation in teaching the sacred tongue.

As Jerome Friedman has pointed out in his history of the flowering of Christian Hebraism in sixteenth-century Europe, "Essentially, Christendom suffered from an approach-avoidance complex when dealing with things Jewish."[15] More than a century before Nordheimer was appointed to teach at New York University, Judah Monis, a Jew of Marrano extraction whose story I told in Chapter 2, had chosen to convert to Christianity in order to receive an appointment as instructor of Hebrew at Harvard College. His conversion, however, did not allay the fears of his colleagues, who suspected that "Rabbi Monis" had not joined the church for the most high-minded reasons.[16]

In the preface to his Hebrew grammar, Bush remarked that in the America of his day "several hundreds of young men in different stages of a collegiate and theological education are annually engaging in the study of Hebrew, besides a large number of persons of both sexes in private life who are prompted to the enterprise solely by a desire to drink from the pure fountain of revelation." He expressed his hope that Hebrew would recover the place of importance that it had in Protestant Europe during the sixteenth and seventeenth centuries. "Judging from the past, we see no reason to doubt that these hundreds will soon be increased to thousands, if indeed the Hebrew be not, like the Latin and Greek, eventually incorporated into every course of liberal education."[17]

Notes on the Old Testament

The most popular of Bush's works was the series of *Notes on the Old Testament* that he embarked upon in 1840. He published seven volumes of these notes, working his way through the Pentateuch, Joshua, and Judges, before moving on to the Psalms. In these editions, the biblical text appeared in the original Hebrew; next to it was the Septuagint Greek and the Latin of the Vulgate. English translations of these three classical sources were provided. Bush's extensive notes followed this textual apparatus.

Aware that the majority of his readers did not have the training to make use of the ancient languages, Bush explained in the introduction to *The Prophecies of Daniel* that "in placing the Hebrew text, with several accompanying versions, so prominently before the reader, I am aware of the hazard incurred by the somewhat repulsive array of unknown characters, to the popular effect of my expositions." He goes on to say that those who have studied some Hebrew will benefit from reviewing the original, and for those who have not, "I have consulted the convenience of the reader to the utmost practicable degree—by exact translation."

The accompanying notes were written for scholars and educated laymen; one did not have to know the Hebrew and the Greek to follow the thread of the argument and exposition. Some of these volumes, which were weighty tomes of three to four hundred pages each, went through as many as ten editions, attesting to their popularity in both schools and homes.

The Valley of Vision

Despite his high praise for and encouragement of the study of the language preserved by the Jews, Bush, in the tradition of the European humanist scholars, did not have much regard for the Jews as a people. Though his biblical studies eventually led him to advocate the return of the Jews to Ottoman-ruled Palestine, he cannot be considered a philo-Semite. In his *Valley of Vision; or, The Dry Bones of Israel Revived: An Attempted Proof of the Restoration and Conversion of the Jews* (1844), he argued against a spiritual interpretation of the prophecies concerning "the end of days," and advocated instead "the literal return of the Jews to the land of their fathers." And this, he said, was not to be effected by miraculous means.

> Nothing more is implied than that it will be so ordered in Providence that motives will be furnished for such a return, appealing it may be to the worldly and selfish principles of the Jewish mind. It is by no means improb-

able that the affairs of the nations, or the progress of civilization, may take such a turn as to offer to the Jews the same carnal inducements to remove to Syria, as now promote them to emigrate to this country. Indeed when we consider the force of national predilections naturally operating with that people, and drawing them with a mighty attraction to their paternal soil, we can scarcely doubt, that a much less degree of worldly inducement will suffice to turn their faces and their footsteps thither than to any other region of the earth.[18]

Here Bush was arguing against the Adventist predictions of the early 1840s that the Second Coming was imminent. The realism of Bush's call for the return of the Jews was underscored by the inclusion in the book of a map of Palestine with areas marked for the settlement of the returning tribes. This geographic realism exemplifies a shift that we alluded to earlier, from the Puritan concept of American Zion to an advocacy of American support for the renewal of the biblical Zion. The advocacy is scripturally based, but not apocalyptic. The Adventist/Millerite claims are rebutted, but the support for a renewed Zion remains.

The Valley of Vision was well received, as is illustrated by the review in the *Princeton Biblical Repository* of July 1844: "Prof. Bush is now well known, both in Europe and America, not only as a Biblical scholar and interpreter of Scripture, but as one who has for many years devoted his attention, in a special manner, to the subject of prophecy. . . . We need only say, that in the case before us we are not called upon to sit in judgment on a flight of fancy, or an ignorant exposition of the English texts, but on a genuine attempt to lay open the true meaning of the inspired original by the help of the best means to which the author has had access."

Swedenborgian Mysticism

While formulating his view of the coming redemption and of the place of the Jews in it, Bush was deeply influenced by the Swedish scientist and mystic Emanuel Swedenborg (1688–1772), a man whose all-encompassing mystical system exerted enormous influence in European esoteric circles. Swedenborg had himself studied Hebrew and had used the texts of Genesis and Exodus as the structural basis for his massive theological work, *Arcana Caelestia* ("Heavenly Secrets"). In this system of arcane symbols the Jew represents the power of the "external," in contrast to the "internal" religiosity of the Christian. Writing of the Jews, Swedenborg says, "The nature of their fantasies and lusts no one can know. . . . They love themselves and love worldly wealth more than all others; and besides above all others they fear the loss of honor, and also the loss of gain."[19]

By the mid-1840s Bush had become a full-fledged Swedenborgian, a convert to the Church of the New Jerusalem. His advocacy of Swedenborg's ideas caused quite a stir in America. To promote these views he founded a monthly journal, the *Hierophant*, in which he "elaborated on the nature of prophetic symbols." The journal lasted only a year, but during that time it was widely read and quite influential.

Swedenborg's mysticism appealed to academic intellectuals, especially to those laboring in the interpretation of ancient texts. As Ernst Benz noted, "Swedenborg's visions do not occur in church or in the exercise of priestly observances or in connection with the sacrament, but surprise the scholar studying at his desk as he labors over the inner sense of the Bible."[20]

In 1845, in an address at the Odeon in Boston, Ralph Waldo Emerson, who would later write about Swedenborg in his *Representative Men* (1850), challenged Bush's presentation of Swedenborgian doctrine. While recognizing Swedenborg's contributions to modern thought ("No single man can judge of his various works. His wisdom can hardly be estimated"), Emerson questioned the validity of the religious system derived from the mystic's work and called on Bush to rescind his support for it.

In 1847 Bush published *Mesmer and Swedenborg*, in which he attempted to validate the claims of Mesmerism by "spiritual" explanations. This book only served to distance him even more from his academic and clerical associates. Shortly afterwards, in the summer of 1848, Bush was reordained in the ministry of the Swedenborgians' New Jerusalem Church. He consented to do so "although opposed to all ecclesiastical rites."

Despite these changes in his religious outlook, Bush's colleagues still thought highly of him. An associate of his wrote: "His mind was omnivorous and devoured everything that it came in contact with. Gifted with a retentive memory, and ready on any subject, all the stores of literature and science seemed open to him. . . . His conversational powers were remarkable, while his amiable disposition and simplicity of manners rendered him accessible to all."[21]

Because of his increased involvement with the Swedenborgian church, of which he was now one of the chief exponents in the United States, Bush left the academy and stopped writing and publishing scholarly works. Abandoning his university post and his large Nassau Street studio, "his den of learning," he set out to build a new life. In 1849 he married for a second time. His wife, Mary W. Fisher, shared his enthusiasm for his work in the new church and they were a close couple until Bush's death in 1859.

Bush spent the last decade of his life furthering the cause of his newly adopted church. In a series of books he defended its doctrines, and toward the end of his life he published what is considered his most radical treatise, *Priesthood and Clergy Unknown to Christianity; or, The Church a Community of Co-equal Brethen*. Divested of his library, which he had sold, and of his academic post, from which he had retired, he moved to the small New Jerusalem Church community in Brooklyn. A close friend, visiting Bush there several months before his death, found the former "controversialist" a changed man. "I do not think he ever loved controversy except as an instrument for the discovery or establishment of truth; but *now* his liking for it he declared to be gone. . . . His whole character had become softened and spiritualized; and, although then but slightly ill, he seemed like one getting ready to depart."[22]

In later years both Dartmouth and New York University seem to have been embarrassed by Bush's association with them. The college histories refer to him as a promising academician who was led astray by his unconventional beliefs. The Dartmouth alumni records note his conversion to Swedenborgianism and his adoption of "the modern myth of spiritualism. These changes were much lamented owing to his high character and distinguished scholarship."[23]

One wonders whether Bush would have been surprised by the realization of the dream of the Return to Zion, then advocated only by a small group of "Christian Zionists"? Could he have imagined that two of his relatives would someday become presidents of the United States?[24] Surely he must have felt that the Divine Plan manifests itself in unusual ways, and that these ways may not appear to be miraculous. In the concluding pages of *The Valley of Vision* he wrote, "While I anticipate, moreover, the most august developments of providence on the field of human destiny, of which the dawning's may even now be perceived by the enlightened eye, I look with equal confidence for a gradual accomplishment of all the splendid purposes of Infinite Wisdom."[25]

11

THE CAREERS OF SELAH MERRILL
NINETEENTH-CENTURY CHRISTIAN
HEBRAIST, PALESTINE EXPLORER,
AND U.S. CONSUL IN JERUSALEM

Palestine is not ready for the Jews, and the Jews are not ready for Palestine.
Selah Merrill

Selah Merrill and the Jews of Palestine

"The Jew needs to learn that his place in the world will be determined by what he can do for himself, and not so much by what Abraham did for himself four thousand years ago. It has a most mischievous effect to be always associating the modern Jews with eminent men and deeds in the remote ages of the past." So wrote Selah Merrill, U.S. consul in Jerusalem, in an official report on Palestine. Merrill felt impelled to include in his report a long section entitled "Jews and Jewish colonies in Palestine" in response to the Blackstone Memorial of 1891, which petitioned President Benjamin Harrison to support the convening of an international conference to discuss Jewish claims to Palestine. The Blackstone Memorial, a founding document of American Christian Zionism, had more than four hundred prominent signatories, the great majority of them Protestants; for many of them the contemporary Jews *were* the natural heirs of the ancient Hebrews: "Why not give Palestine back to them again? According to God's distribution of nations, it is their home, an inalienable possession, from which they were expelled by force."[1]

It was just such restorationist sentiment that Merrill so vehemently opposed. His report called the memorial "one of the wildest schemes brought before the public." The "character and habits of the modern Jews" would doom their Palestine settlement efforts to failure. According to Merrill, the originators of the petition "appear[ed] to be ignorant of two great facts, (1) that Palestine is not ready for the Jews and (2) that the Jews are not ready for Palestine."

Selah Merrill (From Vogel,
To See a Promised Land)

Merrill's sentiments were not unusual among American Protestant elites, especially among those serving in the diplomatic and consular services. As Ruth Kark has noted, Merrill's first term as consul (1882–84) coincided with the beginnings of Jewish agricultural settlement in Palestine. Merrill was in the unique position of being able to respond negatively to Jewish immigration, to oppose Jewish settlement, and to shape State Department attitudes toward these settlement efforts. As Peter Grose writes in *Israel in the Mind of America*, Merrill's 1891 report was "the first considered assessment of the Jewish restoration in the State Department files." Merrill's assessment, articulated by a man considered "the most serious and influential of the nineteenth-century Jerusalem consuls," was highly negative. Its conclusion, that the United States should not lend any support to the settlement of Palestine by Jews, was taken to heart by many of Merrill's colleagues at the State Department.[2]

When examining Merrill's attitudes toward Jewish settlement in Palestine it is worth noting that Merrill's twenty-five-year career as a U.S. diplomat (1882–1907) was preceded by three other careers. He had served as a Congregationalist minister, a teacher of Hebrew in a theological seminary, and an archaeologist in Palestine. Up to the time of his appointment to the Jerusalem consulate by President Chester A. Arthur, Merrill's life was devoted to the study of the Bible and the Holy Land and those very "eminent men and deeds in the remote ages of the past" whose modern descendants he so heartily disdained.

Merrill's study of the ancient Hebrews did not stop when he entered the consular service. During his tenure as consul in Jerusalem he deepened his knowledge of the biblical world through study of ancient languages and recovery of lost artifacts. His books and articles—among them *East of the Jordan* (1881), *Galilee in the Time of Christ* (1881), and *Ancient Jerusalem* (1908)—demonstrate a flair for writing and an ability to popularize new discoveries. His influence on other archaeologists and biblical researchers was considerable, though to a large extent unrecognized.

This combination of acute interest in the ancient Hebrews and intense disdain for their modern descendants bears examination. While Christian writers on Judaism often displayed ambivalence toward Jews, Merrill's case is especially intriguing because his attitude toward Jews had political consequences. With the advent of Zionism, these ambivalent attitudes affected American consideration of Jewish claims to the Holy Land.

Though Merrill was neither a profound thinker nor a highly original scholar, his place at the center of political events and his role in the transmission of ideas makes his career a fruitful locus of inquiry. Merrill's career and writings provide us with an opportunity to clarify the relationships among four factors and to question some common assumptions about those relationships. The history of Christian Hebraism, with its roots in the sixteenth century, significantly influenced European intellectual life in the seventeenth and eighteenth centuries. While the teachers of the early Christian Hebraists were often Jews, an independent Christian tradition of Hebrew study soon developed. As we have seen in preceeding chapters, this tradition developed in isolation from Jewish traditions of Hebrew study and was at times hostile to traditions of Jewish learning.

Second, the effect of Christian Hebraists' ideas on Protestant attitudes toward the Jews was considerable, especially in the seventeenth and eighteenth centuries. In contemporary Jewish historiography Hebraism is often described as a factor in promoting philo-Semitism and encouraging restorationist ideas. But as Frank Manuel has pointed out, Hebraism is not synonymous with philo-Semitism. Many eminent Hebraists were unsympathetic or actively hostile to the Jews of their day.

For Christians, the emergence of biblical archaeology and biblical research in the first half of the nineteenth century changed the concept of the Holy Land. Palestine was still a spiritual center and place of pilgrimage, but it was now also a place where scientific research on "biblical origins" could be conducted.

Finally, the emergence of proto-Zionist plans for the restoration of the Jews to Palestine and the subsequent reactions to these plans by Protestant scholars, clergymen, and statesmen resulted in political activity that either promoted or resisted the development of a Zionist project. With the development of Jewish political Zionism at the end of the nineteenth century the interaction between Jewish leaders and Christian Zionists became even more complex. Merrill, heir to and transmitter of some of these ideas about the Jews and an active participant in the events transpiring in Palestine, stands at the intersection of an important set of ideas and a significant series of events.

The development of the mindset Peter Grose has dubbed "Israel in the mind of America" is intimately linked to this cluster of ideas. From the earliest English settlement, ambivalence toward Jews manifested itself in British North America. The New England Puritans combined an intense interest in both Jewish learning and the religious lives of the few Jews living in the colonies with a strong desire for the Jews' speedy conversion. The political and cultural break with England did not resolve these contradictory attitudes. As Grose notes: "The old ambivalence toward Jews in the United States grew more pronounced by the middle of the nineteenth century. . . . If, in the early decades of the republic, most Americans never had occasion to know a Jew, this was not true for the second American generation."[3]

This already complex set of attitudes concerning the Jews was soon affected by events in Palestine, and events in Palestine were to some degree influenced by American attitudes. Thus, a reciprocity of events and ideas was set in motion. Merrill, heir to and transmitter of some of these ideas about the Jews, was also an active participant in the events transpiring in Palestine.

Perhaps it is naive to express surprise at the fact that Merrill's intense interest in ancient Israel was coupled with antipathy to modern Jews. For some scholars such ambivalence lies at the heart of the enterprise of Christian Hebraism. As Raphael Loewe has noted, Hebraism "could easily slip into anti-Semitism and the unscrupulous exploitation of rabbinic literature for purposes of anti-Jewish propaganda."[4] Thus, if Hebraism and anti-Semitism are not necessarily antithetical, what seems an inherent contradiction in Merrill's views may turn out to be nothing of the sort.

American Protestant observers of the Holy Land in the late nineteenth century were struck by another apparent paradox in Merrill's behavior: It was not only the Jews of Palestine who raised his ire. Protestants who were out of the American mainstream also suffered his attacks. Though he was an ordained clergyman and a Bible scholar, he became the constant nemesis and vociferous opponent of the largest American Protestant settlement in Ottoman Palestine, the American Colony in Jerusalem. An American journalist who visited the American Colony in 1906 noted that Merrill, who should have been the colonists' closest friend, was in fact their worst enemy: "While enjoying the respect and friendship of the 'infidel' Turkish government, [the colonists] have been subject to renewed controversy with one of their own creed and country; one who should, of all others in the wide worlds, be their best and truest friend, counselor and protector. For not only is this man a duly ordained minister of the Gospel, but he is America's consul in Jerusalem, with far-reaching powers to help or harm his fellow citizens in the Holy City."[5]

The American colonists and their antagonist at the consulate had arrived in Palestine within a year of each other—the colonists in 1881 followed by Merrill in 1882. Coincidentally, this marked the beginning of the first *aliyah*, in which approximately eight thousand Eastern European Jews established agricultural settlements in Palestine between 1882 and 1884.

Consul Merrill and his enemies, the Spafford family, founders of the American Colony, represented the extremes of the American Protestant ideological spectrum, with Merrill (associated with Andover Theological Seminary) on one extreme and the Spaffords (associated with the Chicago Baptists and the Millerites) on the other. Newly arrived in Jerusalem, the two were bound to clash, and both were to be troubled by the new Jewish immigration to Palestine—how were they to understand it? How were they to respond to it?

In the spirit of early-twentieth-century American Protestant liberalism and ecumenicism, Alexander Hume Ford speculated that the East was to blame for such religious intolerance. "Perhaps it is in the air, these religious feuds on sacred soil, where Mohammedan soldiers still patrol the Church of the Nativity, so that Christians of different sects may not cut each other's throats at the very manger where their God became man."[6] Of course it was not the East and its air that were to blame. In their antagonism to religious dissidents and enthusiasts, Merrill and many of his prestigious American visitors were espousing a highly conservative New England ideology, the legacy of opposition to the New Lights of the mid-eighteenth century.

So we cannot simply dismiss Merrill as a crank. In his worldview Jews were as objectionable as "enthusiastic" Protestants. (Unorthodoxy in Protestant circles has often been characterized as a Judaising tendency, just as the Catholic Church deemed the Reformation a Jewish heresy.) Merrill, a product of New Haven Theological Seminary and a member of the faculty at Andover Theological Seminary, objected equally to the extension of American consular protection to American Protestant "cranks" and "Russian" Jews, even if the latter had previously been accorded American consular protection.

The U.S. Consulate in Nineteenth-Century Jerusalem

During the final decades of Ottoman rule in Palestine, the office of U.S. Consul in Jerusalem was occupied by a series of intriguing and unconventional men. The Jerusalem consulate was itself an unusual post. Jerusalem was not a commercial post of importance, and the establishment of a consulate was regarded as an aid to tourists and pilgrims. In the early years of the office the Jerusalem consul was unpaid, as were all U.S. consuls. This was before the professionalization of the U.S. consular service, a process that took place in the last two decades of the nineteenth century. With the appointment of John Warren Gorham in 1856, a regular salary was allocated for the holder of the Jerusalem post. Prior to professionalization an appointment enabled the consul to engage in his primary interests, be they commercial, scholarly, or religious. Many of the American consuls were ordained Protestant clergymen, and they often hosted traveling church dignitaries and missionaries who visited Palestine.

Between 1844 and the end of Ottoman rule in 1917, there were eighteen appointments to the Jerusalem American consulate. The officeholders ranged from the self-appointed Warder Cresson, who later converted to Judaism and settled in Palestine, to the less colorful but more professional Otis A. Glazebrook, a personal friend of President Wilson's and a man who brought considerable diplomatic experience to the delicate post. Merrill entered the consular service in the middle of this period, at a time when great changes were taking place in the American diplomatic community.[7]

The American consuls took a lively interest in attempts by foreigners to establish colonies in Palestine. The fate of American groups, such as the Adams colony of Jaffa (1867), which had over 150 members, was of special concern to the consuls. Most often the consuls were hostile to American settlement efforts, whether Christian or Jewish. Along with reports about the economic state of Palestine and updates on recent archaeological and scientific studies, negative assessments of colonization efforts filled the annual reports to the secretary of state.

The diplomat who held the post for the longest period of time—he was appointed to three terms, for a total of sixteen years between 1882 and 1907— was Selah Merrill. Like some of his predecessors and all of his successors, Merrill had many an occasion to comment on and influence Jewish settlement in Palestine. As historian Frank Manuel has remarked: "Merrill considered himself an authority on all matters ancient and modern relating to Palestine and the Near East. Though he had graduated from a theological seminary, he preferred not to have the title 'reverend' used and chose to describe himself as a scientist, naturalist and explorer. His travel books and antiquarian studies are in the popular style of the period and show no great distinction; but he had an inquisitive mind and, whatever his prejudices, learned and reported a good deal about the Jewish community in Palestine."[8] His attitude toward Jewish settlement seems to have been formed long before he wrote the hostile report quoted at the beginning of this chapter.

The pre–World War I U.S. consuls were involved with the Jews of Palestine for three main reasons: (1) The Ottoman Empire had granted to the Western powers legal jurisdiction over their citizens resident in the Ottoman lands. Though their numbers were few, American Jews resident in Palestine thus fell under the American consul's jurisdiction. Any disputes between American Jews and Jewish nationals of other states also fell within the consul's purview. (2) In the last decade of the nineteenth century, American Jewish contributions to the *halukah*, those monies collected by Jews in the Diaspora for members of the Old Yishuv in Palestine, increased greatly. The consuls were often involved in local disputes over the disbursement of the *halukah* monies. (3) Several hundred Russian Jews in Palestine had gained U.S. consular protection under Merrill's predecessors. Some State Department officials were unhappy with this situation. Merrill, who agreed with them, argued that the protection extended to these Russian Jews was temporary and had lapsed. His view prevailed during his tenure; later the situation would change.

The attitudes of the consuls toward the Palestine Jewish community, toward both the Old Yishuv (the pre-1880 Orthodox community) and the New Yishuv (the more secular, post-1880 pioneer community), varied greatly, and it is difficult, if not impossible, to characterize a general attitude on the part of the consulate. But, as Frank Manuel has noted, Selah Merrill "was the most acrimonious reviler of the Jews who ever occupied the post of consul."[9] Merrill's hostility toward Jewish settlement, which he forcefully conveyed to his colleagues at the State Department, had a considerable effect on U.S. policies toward Jewish settlement. His attitude toward the Yishuv was in marked contrast to that of Henry Gilman, who succeeded Merrill in 1886. Gilman, with the support of the U.S. State Department, was instrumental in pressuring the Ottoman authorities to ease restrictions on Jewish immigration and land acquisition.[10]

It was not only as consul that Merrill left his mark. His scholarly output was extensive and influential. He was a pivotal figure in the development of Palestinian archaeology, both as an explorer of biblical sites and an organizer of American institutions in the Middle East, including the American Palestine Exploration Society and the American School of Oriental Research in Jerusalem. What impelled Merrill to visit Palestine in 1869, when he was in his early thirties, was his passion for what was then loosely defined as biblical research.

The father of this new field, as we saw in Chapter 7, was Edward Robinson. Robinson's enormously popular *Biblical Researches in Palestine*, based on his explorations of 1838 and 1852, spawned a new generation of American enthusiasts for Holy Land exploration. As one historian of the period put it, "Robinson's book is a cornerstone of nineteenth century Palestine exploration: whoever wished to understand the Palestine of that period had to follow him along its highways and byways."[11] While Robinson articulated no one particular method of inquiry, he emphasized that knowledge of the ancient and modern languages of the Near East was essential to the biblical researcher's efforts.

Central to Robinson's approach was a knowledge and use of comparative philology. On his first visit to Palestine, he enthusiastically noted the abundance of Greek inscriptions and copied many of them in his notes. In assessing the probability of correct geographical location he often made reference to the way the Septuagint, the third-century B.C.E. Greek translation of the Hebrew Bible, rendered the place-name. The centrality of philology in Robinson's method derived from his training at the University of Berlin. This training, combined with his American utilitarianism and a streak of New England stoicism, produced a formidable scholar-adventurer.

Merrill, who first visited Palestine seventeen years after Robinson's second journey, followed Robinson's route along many of the same "highways and byways." Merrill's whole life had prepared him for this initial three-month journey, which, like Robinson's, was short but had a momentous effect on Merrill's life. Like many an American seminary graduate of his day, Merrill was caught up in the romance of Holy Land exploration. Unlike many others, however, he persisted beyond the initial burst of enthusiasm and made the study of the Holy Land a lifelong endeavor. Much as mid-twentieth-century American Jewish students with a Zionist education might be led to visit modern Israel and, if of a scholarly bent, to devote their lives to study of the land, nineteenth-century Protestant students making an earlier version of that journey would dedicate themselves to biblical research and the affirmation of the "scriptural truth."

Merrill's Youth and Education

Selah Merrill's English ancestor Nathaniel settled in Newsburg, Massachusetts, in 1635. The family moved to Connecticut, where it supported itself through farming for much of the next two centuries. Selah was born on May 2, 1837, on his family's farm in Canton Centre, Connecticut. The farm, purchased from Native Americans, had been in the family for four generations, but after the death of Selah's father, Daniel Merrill, it passed out of the family.[12] Merrill's given name, the untranslatable word that marks the end of many Psalms, was an unusual but not unknown Puritan name. It has also been suggested the name "Selah" is the transliteration of the Hebrew word for "rock."

Of Merrill's childhood we know little; he was prepared for college at Williston Seminary in Massachusetts and entered Yale College in 1859.[13] He left his class the following October to enroll in New Haven Theological Seminary.[14] Though he left Yale College after only one year, he remained loyal to the institution throughout his life. When he was on leave in the United States he participated in Yale alumni activities, contributed articles to college publications, and kept up a steady correspondence with college officials.

It seems that the excitement generated by the impending Civil War, combined with his family's financial difficulties, led Merrill to choose the ministry as his vocation. At the New Haven seminary he concentrated on the study of biblical Hebrew. He completed his theological studies in 1863 and preached in a church in Chester, Massachusetts, for less than a year. In 1864 he was appointed chaplain of the 49th Regiment, U.S. "Colored Troops," stationed at Vicksburg, Mississippi, and remained in that post until the end of the war. The officers and clergy of these African American units, organized in 1862, were white. Unfortunately we have no record of Merrill's comments on his service in this unit. During the immediate postwar period Merrill was beset by tragedy. He was married in 1866 to Fanny Lucinda Cooke, who died the following year. In 1868 he married Phila Fargo, who died only two years later. For the next five years he remained alone and unmarried.

Following the Civil War Merrill spent three years in the ministry. After serving as the minister of Congregational churches in New York and San Francisco, his interests shifted from the ministry to the academy. Graduate education did not yet exist in the United States; students pursued advanced degrees in the great German universities. In the late 1860s Merrill spent two years at the University of Berlin, where he studied Near Eastern languages and the fledgling science of archaeology. But his training in Berlin was less than comprehensive. In 1869 a three-month vacation to Greece, Egypt, and Palestine supplemented his biblical education and decided his future. As the historian of his Yale class put it, "His special interest in Oriental Studies dates from this period."[15] Merrill was following a pattern set by fellow Americans: graduate study in Germany combined with travel in the Near East followed by an academic career in "oriental languages" or biblical studies.

Merrill's orientalist training in Germany and his subsequent journey to Palestine inspired him to explore further the biblical lands and follow in Edward Robinson's footsteps. But no opportunity for exploration afforded itself. Disappointed, he returned to the United States and again assumed the leadership of a Congregationalist church, this time in New Hampshire. He did not remain there long.

While serving in the ministry Merrill wrote articles for the emerging scholarly journals in biblical studies and archaeology. He was a fluid and engaging writer. Edward Robinson's influence is evident in these early pieces. Merrill's first articles appeared in *Bibliotheca Sacra*, the successor to *American Biblical Repository*, the journal founded by Robinson in the late 1830s. As N. A. Silberman has noted, the journal was conceived "as a counterweight to the numerous liberal periodicals" of the time. Merrill's articles ranged from surveys of recent Assyrian discoveries to detailed reports on some of the many artifacts and monuments brought to the United States by missionaries and biblical researchers.

In 1873 Merrill wrote to President Woolsey of Yale. Mentioning his progress in the study of Assyriology and Semitic studies, Merrill suggested a series of lectures on these topics at the various theological seminaries, and asked for Woolsey's help: "I would like to make these studies more of a specialty than I have yet been able to do. But I am not able to live without doing something—either preaching or teaching—which shall bring me an income. It may be in your way to introduce me, or mention my name in some school or seminary where they need a Hebrew teacher. I have felt that if I fitted myself for such work, or such a position, some place would open: which I hope will be the case."[16] We do not know if Woolsey responded. In any case, Merrill was not invited to teach at Yale.

Three years earlier, in 1870, a group of prominent academicians and clergymen had founded the American Palestine Exploration Society. It was modeled on its British namesake, the Palestine Exploration Fund. Though Merrill was not involved in founding the American organization, he soon became its most active and dedicated promoter, and through his books and articles he preserved the society's work for posterity.

In the 1920s, when Palestinian archaeology had been firmly established on a scientific basis, its dean, William F. Albright, acknowledged Merrill's pioneering contribution to the field, though his praise for Merrill was somewhat reserved. As Albright saw it Merrill had two flaws: his education did not prepare him for the task of mastering a new field, and his "strong prejudices" interfered with his scientific work. "Though he received the honorary degree of A.M. from Yale 'for special services in Biblical learning,' and spent two years (1868–70) at the University of Berlin, his lack of an adequate academic training was later to affect the value of his work very seriously." Albright felt that Merrill's lack of training manifested itself in his work for the American Palestine Exploration Society. "He possessed a respectable knowledge of the documentary and philological material, and indeed surpassed his English colleagues of the Palestine Exploration Fund in this respect. Had he been able to follow in the footsteps of Edward Robinson, the founder of the scientific study of Palestinian geography, and to combine a sound philological training with his New England endurance and practicality, his work might have been epoch-making." [17]

Merrill at Andover Theological Seminary

In the mid-1870s Merrill was employed as instructor in Hebrew at Andover Theological Seminary. Since the founding of the school by Eliphalet Pearson in 1809, Hebrew instruction had been one of the cornerstones of the Andover curriculum. Andover was established in opposition to Harvard's perceived liberalism, and its trustees insisted on perpetuating a text-oriented philological approach to Bible study. From 1827 to 1837, when Moses Stuart was the institution's professor of sacred literature, a Hebrew rule had been instituted, requiring all applicants to the seminary to demonstrate competence in Hebrew. Just as a reading knowledge of Latin and some knowledge of Greek had been prerequisites for admission into the New England colleges in the eighteenth century, Stuart intended to make Hebrew a prerequisite for theological studies at his institution.[18]

Merrill served in a distinguished line of teachers. Moses Stuart, Andover's first Hebraist, had been the dominant intellectual and theological voice at the seminary in the years between his appointment in 1812 and his death in 1847. Stuart's protégé, Edward Robinson, had served as instructor in Hebrew at Andover before his appointment at Union Theological Seminary in 1836. We have noted his central role in Palestine exploration. From 1852 to 1864 Calvin Stowe was the seminary's professor of sacred literature. His success as a teacher, not to mention his wife's fame (Harriet Beecher Stowe published *Uncle Tom's Cabin* in 1852), brought him considerable renown. Later in the century George Foot Moore would grace Andover's faculty before moving on to a distinguished career at Harvard.

When Merrill arrived at Andover in the late 1870s, Hebrew no longer held the same central place in the curriculum. The emphasis had shifted to systematic theology and to the employment of that theology in defense of the accuracy and historicity of the biblical text. In addition to his duties as instructor in Hebrew, Merrill founded and organized Andover's Biblical Museum, which he filled with artifacts that he brought back from Palestine. This museum housed a large collection of stuffed birds and animals and many Egyptian, Mesopotamian, and Palestinian artifacts, all in the tradition of the European "wonder cabinet." Merrill's cabinet, which illustrated the biblical world, was informed by the idea of the "unchanging East": By looking at the peoples and places of the Middle East of the nineteenth century, the contemporary viewer could see the Bible come alive.

Merrill's collection was large (over two hundred items) and unusual. The Biblical Museum grew considerably over the years; it would later become the focus of a bitter controversy between Andover and the Hartford Theological Seminary. Merrill had hoped to sell his collection for a considerable price and to find a permanent and distinguished home for it. While at Andover he wrote and published many articles on biblical research, broadly defined. In these articles he took particular delight in comparing the United States, with its newly found sense of itself as a world power, to the ancient Mesopotamian civilizations then being uncovered by his fellow archaeologists and biblical researchers.

While Merrill was at Andover his book *East of the Jordan* was published, first in London (1881) and later in New York (1883). Reviewers praised it for its readability and informativeness, and the book went into a number of printings in the United States and England. As a member of the seminary faculty Merrill aligned himself with the Andover Theology, and his conservative religious viewpoint later manifested itself strongly in Jerusalem. At Andover Merrill was a member of the Hebrew Club of Lowell, Massachusetts. Its members were Protestant clergymen and intellectuals who met on a regular basis to study biblical Hebrew and apprise themselves of the newest scholarly literature in the field. They were associated with William Rainey Harper's journal the *Hebrew Student*, which was published in the last two decades of the nineteenth century. Harper's journal published reports of Hebrew clubs around the nation. Many of the members had been participants in Harper's summer Hebrew schools, held near Chicago.

The academic life was neither active enough nor exciting enough for Merrill's temperament, so he cultivated ties to powerful figures in the Republican Party. With the election of Chester A. Arthur in 1882, Merrill was appointed U.S. consul in Jerusalem. Merrill's successor at Andover was George Foot Moore, who served as professor of Hebrew from 1883 until 1902, when he was appointed professor of the history of religion at Harvard. For almost a century the Andover Hebraists had a profound influence on the development of American biblical studies, on the development of American theological studies, and on the emergence of the comparative study of religion. Merrill's contribution to biblical and Near Eastern studies, though not of the depth or breadth of Stuart's, Robinson's, or Moore's, was nevertheless considerable.

Merrill was forty-five years old when he was appointed U.S. consul in Jerusalem. He had lobbied hard for the post and he must have seen his new position as the culmination of his life's efforts. His time in the ministry, where he had served in both civilian and military pastoral posts, was his first calling. His decision in his early thirties to pursue graduate education in Germany led to his 1869 sojourn in Egypt, Syria, and Palestine. This interlude led to another career, that of biblical researcher. His academic training, limited though it was, enabled him to join the American Palestine Exploration Society as its archaeologist. This second career, much of it carried out in Eastern Palestine, led to his third calling, instructor in Old Testament Hebrew. The combination of service in the ministry, biblical research in Palestine, and membership on the faculty of a prestigious Protestant seminary made Merrill a strong candidate for the Jerusalem post. He served three terms: 1882–85, 1891–94, and 1898–1907. During Democratic president Grover Cleveland's two nonconsecutive terms in office Merrill moved back to the United States and renewed his association with Andover Seminary.

After his appointment Merrill embarked on various research projects. Characteristically, he was soon caught up in controversy, and the "strong prejudices" to which Albright referred manifested themselves. In Jerusalem Merrill saw himself as arbiter of matters scholarly and academic, a general authority on history and archaeology, and host to visiting American and British scholars. Constantly traveling, he enlarged his collection of ancient and contemporary artifacts and of stuffed birds and animals. He was a keen observer of the natural world, recording many of his observations in journal articles. *Gazella merrelli*, a rare species of gazelle, was one of his many discoveries. An avid student of bird life, he published an important article on the birds of Palestine in A. M. Luncz's journal *Jerusalem*.

Possessed of considerable arrogance, Merrill often took the law into his own hands. The most flagrant demonstration of this propensity was his part in what was later dubbed the "War of the Graveyard." In Jerusalem Merrill was notorious for excavating any place that aroused his interest. One of the more sensitive spots that he chose was the American Protestant Cemetery on Mount Zion. In what strikes the modern reader as a bizarre act, Merrill's workers dug up the grave of Horatio Spafford, founder of the American Colony. As Merrill had been a fierce and vocal opponent of the colony during his first term in office, this unwitting desecration of the founder's grave had serious repercussions. The antagonisms that the incident aroused were to drag out for seventeen years and eventually lead to Merrill's removal from office. For the many members of the colony and their American supporters, Merrill was the enemy, a consul who could not be trusted, who might betray them to the Ottoman authorities and defame them in the presence of American visitors.

American visitors to Palestine naturally sought out Merrill when they arrived in the Holy City. Those with "acceptable" religious and educational affiliations were well received by him. All others were slighted. If a visitor expressed a positive interest in the American Colony and its activities, he or she was cut off from all further contact with the consulate. The scholarly, the wealthy, and the well connected were well received as long as they acquiesced to Merrill's ban on contact with the colonists and other "cranks."

Despite Merrill's campaign, the American Colony grew in size and prestige. In the 1890s its numbers were supplemented by a group of Swedish colonists. Among them was Selma Lagerloff, novelist (and Nobel laureate) who, after a short sojourn in Jerusalem, took up the case against Merrill.[19]

Merrill's Decline

Merrill's dispute with the American Colony, which began as soon as he reached Jerusalem in 1882, continued throughout his three terms as consul. Though his early accusations against the Americans did have the desired negative effect (they were denied consular representation and the opportunity to appeal for U.S. government help), with the passage of time American visitors and the public back home realized that the accusations were false and that the American colonists were exemplary Protestant ambassadors of good will.

Many Americans began to see the colonists as Christian martyrs persecuted by Merrill, a modern manifestation of a Roman consul. The children of the first group of colonists remembered Merrill as their parents' nemesis. As the dispute between the consul and the colonists went on for two decades, some of these children grew into adulthood never having met, but always having feared and resented, Selah Merrill. Anna Spafford Vester, daughter of the founders of the American Colony and author of the engaging memoir *Our Jerusalem*, refers to Merrill many times in her book, noting that his "resentment of Father and the American Colony tormented us for eighteen years."[20]

With the growth of American tourism to Palestine, American journalists began taking a lively interest in the Merrill–American Colony battle. Merrill was then, at the end of the nineteenth century and the first years of the twentieth, in his third term as consul. Visiting American journalist A. H. Ford called the colonists "an undaunted body of American citizens; a body that, with the hand of its own government repeatedly and inexplicably raised against it, has persevered to the end." The villain of Ford's article is clearly and immediately identified. It is none other than the American consul who has defamed the colonists for years. Their accuser, the American consul, "has not crossed the threshold of the little band he condemns, for more than a score of years . . . he stoutly maintains to all who will hear him that the American colony is the home of midnight orgies in which its founders, now white haired men and women who have passed their sixtieth and seventieth birthdays, still take an active part. . . . It had been said by the enemies of the American colony, as it was of the early church at Jerusalem, that the members lived in common, were adulterers, and forbad marriage."[21]

Accusations of sexual impropriety were commonly used against dissident Protestant sects in America; enemies of the colony were extending this smear technique to the Americans in Palestine. Merrill also disseminated an alternative and contradictory slander: the colonists were practicing celibacy. According to Bertha Spafford Vester, the basis for this claim lay in a decision by her parents, who had lost four children at sea, to have no other children.

> Some time after my parents came to Jerusalem, Father told Mother in private that he wanted to live Matthew 19:12, "and there are eunuchs which have made themselves eunuchs for the kingdom of heaven's sake." Nothing about this resolution was mentioned at the time to any of the other members of the Group. When, finally, Mother spoke of it to Mrs. Whiting, she found that the Whitings had made much the same choice.
>
> It was a solemn undertaking, a personal dedication which did not concern any except those who chose to live it. Celibacy was never meant to become a governing canon of the Group.
>
> Somehow this had leaked out. It was misinterpreted and degraded by our opponents.
>
> After Father died Dr. Merrill became less cautious in his attacks and accused us of forbidding marriage. There were no young people in the Colony at the time to get married, so we had no means of disputing this new charge. Mother went to Dr. Merrill to try to explain, saying that she believed if he knew it was false, he, being a Christian gentleman, would cease to repeat such statements. "Why don't you get married?" he demanded rudely.
>
> Mother's reply was that she still felt close to Father.
>
> Dr. Merrill's next accusation was that we were spiritualists who claimed communication with the dead![22]

In the United States the colonists' supporters rallied against Merrill and called for his removal from his post. It is also possible that his opposition to Jewish settlement had antagonized those few diplomats within the State Department who were sympathetic to Jewish causes. Foremost among these was Oscar Solomon Straus, who represented the United States in Ottoman Tur-

[*Scholars, Prophets, Mystics*]

key between 1887 and 1900. Though opposed to political Zionism, Straus was instrumental in circumventing some of the Ottoman restrictions on Jewish settlement in Palestine, and he was aware of Merrill's tacit support of those restrictions. Ford's article also contributed to Merrill's downfall. It was so sympathetic to the much-maligned American colonists and so damning of Merrill that, as Mrs. Vester said, "It caused many of our friends in America and the Holy Land to write to the State Department."

Merrill sparred with his opponents, but he had gone too far and was seriously ill. Cancer of the throat, which had long plagued him, advanced, and he lost the ability to speak. The American colonists considered his cruel illness an act of divine retribution. In 1907 he left his Jerusalem post and was assigned to the American consulate in Georgetown, British Guiana. He served as American consul there for a little over a year. In January 1909 he died in Oakland, California. His wife, Adelaide Brewster Taylor, survived him and endeavored to keep his memory alive and his works in print. In 1915 she presented his unique Josephus collection to Yale, and we can assume that she shepherded his *New Comprehensive Dictionary of the Bible* (1922) through publication.

Merrill's Legacy

In addition to the many books and articles he wrote, Merrill bequeathed to the scholarly world three enduring legacies. All have proved to be estimable resources for future researchers.

The Merrill Museum, his large collection of artifacts and natural history specimens from Palestine, was housed at Andover Theological Seminary for many years; much of this collection is now in the Harvard Semitic Museum. Merrill's widow donated the "impressively sizeable collections of 1500 volumes pertaining to Josephus" to the Yale library in 1915. This gift constituted the first large contribution to the Yale Judaica Collection. Later that same year George A. Kohut, a scholar mentioned earlier (Chapter 2) in regard to Judah Monis, presented his father's library to Yale. Together with the Merrill Josephus collection, these five thousand volumes became the cornerstone of Yale's great collection of Hebraica and Judaica. Finally, Merrill's collection of photos of Jerusalem and Palestine, presently in the Photographic Archives of the Israel Museum, preserve landscape and architectural details that have helped modern researchers construct an accurate portrait of nineteenth-century Jerusalem.

While the donation of the Josephus collection was a straightforward matter—the gift came six years after Merrill's death—the fate of the Merrill Museum proved more complicated. Its disposition was attended with contentiousness and rancor. During his first visit to Palestine, in 1869, Merrill had collected artifacts and samples of the local flora and fauna. In a report on "Birds and Animals New to Palestine," Merrill noted his archaeological experience and made reference to his "residence of nearly seven years in Palestine" and the opportunity afforded him to carefully observe and record the natural life of the country. He not only observed, he collected. In an autobiographical sketch written in 1905 Merrill claimed to have "the largest known collection of the fauna of Palestine."[23] This was not empty boasting on his part. Modern authorities concur: Only the collection of the British savant Henry Baker Tristram, author of *Fauna and Flora of Palestine* (London, 1884), rivaled Merrill's collection of Palestinian birds and animals.

After each of his stays in Palestine, first as archaeologist for the American Palestine Exploration Society and later after each of his terms as consul, Merrill shipped his artifacts and specimens back to the United States. At his home in Andover, Massachusetts, the collection grew, and he endeavored to make it a permanent part of the Andover Theological Seminary. Then instructor in Hebrew at the seminary, Merrill housed his growing collection in one of the school's lecture halls and in a nearby barn.

The Andover trustees assumed that the collection would some day legally belong to the seminary, but Merrill had other plans. Engaged by the officers of the Hartford Theological Seminary to deliver two lectures on his explorations east of the Jordan, Merrill went to Hartford, Connecticut, in February 1881. There, while delivering his lectures, he entered into negotiations with the Hartford trustees to sell his collection to them. They sent an expert to examine the artifacts, and within a few weeks Merrill received a $200 deposit from Hartford. By early March, however, he had returned the check. On the back he had scrawled: "I have not and will not have any interest in this. I will not receive it and I return it to the drawer." Accompanying the check was a short note that opened as follows: "I am pained and ashamed to be obliged to write about what I must." Merrill went on to explain that the Andover trustees had claimed their right to acquire the collection pursuant to an agreement concluded with him in 1877. "They regret that I have gone so far with you but positively refuse to release me. The disgrace of the unpleasant affair I must bear alone. And I hardly know how to face you in your disappointment."[24]

Unfortunately for Merrill, this "unpleasant affair" did not end with his returning the check to Hartford. A full year later, in February 1882, the boards of Andover and Hartford were still engaged in a dispute, which was carried out in a lengthy correspondence. In an eight-page letter the Hartford board recounted the yearlong history of the dispute and placed the blame on Merrill. Hartford had "instituted suit in the Court of Equity . . . to secure a fulfillment of the contract." But now the trustees decided to withdraw their suit "rather than endanger the fraternal relations and spiritual interests of both seminaries, and to avoid the damaging criticism which the enemies of religion are always ready to offer."[25] It seems that the dispute had come to the public's attention.

Soon afterwards, Merrill was on his way to Jerusalem to serve his first term as consul and thus avoided the unpleasantness surrounding this affair. The collection remained at Andover, but the seminary did not legally take possession of it. Seven years later, between his first and second terms as consul, Merrill continued to promote his museum and endeavored to find a permanent home for it. The Religious Outlook column of the *Boston Advertiser* noted that "probably few people who read this column are aware that within 20 miles of Boston can be found the most extensive collection of Palestinian antiquities that exists anywhere in the world, yet such is the fact. This collection is owned by Selah Merrill, D.D., L.L.D., the distinguished archaeologist, and is now kept in a building connected with his residence at Andover." Several enthusiastic paragraphs later the columnist concluded with Merrill's pitch for a purchaser who would both keep the collection intact and give it a permanent home. "Dr. Merrill has been importuned by many collectors of rare and curious specimens to sell separate articles. But he refuses nearly all such solicitations, tempting as some of them are. His idea is that the collection, substantially unbroken, should be secured for an oriental and sacred museum by some institution of learning, or better still, established in some proper building in a city like Boston, and made accessible to all who wish to avail themselves of its opportunities."[26] One wonders how the trustees of the Andover and Hartford seminaries reacted to this bit of self-promotion on Merrill's part.

Eventually the Merrill Museum found its way to Harvard. With the establishment of the Semitic Museum in 1902 (supported by Jewish philanthropist Jacob Schiff's donation), Merrill's collection found a permanent home. The items of biblical interest were stored in the Semitic Museum. Items illustrative of the natural life of nineteenth-century Palestine were kept in the Harvard Museum of Comparative Zoology.[27]

Conclusion

Consideration of Merrill's careers and writings raises questions about some of the basic assumptions about Christian Hebraism, Christian Zionism, and American support for, or hostility toward, Zionism. That Merrill, a Hebraist and biblical researcher, displayed antipathy to Jews should not surprise us. American Christian Hebraists, like their European counterparts, expressed a wide range of opinions on Jews and Judaism. When we look at the pronouncements of eighteenth- and nineteenth-century American Christian scholars who devoted themselves to Hebraic studies we find philo-Semites, such as Calvin Stowe; scholars who were ambivalent about the Jews, such as Yale's Ezra Stiles; and researchers such as Selah Merrill, who vilified the Jews of his day. Was Merrill hostile to the Jews he encountered in the United States? Was his hostility to Jews exacerbated by his contact with European Jewish immigrants to Palestine? I have found no specific reference to encounters between Merrill and American Jews. On the other hand, the harshness of his depiction of Palestine's Jews was extended to Jews the world over. In his 1891 report to the assistant secretary of state, he stated that "not only in Jerusalem, but in every other city of the world where Jews congregate they are clannish beyond any other people that claim to be civilized." They would not settle in farms in Palestine because "no amount of money or persuasion would induce Jews to settle in this manner, and were the proposition made to them it would be spurned with contempt. Rather than do this and be independent, a Jew would prefer a starvation existence in the filthiest quarter of New York, London or Jerusalem."[28]

Merrill—lifelong student of Hebrew and the Bible, instructor in Hebrew at Andover, and member of the Lowell, Massachusetts, Hebrew Club—displayed little tolerance for the Jews of his time and place. In this he was not alone. Many Christian students of Jewish texts and history disdained the Jews as a living people. Respect for the ancient Hebrew could go hand in hand with contempt for their descendants. As Frank Manuel observed, "The tendency of popular Jewish historiography to equate a knowledge of Hebrew with Judeophilia is based on an old misconception that goes back to those prominent Amsterdam rabbis who argued, like Manasseh ben Israel, that the fascination of the Hebrew language itself would lead to tolerance, respect and even affection."[29]

In a similar fashion, we have to treat with great caution the notion that Christian participation in Hebrew studies for biblical research led to support for Zionist aims. Just as the Hebraist Judeophilia misconception must be questioned, the extension of this notion to the idea that Hebraism implied support of Jewish restoration to Palestine must be examined. The complexity of the relationship between these tensions in American religious and political thought is well illustrated in the career of Selah Merrill.

A large literature has developed that ties together Anglo-American Hebraism and biblicism with British and American support for the Zionist idea. The most cogent and persuasive expression of this connection is Barbara Tuchman's *Bible and Sword: England and Palestine from the Bronze Age to Balfour*.[30] But as recent scholars have pointed out, Tuchman's argument is flawed and programmatic. Tuchman conveniently leaves out of her discussion many eminent Englishmen who vigorously opposed the very notion of Jewish restoration to Palestine. These include Thomas Fuller (1608–61), author of *A Pisgah Sight of Palestine*; the poet (and Hebraist) John Milton; and Richard Baxter, arguably "the greatest Presbyterian theologian in seventeenth-century Britain." As Nabil Matar put it in a recent issue of the *Journal of Palestine Studies*: "That twentieth-century scholars should deliberately ignore this criticism reveals the bias that has informed their search. Their scholarship has clearly been dominated by ideological expediency and not by intellectual integrity."[31] Matar, an advocate for Palestinian nationalism, has his own ideological agenda to promote. But his critique of Tuchman is valuable because it calls into question the assumption implicit in much historical writing about proto-Zionist ideas—the notion that interest in matters biblical and Hebraic predisposed scholars to support the idea of Jewish restoration to Palestine.

Merrill, despite his lifelong association with the Hebraic, displayed antipathy toward Jewish aspirations for full participation in the social and political arenas. He displayed contempt for the Jews of the large American and European cities, and he campaigned vigorously against plans for Jewish settlement in Palestine. There were other nineteenth-century American Protestant scholars who displayed antipathy toward the Jews as a people but who supported proto-Zionist ideals because these ideals mapped on to their religious expectations. As we have seen, Professor George Bush of New York University was one such scholar. But Merrill, conservative Congregationalist, disdained all restorationist ideology.[32]

Raphel Loewe noted in the late 1960s that "the history of gentile Hebrew scholarship cannot be properly written until the careers and achievements of its practitioners have been not only assessed but also correlated."[33] Chronicling Merrill's multifaceted career and placing his views within the context of nineteenth-century American religious and social thought has, I hope, illuminated the history of the enterprise of American Hebraism, a tradition with its roots in the Puritan intellectual tradition. In late-nineteenth- and early-twentieth-century America, this tradition would be transformed into the academic discipline of Semitic studies and would continue to affect the development of American Christian reactions to political Zionism. Here too Protestants and Jews would clash and interact in a creative manner. The concluding section of this book investigates the twentieth-century history of the relationship between Hebraism and Zionism.

III

CHRISTIAN ZIONISM,

THE JEWISH STATE, AND AMERICA'S

BIBLICAL BACKGROUND

TWENTIETH CENTURY

In Part III we take up the remarkable story of American Christian Zionism and its relationship to Christian Hebraism. In the late nineteenth and early twentieth centuries, political Zionism found its strongest support among American Jews. Zionist groups found powerful allies among members of the Protestant elites. Some churchmen, legislators, and scholars were drawn to the Zionist idea; others opposed it. Classical Hebraism and the attraction of biblical studies were factors that influenced both Zionism's detractors and its supporters.

In the following chapters the connections between Hebraism and Zionism are illustrated through biographical portraits of American scholars and religious leaders. These individuals represent the worlds of higher education, Protestant church leadership, and literary criticism.

As we saw in Part II, during the last decades of the nineteenth century interest in the newly rediscovered Holy Land was considerable. Books on Palestine archaeology were among the first American bestsellers. Protestant missionaries, at work in the Middle East since the early nineteenth century, forged strong ties with local Arab and Christian officials and other members of the educated elite. U.S. diplomats assigned to Middle Eastern cities developed parallel ties with local inhabitants. Missionaries, diplomats, and American visitors to the region worked together to establish educational institutions that would later have a profound effect on Middle Eastern elites. Among these institutions were Robert College in Istanbul, founded in 1863, and the American University in Beirut, founded as the Syrian Protestant College in 1866.

Many of these missionaries, diplomats, and "biblical researchers" viewed the peoples of the Middle East as the natural heirs to the cultural and religious traditions of the ancient Near East, a set of cultures that was undergoing rediscovery in the nineteenth and twentieth centuries. For some biblical researchers the Arabs of the Middle East generally, and the Arabs of Palestine more particularly, were the current representatives of the peoples of the Bible. In Part II we learned that Selah Merrill, U.S. consul in Jerusalem and biblical scholar, was a fierce opponent of Jewish settlement in Palestine. Other Americans were sympathetic to the Zionist cause. For them, the Jewish return or "Restoration to the Holy Land" was both the fulfillment of biblical prophecy and the logical conclusion to their understanding that the Jewish role in history was still unfolding. This loyalty to the emerging Zionist movement grew over the course of the late nineteenth and early twentieth centuries. Powerful personalities in twentieth-century American culture advanced competing ideas about the future of the Holy Land, and about the role the United States should take in influencing that future.

A figure who bridged the discourses of Puritan Hebraism and early political Zionism was Louis D. Brandeis (1856–1941). David Ben Gurion, acknowledging Brandeis's pivotal role in American Zionism, eulogized him in this manner: "Brandeis was the first Jew to be great both as an American, quite apart from what he did for the Jews, and great as a Jew, quite apart from what he did for America."[1] At Harvard Law School, which he entered at eighteen, and at the Boston law firm that he cofounded, Brandeis found himself far from the concerns of the American Jewish community. It was only in his fifties that he experienced a conversion to the Zionist cause, a cause for which he became a most articulate spokesman. "Zionism," Brandeis stated, "is the Pilgrim inspiration and impulse over again. The descendants of the Pilgrim fathers should not find it hard to understand and sympathize with it." When he was appointed to the Supreme Court in 1916 Brandeis relinquished his leadership roles in Zionist politics, but continued to support the movement in a less public manner. Brandeis's "conversion" to political Zionism at the beginning of the twentieth century serves to remind us that in the early years of political Zionism only a minority of American Jews supported that cause. Zionism drew its greatest strength from Russian and Polish Jews who came to the United States in the great immigration of 1880–1920. German and Sephardic Jews, the ancestors of whom arrived on these shores before the Civil War, were somewhat reluctant to join a nationalist cause that might compete with their sense of American identity. It took a full half century, from the First Zionist Congress of 1897 to the United Nations Partition of Palestine in 1947, for American Jewry to be fully drawn into the Zionist movement. During that

[*Christian Zionism and the Jewish State*]

same period many American Christians were also drawn to the Zionist cause. Some took direct action to facilitate the creation of a Jewish state in what they saw as the land holy to both Jews and Christians.

The leaders of a number of American Protestant denominations were engaged with the question of the fate of the Holy Land in the last years of the nineteenth century. "Details of the belief varied considerably, but the basic approach centered on the notion that the return of the Jews to power in the Holy Land was a sign from God that time was coming to an end. . . . Wars and rumors of wars, social turmoil and violence, corruption and growing materialism all combined to convince many that the dire predictions from the Revelation were true."[2]

A remarkable expression of American support for "the Restoration of the Jews to the Holy Land" was the Blackstone Memorial of March 1891. This petition, presented to President Harrison and signed by four hundred Americans prominent in government, business, and the academy, called for the restoration of the Jews to Palestine. "According to God's distribution of nations, it is their home, an inalienable possession, from which they were expelled by force."[3] An addendum in the middle of the petition notes that "several petitioners wish it stated that the Jews have not become agriculturalists because for centuries they were almost universally prohibited from owning or tilling land in the countries of their dispersion." Remarkably for its time, this letter to the president addressed the issue of political and religious differences within the Jewish community. "That while a very few, of what are termed ultra radical, reformed, Jewish Rabbis have renounced their belief in ancient Scriptures, and openly proclaim that the Jews should amalgamate with the various nations, wherein they are scattered, the great body of the Jews, both clergy and laity, still cling to their time honored hopes of national restoration and will quickly respond to any such opportunity with abundant energy, means, and enthusiasm."

William Blackstone, the author of the petition to President Harrison, was dismayed to learn that Theodore Herzl and many other Zionist leaders were secularists. He sent Herzl a copy of the Hebrew Bible with the passages concerning the Promised Land carefully marked. Herzl's Zionism may have been nationalist and modern; Blackstone's was deeply religious and premodern. A century later this conflict between Christian Zionists' idealized images of Israel and secular Israeli understandings of their modern state is still playing itself out.

Louis D. Brandeis understood that these tensions between religion and secularism had to be mediated for the Zionist cause to make inroads in the post–World War I United States. In 1916 he and Blackstone joined forces and authored a second Blackstone Memorial. A quarter-century after the first petition it reiterated and restated a particularly American understanding of the need for a Jewish state in Palestine.

The idea of a Jewish state in Palestine held a powerful attraction for American leaders. Brandeis helped to win President Wilson's support for Zionism, a cause bolstered by the Balfour Declaration of 1917, which Wilson supported. Twenty years later, when Brandeis was in his eighties, he met Senator Harry Truman and the two formed a close friendship. A decade after that, in the fall of 1947, Truman would be faced with a momentous set of decisions about U.S. engagement with that legacy of the British Mandate, "the Question of Palestine." Among the factors that affected Truman's decision to support the U.N. Partition Plan and recognize the state of Israel were his friendship with Jewish spokesmen and his biblically based belief that Israel, promised to the Hebrew people in the Bible, should be restored to them.[4]

While politicians, diplomats, and Protestant theologians were in the forefront of the debate over America's role in the Middle East, other American cultural figures were also engaged in these questions. William Rainey Harper (1865–1905), Reinhold Niebuhr (1892–1971), and Edmund Wilson (1895–1972) each thought deeply about the relationship between Hebraism, American culture, and the fate of the Jews in the modern world. These were pivotal figures in American religious, cultural, and literary life. Harper, founder and first president of the University of Chicago, started his academic career as professor of Hebrew and the Bible at Yale. He also founded the American Institute of Hebrew, which endeavored to teach Hebrew and biblical texts to thousands of American Protestants. The institute organized annual summer schools held throughout the United States during the 1880s and 1890s, long before any nationwide Jewish educational effort to teach Hebrew and the Bible.

Reinhold Niebuhr was one of the most influential Protestant theologians of the twentieth century. His concern for social justice for all Americans was linked to his understanding of the message of the Hebrew prophets. He wrote, "I have as a Christian theologian sought to strengthen the Hebraic-prophetic content of the Christian tradition."[5] Unlike many politically conservative Christians, Niebuhr's support for a Jewish state in Palestine was not based on eschatological expectations. Rather, his support for Zionism was thoroughly pragmatic and ethical. As the rise of Nazism threatened the Jews of Europe, Niebuhr asserted that America was ethically bound to establish a refuge for them. Some could immigrate to the United States, but the vast majority of refugees would need a state of their own. Niebuhr vigorously supported the emergence of a Jewish state. In 1967 the Hebrew University of

Jerusalem granted him an honorary doctorate in honor of his scholarly contributions to the study of theology and his efforts on behalf of the Jewish state.

The ceremony at which Niebuhr was granted his honorary degree was held in the context of the celebrations of the Israeli victory in the 1967 war. As one acute observer of Israeli-American relations has noted, "The Six-Day War had a dramatic effect on American evangelical attitudes towards Israel. . . . The dramatic and unexpected Israeli victory and the territorial gains it brought with it, strengthened the pre-millennialists' conviction that Israel was created for an important mission in history and was to play an important process that would precede the arrival of the Messiah."[6] This scripturally based apocalyptic ideology replaced to a great extent the more liberal pro-Israel sentiment espoused by Niebuhr and other progressive thinkers.

In contrast to Niebuhr's support of Zionism based on a liberal political and religious stance, much of current Christian Zionism is articulated by exponents of conservative ideologies and hearkens back to nineteenth-century dispensationalist ideas about the End Time. A careful reading of Niebuhr's stand on Israel indicates that his support for the Jewish state was not unconditional. Along with other mid-twentieth-century liberal supporters of Israel he called for recognition of the rights of the Palestinian refugees and a solution to the problems generated by their displacement. The refugee issue is not one that concern's the current Evangelical adherents of Christian Zionism, a group sometimes referred to as "Born again Zionists."

The cultural manifestations of Evangelical Christian Zionism have had a remarkable effect on American reading habits. Many observers have noted that among the greatest bestsellers of the last quarter of the twentieth century are books that promote a millennialist view of current events. Hal Lindsey's *The Late Great Planet Earth*, first published in 1970, has sold over ten million copies. It portrays the Israeli victory in the 1967 Arab-Israeli war as divinely ordained, and the two Cold War adversaries, the United States and the Soviet Union, as the Gog and Magog of biblical prophecy.

In the 1990s and the early years of the twenty-first century, the *Left Behind* series by Tim LaHaye and Jerry Jenkins has been an unparalleled publishing phenomenon. In some respects it fictionalizes Lindsey's millennial tract. Over fifty million copies of this series, now in its tenth volume, have been sold. The plot of each novel revolves around the events of the impending Rapture. Jewish and Israeli characters are central to the unfolding of these stories, and their actions replicate Evangelical understandings of the role of Jews in the events of the Final Days.

Literary critics of an earlier era would have been bemused and appalled by the popularity of these millennialist tracts in fictional form. Not that these critics neglected the biblical background of English and American literature. But they did hold readers and writers to high standards of language and structure. Edmund Wilson was, arguably, the most influential of twentieth-century literary critics. His biographical portrait is the closing chapter in *God's Sacred Tongue*. He admitted to a "lifelong romance" with the Hebrew language and its literary influence. For Wilson, unlike Harper, the value of Hebrew was not limited to its usefulness as a guide to interpreting the Bible. Wilson sought out the Hebraic underpinnings of much of English poetry and prose, and in his later years took up the study of the Dead Sea Scrolls. His book on the subject, based on his popular *New Yorker* articles; became an American best seller. His Hebraic interests occasioned two journeys to Israel, both of which are chronicled in his literary essays. In Israel he met with S. Y. Agnon, Nobel Prize–winning novelist and the dean of Israeli writers. As a sort of "Secular Christian Hebraist," Wilson's life and work exemplify the centuries-old ties between the United States, Land of Promise, and Israel, Promised Land. The Hebrew Bible/Old Testament, a text for which the American people have such a remarkable affinity, was a central document in the lives of the theologian Reinhold Niebuhr and the biblical scholar William Rainey Harper. This should not surprise us. That an affinity for Hebrew scripture can illuminate the life and writings of Edmund Wilson, arch secularist, may come as something of a surprise.

12

THE UNIVERSITY AS MESSIAH

WILLIAM RAINEY HARPER AS
HEBRAIST, EDUCATIONAL REFORMER,
AND VISIONARY

The Hebrew Scriptures had never been far from the consciousness of Americans
who had interpreted their reality with Old Testament images.
J. P. Wind

Scripture and Higher Education

"The most serious blunder in American education of the last half-century was ignoring the Bible in higher education." These are not the words of a late-twentieth-century cultural conservative bemoaning the disappearance of "traditional values" among America's youth. William Rainey Harper, newly appointed professor of Bible in English at Yale University, penned these sentiments over a century ago, and the decades he was referring to were those of the mid-nineteenth century. In 1890, at age thirty-four, Harper became the first incumbent in this new post. For the preceding five years he had taught Semitic languages at Yale. His courses included offerings in Hebrew, Arabic, Assyrian, and Aramaic. In these language courses, he focused constantly on philology as the key to unlocking the multiple meanings of the sacred texts. Harper's ability to "bring the ancient texts to life" and provoke and inspire his students made these courses among the most popular classes at the university. His success as a language and text teacher encouraged the Yale administration to widen his responsibilities to include the teaching of the Bible in English. Harper responded by presenting the Bible as a literary and historical anthology, one with a unique appeal to American audiences.

Thus Harper's 1890 call to return the Bible to the curriculum was not the call of a moralist bemoaning the decline of values. He was operating within an American Protestant context in which Bible study was understood to be ennobling and edifying, but Protestant edification was not his stated purpose.

William Rainey Harper (From
Thomas Goodspeed, William
Rainey Harper: First President
of the University of Chicago
[Chicago: University of Chicago
Press, 1928])

His educational plan was much more expansive. He chose to work by indirec-
tion; his courses were part of a grand, national vision, which he first articulated
in his early years at Yale. In its initial stages this vision included a "Hebrew
revolution"—a plan to teach the Hebrew language to millions of American
Christians. Later, the plan would expand to include both the teaching of the
Bible as literature and the establishment of the Bible as a reference point for
a particularly American understanding of history. In its final form, Harper's
educational master plan subsumed all cultural topics in a biblical worldview.[1]

On the way to fulfilling his vision, Harper and his backers, foremost among
them John D. Rockefeller, created some remarkable American institutions,
including the University of Chicago and the Hebrew and biblical lectures
at the Chautauqua Summer Schools. In the mid-1880s an average of three
hundred students studied Hebrew each summer under Harper's direction. As
his activities expanded, he influenced, both directly and indirectly, tens of
thousands of Americans. Many of his students were ministers and lay leaders
in mainstream Protestant denominations, and they transmitted Harper's enthusiasm and teaching methods to their parishioners and co-religionists. Just
as Moses Stuart of Andover Theological Seminary had influenced American churchgoers a half-century earlier through the hundreds of missionaries

[*Christian Zionism and the Jewish State*]

he trained, Harper endeavored—and eventually succeeded—in influencing far greater numbers of American Protestants through his adult education classes. His first and most beloved subjects were Hebrew and the Bible, but he would develop lectures and a curriculum that encompassed all of emerging American culture. As at Harvard and Yale, the University of Chicago too would be shaped by a Christian Hebraist with a far-reaching educational vision crafted to fit a culture in formation.

Many of the subjects of our earlier chapters, such as Ezra Stiles (Chapter 3), were Christian Hebraists whose Hebrew teaching stemmed from their exegetical and theological projects. They were "clergyman educators." Harper was different. He was the product of a more scientific and literary approach to Hebrew and the Bible. Though he was not an ordained minister, his social and educational ideas were nevertheless deeply religious. He sensed that American higher education would benefit from his transformative vision.

In his personal life Harper was a deeply religious man, and his adoption of the Baptist faith will occupy us later in this chapter. But in his crusades—and crusades they were—to reform American education he chose to cast his net widely, appealing at first to all of Protestant America regardless of denomination or doctrinal affiliation. Later, he would direct his crusades even more broadly toward all Americans, regardless of religious background, tradition, or affiliation.

On a number of levels Harper was a mediating and transitional figure. He mediated between two tendencies in biblical studies: the Reformation project to read the Greek and Hebrew biblical texts with honesty and rigor, unencumbered by the theological encrustation of centuries of Scholasticism and dogma ("to drink from the pure fountain," in Luther's metaphor), and the scientific, philological approach pioneered by German Protestant biblical scholars of the generation that preceded Harper's. He was, in a sense, mediating between religious belief and scientific skepticism about the claims of Scripture. By Harper's time the crisis of belief occasioned by nineteenth-century science had become acute. Geology and its challenge to the biblical account of the age of the earth were followed by the challenge of the developing theory of evolution. In 1830 Lyell published his pioneering work on geology and the age of the earth's crust; in 1859 Darwin published *The Origin of the Species*. That Charles Darwin had begun his scholarly-intellectual life as a seminary student renders the story of the Western crisis of belief all the more dramatic and Bible-centered.

One response to the emerging conflict between religion and science was to construct a "scientific" approach to the study of the Bible that would shore up the foundations of Christian belief. Several possible methods evolved, including the use of recently discovered "ancient monuments" of the Near

East as evidence to buttress claims of biblical accuracy, and the employment of recently deciphered ancient Near Eastern languages to "demonstrate the biblical truth." Another "scientific" approach later called source criticism developed from earlier European readings of ancient texts—the model being eighteenth-century analyses of the Homeric epics. Each of these methods, however, proved to be a double-edge sword. For the very same material or textural-epigraphic evidence used to "prove" the accuracy of the Bible could also be used to challenge the veracity and historicity of the biblical narrative. No simple solution presented itself.

For Harper the work of biblical interpretation could begin only after one had mastered both the extrabiblical material and the modern investigative scientific method. As he saw it the aspiring Bible student should first study Hebrew and its cognate languages. "Next, the history of the biblical material should be carefully investigated. Finally each particular section of scripture had to be viewed as a piece of literature and compared with other similar types of literature."[2] In retrospect we may situate Harper as an American pioneer of the comparative method. This is true not only in regard to the study of the Bible, but also in regard to the study of the sacred texts of other traditions. Harper's approach, which stemmed from his philological training, included the classical languages, the Semitic languages, and Sanskrit, all of which he had studied at Yale with William Dwight Whitney. Harper had presented his Ph.D. thesis, "A Comparative Study of the Prepositions in Latin, Greek, Sanskrit, and Gothic," which he wrote under Whitney's supervision, when he was but nineteen years old. The comparative method, with a philological underpinning, would inform all of Harper's work to come.

The development of comparative religion as a discipline emerged at the University of Chicago under Harper's stewardship. Harper appointed G. S. Goodspeed as head of comparative religion at the Divinity School—the first comparative religion appointment in the United States. In 1902 Harvard followed suit and appointed George Foot Moore. As the University of Chicago's Joseph Kitagawa noted in the 1950s, the study of the history of religions originated in the philological method. "The key to the scientific investigations of religions was philology." The great nineteenth-century scholar of Indian religions, Max Muller, had pioneered the interpretation of philological method and a comparative approach to the study of religion.

A Biblical Worldview

Harper's criticisms of American education were not limited to the curricula of American colleges. He also scrutinized the curricula of the Protestant seminaries. From Harper's vantage point real biblical knowledge had been crowded out of the seminary curriculum. He sarcastically prophesied that the day was coming when seminary graduates would have to know something of the Bible.

In 1891, only one year after the expansion of his teaching responsibilities at Yale, Harper accepted the presidency of the new University of Chicago. To the Baptist leaders of the university committee (and to John D. Rockefeller, who funded the effort and eagerly sought Harper's appointment), he made clear that "there should be entire freedom of teaching and investigation both for himself and the university." More specifically, Harper insisted that there be no doctrinal limits on the teaching of the Bible. Faculty members would not have to sign a statement affirming their adherence to a body of Christian doctrine, a practice then in place in many institutions of higher learning. For Harper, then only thirty-five years old, the presidency of a new university was an opportunity to combine all of his interests. As one astute observer of the history of American education noted: "The University of Chicago became Harper's chosen vehicle for continuing his effort to develop a new biblical world for moderns. In his new institution in Hyde Park Harper strove to unite all his programs into a larger whole, one that could lift a nation to the higher life."[3]

J. P. Wind noted that "Harper turned to the Hebrew Scriptures for his basic construction of reality." By the mid-nineteenth century a Hebraic construction of American religious history was no longer in fashion. As we have seen in the publishing and teaching careers of earlier American Christian Hebraists, Harper's vision was not original, and he would have been the last to make such a claim. In the years between Moses Stuart's death and Harper's ascendancy to the presidency of Chicago, many educators had called for a return to a biblically based educational system. Harper echoed this call for the renewal of an earlier American idea, refashioned to encompass traditions of free inquiry. By the late nineteenth century, theological education was identified with reaction, narrow mindedness, and antiscientific thought. Harper sought to change all that.

Harper claimed in 1886 that "the Bible does not occupy the place in the theological curriculum which it deserves." If Harper's critique of American seminaries was accurate, what then did occupy the time of most seminary students? If they did not study the Bible, what did they study? For it was the seminaries that Harper first sought to reform—after he had moved from Morgan Park Seminary in Chicago to teaching Hebrew and the Bible at Yale. The classical Protestant seminary model, the origins of which lie in eighteenth-century Germany, was organized around a "theological encyclopedia" with a four-fold curriculum: sacred literature, Christian theology, ecclesiastical history, and sacred rhetoric.[4] Many seminaries emphasized theology and rhetoric at the expense of the other two areas. Harper and other critics called specifically for a renewed emphasis on sacred literature, to which seminary students should devote at least half of their time. The study of Hebrew was essential to this reformist effort. But Harper did not intend merely to place all seminary students in Hebrew reading classes. He wanted incoming students to have a reading knowledge of Hebrew before seeking admission to seminaries. They could then embark immediately on the study of the biblical text in its original language.

Harper was not the first American educational reformer to suggest this. Moses Stuart, professor of sacred literature at Andover Theological Seminary (founded in 1809), had first instituted the "Hebrew rule" at that large and influential seminary in the years between 1827 and 1837. In an earlier chapter we saw how Stuart's student Edward Robinson further revived Hebrew Studies. By transmitting the scientific approach of German scholarship to the American academy he increased the prestige of philologically rigorous study. Then, not content merely to master the textual apparatus, Robinson embarked on his mid-nineteenth-century "biblical researches," which led him to Palestine.

By the end of the nineteenth century, Harper was building on Robinson's pioneering work and pushing beyond the realm of philology. His earlier calls for educational reform had begun to draw a wide response. Hebrew language study was again made compulsory in most seminaries, and in many of those seminaries a quarter of the students' time was spent studying the Old Testament text in its original languages—Hebrew and Aramaic. Reform of American theological education was so successful that a decade later Harper, now at the helm of the University of Chicago, modified his earlier view and called for less emphasis on Hebrew study. In his new view too much time was being spent on philology, and not enough on an overall view of the Bible's development and interpretation. He feared that the theological seminaries were not preparing students adequately for the ministry, and that graduates lacked knowledge of biblical thought.[5] But then not all students had Harper's training. His course of Hebrew study had begun when he was ten years old and a student at the town school in New Concord, Ohio.

Harper's Youth and Education

An intellectually precocious child, Harper entered Muskingum College, in his hometown of New Concord, Ohio, at the age of ten. In this small school, established by the local Presbyterian laity, he excelled in all subjects, especially in the study of ancient languages. When he graduated at age fourteen he delivered a Hebrew oration at the commencement ceremonies. These ceremonies were in emulation of colonial-era college orations in the "learned lan-

[*Christian Zionism and the Jewish State*]

guages"—Latin, Greek, and Hebrew. Though the fiction that the audience understood these orations was maintained, and no translation or paraphrase of the orations was provided, it is doubtful whether anyone but Harper and his Old Testament teacher understood the contents of this Hebrew language speech.[6]

William Harper was a decade younger than the other students in his college class, and his parents were both proud of and concerned about their son. Samuel Harper, William's father, owned a dry goods store in New Concord. On his son's graduation day he noted in his diary, "I attended store and commencement. Willie graduated. It was a very solemn matter to me. Think of having a son to graduate before he was fourteen years old."[7] Following graduation the young Harper worked in his father's store, devoting his spare time and his considerable artistic and intellectual energies to two pursuits— organizing and performing in the local marching band, and continuing to study the Hebrew language.

After two years at the family store Harper eagerly accepted an offer to teach Hebrew at his alma mater. During the two years that he taught at Muskingum College, he developed "the inductive method that later made him famous."[8] The original text of the Bible served as the textbook for both teacher and student. Harper did not advocate using a manual of grammar, though later in his career he would write a series of such Hebrew grammars. Rules of grammar and syntax could be derived from the text, rather than imposed on it; the student would concentrate on analyzing the structure of each verse, not on memorizing verb paradigms. Harper's inductive method was to prove successful in both the public education and university spheres. It focused attention on the primary texts, the Hebrew Old Testament and the Greek New Testament. Harper expected his students to master both the content and the form of the text, absorbing its message and its structure. Those enrolled in the American Institute of Hebrew, or in one of Harper's university courses, received both a philological education and a religious education. The point of the philological exercises was to make the meaning of sacred scripture clearer.

Young William's success as a teacher convinced his parents that he should continue his education. From 1873 to 1875 he studied as a graduate student at Yale College. He received his Ph.D. there in 1875, at age nineteen. Harper's mentor at Yale, as we have seen, was William Dwight Whitney, whose specialty was Sanskrit language and texts, particularly the Vedas. As historian Bruce Kuklick has noted, Whitney and his student Harper "put American training in ancient languages on a level with that of Europe." With Whitney, Harper and his few fellow students read widely in the religious literature of the ancient world. This included a seminar in the Rig Veda. A series of teaching appointments followed: at Denison University in Ohio, at the Baptist Union

Theological Seminary in Chicago, and—after a decade of distinguished and innovative teaching—at Yale in 1886. During this period from 1875 to 1886 Harper also founded the American Institute of Hebrew, an organization devoted to the promotion of the Bible and the study of the Hebrew language through summer schools, correspondence courses, and adult education lectures. Under the auspices of the institute Harper launched—and edited—two journals: the *Hebrew Student*, (later renamed the *Biblical World*) and *Hebraica* (later renamed the *American Journal of Semitic Languages and Literatures*). In other later incarnations, both of these journals—one published as the *Journal of Religion* and the other as the *Journal of Near Eastern Studies*—would accrue great prestige in the American academy. At the end of the twentieth century these journals were among the premiere scholarly journals in their respective fields.

Harper, the Institute of Hebrew, and American Jewry

In the inaugural issue of *Hebraica: A Quarterly Journal in the Interests of Hebrew Study* (March–April 1884), Harper identified the audience he had in mind for this new journal. Bemoaning the state of Hebrew studies in the United States, he called on scholars, Protestant clergyman, and the educated laity to teach the Bible, Hebrew, and its cognate languages in seminaries and colleges. Harper noted that though Hebrew was taught in the nation's divinity schools, "the time of both instructor and student is occupied largely in the discussion of questions strictly theological. Discussions of a philological nature are neither required, nor expected." This situation, said Harper, must change. He urged American professors of the Bible to engage textual and linguistic issues and enter into "the literary and philological fields." For Harper the challenges to belief offered by geology and the theory of evolution could only be countered by a discourse that was equally scientific, the discourse of philology and textual analysis. This is a theme we encountered in earlier chapters, particularly with regard to Edward Robinson and his circle.

As for members of the Protestant clergy: "That Christian ministers ought to know Hebrew, is a generally accepted truth. . . . *Hebraica* will endeavor to interest these ministers more deeply in the study of Hebrew. . . . It will aim toward a better understanding of the principles and structures of that language in which is written three-fourths of God's revelation to man." That the other fourth, the Greek New Testament, would also be studied, was a given. Students in all Protestant Seminaries studied New Testament Greek, but Hebrew and the Old Testament, in Harper's view, were still somewhat neglected.

For the Jewish reader of Harper's time, this Christian call to Hebrew study was somewhat problematic. Was Harper purposefully avoiding mention of Jewish readership and participation? Or was their participation deemed improbable, if not impossible? Later, there would be some Reform Jewish involvement in Harper's multifaceted Hebraic efforts, but in the early volumes of *Hebraica*, the tone and content was thoroughly Protestant. The journal evaded and avoided the Jewish connection to the Hebrew language.

A curious exception, and one that strikes today's reader as quite humorous, is William Sproul's "Hebrew and Rabbinical Words in Present Use" (*Hebraica* 7, no. 7 [Oct. 1890]). Sproul, who taught Hebrew at the University of Cincinnati, opens his article in this way: "We shall give a few of the most common Hebrew and rabbinical words with some of their meanings in present colloquial use among the English-German speaking Jews." The forty words that follow are, in reality, Hebraisms that appear in Yiddish speech. Sproul's "translations" of these Hebraisms are imprecise at best—and some are quite amusing. While the first item *apikorus* may connote "one who does not care for religion," the second item *behamah* means "a stupid person" in colloquial Yiddish only (the Hebrew means "animal"). *Goy* and *Gonif* follow. This odd list closes with *Shiksah* "a gentile servant girl," and *Beitzmer* "meaning an Irishman," an appellation that Professor Sproul derives from the Hebrew for egg and its "suggestion of sound" that ties it to the Yiddish "eye"—the first syllable of Irish! As we can see this was not a scholarly article and is the only one in the journal on contemporary Jewish uses of Hebrew.[9]

In its second year *Hebraica* published a Hebrew-language Christian prayer with which a teacher could open a Hebrew classroom session. It seems that during its first year Harper's Hebrew Summer School classes opened with an English-language prayer. One of the lecturers suggested "that it might stimulate some of the students to the more earnest study of the Holy tongue if he should offer the usual opening prayer in Hebrew." The prayer that followed was a rendering of the Lord's Prayer in rabbinic Hebrew. It opened with an invocation of the Trinity and a quotation of the Sanctus, the prayer Jews would know as the Kedusha.[10]

Hebraica, in its early issues, took no cognizance of Jewish readers. It was not afraid of offending their sensibilities; it simply ignored them. *Hebraica* had Jewish contributors and readers, but their presence as contributing writers and readers was never acknowledged, at least not directly. This situation recalls the idea, developed in John Murray Cuddihy's *The Ordeal of Civility*, of Jewish entrance into European modernity. While nineteenth-century American Jews participated in, and often actively supported, American cultural and religious efforts, they kept a low profile and did not trumpet their support for cultural and educational causes.[11] It is only in the twentieth century that American Jewish intellectuals, offering a secularized form of the Jewish tradition, became full partners in the nation's cultural life.

Some articles and reviews were overtly hostile to Jewish traditions of Hebrew study and biblical interpretation. In "The Divine Name Adonai and Its History," a review of Gustav Dalman's German-language work of that name, Philip Nordell presents Dalman's main points and then moves to attack Jewish understandings of the divine names in the Hebrew Bible. In a discussion of the traditional Jewish reluctance to pronounce the divine names, Nordell, following Dalman, offers a number of explanations. He concludes his summation of Dalman's work in this way: "The Jewish dread of pronouncing the name *Yahweh*—is traceable to that extraordinary degeneracy of the Mosaic religion into rabbinical Judaism which annihilated the free and lofty spirit of the Law beneath a grinding bondage of the letter."[12]

An assertion like Nordell's would not be surprising or remarkable in a Christian anti-Judaic polemic of earlier centuries. Along with Hebrew-language renditions of Christian prayers (like the prayer that appeared in *Hebraica*), such condemnations of Judaism were commonplace in Christian Hebraist anti-Judaic polemics. But the appearance of such a statement in a late-nineteenth-century American journal devoted to the "scientific" study of Hebrew—a journal which in fact published articles by a small but significant number of prominent Jewish academicians—demonstrates that the old Christian ideas about the Jews and the Bible were not yet dead. There were still some Christian exegetes who searched Jewish texts for philological tools that guaranteed "correct" readings of the biblical text. Then, utilizing those tools, they would denigrate the Jewish tradition.

Harper's Rabbis

In 1891 Rabbi Emil G. Hirsch of Chicago joined the editorial board of *Hebraica*. In the seven years since the journal's founding, years in which Harper had moved from Yale to the University of Chicago, Harper had worked steadily to restrain the remarks of his journal's more anti-Judaic contributors. For this restraint there were both practical and moral reasons. Chicago's Reform Jewish community, with Rabbi Emil Hirsch as its leader, played a pivotal role in gaining John D. Rockefeller's assent to fund the establishment of the renewed University of Chicago. Rockefeller agreed to a matching grant of $600,000 if Chicago businessmen contributed $400,000; with Rabbi Hirsch's help this money was raised from among the wealthy members of Chicago's

Reform Jewish community—among them Julius Rosenwald, the founder of Sears, Roebuck. When Harper set about organizing the university, he appointed Hirsch to the faculty, as professor of rabbinic literature and philosophy. Rabbi Hirsch had considerable influence on Harper, as did other figures in American Reform Judaism.

Earlier in this chapter I described Harper as a transitional figure, particularly with regard to his ability to mediate between the older, more dogmatic approach to biblical interpretation and the newer, scientific and literary approach to reading Scripture. But Harper was also a transitional figure in the larger arena of American culture. He propelled the shift in higher education from the American notion of the local college devoted to undergraduate education to the German model of the university—an institution that offered graduate and professional training while maintaining its commitment to an undergraduate education anchored in the liberal arts. Some American colleges—Harvard and Johns Hopkins among them—were moving in this direction, but Harper at Chicago would create a university ex nihilo, rather than expand a college to create one.

Harper also proved to be a catalyst in the emerging American sphere of improved Christian-Jewish relations. He hired Jewish professors and admitted Jewish students to the newly founded university. *Hebraica* and his other journals featured articles by Jewish scholars. This shift from Protestant exclusivism to greater openness was subtle, not dramatic. Major figures in American Reform Judaism quietly associated themselves with the university and with his journals. Besides Emil Hirsch, other Jewish authors who contributed to *Hebraica* included Richard Gottheil, Columbia University professor of Semitic languages, and Marcus Jastrow of the University of Pennsylvania.

In the fifth volume of *Hebraica*, Rabbi Kaufman Kohler of New York City favorably reviewed Jastrow's magnum opus, *A Dictionary of the Targumim, the Talmud, and Midrash Literature*. Kohler along with Emil Hirsch and his fellow clergyman Bernard Felsenthal were Reform rabbis and scholars who saw good reasons to contribute to Harper's journals—despite the manifest Christian tone of those journals. In Rabbi Felsenthal's 1893 review of Alexander Kohut's *Arukh Completum* (an amplification and expansion of the great twelfth-century Talmudic lexicon of Rabbi Nathan of Rome), he calls the work "epoch-making, one of the foremost works in Semitic lexicography. . . . It is a great work." Felsenthal's detailed and laudatory review provides a short history of Talmudic lexicography, before ending with a sentiment new to the pages of William Rainey Harper's journal. For Felsenthal takes pride in the author's Jewish origin and his use of Masoretic traditions of scholarship. He hopes that the new lexicon will "contribute toward stimulating a love for a branch of study, which, after all, has had thus far not many devotees, and which has been thus far almost exclusively fostered and cultivated by Jewish students."[13]

The Chicago rabbis who joined Harper in his Hebraic efforts were affiliated with the more radical wing of American Reform Judaism. As rabbi of Temple Sinai, Hirsch called for the addition of Sunday worship to the traditional Jewish Saturday services, and this was put into practice in his congregation. From 1874 to 1887 both Saturday and Sunday worship services were offered; from 1887 onward, only Sundays were observed.[14]

Rabbi Bernard Felsenthal, like Hirsch, was trained in Germany and came to the United States in his thirties. Felsenthal had preceded Hirsch as the rabbi of Chicago's Temple Sinai. He too wrote articles and book reviews for Harper's journals. Already a senior scholar and rabbi by the time Hirsch and Harper rose to prominence, Felsenthal lent the journal his prestige and its pages benefited from his considerable erudition. Like Emil Hirsch he was a proponent of Radical Reform. "He maintained that the Bible was the product and not the source of Judaism, and he emphasized the right of the individual and of the congregation to autonomy in religious affairs."[15]

Both Hirsch and Felsenthal had been students and followers of David Einhorn, "the first ideologue of European radical Reform Judaism in America." Hirsch, whose father Samuel Hirsch had also been an eminent Reform rabbi, envisioned an American Judaism that would be "a religion of reason." Forging alliances with Christian clergyman was important to him as a means to effect social change. As a nineteenth-century liberal social reformer Hirsch was an advocate of progressive social change, though he steered clear of socialist ideas. In his authoritative history of Reform Judaism, Michael Meyer noted that "Hirsch regularly took stands and participated in projects with local non Jewish social and economic reformers." Social justice was at the core of Hirsch's understanding of Reform Judaism, and it was he who wrote the famous concluding paragraph of the Reform movement's Pittsburgh Platform of 1885: "It is a Jewish obligation to participate in the great task of modern times, to solve on the basis of justice and righteousness the problems presented by the contrasts and evils of the present organization of society." Meyer again noted that "had Emil G. Hirsch not insisted at Pittsburgh that his colleagues take note of contemporary social injustice, it is unlikely they would have done so."[16]

Emil Hirsch recognized in William Rainey Harper a fellow social reformer. He was the rabbi whom Harper chose as the first Jewish representative on Chicago's faculty, and as a coeditor of *Hebraica*. David Einhorn Hirsch, Emil Hirsch's son, situated his father's social justice advocacy in the context of American religious history: "What Graham Taylor and Jane Addams did within the churches of Christendom, Hirsch did for the Synagogue of Israel. He reaffirmed its moral theses. He restressed with thunderous power its ethical imperatives."[17]

Under Hirsch's coeditorship more articles by Jewish savants and more articles on Jewish topics began to appear in the journal. The great Hungarian Jewish scholar Wilhelm Bacher, who was one of the first European scholars to engage in the scientific study of Aggadah and midrash, contributed an article on "The views of Jehuda Halevi concerning the Hebrew Language." Bacher surveyed the wider subject of Jewish attitudes toward the antiquity and sacred character of Hebrew; it provided readers of *Hebraica* with a first glimpse into the Jewish scholarly relationship to the Hebrew language.[18]

Throughout Harper's Hebraic work—and especially in the pages of *Hebraica*—the Masoretic text of the Old Testament was the constant point of reference. Harper's method of study called for mastery of both the vocalized text and its Masoretic apparatus: "To one who has not practiced reading the unpointed text, the work may seem unimportant, and the results of small consequence. There is, however, no better way of teaching Hebrew grammar, no better way of teaching the language, than to require of the student the pronunciation of the Masoretic text with only the unpointed text before his eyes."[19]

Whether he was aware of it or not, Harper was emulating the traditional Jewish system for learning to chant the weekly Torah portion in the synagogue. In that system the student first learns the text and its Masoretic apparatus from the printed page. Only then does he or she proceed to read the unpointed text of the Torah scroll—pronouncing it as it is pronounced in the reading of the Masorah.

Despite these references to Jewish traditions and gestures toward Jewish participation in university life, Harper's view of his great project was assertively Christian. At the 1902 tenth anniversary celebration of the founding of the University of Chicago, Harper stated:

The position of the University of Chicago religiously has been definitely and professedly Christian. Any other attitude would have been false to the auspices under which the institution was established, and particularly to the hopes and desires of its founder. It is not forgotten that in the earliest days, when there was great question whether the first four hundred thousand dollars could be secured, the Jews of Chicago came forward, and by their splendid gift made the effort successful. A representative of the Jews has been on the Board of Trustees, several Jews are members of Faculties, large numbers of Jews have been matriculated as students; but in the large and true sense of the word "Christian" the University has maintained urgently and strongly its professed position as Christian. The various Faculties have contained members of almost every communion, and many who were not members of any church. The question of the religious faith of an officer has not been raised by the Trustees in connection with the appointment of any officer of the University. No one, so far as I am aware, has ever taken the trouble to make a calculation of the representation of the various denominations either in the Faculty or among the students. As the country of which we are citizens is a Christian country, so the University of Chicago is a Christian institution. The drawing of a narrower line than this would be fatal to the growth of the University. Here lies the distinction between a college and a university. The one may be controlled by the ecclesiastical or political spirit; the other may not be.[20]

Harper's Intellectual Legacy

Harper died in 1905 at the age of forty-nine. He led and shaped the University of Chicago until the day of his death. His mission—to establish a great American university—was eminently successful and it established one model for American graduate education.

Scholars of the history of American higher education have debated the question of Harper's relevance to the development of American education in the twentieth century. Some prominent historians of American education see Harper as a pivotal figure. Others minimize Harper's relevance. There is greater consensus about Harper's contributions to the teaching of Hebrew and the study of the Bible in English. Harper's Hebrew institutes and schools reawakened an American interest in that language, and, for the first two decades of the twentieth century, those institutions satisfied that interest. Harper's Hebrew textbooks, and the inductive method they promoted, had a longer life than his journals and institutes. One American intellectual historian has called Harper's method of teaching Hebrew "both revolutionary and enduring." Of *Harper's Elements of Hebrew by an Inductive Method*, J. Rylaarsdam wrote, "Ninety years after he began as an instructor, the influence of Harper's principles and methods continues to grow."[21] At the end of the twentieth century Harper's textbooks were still in use in university Hebrew courses.

Despite the revival of modern Hebrew and the growth of Jewish studies, teaching tools and methods remain unchanged in Christian seminaries and many Bible colleges. The emergence of the State of Israel and the growth of Hebrew study among American Jews have not lead to a revolution in the study of biblical Hebrew among Christians. Old Testament Hebrew continues to be taught in the traditional manner. Thus the divide between Christian study of Hebrew and Jewish study of Hebrew has been maintained. But perhaps it could not be otherwise. The continuity of pedagogical traditions in Protestant seminary education has assured a continuity of methods. The emergence of Jewish nationalism, with Hebrew language instruction as a corollary, would keep Jewish Hebrew learning a separate endeavor. Though a distinct and assertive Christian Hebraism was a thing of the past—and "Hebrew knowledge" no longer a missionary or polemical tool—Jewish and Christian study of Hebrew and the Bible did not converge. There are exceptions to this dichotomy. The founders of NAPH, the National Association of Professors of Hebrew (ca. 1950s), included both Christian teachers of Hebrew from Protestant seminaries and Jewish teachers of Hebrew from American universities, though the majority of the organization's membership during its first decade were teachers in Protestant seminaries.

Harper's work as biblical exegete and critical scholar was not as significant as his work in Hebrew pedagogy. As Rylaarsdam put it: "Professor Harper was a philological and historical exegete of the first rank who was productive on many fronts. So to place all of them in the 'first rank' of scholarship seems hyperbolic. But he devoted his gifts for originality to the development of methods for teaching Hebrew."[22] Harper's articles on biblical exegesis strike today's readers as dry and unexciting. They are thorough, technically precise, but uninspired. For the most part his historical and exegetical studies on the Bible are now of antiquarian interest only, but his Hebrew teaching methods had staying power.

In *Hebraica*, the journal he intended as a showcase for new approaches to biblical scholarship, Harper published articles on the precise application of the critical method to biblical texts. His focus was on the documentary hypothesis and its application to discrete words, phrases, and verses of the Old Testament text. One could then examine what these elements reveal about the dating, writing, and editing of that text. One concern of nineteenth-century textual criticism was the identification of the "original" words of biblical personages and the separation of those words from late "accretions." A late-twentieth-century version of this approach is the famed Jesus Seminar and its rigorous search for the original words of Jesus. In Harper's work he provided the exegetical ideological framework for the search for the "original" text. In his *Critical and Exegetical Commentary on Amos and Hosea* (1905), Harper stated that "nowhere is it more necessary to distinguish sharply between the actual words of an author and those that have been added by later writers than in the case of Amos and Hosea. The history of the Messianic idea, in whatever sense we employ that term, is fundamentally involved in that distinction." For Harper exegesis developed from philological analysis of the text. That analysis, especially in its comparative mode, was based on the then recently deciphered and analyzed ancient Near Eastern languages.

The workshop for Harper's Amos and Hosea volume (published in the distinguished *International Critical Commentary Series*) was in the pages of *Hebraica*. Harper was stimulated by the articles of senior scholars in the field of biblical exegesis, and he contributed a number of such articles himself. Some of these articles constituted a conversation with William Henry Green of Princeton Theological Seminary. In "The Pentateuchal Question," the most famous of these articles, Green attacked the documentary hypothesis, calling it "the divisive hypothesis." According to Green even if scholars can demonstrate that Genesis is composed of different strands joined together late in Israelite history, the inference that the text is of human, not divine origin, will shake the belief in the text's divine origin; "thus the credibility of Genesis is undermined."[23]

Green was representing a rear-guard action against the emerging academic disciplines that favored the Higher Criticism of Scripture. This action based itself on a detailed refutation of the documentary hypothesis analysis of Genesis. Harper's response to Green was lengthy, detailed, and sustained. He did not engage Green on the level of abstraction (concern with the implications of documentary hypothesis for questions of belief) but rather, responded to him on philological, technical grounds. In this debate and others, Harper was on the side of "science"—but his advocacy of modern methods was combined with a religious view, and this in turn was related to his vision of American education.

Harper's Legacy to the American Jewish Community

Harper's intellectual legacy touched the American Jewish world in a number of ways. We have seen how late-nineteenth-century Reform Jewish scholars, enamored of the idea of progress, were attracted to Harper's educational and religious vision. The 1885 Pittsburgh Platform, the defining document of early American Reform Jewish theology and practice, stated that "we recognize in Judaism a progressive religion, even striving to be in accord with the postulates of reason. . . . We recognize in the modern era of universal culture of heart and intellect the approaching of the realization of Israel's great Messianic hope for the establishment of the Kingdom of truth, justice, and peace among men." We can imagine that Harper read these statements—and approved of them. For they echo and amplify trends then current in liberal Protestant circles. Harper was "one of the early proponents of a new form of public religion which could respond to the new social and religious realities of his day."

Rabbi Emil Hirsch, Harper's close friend, rabbi of the Chicago Sinai congregation, member of the *Hebraica* editorial board, and faculty member at the

University of Chicago, was instrumental in adding the capstone statement to the Pittsburgh Platform: "In full accordance with the spirit of Mosaic legislation, which strives to regulate the relation between rich and poor, we deem it out duty to participate in the great task of modern times, to solve, on the basis of justice and righteousness, the problems presented by the contrasts and evils of the present organization of society." Here again we can see the influence of Hirsch's mentor and father-in-law, Rabbi David Einhorn. Einhorn, who emigrated from Germany to the United States in 1855, was a vociferous opponent of American slavery. He called it "the cancer of the Union" and preached against that institution from the pulpit. "It was his outspoken stand on slavery that forced Einhorn to flee Baltimore (where he was a rabbi) for his life in 1861."[24] Twenty years after the Civil War, Hirsch, Einhorn's successor, placed social justice at the head of his religious agenda. Hadn't his father-in-law, David Einhorn, challenged his anti-Abolitionist colleagues who urged him to keep politics from the pulpit: "Is not the question of slavery above all a purely religious issue?"

In similar fashion "Harper was a meliorist who sought to convert the culture to a biblical way of life." Harper's instrument for achieving that transformation was study of the Hebrew language and the biblical text. At first his vision was focused on teaching the Hebrew language to scholars and clergymen; later it widened to encompass all of America's citizens, whatever their degree of education or ability. For the country as a whole he prescribed the Bible in English. In an 1895 letter to J. M. Taylor, president of Vassar College, Harper—who had devoted almost every waking moment of the previous five years to the establishment and expansion of a new university—wrote that "my special business in the world is stirring up people on the English Bible. The University of Chicago is entirely a second hand matter."[25] This is an astounding assertion, but within it lies the key to Harper's vision. For him, the university, great and influential as it might become, was but an *instrument* of influence, a secular pulpit of sorts. In the last year of his life (1905) Harper wrote a short book on *The University and Democracy*. In it he praised American democratic ideals and made the case that only through biblical education could the progress of democracy be ensured. "I wish to show that the university is the prophet of this democracy, and as well, its priest and its philosopher; that, in other words, the university is the Messiah of the democracy, its to-be-expected deliverer."

While this statement might strike today's reader as a piece of fund-raising hyperbole, in the context of its time, and in the mouth of its author, it should be taken at face value. A sustained analysis of Harper's terms—prophet, priest, Messiah—will demonstrate that he was offering a cogent and consistent modernization of the biblical messianic ideal. Harper's vision for Chicago was that the university be so well organized and so intellectually grounded that it would not have to develop into greatness. Rather, it would emerge fully formed and prepared to influence the nation and its culture. This was a revolutionary and "messianic" idea rather than a gradual and evolutionary one. As Harper wrote to John D. Rockefeller in 1890, "It seems a great pity to wait for growth when we might be born full-fledged."[26] One could say that Harper had a "Messiah complex" about his own role in the emergence and influence of the university. And he saw his newly founded university as the fulfillment of biblical ideals.

Harper's life and work were profoundly influenced by the Hebraic tradition. The Jewish community of Chicago, where he founded America's first great university, responded to the Hebraic in Harper's vision. Rabbi Emil Hirsch wrote after Harper's death: "We Jews owe him a great debt of gratitude. He brought the Hebrew Bible again to the notice of the nation and did a giant's work to open it to the understanding of the best."[27]

[*Christian Zionism and the Jewish State*]

13

REINHOLD NIEBUHR,
THE JEWISH TRADITION, AND
POLITICAL ZIONISM

No man has had as much influence as a preacher in his generation;
no preacher has had as much influence in the secular world.
Arthur Schlesinger Jr. on Reinhold Niebuhr
The Jewish people have long ago found their authentic way to God.
Reinhold Niebuhr

Beginnings

In the small midwestern town of Wright City, Missouri, in the 1890s Pastor
Gustav Niebuhr of the German Evangelical Church began each day with readings in Hebrew and Greek from the Old and New Testaments. But Pastor
Niebuhr felt very much alone in rural Missouri. He found no other scholars
of the biblical languages with whom he could share his passion for biblical
philology; if Niebuhr wanted company in his studies he would have to create
and cultivate his own students. And that is exactly what he did—he taught
his five children the ancient languages and texts, and he and his wife Lydia
instilled in their children a love of scholarly inquiry, debate, and theological
reflection. Three of their offspring—Hulda, the eldest daughter, and the two
youngest sons, Reinhold and Helmut Richard—became household names in
American Protestant circles, dominating the academic and pastoral scenes for
the first two-thirds of the twentieth century. In 1958, in an article on Reinhold
Niebuhr, *Time*'s "man of the year," the magazine dubbed the Niebuhrs "the
Trapp family of theology." As of yet, Hollywood has not made a movie about
them. This might have brought them the celebrity that the *Sound of Music*
brought the Trapp family.

For American Protestant liberals of the late 1950s Reinhold Niebuhr articulated a worldview that criticized the excesses of capitalism and supported civil

rights. He was also fiercely critical of communist governments. As a founder of Americans for Democratic Action he influenced intellectuals such as George Kennan and Arthur Schlesinger Jr. A pioneer in furthering Jewish-Christian relations, Niebuhr saw himself as influenced by "the Jewish passion for justice," opposed missionizing, and favored Zionism at a time when it was unpopular among mainstream American Protestants.

The Niebuhr tradition of integrating Bible reading with family education had venerable European and American roots. In the German Lutheran tradition in which Gustav had been reared, Bible study, translation, and mastery of the Bible's "sacred languages" were accomplishments to which the clergy aspired. Earlier in this book I described a similar tradition in the home of Ezra Stiles, pastor of the Newport, Rhode Island, church. Stiles, the eighteenth-century polymath, did not limit himself, or his wife and seven children, to the Hebrew and Greek of the Old and New Testaments. After breakfast Bible readings the Stiles family would remain sitting around the table and perform a short exercise in Arabic. While reading the Quran would have proved too much of a theological stretch for Stiles, Arabic renditions of the Church Fathers were found to be edifying and instructive, and they served to illuminate his philological study of biblical text.

The level of intellectual engagement at the Niebuhr breakfast table was not quite so sophisticated, wide-ranging, or erudite. As one late-twentieth-century scholar of American religion noted, the quality of Niebuhr's formal education was not spectacular. Young Reinhold aspired to serve in the ministry. To prepare him for the seminary, his father tutored him in the biblical languages. As one wit remarked, "A century ago you needed these languages to get into seminary, today you have to know something of them to get out." The family's daily readings in Gustav's Polyglot Bible gave Reinhold an edge in language study. At age ten he was sure he wanted to be a pastor. Asked by his very pleased father as to the reason, Reinhold answered, "Because you're the most interesting man in town." In his short "Intellectual Autobiography" written in the 1950s, Niebuhr noted that "the first formative influence on my life was my father, who combined a vital personal piety with a complete freedom in his theological studies."[1]

Growing up in a series of midwestern farm communities (his father's success meant frequent offers of new pastoral jobs), Reinhold referenced his rural childhood experiences to biblical scenes and cadences. In an autobiographical fragment Niebuhr recalled an experience of his boyhood: "We ran to the barn threatened by the ominous clouds of an approaching storm, and then heard the wind and the rain beating outside while safe and dry under the eaves of the haymow. The experience had actual religious overtones. The words of the Psalmist, committed to memory, achieved a sudden and vivid relevance:

'Thou shalt not be afraid for the terror by night; nor for the arrow that flyeth by day . . . there shall no evil befall thee.'"[2]

Both Reinhold and his brother H. Richard attended Elmhurst College in Elmhurst, Illinois, and then went to the Lutheran Eden Theological Seminary in Webster Grove, Missouri. Their sister Hulda was educated closer to home. At Eden Seminary, Reinhold fell under the spell of Dr. Samuel Press, professor of Bible. Toward the end of his life Niebuhr told an interviewer that "the seminary was influential in my life primarily because of the creative effect on me of the life of a very remarkable man, Dr. S. D. Press, who combined a childlike innocence with a rigorous scholarship in biblical and systematic subjects."[3]

In 1913, when the Niebuhr brothers were highly motivated students at the Lutheran Eden Theological Seminary, Gustav Niebuhr died unexpectedly. One of the brothers was expected to take their father's pulpit. The mantle fell on Reinhold. It was a role for which he had been preparing since the age of ten.

Returning briefly to minister to his late father's congregation in Lincoln, Illinois, Niebuhr applied to Yale Divinity School and was accepted as a scholarship student. At Yale he realized that virtually all of his Lutheran education had been elementary—and narrowly theological. To Professor Samuel Press, Reinhold Niebuhr wrote from Yale, "The more I see how highly scholarship is prized in other denominations the more the penny-wise attitude of our church makes me sore. . . . The more I look at the thing the more I see that I have been cheated out of a college education."[4]

Determined to overcome these intellectual handicaps, Niebuhr worked hard and did well at Yale, but as he himself admitted, "not brilliantly." Again, in a letter to Press, he wrote, "I have bluffed my way through pretty well by industrious reading, but I feel all the time like a mongrel among the thoroughbreds and that's what I am."[5]

Despite these perceived lacunae in his education (or perhaps because of them), Niebuhr succeeded at Yale and was awarded his Master of Divinity degree in 1915 at the age of twenty-one. In a memoir of her husband, Niebuhr's widow Ursula recalled, "I used to hear about your coming to Yale. . . . You described yourself as a yahoo from the Midwest arriving at this seat of education and culture." Niebuhr left Yale still loyal to his Lutheran denomination, but he was now passionately critical of it, especially of its limited intellectual aspirations. To Dr. Press he again wrote, "I don't know if I'll ever have a voice in our church but if I will have it will never be silent until our ministry receives an adequate education. . . . This substitution of piety for critical enquiry shows where scholarship stands in a great part of our church."[6]

In his personal and pastoral lives Niebuhr sought to emphasize scholarship, especially the study of the sacred texts, and to develop an effective manner in which to speak out on social issues. Frustrated that he could not find these qualities in early-twentieth-century Lutheran circles he was determined to import them from places outside his tradition. His search would lead him to an unexpected source.

Leadership

In Detroit, where he accepted the leadership of the Bethel Evangelical Church, Reinhold Niebuhr was to encounter both the engagement with social issues that he sought and the spirit of critical inquiry that he felt was lacking in his church. Curiously he found both of these outside his denomination—and outside of Christian circles—among the Jews of Detroit. This was the first group of Jewish people that Niebuhr met; his encounters with them would leave a profound mark on his life and work.

The prominent social activists in the city were Jews. When Niebuhr arrived in Detroit, his mentor, Episcopal bishop Charles Williams, told him that "in the weightier matter of social justice there were only two Christians in Detroit, and they were both Jews." Niebuhr understood this to mean that in the Christian churches social justice did not get the attention it deserved. Williams was pointing out that many Christians were derelict in their duties toward other Christians, especially toward the impoverished black population of 1920s Detroit. Perhaps some non-Christians could provide a living example of what needed to be done.

The tense racial situation in Detroit first attracted Reinhold Niebuhr's energy and participation. With the growth of the auto industry many African Americans had moved to Detroit to work in the Ford motorworks. In Detroit they found themselves marginalized and discriminated against, despite the progressive policy of integration within the Ford Company itself. Soon after arriving in the city Niebuhr became the chairman of the mayor's committee on racial relations. "We had a rather long struggle to provide what one might call elemental justice to a growing Negro group, emphasizing equality in jobs, housing, and so forth," Niebuhr recalled many years later. The preoccupation with civil rights for African Americans would stay with Niebuhr throughout his life. According to Niebuhr biographer Richard Wightman Fox: "In the early 1930s, before he had discovered the virtues of the open society, Niebuhr had asserted that 'the white race in America will not admit the Negro to equal rights if not forced to do so.' While he cautioned against violent rebellion on the part of blacks he understood that nonviolent resistance to racism would be effective."[7]

In 1943 Niebuhr joined the "Committee of One Hundred" prominent Americans who supported the NAACP Legal Defense Fund. Niebuhr's vision of a just society would strongly influence Martin Luther King Jr. Recalling his years as a King aide, Andrew Young told an interviewer that "King always claimed to have been much more influenced by Niebuhr than by Gandhi; he considered his nonviolent technique to be a Niebuhrian strategy of power."[8] Congruent with his stand on racial issues, Reinhold Niebuhr's sympathies were with labor and against management. These sympathies often brought him into conflict with the wealthier members of his congregation. Niebuhr's first biographer, June Bingham, noted that in Detroit "Niebuhr could see at first not only the sufferings of labor, but also the spiritual blindness of the successful industrialists. Ford was the most extreme of these—but he was not the only one, nor was the form of blindness he exhibited the only one."[9]

While serving on the Detroit mayor's committee on race relations Niebuhr met "the most remarkable man I have ever known," Fred Butzell, a Jewish law-yer who served as the vice-chairman of the committee. Niebuhr made a clear connection between social activism among Jews and the message of the bibli-cal prophets. This linkage would have been questioned by many of these same Jewish social activists; almost all of these Jewish social activists were asser-tively secular. Butzell expressed his skepticism about the vitality and relevance of the Jewish religious tradition in a comment to Niebuhr that when he at-tended Jewish religious services it was out of habit rather than conviction, and that most rabbinic sermons were "second rate book reviews." Butzell became Niebuhr's friend and confidant. "Through him I established contacts with the Jewish community and from him I learned another aspect of American demo-cratic life—cooperation across a religious line."[10]

Christian Pragmatism and the Judaic Tradition

Another lesson that Niebuhr attributed to Butzell was the following: "I learned, incidentally the very great resources that the Jewish community has in its passion for practical justice." "Practical" is a key word here. Later, Rein-hold Niebuhr would call for "Christian Pragmatism" (which he later dubbed "Christian Realism")—and he expounded this philosophy on the pages of *Christianity and Crisis*, the journal he founded in the early 1940s. For Niebuhr, what was missing in contemporary Christian life was a hard-nosed sense of how to be effective in the real worlds of politics, business, and diplomacy. He contrasted the "concrete communal situations in which Jewish norms were established," with "a Christian universalism that often times tended toward vagueness and irrelevance." Niebuhr was well read in the Bible and later Jewish sources and was conversant with Jewish legal discourse. Though his earlier writings reflected an impatience with "Jewish legalism," he later modified his view of the New Testament condemnation of the Pharisees. Along with other twentieth-century scholars of early Christianity, he came to see these New Testament condemnations of legalism as part of an internal polemic within first-century Jewry. As his concept of Judaism changed, Niebuhr began to view Jewish law as a vehicle for the expression of the Jewish passion for justice. Through his friendship with Rabbi A. J. Heschel, a friendship that developed during Niebuhr's New York period, which I explore in detail later in this chapter, Niebuhr gained an appreciation of both the specificity and flexibility of rabbinic law. He was aware of that law's specificity in the realm of charity and other good works. Even if Fred Butzell and his Jewish colleagues were not consciously following Jewish law when they engaged in good works, for Niebuhr they were nevertheless still squarely in the Jewish tradition. Niebuhr remarked that, "Fred Butzell's capacity for magnanimity and social shrewdness was so impressive that it began my long love affair with the Jewish people."[11]

Niebuhr's fifteen years in Detroit brought him into contact with American minorities and their advocates. Their methods of advocacy, and the philosophies underlying these traditions of protest against injustice, had a profound effect on his role as a pastor and emerging public intellectual. In Niebuhr's "Intellectual Autobiography" he noted that "the obscurantism of historic faiths is aggravated by the fact that a type of religious orthodoxy betrays man's natural skepticism about the truths of love and faith. Christianity is, in principle, a religion of the spirit rather than of law. . . . But actually the excessive conventionality, the frantic respectability and the devotion to the minutiae of propriety in historic Christianity stand in sharp contrast to the love, joy, and peace which characterize a genuine conversion. They sometimes compare unfavorably with the freedom of the best secular idealists."[12] For Niebuhr secularists working for the common good had a distinct advantage. They were free of the cant and hypocrisy that often accompany the "doing of good works." Religious Christians, then, had much to learn from secular idealists, whatever their ethnic and cultural roots.

Niebuhr's ability to examine alien ideologies had been in evidence decades earlier when he read widely in Marxist theory. In the late 1920s and early 1930s he sought a fusion of Christian and Marxist ideals. As Arthur Schlesinger noted, "The appeal of Marxism to Niebuhr was a measure of his recoil from the optimism and moralism of Christian liberalism." In the 1920s Niebuhr joined the Socialist Party and became very active in the labor movement. His activism was spurred by his observation of Detroit's auto industry. Niebuhr recalled years later, "I cut my eyeteeth fighting Ford." As Jack Allen noted, "While the world was focusing on the opportunities Ford was bringing to Detroit, Niebuhr was focusing on the injustices that followed in the wake of industrialization." But his sense of realism about developments in the "worker's paradise" of the Soviet Union soon tempered his enthusiasm for the full implementation of Marxist ideals. Throughout this process of identifying with, and later distancing from, Marxist ideals, Niebuhr emphasized what he saw as the Hebraic roots of Marxism. Here we touch upon a wider phenomenon: the tendency of intellectuals, both Marxist and anti-Marxist (and all shades in between), to identify a Hebraic/Judaic background in the Marxist critique. As we shall see in a later chapter, literary critic Edmund Wilson emphasized the "rabbinic" aspect of leftist politics. Wilson remarked that Marx was "the great secular rabbi of his time," a role influenced by his ancestry: he was the descendant of a long line of German rabbis. For Niebuhr the connection between the Jews and socialism was biblical, not rabbinic. He found "the Marxist appreciation of the fact of judgment and catastrophe in history closer to the genius of Hebrew prophecy than liberalism, either secular or religious."[13]

Niebuhr highlighted the Judaic roots of both socialism and early Christianity. "The Hebrews took the correct middle ground between the optimism which conceived the world as possessing unqualified sanctity and goodness and the pessimism which relegated historic existence to a realm of meaningless cycles." Niebuhr's tendency to emphasize the Judaic content of early Christianity troubled some theologians. Today we might view Niebuhr's work as presaging a late-twentieth-century shift in Christianity's understanding of its Judaic roots. Paul Tillich wrote that "Niebuhr emphasizes increasingly the conflict between the Jewish and Greek elements in Christian thought, trying to remove the latter and to strengthen the former. . . . Christianity cannot give a preference to the Jewish in contrast to the Greek encounter with reality. It transcends this contrast."[14]

Recondite theological and political issues aside, Niebuhr's emphasis on Christian good works drew him inexorably to Jewish models of engagement with social problems. This exposure to minority concerns led Niebuhr to question the provincialism of his own German American upbringing. During World War I, Niebuhr supported the American war effort, though many German Americans opposed American entry into the war. Soon after his graduation from Yale Divinity School, he had his first major article published. For its July 1916 issue the *Atlantic Monthly* selected Niebuhr's essay "The Failure of German-Americanism." It was "a ringing repudiation of his own past, a firm assertion of his adult course, a promise of adherence to liberal ideals." Niebuhr chastised his fellow German Americans for supporting the kaiser against the British and the French (this was the year before America entered the war).

If America looked upon German Americans with "suspicions of disloyalty," such suspicion was justified, he argued. Making a case for the liberal political traditions of German thought, Niebuhr lamented the conservatism of German Americans. If the American public was suspicious of German American disloyalty this could have been mitigated if his fellow German Americans had been "less indifferent to the ideals and principles of this nation, and more true to its own."

In the postwar period Niebuhr supported the ideals of Wilsonian democracy. President Wilson's liberal foreign policy fully engaged his support and attention. The "reluctant citizenship" of many German Americans during the war dismayed him. He complained that "the great moral, political, and religious questions had aroused no greater interest on the part of German Americans." Niebuhr contrasted the Jewish contribution to progressive social reforms with the German American failure to address these same issues.

Niebuhr's concern for minority rights engaged questions of minority identity in white Christian culture. Speaking of the attitudes of those who would repress minorities, he wrote that "the majority group expects to devour the minority group by way of assimilation. This is a painless death, but a death nevertheless."[15]

At Union Theological Seminary

In the mid-1920s, Niebuhr was invited to teach at Union Theological Seminary (UTS) in New York. There he occupied the Chair of Christian Ethics, a position created for him. At UTS, and in the larger New York City scene of the 1930s, Niebuhr came into close contact with the rich cultural lives and difficult economic situations of the city's ethnic minorities. In *Saints and Villains*, Denise Giardina's 1998 novel based on the life of Dietrich Bonhoeffer, Niebuhr meets a black student from the South at a seminary reception. Niebuhr introduces himself. "'Reinhold Niebuhr, Professor of Applied Christianity.' 'Applied Christianity?' The Negro had raised his eyebrows. 'Sounds like "How to Put on a Bandage."' Only then did he take Niebuhr's hand. 'Albert Frederick Bishop,' he said, 'from Birmingham Alabama. They call me Fred.'" In the novel and in reality it was through Bishop and other black students at UTS that Niebuhr became familiar with the emerging struggle for civil rights. As the clashes with entrenched segregationists intensified, this was a struggle with which he would later identify.

Niebuhr also identified with the persecuted Jews of Europe. Living in New York and coming into contact with Jews made him more aware of their European situation. With the rise of fascism in Europe, "Niebuhr was among the first of the leading Protestants to direct attention to the rising wave of anti-Semitism in Nazi Germany. Throughout the decade of the 1930s Niebuhr warned of the threat to Jewish survival in Germany."[16] For Niebuhr the fight against racism in the United States was linked to the struggle against fascism and anti-Semitism in Europe. His concern for the Jews of Europe, and his later support for a Jewish state in Palestine, were not dictated by a theological reading of Christian-Jewish relations, and in this respect his worldview differed radically from the "religious" Christian Zionist views of many American thinkers. Rather, Niebuhr's thinking on anti-Semitism and many other issues was pragmatic. In the mid-1930s Niebuhr condemned the churches of Hitler's Germany for their failure to combat fascism and anti-Semitism. He angrily stated, "Probably seventy-five percent of the church population is avowedly Nazi."

From his growing position of influence at Union Theological Seminary, Niebuhr set out to help European intellectuals who sought refuge and an academic home in the United States. Paul Tillich was the first of many distinguished refugees from fascism whom Niebuhr helped settle in the United States. Dietrich Bonhoeffer, a German Lutheran pastor who was a postgraduate student at UTS in the early 1930s before the rise of Nazism, became a student and friend of Niebuhr. Among the solutions that Bonhoeffer proposed to Hitler's ascent to power was to organize passive resistance to the German regime. In Denise Giardina's *Saints and Villains*, the author imagines the following conversation between Bonhoeffer and Niebuhr:

"I'm thinking of going to India, I've already written to Gandhi."
"Really? Why?"
"To learn about his movement. Perhaps it can be applied to the situation in Germany."
Niebuhr squints at him, "You've got to be kidding. What do you expect Hitler would do, faced with a Gandhi?"
". . . but if moral force were the obvious impetus?"
"Moral force my ass. Are those poor souls rotting in Dachau because they're immoral? . . . you wouldn't last a week as a German Gandhi."[17]

On this issue, pragmatism in its utilitarian, not its philosophical, sense was at the forefront of Niebuhr's ideas. As John C. Bennet notes: "Niebuhr came to emphasize the irresponsibility in relying on non-violent resistance when there was no ground to believe that it would be successful in preventing the spread of totalitarian tyranny. It could only be successful when those who are resisting have a potential ally in the consciences of their opponents, as was the case in Gandhi's struggle against the British." Daniel F. Rice also notes, "The pragmatic element is present throughout Niebuhr's thought and is apparent in his long-running dialogue with Judaism." This dialogue with Judaism compelled Niebuhr to respond to Jewish concerns—long before they became the stuff of public debate. This was especially true of the looming question of Jewish statehood.[18]

In addition to Dietrich Bonhoeffer there was another foreign student at UTS during the 1930–31 academic year who would make a claim on Niebuhr's attention and affections. Ursula Keppel-Compton was a scholar from England who had recently completed her theology degree at Oxford. In New York for only a year, she had intended to devote her time to studying with Niebuhr. As R. W. Fox put it, "As the year progressed she settled her own gaze on the most confirmed bachelor at Union, one who appeared never to give women a thought." An eloquent public intellectual, Niebuhr was taciturn about his private life. Perhaps we can learn something of what transpired in that year from an adage that Niebuhr was later known to use often in the lecture hall. "In courtship it is the man who pursues—until the woman catches him." At the end of the school year Ursula returned to England. A year later Niebuhr traveled to England to marry her. Back in New York Ursula Niebuhr had a successful academic career. She was appointed professor of religion at Columbia's Barnard College and later served as chair of that department. She shared Reinhold's Zionist sympathies and in the late 1960s was tapped by Jerusalem Mayor Teddy Kollek to serve on his Jerusalem Committee.

Niebuhr, World War II, and Zionism

Earlier, I noted that Niebuhr's support for a Jewish state was not explicitly theological. Unlike many theologians among Christian Evangelicals he did not see the "Restoration of the Jews" as a fulfillment of biblical prophecy, or as a precursor of the "End of Days." That was the "biblical" reading of Zionism that so many American Protestant leaders, especially those on the Evangelical Right, would develop in the second half of the twentieth century. This Evangelical Christian Zionism went hand in hand with a parallel "biblical" reading of recent history: the Nazi murders of the Jews were part of the unfolding End Time. For some Evangelical thinkers, the meaning of those murders was sacrificial; the Jews had been sacrificed on the "altar of history." Implicitly rejecting these stances, which clashed with his liberal political views, Niebuhr based his support for Jewish statehood on clearly pragmatic grounds, and did so long before World War II. Niebuhr's articulation of the argument for Zionism was decidedly nontheological. It did not appeal to Christian evangelical impulses or to Jewish messianic yearnings. The Zionist thinker who most deeply influenced Niebuhr was Justice Louis Brandeis. According to Niebuhr: "Brandeis understood in 1916 what many a Gentile liberal will never learn. 'We Jews,' he said, 'are a distinct nationality of which every Jew is necessarily a member. Let us insist that the struggle for liberty shall not cease until equal opportunity is accorded to nationalities as to individuals.'"[19]

Niebuhr encountered Zionist political activism for the first time in the mid-1920s, when he arrived in New York to join the faculty of Union Theological Seminary. The variety of opinions within the Zionist world intrigued and amused Niebuhr. Within these contending groups he found pro–Jewish state ideologies that fit with his already formulated concepts concerning the place of morality in political action. He was drawn to a pacifist approach to nationalism, one that could be achieved with the use of coercion. Yet, within a few years he became convinced that a peaceful resolution of the emerging conflict between Jews and Palestinian Arabs was unlikely, and moved to a more activist approach. In his meditations on Zionism he made a remark that encapsulates much of his later writing and action on the question of Jewish statehood: "The idea of a political homeland for the Jews is so intriguing that I am almost willing to sacrifice my convictions for the sake of it."[20] For critics of American Christian support of Israel, this was a self-incriminating statement. Why would a principled commentator and activist exempt Zionism from the rigorous scrutiny he applied to other questions? Within a few years Niebuhr would attempt to lend some clarity to this conundrum.

After Pearl Harbor, Niebuhr, fully engaged in supporting the American war effort, wrote articles for the *Nation* that privileged unity during wartime over concerns about the infringement of the civil liberties of political and ethnic minorities. The American Civil Liberties Union complained in a rejoinder that Niebuhr seemed "much more solicitous of unity than liberty." An even stronger set of responses was generated by a subsequent Niebuhr series in the *Nation*, "Jews after the War." Richard W. Fox called these articles "an eloquent statement of the Zionist case: the Jews had rights not just as individuals, but as a people, and they deserved not just a homeland, but a homeland in Palestine." These articles were published in the *Nation* in February 1942; by the spring of that year Niebuhr had two hundred invitations to address Jewish groups throughout the United States.[21]

In the middle of World War II Niebuhr reiterated his call for American support of Zionism. The situation of the Jews of Europe demanded America's help by accepting "the Zionist program as correct in principle, however much it may have to be qualified in application." This pragmatic approach to Zionism enabled Niebuhr to articulate a more nuanced approach to the emerging Arab-Jewish conflict. Daniel Rice has noted that "as early as 1936 Niebuhr pondered the bewildering ethical complexities attending the rivalry between Jews and Arabs in Palestine." In an eerily prescient meditation on religion and conflict, Niebuhr asked, "How is the ancient and hereditary title of the Jews to Palestine to be measured against the right of the Arab's present possession? . . . The participants cannot find a common ground of rational morality from which to arbitrate the issues because the moral judgments which each brings to them are formed by the very historical forces which are in conflict. . . . The effort to bring such a conflict under the dominion of a spiritual unity may be partly successful, but it always produces a tragic by-product of the spiritual accentuation of natural conflict. The introduction of religious motives into these conflicts is usually no more than the final and most demonic pretension."[22]

In 1941 Niebuhr spoke at the annual convention of the B'nai B'rith organization. There he came out in favor of U.S. support for a Jewish state in Palestine. He repeated this call in a speech the following year to the leadership of the Reform movement, the Union of American Hebrew Congregations. Toward the end of World War II Niebuhr joined other prominent Christian leaders to found the American Christian Palestine Committee. As its representative he lectured on its behalf in many cities across the nation in 1945 and 1946. The committee printed ten thousand copies of his articles "Jews after the War" for distribution throughout the United States.

While he was deeply concerned about finding a refuge for the Jews who had survived the Nazi terror, Niebuhr also expressed concern for the fate of the Palestinian Arabs. As Niebuhr biographer June Bingham noted, "At no time, however, was Niebuhr an uncritical Zionist."[23] This nuanced approach was unusual among supporters of the emerging Jewish state. In some matters Niebuhr aligned himself with the proposals of Brit Shalom, a peace group formed by Martin Buber, Judah Magnes, and Ernst Simon. These Jewish intellectuals, resident in Palestine, called for a binational state. Niebuhr was attracted to the idea, but eventually deemed it "unrealistic." For as we have seen realism (or "pragmatism") was at the core of Niebuhr's idea of operating in the world. In the 1920s Niebuhr had rejected pacifism, and this rejection was strengthened after the rise of fascism in Europe. Niebuhr's brother, H. Richard, differed with him publicly on the question of pacifism—one of the very few times that the brothers allowed a disagreement to become public.

The Anglo-American Commission on Palestine proposed its own postwar version of a binational state in Palestine in which both Arabs and Jews would share power. In January 1946 the commission members imagined that this proposed state would remain under the administration of the British mandate. Committee member Richard Crossman, a British member of Parliament, questioned Niebuhr and then attempted to summarize Niebuhr's position: "Your view would be to go ahead on the establishment of the Jewish home and then the mandatory power must see to it that they do not exceed their powers and rights over and against the other group of the state." Niebuhr responded affirmatively with the following qualified statement:

> That is right. I would make one criticism, I think, of some of the propa-
> ganda and the work that the Jews have begun. They have insisted that to
> give them justice in Palestine would not infringe upon Arab justice. I can
> see why they say that, because the introduction of a democratic technical
> society has produced benefits, and they have rightly emphasized that point.
> But I think they should be realistic and say, "Even if you give economic
> benefits to the Arab world, and you subtract political inheritance from it,
> that is at least, say from their perspective unjust." In other words, I would
> proceed upon the assumption that there are no perfectly just solutions for
> any of these problems where there are great conflicts of right. We mustn't
> say that our solution is absolutely a just solution for the other person, but
> try to make it as near perfect as possible.[24]

Again we see that Niebuhr's support for the idea of a Jewish state was not theological but pragmatic. Yet realism and pragmatism were for Niebuhr theological imperatives. We need to contextualize Niebuhr's concern and work for a Jewish state with his overarching concern for all the victims of World War II. "After the war Niebuhr continued to labor tirelessly in refugee organizations and in groups sending aid to Europe." In both the European and Middle Eastern spheres of influence, Niebuhr saw a need to affirm American ties and establish American style governments. In November 1947, on the eve of the United Nations vote on the partition of Palestine, Niebuhr and six other prominent American intellectuals wrote a long letter to the *New York Times*. The letter examined the ways in which a Jewish state in the Middle East would serve American interests. "Politically, we would like to see the lands of the Middle East practice democracy as we do here. . . . Thus far there is only one vanguard of progress and modernization in the Middle East, and that is Jewish Palestine."[25] This comment, which seemed so politically progressive in post–World War II American discourse, would later, in the 1970s, be read very differently.

For Niebuhr, World War II brought "home to Americans, the way the First World War had done for Europeans, the refutation of all optimistic estimates of man's moral capabilities."[26] Before World War II, and as early as the late 1920s, Niebuhr warned of the dangers inherent in an unstable Germany. With the rise of Hitler to power in 1933 Niebuhr protested against the German government's infringement of human liberties. The anti-Jewish policies of the German state outraged him and he attacked the German churches for their failure to criticize the government and educate their church members as to the dangers of espousing race hatred. In 1940, asserting that the journal with which he had been associated for many years, the *Christian Century*, was not forceful enough in its condemnation of Nazism, Niebuhr resigned from its editorial board. *Christianity and Crisis*, the journal that he founded in 1941, focused on the threat, and non-Christian character, of European fascism. In the first issue of the new journal he warned of the imminent danger to European Jewry posed by German fascism. He was convinced that "Nazi tyranny intends to annihilate the Jewish race." Unlike most American Christian supporters of Zionism (among them Johns Hopkins University's William F. Albright, dean of American archaeologists), Niebuhr understood Zionism as a largely secular response to the threat of annihilation. For Albright and many other Christian supporters of Israel, the issues were "biblical." God had promised Palestine to the Jews. Now the United States had the opportunity to fulfill God's will.

For Niebuhr and other liberals the issues were those of justice and pragmatism. In a remarkably accurate reading of Zionism's roots, one that emphasized the secular nationalistic roots of the movement and not its religious background, Niebuhr noted that "Zionism is the expression of a national will to live that transcends the traditional orthodox religion of the Jews." A Jewish state was a necessity because "the bigotry of majority groups toward minority groups that affront the majority by diverging from the dominant type is a perennial aspect of man's collective life. The force of it may be mitigated, but it cannot be wholly eliminated."[27]

Niebuhr's encounters in the 1920s with liberal Jews in Detroit had confirmed his preference for liberal Judaism, and he extended this preference to his hopes for the role of religion in the young State of Israel. In 1957 he warned that the forces of Jewish orthodoxy would endanger Israeli democracy. He predicted that orthodox rule in Israel "would fasten upon this essentially secular community political standards directly derived from the book of Deuteronomy." In a 1984 essay Egal Feldman characterized Niebuhr's misgivings on this subject as an "exaggerated fear." Some observers of early-twenty-first-century Israeli life would disagree.

Neither Niebuhr's concern for the fate of the Arab refugees nor his fear of Orthodox encroachment on the lives of citizens in a secular state weakened his support for Israel. The Suez Crisis of 1956, in which Britain, France, and Israel invaded Egypt after the Egyptian nationalization of the Suez Canal, elicited strong American condemnation of the invading powers. President Eisenhower led the demand to reverse the results of the conflict, a demand which led to a UN resolution calling for Israeli withdrawal from the Sinai Peninsula. During the Suez Crisis Niebuhr's was one of the few influential American Christian voices calling for American support of Israel. As the Soviet Union supported Egypt with arms, Niebuhr felt that the United States should support Israel, for "the very life of the new nation of Israel is at stake."

While Niebuhr clamored for U.S. support for Israel, most American liberal public opinion considered the Suez invasion a colonial endeavor. Niebuhr's support of Israel was nevertheless nuanced by his often-expressed concern for the effect of the establishment of Israel on the Palestinians and the citizens of other Arab states. As Daniel Rice noted, "Niebuhr grasped the intractable and ambiguous elements in the historical process of the conflict." A year after the Suez Crisis Niebuhr pointed out that "the West and the Jews may claim the previous Jewish right to the soil of Palestine, but we tend to forget that this right evaporated thousands of years ago and that the Arabs are not impressed by the prophecies of the Old Testament, at least not by the political relevance of these prophecies." This was a nuance that the more "theological" of his fellow Christian Zionists failed to see. They heatedly disagreed with Niebuhr's assertion that there cannot be a "simply just solution of such a conflict, when competing claims move on such various levels."[28]

An early-twenty-first-century survey of the deepening conflict between Israel, the Palestinians, and the Arab world confirms the stunning accuracy of Niebuhr's reading of the direction in which the conflict was headed. The period since the 1967 Arab-Israeli war has seen a definite "spiritual accentuation of natural conflict." And "demonic pretension" would not be hyperbolic as a description of the pronouncements of Jewish, Muslim, and Christian spokesmen on the scripturally based claims to the Holy Land. On both the Israeli and the Arab sides of the conflict nationalist claims have been buttressed by religious claims. With the growing assertiveness and popularity of religious nationalism we witness a diminished secular idealist voice.

Some observers have questioned the sincerity of Niebuhr's expressions of concern for the Arab population of Palestine. In Edward Said's *The Question of Palestine* (1979), Niebuhr and literary critic Edmund Wilson, the subject of our next chapter, are cited as exemplars of American one-sidedness with regard to the issue of Israel and the Palestinians. Though Niebuhr's support for the Jewish state was often qualified by expressions of concern for the fate of the Palestinians, Said sees these expressions of concern as mere rhetorical flourishes. According to Said, Niebuhr, in joining the Zionist cause, and in tying Zionist aspirations to American interests, was promoting a worldview that "Zionism on its own merits is a marvelous, admirable thing which is accountable to no one and nothing, mainly because it corresponds so completely with Western ideas about society and man."

"Niebuhr's intellectual authority has been very great in American cultural life," Said adds. "What he says, therefore, has the force of that authority." To demonstrate this authority, Said points to the 1947 group letter to the *New*

York Times, where Niebuhr and his colleagues had identified "Jewish Palestine as the vanguard of progress and modernization in the Middle East." Said reads this passage from the letter as "the appropriation of quasi-Marxist language to promote a fundamentally colonialist scheme." For Said, what Niebuhr et al. had called "these two islands of western civilization"—Jewish Palestine and Christian Lebanon—are in fact "western colonies." In praising the governments and peoples of these two "islands," "Niebuhr doesn't feel it necessary to say what should be evident to any civilized western. Islam is the enemy of Judaism and Christianity and therefore 'our' policy ought to be the support of Jewish Palestine and Christian Lebanon."[29]

Until the Conversion of the Jews

For Protestants and Roman Catholics in early-twentieth-century America, the degree to which a specific Christian community might endeavor to bring local Jews into the Christian fold differed considerably according to place and time. In modern Europe and the United States many churches did not directly engage in missionary activity but were content to have church-supported missionary societies devote their energies to this project. The early nineteenth century had seen a flourishing of these societies in the United States. As we saw in an earlier chapter, there were two hundred chapters of the American Society for Meliorating the Condition of the Jews by 1850. In the early twentieth century, Chicago specifically, and the Midwest generally, were centers of missionary work directed at Jews, though missions operated in all Jewish population centers.

Niebuhr and his Detroit congregation of the 1920s were no different in this respect from other midwestern churches. In 1923, Niebuhr preached on the necessity of increasing the number of Jews who would join the Christian fold. There were two reasons why Jews did not convert: "The unchristlike attitude of Christians" and "Jewish bigotry." Yet Niebuhr would soon reconsider his position on this issue. No doubt he was influenced by his experience of and insight into the local Jewish community's commitment to better the welfare of the poor, the unemployed, and those who suffered from racial discrimination. In 1926 Niebuhr rejected completely the idea of a mission to Jews. As his biographer R. W. Fox noted, Niebuhr understood by this time that "Christians needed the leaven of pure Hebraism to counteract the Hellenism to which they were prone." Niebuhr now argued forcefully that Christians had no business trying to convert Jews, in part because of the "secular fruits of Jewish piety."[30]

Niebuhr's brother H. Richard shared this opposition to the idea of making the Jews Christian. A professor at Yale since 1931, he had criticized in private many of Reinhold's emerging theological and political stances. To some extent H. Richard moderated Reinhold's radicalism and influenced his shift from engagement with political issues to a renewed focus on theological issues. A question on which the brothers agreed was Christianity's relationship to the Jews as a living religious community, a community with its own theological integrity and not in need of "spiritual advice." Many years after the Niebuhr brothers joined forces to oppose entrenched anti-Judaic attitudes in American Christian circles, Niebuhr wrote an essay on "The Unsolved Religious Problem in Christian-Jewish Relations" (*Christianity and Crisis*, April 1966). Niebuhr's essay was inspired by the Catholic Church's Vatican II deliberations. Arguing that the Gospel's depiction of Jesus' life "is obviously influenced by Christian ideological viewpoints prompted by the contest in the early church" placed Niebuhr decades ahead of his time. Daniel Rice noted in 1970 that "here he touched upon the problem of scriptural anti-Semitism which is being explored in such earnest today." Niebuhr's insight that the anti-Jewish polemics of the New Testament relate to debates and struggles within first-century Palestinian Jewry, and should not be understood as condemnations of the Jews of our time, had far-reaching implications. The theological and literary insights that Bruce Chilton and James Carroll articulated in the late 1990s, thirty years after Niebuhr published his essay and sixty years after he first articulated his opposition to missions to the Jews, are highly relevant in this regard.[31]

Protestant insistence on the primacy of scriptural authority, and its opposition to clerical absolutism, had a curious and paradoxical effect on the understandings of the "anti-Jewish" diatribes within the New Testament, diatribes that Niebuhr and more recent scholars have recognized as intra-Jewish community diatribes. While Catholic churchmen may have been able to mitigate the force of those New Testament texts read as anti-Jewish, Protestants considered these texts to have unchanging relevance. Niebuhr correctly understood that Vatican II was undercutting, or rather "ignoring the Pauline cry of anguish: Brethern, my heart's desire and prayer to God for Israel is, that they might be saved. (Romans, 10:1). . . . The Pauline hope for the conversion of the Jews has been the root of a Christian disposition more authoritative among scripturally-minded Protestants than among Catholics: to regard tolerance of Judaism as merely preliminary to its final absorption in the Christian faith."[32]

Fully aware that by rejecting the idea of converting the Jews he was challenging a sanctioned and previously unchallenged concept in Christian life, Niebuhr used his aversion to missionizing the Jews as a way to understand the historical and theological relationship between Judaism and Christianity.

For Niebuhr the removal of Christian animosity toward the Jews would allow genuine dialogue between the members of the two faiths. The philosophical underpinning of his stance was this: As both the Jewish and Christian ideas of covenant base themselves on revelation in history, members of each faith community must admit that no objective view is possible within the context of a faith commitment. For Niebuhr the Gospel's portrayal of the Jews of Jesus' time as Pharisees, legalists, and betrayers is the *subjective* view of one historical *Jewish* party—a party that later developed into Christianity. By the late 1950s Niebuhr was suggesting that contemporary Christians engaged in dialogue with Jews move away from making claims to absolute truth toward a stance that emphasizes the notion of "a double covenant."

To make the case against missionizing the Jews, Niebuhr enlisted the authority of his brother H. Richard. He was "the first Protestant theologian to affirm unequivocally that the religious affinities of Jews and Christians were so great that Christians must leave the Jews to solve their moral and religious problems without any help from these missions." Both Niebuhr and his brother felt that attempts to Christianize Jews "negated every gesture of our common biblical inheritance." Yes, there was a theological point to be made here—but, also, a pragmatic one. Both Niebuhrs recognized that the mission to the Jews was, for the most part, a dismal failure. (My discussion of nineteenth-century American missions to the Jews in Chapter 6 made clear that "failure" was not in the missionary's vocabulary. The very resistance of Jews to apostasy only strengthened missionary activities.) Reinhold Niebuhr wrote that "when some of us questioned the ecumenical wisdom of those not too successful missions to the Jews, we were met with sympathy, as well as a warning that our concern was 'heretical.'" His opposition to missionizing the Jews has to be seen in the wider context of his trenchant analysis of America religion. While the United States was highly secular, it was also highly religious. "The best of its secularism drew on deep religious roots—as in the civic virtue of secular Jews . . . its popular religion aped the worst of secularism, the frantic pursuit of success."[33]

This anticonversionist stance generated considerable opposition in conservative Christian circles. By 1962 Niebuhr had made his antimissionizing stance explicit in his preaching. At Easter of that year he told a group of worshippers that, "Since the ethical impulses of the Christian faith are inherited from the Jewish faith, with its sense of justice, with its law of love, with its emphasis on historical responsibility, it is not our business to convert Jews to Christianity."[34]

The Niebuhr brothers' stance on missions did not go unopposed. *Christianity Today* ran a series of articles that challenged the Niebuhrs' liberal stance on the issue. Reinhold Niebuhr made it clear in these exchanges with his critics that he did not oppose missions to non-Jews; it was the "shared biblical tradition" of Jews and Christians that rendered conversionist efforts unnecessary. The controversy continued after Niebuhr's death in 1971. Conservative Christian critics of the 1970s and 1980s wondered whether Niebuhr's position on the Jews was erasing the lines between the two traditions. Jeffrey Hart, a *National Review* columnist, wrote in his 1982 book, *When the Going Was Good: American Life in the Fifties*, that Niebuhr, in attempting to improve Christian-Jewish relations, was betraying the Christian traditions, and that betrayal constituted "a regression to the tribal theologies of the ancient world."[35]

Jewish Reception of Niebuhr's Work

In the mid-1950s twenty prominent American theologians—Protestant, Catholic, and Jewish—were invited to write essays for a volume celebrating Niebuhr's religious, social, and political thought. The occasion was Niebuhr's approaching sixty-fifth birthday. Published in the "Library of Living Theology" in 1956 and edited by Charlesz Kegley, the volume included an essay by Niebuhr in which he replied to his interpreters and critics. Responding specifically to Paul Tillich's assertion that he overestimated the importance of the Judaic background of Christianity, he wrote, "Professor Tillich thinks that my trouble is that I have capitulated to a Hebraic mode of thought in preference to the Hellenic. But my thesis is simply that both modes of thought are necessary. . . . The Hellenic component of our culture generated our sciences and philosophies. My point is simply that when we deal with aspects of reality which exhibit a freedom above and beyond structures, we must resort to the Hebraic dramatic and historical way of apprehending reality."[36]

The volume closes with essays by two Jewish scholars, Rabbis Alexander J. Burnstein and Abraham J. Heschel. These two essays by Jewish admirers of Niebuhr are instructive with regard to the variety of Jewish responses to Niebuhr's theological and political writings. Jewish figures were unanimous in their praise for Niebuhr's support of Zionism and his opposition to missionizing. Where Alexander Burnstein and others differed with Niebuhr was on his emphasis on original sin. "Let me begin with the most fundamental of Niebuhr's ideas, the doctrine of man as sinner, which dominates all his religious thinking." For Burnstein "this grim and gloomy view of man, and the great stress he places on man's inveterate liability to sin . . . makes his otherwise profound and stimulating teaching difficult to reconcile with the main stream of biblical and religious Jewish thought."[37] To the "gloominess" of Niebuhr's idea of human behavior Burnstein contrasted the Jewish idea of *teshuvah*, repentance. Seymour Siegel noted that "Niebuhr's impressive analysis of the ambiguities of human nature did not receive the response which it deserved from the Jewish community. Part of the reason was his use of the term 'original sin.'" For Siegel and his Jewish Theological Seminary colleague Abraham Joshua Heschel, Niebuhr's conception of the tendency of humans to fall into error was closer to the rabbinic idea of *yetzer ha-ra* (the evil inclination) than to classical Christian models of man's inherent "sinfulness."[38]

Niebuhr and A. J. Heschel, intellectual and spiritual luminaries of two neighboring institutions, Union Theological Seminary and the Jewish Theological Seminary, forged a strong friendship in the 1950s and 1960s. Students of both masters built on the foundations of this amor intellectualis. After a 1958 talk by Niebuhr, one of Heschel's colleagues, Professor Shalom Spiegel, remarked to the assembled Christian and Jewish scholars, "After listening to this remarkable lecture I know why the slogan at J.T.S. is 'Love thy Niebuhr as thyself.'" We might see this friendship as a twentieth-century version of the rare nineteenth-century Christian-Jewish friendship between Edward Robinson, professor of Hebrew at Union Theological Seminary in the 1830s, and his Jewish associate Isaac Nordheimer. But in the 1830s there was no *Jewish* Theological Seminary; that institution was not founded until the 1880s. Furthermore, the Robinson-Nordheimer relationship did not affect other Jewish scholars or the wider Jewish community. In contrast, the friendship between Heschel and Niebuhr opened up the possibility of friendships both social and intellectual between Jewish and Christian scholars.

It is important to contextualize Niebuhr's cultivation of friendship with Jewish thinkers and his insistence on including Jews in a wider American theological conversation. "Fortunately, we have two contributions from Jewish sources," wrote Niebuhr in the 1956 volume. Why was this small Jewish contribution so important to Niebuhr? I think that Daniel F. Rice catches the essence of it. "Niebuhr regarded the problem of the genuine autonomy of the Jews as the final problem facing the Christian community. Authentic toleration whereby unqualified acceptance of the Jew as Jew is recognized, marks the final issue with which the church must come to terms."[39] In the same period, some in the hierarchy of the Catholic Church were grappling with similar issues. They were confronting the wider implications of the church's troubled relationship with the Jews, especially with the fate of the murdered Jews of twentieth-century Europe. But it was only at the very end of the twentieth century that the Catholic church more fully articulated its new understanding of its relationship with the Jewish people.

In 1951 at the age of fifty-eight, Niebuhr suffered a series of debilitating strokes. He had to give up teaching and writing for over a year, and only by remarkable force of will was he able to return to some of his many duties by mid-1953. He was then faced with severe depression, for which he reluctantly sought psychiatric help. It was not until the late 1950s and early 1960s that he returned to his early engagement with minority concerns. I have cited Martin Luther King Jr.'s indebtedness to Niebuhr's ideas and noted that King considered his own nonviolent technique a "Niebuhrian strategy of power." King, Niebuhr, and Heschel all invoked and hearkened back to the social justice message of the prophet Amos. In the early to middle 1960s Niebuhr was a strong vocal supporter of King's policies, especially on the issue of nonviolence. King was being challenged daily by advocates of "Black Power" to take a stand, which would have condoned violence against whites. He refused. Niebuhr, allied with both King and A. J. Heschel on civil rights, opposed the war in Vietnam. Though now beset by multiple illnesses, Niebuhr actively supported a new organization, Clergyman Concerned about Vietnam. In 1966 Niebuhr said of Martin Luther King Jr., "He was still the most creative Protestant, white or black."[40]

In 1967 the Hebrew University of Jerusalem awarded Niebuhr an honorary doctorate. His health prevented him from accepting the award in person. The award was in recognition of Niebuhr's intellectual achievements as well as his lasting contribution to promoting Israel's image in the contemporary American mind. Though Niebuhr's commitment to political Zionism was somewhat qualified, his support for the Jewish state never wavered. In the 1950s he often invoked the metaphor of David and Goliath to describe Israel and the Arab states. In a 1956 essay in *Christianity and Crisis* Niebuhr proclaimed that "the state of Israel is, whatever its limitations, a heartening adventure in nationhood. . . . Whatever our political or religious positions may be, it is not possible to withhold admiration, sympathy and respect for such an achievement." I think it is fair to say that this statement both reflected and helped shape liberal opinion in 1950s America. By the time the 1967 Middle East war broke out, most Americans had no doubt as to who was David and who was Goliath in the unfolding conflict.

Beset by his worsening physical condition, Niebuhr, in his mid-seventies, made detailed plans for his death and funeral. A bout of pneumonia in early 1971 weakened him considerably. With his wife Ursula he decided that Rabbi Heschel would speak at the funeral. When they learned that Heschel too was quite ill (having suffered a heart attack a few months earlier) they were deeply upset. In a conversation with Heschel's colleague and student, Seymour Siegel, Niebuhr broke down in tears and told Siegel of the great influence Heschel had on him; "how through their association he had come to understand Jewish spirituality and the meaning of Jewish law; how he had deepened his appreciation of prophetic religion."[41]

On June 1, 1971, Niebuhr passed away, at the age of seventy-eight. Abraham Joshua Heschel was well enough to deliver the eulogy at a memorial service in Stockbridge, Massachusetts. On June 4, he opened in this dramatic manner: "This is a critical moment in the lives of many of us, in the history of religion in America: to say farewell to the physical existence of the master and to pray. Abide, continue to dwell in our midst, spirit of Reinhold Niebuhr." Seymour Siegel described the eulogy in this way: "Recounting Niebuhr's work on behalf of all peoples, and noting his particular attachment to Jewish texts and themes, Heschel's eulogy moves from the universal to the particular—and back again to the universal." Heschel noted that "Niebuhr began his teaching at a time when religious thinking in America was shallow, insipid, impotent—bringing life and power to theology, to the understanding of the human situation, changing the lives of many Christians and Jews."[42]

Heschel closed his lament for Reinhold Niebuhr with readings from Job and from the Psalms. But before he turned to the Bible for consolation and praise, Heschel masterfully summed up Niebuhr's accomplishment and influence: "He appeared among us like a sublime figure out of the Hebrew Bible. Intent on intensifying responsibility, he was impatient of excuse, contemptuous of pretense and self-pity."[43]

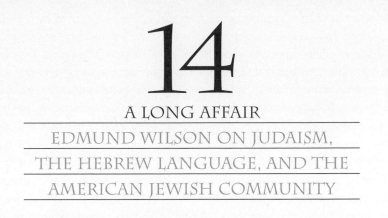

14

A LONG AFFAIR

EDMUND WILSON ON JUDAISM, THE HEBREW LANGUAGE, AND THE AMERICAN JEWISH COMMUNITY

Toward the end of his long and productive life the literary critic Edmund Wilson wondered aloud if perhaps he had been too wide ranging in his interests. "It takes me some time nowadays to get through the literature sent me in connection with the subjects that I've written about. I am inundated with books and papers. I wish sometimes that I hadn't been so various." But one senses that this very complaint was an act of artifice. The now greatly missed man of letters was, to borrow a set of Talmudic metaphors that I am sure he would have enjoyed, both a "Sinai" (a scholar who has achieved mastery of the law) and "an uprooter of mountains" (one whose depth of knowledge is as great as his breadth). Wilson's 1995 centenary provided an opportunity for homage, reassessment, and revisionist challenge to this esteemed critic's reputation.[1]

Yet in all the celebration and commemoration one highly significant aspect of Wilson's life and work was overlooked: his intense interest in, and study of, Jewish languages, texts, and cultural traditions. However we take Wilson's above-quoted complaint, it is difficult to overlook what Lewis Dabney termed Wilson's "long affair with Judaism."[2] Edmund Wilson's intensive study of the Hebrew language and use of Hebrew knowledge to explicate ancient and modern literary texts was coupled with an interest in the Jews of his time, particularly with the Jews of the United States and Israel. The range of Wilson's "Hebraic" interests, and the elegance and intensity with which he expressed those interests are indicated in the titles of two of his essays: "On First Reading Genesis" and "S. Y. Agnon."[3] Rereading those essays in the mid-1990s, I was inspired to explore Wilson's unusual infatuation with Jews and Judaism, and more particularly, his interest in the many varieties of American Judaism.

Perhaps of all of Wilson's "various" obsessions, his Hebraic and Judaic studies were of the greatest relevance to his personal development and sense of intellectual mission. A banner-like inscription in biblical Hebrew hung over his desk in Wellfleet, Massachusetts, and this phrase—*Hazak Hazak Venitha-zek* ("Be strong and be strengthened," in Wilson's translation)—is engraved on the base of his tombstone. He found such encouragement in this phrase that it became his constantly evoked motto. He was even known to use it as a short grace before meals. This Hebrew language exhortation to be strong in one's studies extended to the entire range of Wilson's interests. Apparent in his essays is a sense of struggle with the literary and historical material out of which a particular review or essay was crafted. In the Jewish intellectual tradition he found methods with which such a struggle might be conducted. His wife Elena noted that "to the very end of Edmund's life, he would be found at his desk surrounded by Bibles and dictionaries, keeping with the new developments, deciphering the Old Testament and a facsimile of fragments of the scrolls."[4] For Wilson the Bible was central. Its cadences and its powerful images were "part of the texture of our language: the culture of no other Western people seems so deeply to have been influenced by these: something in the English character, something mystical, tough and fierce, has a special affinity to Hebrew."[5] With these words Wilson places himself squarely in the English Hebraist tradition. The medieval scholastics at Oxford and Cambridge, the great collectors of Hebrew manuscripts at the Bodleian Library, and the scholars who worked on the King James Bible were Wilson's intellectual forebears in this area. He was aware of this intellectual lineage, and proud to be a product of it.

Some critics have argued that Wilson's interest in Hebrew and the Jews was a late, and minor, development in his work and one that came after the high points of his career as critic—his examination of symbolism and modernism in *Axel's Castle*, his magisterial study of Marxist thought and history in *To the Finland Station*, and his survey of the literature of the Civil War in *Patriotic Gore*.[6] Edmund Wilson's studies of Hebraism and Judaism did come late in his career, but they were the more mature and personally relevant products of his critical intelligence. Furthermore, a close reading of his "Judaic" material and a careful study of his vast oeuvre demonstrate a lifelong interest in the Jews and their culture. This was not an interest that flowered after his other interests had withered. Wilson's early interest in American Jews, though now largely forgotten, was widely known to his friends. Some of his Christian friends, amused and bewildered by this obsession, often kidded him about it. After an article of Wilson's was published in *Commentary*, John Dos Passos wrote him to say that he thought that Wilson was "carrying out his role of uncircumcised rabbi very well."[7] Often, it seems, he sought to act as "rabbi" not only to fellow Protestants whom he wanted to teach about Jews, Judaism, and Israel, but also to American Jewish intellectuals as well.

In the early 1950s Wilson's young Jewish friends, many of whom were attempting to Americanize themselves and deemphasize their Jewish backgrounds, chose not to comment on the master's study of Hebrew and the Bible. This silence is noteworthy for it was in this area of inquiry that Wilson would write what was to be his only best-selling book, the collected essays on the Dead Sea Scrolls. Wilson's Jewish friends knew little Hebrew and were reluctant to recall whatever Hebrew they may have learned as children. These aspiring literary acolytes sought to escape the Jewish immigrant "world of their fathers" and enter into Edmund Wilson's world. The mid-century American Republic of Letters was to a large extent a patrician society presided over by Wilson, a gentleman scholar who enjoyed reminding his readers that he was a direct descendant of the Mathers of colonial Massachusetts and the Kimballs of colonial New York. In the early 1950s, at the point when Wilson's lifelong interest in the Hebraic and the Judaic was finding full expression in his books and articles, his American Jewish acolytes, with whose aspirations he was very sympathetic, were trying to gain entry to the world of literary respectability and academic recognition, a world they saw as ruled by American Protestant critics and professors with what Wilson himself had dubbed the "trinomial names" of the New England aristocracy. For these young writers, Hebrew and Judaic knowledge was something to be jettisoned or hidden, not a talent or interest to be displayed. If their aristocratic Protestant mentor chose to delve into the mysteries of the Jewish past, that was his privilege and concern, not theirs.

Wilson was aware of this ironic intersection of interests and aspirations and delighted in teasing his Jewish friends about it. In a 1952 Christmas card to Alfred Kazin, Wilson added two lines in his recently acquired Hebrew handwriting: "I shall learn Hebrew," followed at the bottom of the card by the impish note, "I'll bet you can't read this!"[8] That same year Wilson conducted a seminar at Princeton University. Among the participants were John Berryman, Saul Bellow, Delmore Schwartz, Irving Howe, Leon Edel, and R. W. B. Lewis. With the exception of John Berryman, who had a Catholic upbringing (but a fascination with Jews and Judaism), these young litterateurs were Jews aspiring to make their mark on American culture. While he was conducting this weekly seminar at Princeton, from which he had graduated almost forty years earlier, Wilson enrolled in the biblical Hebrew course offered at the Princeton Theological Seminary. As he later told Leon Edel, "I was harkening back to my Puritan forebears by studying 'God's sacred tongue.'" Wilson's sense of humor and keen sense of irony allowed him to joke about his Hebrew studies with Jewish friends. To Daniel Aaron, professor of American literature at Harvard, he wrote, "I am taking a course in Hebrew at the Theological Seminary here so that I can lecture to (novelist) Waldo Frank about the Jewish Genesis."[9]

Wilson's lifelong flirtation and involvement with Judaica and Jews served an intellectual function and satisfied an emotional need. It allowed Wilson to affirm his connection to his American Protestant roots while at the same time separating himself from those elements of Christian belief that he found objectionable. As essayist Mark Krupnick noted in 1997, "Turning to Ancient Jewish history was a way for this old-stock American, who had been reared as a Presbyterian, to affirm his links to his ancestral tradition without affirming his ancestors' theology." Not only did Wilson refuse to affirm his ancestors' theology, he consciously rejected all theology. Alfred Kazin pointed out that, despite Wilson's engagement with religious texts and ancient languages, he rejected religion as a guide to behavior. Wilson "made a point of being the foremost atheist of an atheistic generation. . . . He had the anger of a man who came out of that Christian heritage and was disillusioned."[10]

It was American Jews as an ethnic group, and not the study of Hebrew and Judaica as an intellectual endeavor, that first attracted Wilson's attention. Fresh from Princeton and his experience as medic and ambulance attendant in World War I, Wilson arrived in New York and fell in love with the city and its human variety, especially with its sense of sexual freedom. The reader of his memoir, *The Twenties*, can see that Wilson is a young man who has embarked on a campaign to liberate himself from prejudice and preconception. In making his way among the city's bohemians and literati Wilson seems acutely aware of the legacy of social snobbery and class prejudice bequeathed to him as an undergraduate at Princeton. A remarkable passage in *The Twenties* tells of his infatuation with Katze—a young society woman whom he "laid siege to" unsuccessfully. When Wilson cannot get her away from her boyfriend Franz, he tells her in desperation that he is sure that it is because both she and Franz are Jewish. Recounting this episode many years later, Edmund Wilson notes, "I am not at all proud of this, but I include it as an instance of the depth from which such a reaction can spring. I regard it as an example of the way in which a purely superstitious idea, that the Jews are responsible for executing Jesus, instilled in one's unconscious, may irrationally influence behavior."[11]

Not content merely to confront his own prejudices and behavior, Wilson also took exception to anti-Semitic comments made by others. He was quite disturbed when his lovers and confidants made anti-Semitic remarks. Though he did not always respond to these comments personally, he did record them in his journal.

Wilson's early writings are peppered with remarks about New York Jews

[*Christian Zionism and the Jewish State*]

he encountered in the art world. In Wilson's novel of the 1920s, *I Thought of Daisy* (1929), the narrator describes a party at which he met a young man who had recently produced a new ballet. When complimented on the show's success by a friend, the producer "accepted the compliment, with no attempt to turn it off or pretend embarrassment. He seemed serious and complacent: I wondered whether he were Jewish—he was blond, but had a hooked nose." The narrator concludes that the fellow is not Jewish, for "a Jew, no matter how serious, no matter how relentlessly preoccupied with the importance of his own activities, would have veiled with some irony of politeness his human and earthbound ambitions in this Valley of the Shadow under the eye of a jealous God."[12] Though these are comments made in passing, there are many such passages in Wilson's early writings. They reveal an interest in, and general sympathy with Jews that Wilson encountered in Gotham. That sympathy is at times tempered with humor, and the humor is seldom tinged with animosity.

This interest in and familiarity with Jews and Judaism also informed the composition in the late 1930s of *To the Finland Station*, in which Edmund Wilson depicted certain post-Enlightenment Jewish thinkers as "secular rabbis." As he saw it, these thinkers came from within the Jewish tradition and applied their intellectual skills to universal problems and their political solutions. In the wonderful chapter on Marx's student years, Wilson describes Marx as "on his way to becoming the great secular rabbi of his century."[13] Rejecting the raucous and convivial student world of German university life and shaking off "the barbarian social world of the beer-swilling and saber-brandishing German students," Marx returned to the rabbinical world of his forefathers. In his *New Republic* articles of the 1930s, Wilson foreshadowed this depiction of Marx as "rabbinic" with his sympathetic portraits of Jewish activists on the American Left. Critic Leonard Kriegel has noted that in his political reportage, "one sees Wilson's growing tendency to identify with the Jews as a group which struggles against all forms of political and social injustice."[14]

As Wilson's portrait of the young Marx unfolds he makes the case that the rabbinical aspect of Marx had a historical aspect. Wilson was aware, of course, that this was not the actual rabbinical world of European Jewry, but a sort of inherited and imagined rabbinical heritage. Wilson reminds us that "there had been concentrated in Karl Marx the blood of several lines of Jewish rabbis. There had been rabbis in his mother's family for at least a century back; and the families of both his father's parents had produced unbroken successions of rabbis, some of them distinguished teachers of the fifteenth and eighteenth centuries." Wilson knew that the young Marx disassociated himself from his Jewish background and he notes that Marx's parents apostatized to Christianity and had the young Karl baptized. He neglects to mention, however, that Karl Marx's rejection of Jewish religious and cultural traditions was radical and overt, as can be seen in Marx's essays on Jewish issues. But these facts did not dissuade Wilson from emphasizing Marx's Jewish aspects. Thus there is a disturbing, essentialist aspect to Edmund Wilson's analysis of Karl Marx's rabbinical background, a romanticizing of the "Jewish" origins of revolutionary thought. In describing Marx's years as a philosophy student at the University of Bonn, Wilson compares the young Marx to another German Jewish intellectual. "Salomon Maimon, in the century before, had tried to reconcile rabbinical philosophy with modernity. Karl Marx, also a teacher in the Jewish tradition but not quite free of the Judaic system and with all the thought of Western Europe at his disposal, was to play an unprecedented role as a leader in the modern world." As Leonard Kriegel notes: "Wilson ascribes too much to Marx's Jewishness. Occasionally, he is guilty of such dubious assertions as 'nobody but a Jew could have fought so uncompromisingly and obstinately for the victory of the dispossessed classes.'"[15]

To the Finland Station was published in 1940. During the following decade Wilson would shift his attention away from Marxism and toward the history of religious belief and unbelief. Wilson's formal study of Hebrew began in 1952 at Princeton Theological Seminary. In this initial involvement with the Hebrew language he was hearkening back to his colonial American origins. On his mother's death in 1951 he returned to the family home in Talcotville, New York, in order to go through her belongings. Rummaging in the attic he found the divinity school textbooks used by his grandfather, Thaddeus Wilson, a prominent nineteenth-century Protestant clergyman. Among the books were Hebrew study texts, a Bible, and a grammar. As he described this moment of discovery in *On First Reading Genesis*, "I had always had a certain curiosity about Hebrew, and I was perhaps piqued a little at the thought that my grandfather could read something that I couldn't, so finding myself one autumn in Princeton, with the prospect of spending the winter, I enrolled in a Hebrew course at the Theological Seminary, from which my grandfather had graduated in 1864."[16] That Wilson's grandfather studied Hebrew was not unusual. All candidates for the Presbyterian ministry had to study Hebrew and Greek, a practice still followed today at many Presbyterian seminaries. As revealed in preceding chapters here, American Protestant students at scores of colleges and seminaries in nineteenth-century America were engaged in Hebraic leaning. As we have also seen, Christian Hebraism had, independent of its Jewish origins, long-established traditions that went back to the Pilgrim leaders and the founders of Harvard College.[17] Wilson, though alienated from the theology of his Calvinist ancestors, now found himself engaged in the same world of biblical discourse that had engaged both his actual and intellectual ancestors.

This rediscovery of a family legacy, and the subsequent decision to study

Hebrew language and literature, not only tied together two strands of Wilson's family heritage, but also merged two intellectual traditions: his paternal grandfather's preparation for the Presbyterian ministry at Princeton Theological Seminary, and his mother's descent from the Mather family, with its tradition of vast scholarly erudition and a specific affinity for Hebrew studies. Cotton Mather's Harvard thesis had addressed the question of whether Hebrew was the "original language." His many works (350 books and pamphlets) were peppered with Hebrew words and phrases and he had delighted in describing Harvard College as one of the *midrashot* (Talmudic study halls) of New England. When his brother Nathan died, Mather mourned the loss of a promising young scholar of Hebrew. But he was consoled in the certainty that Nathan's knowledge of Hebrew would "ease his way into heaven."[18]

Within a few years of taking up Hebrew, Edmund Wilson became immersed in the literature of the American Civil War, studies later published as *Patriotic Gore*. In typical Edmund Wilson fashion, research on the two subjects—the Civil War and the Judaic tradition—nourished and influenced each other. *Patriotic Gore* is rich in allusions to the Old Testament background of mid-nineteenth-century American letters. The opening essay on Harriet Beecher Stowe sets the tone; we are reminded that Mrs. Stowe's husband, Calvin Stowe, was a biblical scholar and professor of Greek and Hebrew, and that her father, Lyman Beecher, was the most prominent American Protestant theologian of his time. The essay on Justice Oliver Wendell Holmes is a veritable treasure trove of American Hebraica and Judaica. Wilson delights in relating Justice Holmes's comments to Morris Cohen, in which he states his belief that his Dutch Vondal (later changed to Wendell) ancestors had been Jewish. Wilson adds, "Holmes had, in any case, in common with his Jewish friends the same background of Old Testament rigor, and they shared—however secular their faith, however, practical their professional activity—the conviction that what we do in this world must have the sanction of nonworldly values and be acted in the sight of eternity."[19]

As we have seen, the persistence and virulence of anti-Semitism also concerned Wilson. Both in *Patriotic Gore* and in his various essays on the Jews, Wilson "cites examples of a glorification of the Jews that has passed suddenly into a neurotic anti-Semitism." The writings of nineteenth-century of literary figure John Jay Chapman serve to illustrate his point. Chapman was at one time an admirer of the Jews and their culture. Later in life his admiration turned to enmity, and his comments on Jews and Judaism became quite vitriolic.[20]

Edmund Wilson visited Israel twice, first in 1954, on assignment with the *New Yorker* to research the discovery of the Dead Sea Scrolls, and again in 1967, on the eve of the Six Day War. Both visits left a deep impression on him. His visit with and subsequent essay on novelist and short story writer S. Y. Agnon introduced the Israeli writer to the American literary world. Curiously, in a reflection of Edmund Wilson's international influence in mid-century, Wilson's name was used to validate Agnon's stature among his Israeli readership. Upon the 1954 publication of Agnon's collected works, Schocken Publishers issued a Hebrew-language brochure in Agnon's honor. The only non-Israeli included in the list of fourteen literary luminaries who praised Agnon was Edmund Wilson.[21] Thus, Wilson's name appears in the company of the great Hebrew writers of the day, the Israeli Chief Rabbis, and a number of Israeli diplomats, including Abba Eban.

The philosopher Isaiah Berlin, a close friend of Wilson, told the following story about Wilson in Israel: "He went to Jordan and when he came back he had to pass through the Mandelbaum Gate. The Israeli passport officer looked at his passport, noticed it was Edmund Wilson, then said: 'I think your dating of the Dead Sea Scrolls is not quite right. I think it should have been fifty years before.' And Edmund Wilson answered, and the chief officer said: 'Stamp Mr. Wilson's passport. You can't discuss the Scrolls here, not on the government's time.' He talked to me about that afterward, saying, 'Only in Israel would I find a passport officer who wished to question the date of the Scrolls!' That amused him. It pleased him."[22]

In addition to Agnon, another Jewish writer Wilson appreciated and promoted was Isaac Bashevis Singer. The two met at a 1962 Harvard University symposium honoring Singer's work. Singer later wrote about this first meeting with Wilson in his column in the Yiddish-language *Daily Forward*: "Edmund Wilson is no longer a young man and at his age to begin the study of a foreign and difficult language as Hebrew, especially for a non-Jew, requires tremendous willpower, character, and scientific curiosity."[23] In the decade before their meeting, Wilson did much to promote Singer's American career. He penned favorable reviews of the Yiddish master's work, encouraged the *New Yorker* to publish Singer's short stories, and even made attempts to read some of those stories in Yiddish.

Wilson not only appreciated I. B. Singer as a writer, but also greatly admired him as a repository of Jewish knowledge. Here was a Jewish writer thoroughly at home in the Jewish languages and textual sources, someone who lived up to Wilson's expectations of what a Jewish writer should be. After Wilson's death Singer's appreciation of Wilson's intellectual curiosity and integrity continued to grow. As Alfred Kazin remembered in 1995, "One bright fall day during a taxi ride down to the old *Daily Forward* building on East Broadway, which the famous Yiddish paper was leaving, Singer said to me, 'Is it really true that Wilson had those Hebrew characters on his gravestone, that he admired them so much? . . . He really has this on—on his gravestone?' I said 'yes.' He said to me in Yiddish, 'Impossible to believe this is such country,' and I said, 'Bashevis, but it is.'"[24]

As Singer and other admirers noted, Wilson's curiosity seemed boundless. According to his wife Elena Wilson, "In the midst of his work on the Dead Sea Scrolls and his Civil War book, Edmund found still another project." For Wilson's creative excursus into foreign cultures did not stop with his fascination with Jewish writers and Israel. Close to the age of seventy Wilson took up Hungarian ("Hungary has really interested me more than any other country I have been in over here in Europe," he noted in a letter to his wife). He reached a high level of competence in that difficult language and was able to employ it to read novels and write letters. In the tradition of the great thinkers of the European Enlightenment, Edmund Wilson did not give up any of these interests; they were not taken up and then dropped. Rather, they overlapped and enriched each other. This erudition was often intimidating to others, accomplished in their own fields as they might be. As Michael C. D. Macdonald pointed out, personal quirks, "coupled with the scholarly reclusions of the man who had learned Russian at forty, Hebrew in his fifties, Hungarian in his sixties, and was getting up Old Slavonic and Welsh at the time of his death at seventy-seven, made Wilson somewhat trying."[25]

The essays that resulted from Wilson's ability to draw connections between seemingly disparate cultures informed and inspired generations of readers. From the 1920s through the early 1970s he had a large and loyal audience for his writing. The critic David Castronovo noted Wilson's "magnetic hold on average intelligent readers."[26] In the *New Yorker*, the *New Republic*, and the *Nation* (and in scores of other journals and newspapers), Wilson addressed his learned and engaging criticism to "the busy person who still has time for serious ideas, history, and culture, and the pleasures of amateur scholarship."[27]

But while Wilson strove for an accessible writing style and endeavored to tackle subjects with wide appeal (the Civil War, the Dead Sea Scrolls, Russian communism and its philosophical origins), he did not intend for his readers to sit back and simply absorb the material. A faithful and constant reader of Edmund Wilson was expected to work at the task: to read the book or books under discussion, to see what other critics were saying about those books, and to learn something about the history of the controversy that Wilson was either addressing or fomenting. In short, to get the full benefit of his longer essays, one had to be an engaged reader. Wilson also expected his readers to be careful readers. As one prominent critic noted, Wilson did not develop elaborate aesthetic judgments. Rather, "a generous consideration of his reader's interest is an abiding characteristic of his literary criticism."[28] Wilson's extended conversation and argument with Vladimir Nabakov, in which Wilson took issue with the accuracy of Nabokov's English translation of *Eugene Onegin*, drove many an American reader to a first reading of Pushkin's great poem. Similarly, Wilson's presentation of the "meaning" of the Dead Sea Scroll discoveries—opinions tinged with his delight in playing the "Christian heretic"—opened up the subject of early Christian origins for many Americans. What concerned Wilson in the 1960s and early 1970s—when he could see the end of his career looming—was the decline of that "intelligent skeptical reader." As he saw it, the scholar was no longer respected in American culture. Journalism had become cheapened, and the cult of celebrity was ascendant.

It was just such an affirmation of the scholarly, and an openness to criticism, that Wilson found in the Jewish intellectual tradition. He saw himself as a representative of an American cultural tradition that, though fast disappearing, could find an ally in this Jewish tradition. In his mind, what was noble about the American tradition was its "Hebraic" element. In Jewish culture he saw the possibility of American renewal—or at the very least, cultural preservation. He was therefore all the more disappointed when he encountered American Jews who knew little about their own traditions. *The Sixties*, the last volume of his memoirs, is peppered with references to Jewish acolytes and visitors who knew woefully little about the Bible, the Hebrew language, or Jewish religious customs. Even close friends came in for criticism. Critic Alfred Kazin noted that "Wilson took every area for his own. He knew more Hebrew than I've learned since my Bar Mitzvah."[29]

Wilson therefore delighted in making the acquaintance of culturally literate American Jews. While he could teach the "alienated" Jew about his or her own traditions, he could learn from the scholarly Jewish person. One such interlocutor was Jacob Landau of Bogota, New Jersey. Landau, a retired electrical engineer, ran Bob's Tavern, a working-class establishment in a small New Jersey town. In 1956, after reading Wilson's essays on Jews and Israel, Landau wrote him a fan letter. There was no immediate answer from the great critic, who was not an eager correspondent. Two years later, however, Landau wrote a second letter, from which Wilson realized that he was not only a fan, but also a scholar of Hebrew and Judaica. A long and rich epistolary friendship ensued. It lasted until Wilson's death in 1972. The two gentlemen, born within a year of each other, also exchanged gifts—primarily whiskey and books. Landau translated Hebrew and Yiddish articles for Wilson; Wilson kept Landau in touch with new developments in American culture. From this as yet unpublished correspondence we get a sense of the seriousness of Wilson's Hebraic endeavors. Writing to Landau in August of 1969, Wilson thanks his Jewish friend for sending him a new translation of Ecclesiastes. "Thanks so much for the book. I tried to read Koheleth in Hebrew a couple of winters ago, but found it so difficult—so many words that don't occur elsewhere—that finally I gave up. I look forward to reading this new translation." The letters, however, are not all about scholarship. A decade earlier, in August 1959, Wilson wrote to thank Landau for his gift of a case of liquor. "I was delighted to get the bottles which arrived in time for some guests. The gin and most of the brandy are gone, but the Bacardi is still in tact. Belated birthday greetings. I was 64 in May." They met only once, in the middle of their sixteen-year friendship. At that encounter, at New York's 92nd Street YMCA, they "talked books" and raised their glasses of Scotch to say *L'chaim*.[30]

Wilson's Hebraism had a profound effect on a number of American writers. Among them was the poet John Berryman. Berryman had studied with Wilson at Princeton in the seminar Wilson conducted in the early 1950s. In his harrowing novel-as-memoir, *Recovery* (1972), Berryman tells the story of his extended and unsuccessful treatment for alcoholism. A note at the beginning of the novel, which is set in a private psychiatric clinic, insists that "the materials of the book, especially where hallucinatory, are historical; all facts are real, ladies and gentlemen, it's true."[31] One might say that the novel's protagonist, Severance, desperate for a spiritual anchor in his chaotic and crumbling world, seeks salvation of the Jews, though he does not quite put it that way to himself. In extreme emotional distress, he takes up the study of Jewish history and ritual and dabbles in the study of the Hebrew language. Berryman/Severance wonders if he should, like Edmund Wilson, study Hebrew. "Take Hebrew: Never minded my Jewish friends knowing Hebrew, but when Edmund Wilson took it up—after Russian—at age fifty years old, I thought God damn it!"[32] Severance even considers conversion to Judaism. Berryman's role model, in all but this last important detail of contemplating actual conversion to Judaism, was Edmund Wilson. Like Berryman, Wilson drank prodigiously (but could hold his liquor) and was fascinated with the Jews and their culture. In *Recovery*, while bemoaning his own inability to sustain his interest in new languages and cultures, Berryman lauds Wilson's steadfastness, and he sees Hebrew and the Hebraic as a symbolic representation of Wilson's stability. Long before his hospitalizations for alcoholism, Berryman expressed admiration for and identification with Jews and the Jewish intellectual tradition. As a young man Berryman wrote an award-winning short story, "The Imaginary Jew." Published in 1945, it tells of a young writer who is attacked on a New York City street when he is mistaken for a Jew. As critic Denis Donoghue noted: "The Gentile hero, by a great reach of sympathy, becomes an imaginary Jew, fights the Jew's battles, accepts insults. . . . A Gentile who becomes an imaginary Jew by an act of sympathy is perhaps as complete as a modern man can be."[33]

Unlike Severance, the protagonist of Berryman's novel, who picks up Hebrew and then, lacking "staying power," drops it after only a few months, Wilson, whose intellectual staying power was legendary, stuck with the study of the "sacred tongue" and achieved a degree of competence, if not mastery. His intellectual efforts bore remarkable fruit. It was his interest in Hebrew that led the *New Yorker* to send Wilson to Israel. As an outsider, Wilson brought a degree of detachment to the subject of the Dead Sea Scrolls that partisans of religious or academic dogma could not bring to that contentious topic. Two testimonies demonstrate this point. The first is from Israeli archaeologist Yigal Yadin on Wilson's contribution to popularizing the discovery and implications of the Dead Sea Scrolls. The second is from David Flusser on Edmund Wilson's contribution to the comparative study of Judaism and Christianity. (There is other "insider" testimony about the power of Edmund Wilson's insights into foreign cultures. In the 1960s, for example, American Indian activists and writers praised his understanding of Native American culture.)[34]

In a review in the *Times Literary Supplement*, Yigal Yadin, scholar, archaeologist, and former Israeli chief of staff, had this to say about Wilson's *New Yorker* articles: "The Dead Sea Scrolls were not discovered by archaeologists but by the Bedouin, and their importance was brought to the knowledge of the world at large, again not by an archaeologist, but by a very scholarly amateur, Edmund Wilson."[35] Yadin's admiration was reciprocated. Edmund Wilson met Yadin on his 1967 journey to Israel and described him as having "an extraordinary combination of high intelligence, informed authority and almost hypnotic persuasive charm." On that same trip to Israel, Wilson met the "man he admired most in Israel," David Flusser, professor of comparative religion at Hebrew University. According to Flusser, an expert on Christian-Jewish relations in the formative periods of both rabbinic Judaism and early Christianity, "Wilson's book about the Dead Sea Scrolls raised questions which the scholars were forced to answer, and so it changed profoundly the course of research into Essenism and had an important impact upon the study of both ancient Judaism and the beginnings of Christianity. Wilson compelled the scholars to think. . . . He has written a book which is from many aspects a turning point in the research of the history of religion."[36]

While many other scholarly reviewers expressed indignation that Wilson had "blundered" into their territory and made errors of judgment, Flusser was able to see the significance of Wilson's contribution. A "scholarly amateur" could introduce insights into the discussion that seasoned experts might overlook or deliberately ignore. One biblical scholar who revised his thinking about Wilson's contribution to the conversation about the scrolls was James Sanders of Claremont College. "On first reading the 'Scrolls From the Dead Sea' essays forty years ago, I recall thinking how much he did not get quite right. By contrast, when read today his work seems not only engrossing and enthralling but also amazingly balanced and fair, given the fact that he was a self-avowed antireligionist."[37]

From the early fifties until his death in 1972 Wilson was an enthusiastic supporter of the State of Israel and often found himself defending its policies against the attacks of Jewish associates on the American left. Leon Edel noted a furious exchange (ca. 1967) between Wilson and publisher and critic Jason Epstein concerning Israel's military situation. Wilson defended Israel's policies; Epstein found them indefensible. If the Israelis were in trouble, Epstein contended, it was because "they had a talent for causing trouble by being where they didn't belong."[38] Wilson was shocked by Epstein's response. Though Wilson's support of Israel was not unconditional, it was powerful enough to arouse the ire of Edward Said and other supporters of the Palestinian cause.[39]

Wilson's affection for American Jewish life and letters was tempered and balanced by thoughtful criticism of a type usually practiced by insiders. In his rare excursions into short fiction, Edmund Wilson took up Jewish themes. In 1956, Wilson published "The Messiah at the Seder." In that story the Messiah appears in mid-twentieth-century Manhattan on the eve of Passover. He is invited to a Seder on the West Side. There he discovers that the fractious and contentious participants at the Seder—which include a Freudian, a Marxist, and a religious thinker—are unable to accept that he is the Redeemer. Nor are they able to agree on anything else. And, when they come to terms with the reality of his mission to the world, they want to deny their ideological opponents a "share in the world to come." This satire on the multiplicity of opinions in the Jewish world is anything but savage. The satirical effect is achieved with considerable subtlety and verve.[40]

Dos Passos's description of Wilson as "an uncircumcised rabbi," a comment made in response to the publication of "The Messiah at the Seder," was more than a barbed witticism aimed at a friend and ideological adversary. Dos Passos, once an ardent leftist radical, had moved to the far right of American politics. Wilson, though sprung from aristocracy and still an "aristocrat" of sorts, was a thoughtful supporter of leftist causes. A vocal opponent of the war in Vietnam, he sported, in the weeks before his death in 1972, a George McGovern button. Ideologically, the two former radicals could not have been further apart in their views. Wilson's philo-Semitism provided Dos Passos with an opportunity to respond to his old friend's criticism of his support of Barry Goldwater.

Lurking in Dos Passos's barb was a solid kernel of truth. Wilson was enjoying his ability to teach both Christians and Jews about Judaism in general and the Dead Sea Scrolls in particular. In his essays on Jewish life and literature Wilson never forgot that he was an outsider; he reminds the reader constantly that the outsider may provide insights that the insider cannot. Unlike some of his Jewish and Christian contemporaries, Wilson did not blur the sharp doctrinal and historical differences between Judaism and Christianity, or between Jewish and Christian approaches to the histories of the religious traditions. In a letter to novelist Waldo Frank, Wilson noted the following: "In general, the approach to Israel (in the large historical sense) of an Anglo-Saxon of the Old Testament puritan background is something entirely distinct from that of either the rabbinical or the Europeanized Jew."[41] It was Wilson's awareness of difference, and his unwillingness to view the Old Testament as a mere prologue to the New Testament, that sharpened his critical view and enabled him to write sympathetically about Israel and the Jews.

In the 1960s Wilson was dismayed at what he saw as the decline of reading and the shrinking of an audience for serious, accessible literary criticism. He was especially dismayed to meet Jews who knew little of their own culture, however sophisticated they might be with regard to English and American literature and politics. Here his romanticized view of the relationship between Jewish ethnicity and Judaic culture came into play. For he found it difficult to accept that an American Jewish intellectual might be ignorant of his or her "own" cultural traditions. On making the acquaintance of American intellectuals of Jewish origin he would assume, often mistakenly, that they had some "innate" knowledge of Hebrew and Judaic lore. Jason Epstein remarked that Wilson "had convinced himself, completely inaccurately, that I knew Hebrew and could teach him something about it. I knew nothing about Hebrew, but whenever I saw him in those years, he would ask me whether I knew Hebrew or not. I suppose he assumed that in the interval between each occasion I'd learned it, but that's what he was like."[42]

Mark Krupnick observed that "thinking of himself as a kind of Jew gave Wilson a dignified alternative to what seemed to him the cheapness and light-mindedness of twentieth-century American culture."[43] Wilson had predicted this decline of culture long before mid-century, and he saw himself, and other readers and writers committed to exacting cultural standards, as a bulwark against such decline. As early as 1939 he had written, "I know now that the tides of society can give a new configuration to all but the strongest personalities, if they do not sweep them away."[44] He for one would not be swept away—and he would exhort others to hold the tide with him.

Wilson's interest in the Bible, Hebrew, and the Jews persisted until the end of his life. Alfred Kazin, visiting the declining Wilson at his Cape Cod home left us this literary snapshot: "Edmund Wilson, the perfectionist, always correcting a word, a fact. Still obsessed with the word in his old age—bitterly disillusioned with America and shakily confronting the end. In his Wellfleet kitchen he (with more Hebrew than I could ever master) asked me—me!—what the Jewish religion could offer a man in his situation."[45]

Wilson left instructions for the conduct of his funeral, requesting that Old

Testament readings be central to the service. At the funeral, in June of 1972, a number of Psalms were read, as well as the twelfth and final chapter of Ecclesiastes. Despite his frequent anticlerical statements and his declaration that he was "not a Christian," Wilson requested the full ritual of the Presbyterian church in which he had been baptized. The church ceremony had its Judaic aspects (and its comic moments). Wilson's cousin, Charley Walker, the eminent Yale labor historian, opened his eulogy with the phrase "Shalom, Dear Edmund," and above the protestations of Wilson's widow Elena, Walker called Wilson "a religious man."[46]

In the Wellfleet cemetery on Cape Cod, Wilson's tombstone is adorned with the Hebrew phrase he so loved—"*Hazak Hazak Venithazek*," "Be strong and be strengthened"—inscribed in Hebrew on its base. His wife Elena, who died a few years after he did, is buried next to him. At the base of her tombstone, in Greek, is the phrase "the immortal soul." I visited the Wilsons' graves during Wilson's centennial year, and I found a small mound of stones at the base of each tombstone. These markers were in emulation of the Jewish custom of leaving small stones at the grave as a sign of respect and remembrance for the departed. No such stones were to be found at other graves in Wellfleet's sprawling and well-cared-for Protestant cemetery. Wilson's "long affair" with Judaism and the Jews had lasted beyond his death. Deeply moved, I gathered a few pebbles and set them among the beautifully polished beach stones that earlier visitors had left. I bowed my head, whispered "Shalom, Dear Edmund," and slowly walked toward the cemetery gates.

EPILOGUE
AMERICAN BIBLICISM AND
MODERN POLITICS

At the opening session of the Madrid Peace Conference in 1991, Israeli prime minister Yitzhak Shamir forcefully reminded his audience of the case for Jewish sovereignty in Palestine. In doing so he did not cite the Bible or the Balfour Declaration. Rather, he chose an American text—and an unlikely one at that—Mark Twain's *The Innocents Abroad*. Twain, as passenger and observer on an American tourist excursion, presented his legion of readers with an extensive, and hilarious, report on Ottoman Palestine. He remarked on the waste and desolation of the Holy Land and contrasted it with the peaceful and pastoral land described in the biblical narrative. If we accept Mark Twain's report as factual, argued Shamir, it is clear that Palestine was desolate before Jewish settlement restored it to its former glory. Little did Twain suspect that his depiction of Palestine as a wasteland would become a tool in the continuing and bitter debate over the history of Israel and Palestine. For these arguments about the past are often bound up with opinions about the future. Shamir's recourse to a satire written in the 1860s confirms the observation that nineteenth-century views of the Holy Land are of more than antiquarian interest—they now serve as ammunition in the polemics of the Arab-Israeli conflict.[1]

The Madrid Peace Conference created the conditions for the secretly negotiated Oslo Accords of 1993, accords which have since collapsed. The power of Mark Twain's assessment of Ottoman Palestine is still very much alive. Curiously, it has been used to refute documentary evidence from nineteenth-century Palestine that indicates that the country was not "desolate." But it is the Bible and not documentary evidence that is the bedrock of American support for the Jewish state. William Blackstone's petitions of 1891 and 1916, petitions in which he called on the American president to honor the biblical promise to restore the Jews to their land, have succeeded in a remarkable manner. One hundred and ten years after four hundred prominent Americans signed the first Blackstone Memorial, and eighty-five years after the American Zionist movement joined forces with Blackstone and other Christian evangelists to renew support for political Zionism, the president, his administration, and a large segment of the American people are supportive of Israel, its government, and its policies. As this book has demonstrated the story behind this remarkable success is complex and multilayered. Colonial American identification with biblical Israel was one component on which support for the idea of a Jewish state was built.

While Mark Twain and other American humorists may have satirized the Bible and American biblicism, that tradition of identification with the Bible and its narratives resisted satire, held steadfast, and grew stronger. Many American Christians continued to read the Bible and understand it literally. Eventually biblical literacy and a literalist understanding of the bible (or "biblical inerrancy") converged. In the nineteenth century, a degree of biblical literacy was expected of all Americans. In the middle to late twentieth century the percentage of Americans who understood the Bible literally increased dramatically. In his petitions, which presumed biblical literacy *and* a literal interpretation of Scripture, Blackstone referred to the Persian King who enabled the return from Babylon. He called on the American president to act as "a modern Cyrus and help restore the Jews to Zion."

When, in 1948, President Truman, over the objections of the State Department, granted diplomatic recognition to the new State of Israel, he fulfilled that Cyrus role. And this is not a matter of interpreting a presidential act in the light of earlier evangelical expectations. Rather, Truman himself offered an explanation that reflected those evangelical expectations. After he left the presidency, Truman was awarded an honorary degree by New York's Jewish Theological Seminary. Introduced as "the man who helped create the State of Israel," Truman, obviously deeply moved, said; "Yes, I am Cyrus." In his memoirs Truman recounts that during the seven years he was in office he read the Bible seven times. Brought up in the Baptist church and schooled in a biblicist culture, he read the Bible seriously and to some extent literally. As he saw it the Jewish return to Zion was an expectation he as American president could help fulfill. The political and diplomatic considerations of his advisors, especially those in the State Department, could be set aside, for Truman had an historic and—as many at the time understood it—divinely ordained role to fulfill. One of Truman's close advisors, Clark Clifford, wrote that "from his reading of the Old Testament he felt the Jews derived a legitimate historical right to Palestine, and he sometimes cited such biblical lines as Deuteronomy 1:8: 'Behold, I have given up the land before you; go in and take possession of the land which the Lord hath sworn unto your fathers, to Abraham, to Isaac and to Jacob.'"[2] The reader will recall Selah Merrill's opposition to Jewish emigration to Palestine. As American consul in Jerusalem at the end of the nineteenth century he fought the ideas of the Blackstone Memorial. Many in the State Department shared his views. Truman overrode their objections and recognized the State of Israel.

In evaluating President Truman's motives for support of the Zionist cause, historian David McCullough wrote that political considerations, including the wish to win the approval of Jewish voters in the key states of Pennsylvania, Illinois, and New York, were significant factors. But, McCullough notes, "beyond the so-called 'Jewish vote' there was the country at large, where popular support for a Jewish homeland was overwhelming. As would sometimes be forgotten, it was not just American Jews who were stirred by the prospect of a new nation for the Jewish people, it was most of America."[3]

When they considered the idea of a modern Jewish state, many Americans conjured the ancient biblical past. Equally powerful was the memory of America's past. Zionist claims to Palestine echoed U.S. claims to the American West. If the Jewish settlers had to contend with Arab opposition, this was reminiscent of American Indian opposition. The Jews, as westerners (of a sort), signified the ideas of progress, technology, and culture. The Arabs were depicted as the enemies of these values.

Colonial American identification with biblical Israel, an idea whose power had waned in the nineteenth century, returned in the mid-twentieth century. For that idea was now linked to the reemergence of biblical Israel in the form of a modern Jewish state, and that state would pattern itself on the history of the United States—"God's American Israel." Americans had long identified themselves as a people of destiny. The Hebrew Bible provided a narrative with which, and a people with whom, Americans could identify. When Jews, a biblical people, established a modern state, most Americans identified with its struggles.

American Evangelical Christianity and Israel

For the past half-century the State of Israel has had great symbolic significance for American Jews. Support of Israel is part of what we might call Jewish "civil religion." Today, for many Jews, religious and secular, the Jewish state now has religious and spiritual significance. A more scripturally based and religiously oriented view of Israel has emerged, one that parallels the biblicist literalism of Evangelical Christians. To some extent this has moved many American Jews to support religious Zionism and the settlers of the West Bank and Gaza. The turning point in this development was the 1973 Arab-Israeli war, a conflict interpreted by many Jews, Israeli and American, as a wake-up call to religious observance and ethnic identification.

One of the surprising aspects of Christian Zionism is that Israel has become equally significant as a religious symbol for many Christians. In the past few years this attachment has facilitated contacts between Jewish and Christian supporters of the Israeli government, most strikingly in the form of Christian

Evangelical pilgrimages to Jerusalem—where the leadership and rank and file of the movement is addressed by the Israeli political leadership. As historian of religion Martin Marty noted in 1991, "No American can understand foreign policy in respect to the Middle East, especially when Israel is the focus without having to deal with a cohort of the population which is dispensationalist."[4] For that growing group of Americans the current "dispensation" or age is coming to an end, and the millennium is near. But the millennium can only be ushered in by great suffering, the period of "Jacob's Tribulations." Israel is the place where these tribulations will begin, and where they will culminate in the Second Coming.[5]

Strange bedfellows indeed have resulted from the politics of Evangelical support of Israel. In 1981 Israeli prime minister Menahem Begin awarded the Jabotinsky Prize to Evangelical leader Jerry Falwell. Like his predecessors in the office of prime minister, Begin felt that the Christian Zionist support was powerful political capital in the United States. The Evangelical idea that support for Israel was predicated on a vision of the End Time in which Jews suffer and accept Jesus was not taken seriously by Israelis. Two decades before Begin awarded a prize to Jerry Falwell, David Ben Gurion, Israel's first prime minister, spoke before a delegation of visiting American Pentecostalists. He was unaware that the official theology of the Assemblies of God, then the largest Pentecostal group, was very explicit about the need to convert Jews to Christianity. Support for the State of Israel was central to their theology, as the restoration of the Jews to their land was the sign of the imminent Second Coming. A 1950 tract of the Assemblies of God stated that "the final blow upon this unfortunate and stubborn people will come during the Tribulation period; and it will be this awful time of suffering that shall break their will and turn the remnant to acceptance of the once hated Nazarene, the Lord Jesus Christ."[6]

This startling quote can serve as a reminder that Evangelical enthusiasm for Israel has not diminished the missionary fervor of some Christian groups. For some groups, the establishment of Israel provided a renewed impetus to missionize and a new place—the Holy Land—in which to missionize. According to their theology, the Jews have a pivotal role to play in the events of the End Time. Their gathering in the State of Israel, understood as the first stage of the Redemption, served as a catalyst for Christian missionary groups to spread the Gospel, translated into Hebrew, directly to Israeli Jews. To some extents these efforts have borne fruit and there are now thousands of Israeli Jews practicing various forms of Christianity.[7]

Israeli critic Gershon Gorenberg pointed out recently in the *New York Times* that "Israel has intoxicated Christian fundamentalists since the day it was established. In their eyes, the Jewish state provides real-world proof that their reading of biblical prophecies is correct—and that the world is racing toward the Second Coming. Israeli rightists have encouraged conservative Evangelicals like Jerry Falwell and Robertson to translate that fascination into active backing for hardline Israeli positions."[8]

Throughout this book I have presented evidence that this idea is powerful in a number of Protestant denominations. I have also presented a balance to this millenialist stratum in the work of liberal exponents of Christian thought, such as Reinhold Niebuhr. His *Nation* articles of the 1940s in support of Jewish statehood had great resonance among liberals, but the force of these liberal ideas about Israel waned over the subsequent three decades. Liberals tended to criticize Israeli policies that clashed with their worldview and thus they couldn't offer unqualified support for the Jewish state. Unburdened by such issues, Evangelicals could provide that support. In that way they were more politically reliable than liberal American Jews, many of whom support the Israeli state but may be critical of some of its policies.

Evangelical Christian theologies mapped onto a dichotomous/binary view of the Arab-Israeli conflict in a number of fascinating ways. For if the American media and the general public saw the conflict between Israel and the Arabs as a conflict between progressive western values and reactionary Middle Eastern tribal ways, Evangelicals added a startling dimension to this dichotomy. In their view Israel's victories in the Arab-Israeli wars were the triumph of divinely ordained Good over human Evil. God's plan in history, revealed to humanity in the Bible, was now unfolding against the background of the East-West struggle of the Cold War. Destiny was again working itself out in the Holy Land. For millenialist Christians the Jewish people again had a pivotal role in human affairs. Just as they had provided the historical circumstance for the First Coming, the Jews in their land would enable the Second Coming. This theology had been developing before the 1967 war; after that war it placed its hopes on the fulfillment of a quite specific scenario: that the Jewish state would rebuild the Temple and thus set the stage for the End of Days. 'Tribulations' would follow and "Jacob" (the people of Israel) would endure loss and suffering. With the return of Jesus the historic mission of the Jewish people would be fulfilled. Many would perish, and the remnant would become the vanguard of believers in Jesus.

As I noted earlier, this scenario, once held by small millenialist groups within the Protestant denominations, had by the 1970s become widely accepted. The astonishing publishing phenomenon of the *Left Behind* series, which has sold thirty-five million copies, attests to the appeal of End Time scenarios to the American reading public. By 2002, conservative Evangelical churches had millions of adherents. For the leadership of many of these Evangelical churches, the politics of the Israeli right wing are the only acceptable Israeli politics. Much of their venom and disdain is reserved for secular Israelis and liberal American Jews. Evangelical spokesman Jan Willem van der Hoeven, former head of the "International Christian Embassy" in Jerusalem, has stated that opposition to the policy of settling East Jerusalem, the West Bank, and the Gaza Strip and the intent to give up Israeli control of these territories would mark "the second time the Jews rejected God."[9] Neibuhr's liberal perspective, which saw the creation of a Jewish state as a historical necessity after the destruction of European Jewry during the Second World War, has been eclipsed. Support for Israel among both Christians and Jews is now theologized. In keeping with the shift from politics to religion as a mode of explaining regional conflict, historical antipathies between Christianity and Islam are now exploited by American fundamentalists. In 2002 Pat Robertson and Jerry Falwell, leaders of the Christian Right and ardent supporters of the Israeli Right, made defamatory statements about Islam. Robertson criticized President Bush for not recognizing that Islam is "violent at its core." Falwell, in early October 2002, said on the CBS program *60 Minutes*, "I think Muhammed was a terrorist."[10] Against the background of the September 11, 2001, attacks these remarks have found great resonance in the United States. A great many Americans now understand Middle East conflicts as clashes of religion and "civilizations," not clashes between economic and political adversaries.

In a remarkable political shift many American Jewish organizations have welcomed the support of Evangelical Christian Zionists. In 2002 the Anti-Defamation League (ADL) of B'nai B'rith, long at the forefront of liberal and civil libertarian causes, took out an ad in major American newspapers. It reprinted "We People of Faith Stand Firmly with Israel," an article by Ralph Reed, former head of the Christian Coalition. Only three years earlier the ADL had condemned "Christian theological extremism," even if its adherents supported Israel. As of early 2003, the "clash of civilizations" paradigm, and the End Time scenario, its theological counterpart, has a firm hold on many Jewish and Christian groups.

American Jewish Culture, Jewish Studies,
and the Legacies of Christian Hebraism

While this millenialist ideology is the most dramatic and politically powerful consequence of Christian Zionism, it is far from the only effect of Christian Hebraism and Christian Zionism on American culture. The reader will recall the irony of Edmund Wilson's situation when he led a seminar at Princeton in 1952. His students were American Jews who wished to enter the literary circles he dominated. Studying Hebrew and Judaic texts was the furthest thing from their minds. But Wilson, their teacher, was enrolled at the same time in a biblical Hebrew class at Princeton Theological Seminary, the seminary his grandfather had attended. Among Wilson's students that summer were Saul Bellow, Delmore Schwartz, and Irving Howe. As novelist, poet, and critic, these three writers rose to great prominence, signaling the entry of Jewish Americans into the literary world, an entry which made an indelible mark on mid-century American culture. Their work, informed but not dominated by Jewish themes, resonated with other minority groups and served to displace the works of the Anglo-Saxon elites. Other minority writers followed them into the literary establishment. WASP ascendancy ended, to be replaced by a new establishment.

Literature and the arts was one area where American Jews made their mark in the twentieth century. The study of Jewish thought, Hebrew, and the Bible, long the preserve of Protestant elites, was another. Throughout *God's Sacred Tongue* I have noted the ambivalence inherent in Christian Hebraism. In the early twentieth century the Protestant hegemony in biblical studies was challenged by Jewish scholars, and over time traditional Jewish modes of interpretation and discourse slowly entered the academy. This shift was facilitated by the entry of Jewish scholars into the higher reaches of American academic life. How this development influenced academic culture is worth tracing.

As the nineteenth century drew to a close, Christian hegemony in Hebrew studies was soon to meet a formidable challenge in the person of Jewish scholars from Europe. The story of Professor Isaac Nordheimer of New York University, told in Chapter 8, provides us with an early example. While a small band of these scholars was able to enter the American academy as full-fledged members—one thinks of Morris Jastrow at the University of Pennsylvania, and Richard Gottheil at Columbia—their influence was limited. But through their writings, and through their subtle but effective challenge to Christian control over the newly defined field of "Semitics," they enabled other Jewish scholars to enter into the American academy. The "long descendants of the Israelite," acculturated to American life, had now entered the academies founded by colonial-era Hebraists, Orientalists, and other claimants to the heritage of the "Old Israel."

In the first half of the twentieth century a small group of Jewish scholars of Judaica won appointments at prestigious American universities. In my chapter on William Rainey Harper, I profiled Rabbi Emil Hirsch, appointed to the Department of Philosophy at the University of Chicago. At Harvard, Harry Austryn Wolfson taught in the Department of Philosophy from 1928 to 1954. A poor immigrant from Russia, he entered Harvard on a scholarship and remained there for all of his illustrious career. This was the first "Jewish Studies" appointment in the United States. Soon afterwards, at Columbia University (where founder Samuel Johnson had attempted to introduce Hebrew into the curriculum in the 1780s), the decision was made to appoint a Jewish historian of the Jewish experience—Salo Baron. Wolfson and Baron, at Harvard and Columbia, were the first of a long series of appointments of Jewish scholars of Jewish history and literature at American universities. The concept of university Jewish studies evolved under their influence. Almost without exception these teachers were ardent Zionists, and this in turn facilitated a growing academic link to Israeli scholars.[11]

In the second half of the twentieth century Hebrew studies in the United States were directly affected by Israeli culture. Today, modern Israeli Hebrew language and literature is taught in hundreds of American colleges and universities. The great majority of students in these classes are Jewish. In the South and the Midwest, they are joined by students from Evangelical Christian families who are eager to learn the language of Israel. The culture wars of the 1980s, and the identity politics that were part of the ammunition of those wars, created to a situation in which "heritage" language teaching emerged. Students of a given ethnicity would sign up for courses in their "heritage language." The teacher, imagined as a representative of that heritage, would, of course, have to be a "member of the tribe"—whatever the tribe happened to be. This pedagogical situation was problematic but also had its affirming, amusing, and intriguing aspects. While the study of Hebrew was considered a marker of Jewish identity on campus, its identity-linked status didn't ensure that teaching was at the highest level and that competence in the language was achieved.

Language, Identity, and Culture

In 1992 the then exiled president of Haiti, Father Jean-Bertrand Aristide, was invited to address a meeting of the Jewish Community Relations Council of New York City. Aristide, known for his friendships with both Israelis and African Americans, seemed a natural choice in a time of rising black-Jewish tensions in the city. He came well prepared for the meeting; in one sense he came too well prepared. For after short opening remarks in English he proceeded to deliver a speech in Israeli Hebrew. The applause, though polite, was muted. Very few of his listeners understood his remarks. As the president of the Community Relations Council put it in his response, "Mr. President, you gave us more credit than we deserve." Aristide, ordained as a Catholic priest, and trained as a specialist in biblical studies, had studied for a number of years at the Hebrew University of Jerusalem. His audience that day may have visited the Hebrew University, but they hadn't studied the language there, and didn't deem it of sufficient importance to devote their time to mastering it as Aristide had. This story reflects a harsh reality—that knowledge of spoken Hebrew is extremely rare among the leadership of American Jewish organizations.[12]

Though so much of American Jewish identity is wrapped up with its real and imaged connection to the State of Israel, this identification has not extended so far as to raise the level of Hebraic knowledge. Numerous paradoxes play out here. Today modern Israeli Hebrew is taught on hundreds of college campuses. Many college Hebrew teachers are Israeli-born and culturally secularist. But the expectation of many students is that their Hebrew classes will have religious, Judaic content. And it is the hope of many parents of college students that Hebrew classes will reinforce the Jewish identity of their children. For this is the expectation fostered by many college Hebrew classes and by American Hebrew school supplementary education. As social critic Leonard Fein wittily remarked: "Hebrew school is remembered as the place where Hebrew wasn't learnt." What was learned was a strong sense of identification with Jews throughout the world, and especially with the State of Israel. What wasn't learned was the Hebrew language and Judaic texts.

A rich fictional evocation of this Hebrew school paradox appears in the closing pages of Philip Roth's *Operation Shylock*, the first major American novel to have a Hebrew epigraph (though a Hebrew word for "whale" appears in the opening pages of *Moby-Dick*). The epigraph is the verse from Genesis that describes Jacob's struggle with the angel. "So Jacob was left alone, and a man wrestled with him until daybreak." The import of this verse is not clear until the very end of this long novel. Waiting in a Jerusalem yeshiva classroom for a meeting with the head of the Mossad, the Israeli intelligence agency, the novel's protagonist contemplates some Hebrew writing on the board:

> On the blackboard I saw something written in Hebrew. Nine words. I couldn't read one of them. Four decades after those three years of afternoon classes at Hebrew school, I could no longer even identify the letters of the alphabet. . . . But how could anything come of going to Hebrew school? The teachers were lonely foreigners, poorly paid refugees, and the students—the best among us along with the worst—were bored restless American kids, ten, eleven, twelve years old, resentful of being cooped up like this year after year. . . . What could possibly come of these three or four hundred hours of the worst possible teaching in the worst possible atmosphere for learning? Why everything—what came of it was *everything*![13]

For Roth, as for many in the American Jewish community, the fact that so much came of so little is still a mystery. But what came was identification with Jews elsewhere and with the Israeli state, not a knowledge of the language or texts. Text had been replaced by the idea of the reborn nation. Along with other groups in the United States, many Jews had lost connection with the founding texts of their culture. Ethnic pride served as a replacement for textual knowledge. As a character in Saul Bellow's *Humboldt's Gift* states, "Our grandfather was one of the ten guys in the Jewish Pale who knew the Babylonian Talmud by heart. Lots of good that did. I don't even know what it is."

The New England Colleges and the Protestant Seminary Legacy

In the 1980s Dartmouth College, an Ivy League school that proudly highlights its roots in colonial America and the early Republic, decided to establish a program in Hebrew language and literature. The languages and texts of both modern Israeli Hebrew and Classical Hebrew would feature in the curriculum. As the first professor in that program I was often asked (and soon came to ask myself) an important question: Who had taught Hebrew at Dartmouth before me? I did the requisite research and found that the previous professor of Hebrew, one John Smith, had died in 1809! He had also been college librarian and professor of Latin; his grave was in the college cemetery. Smith wrote a Hebrew grammar for the use of his students, but like Judah Monis, Stephen Sewall, and Ezra Stiles, he suffered their insults for trying to impose on them the finer points of Hebrew syntax and grammar. He was a Christian Hebraist in the grand tradition that had been transmitted to the American Colonies from the English universities and churches. I was a Jewish scholar and teacher of Hebrew who was soon to become fascinated by the history and implications of the Christian Hebraist endeavor.

My search for American Hebraist materials led me to the libraries and archives of many of the ten colleges founded before the American Revolution. As I read through the lecture notes, grammar books, and marginalia of America's earliest professors of Hebrew and the Bible, I was struck by the persistence of themes that occupy scholars to this day. Even the age-old question of whether to teach the vowel points was still with us. The most fascinating breaks in continuity were twofold. First was the shift from a Protestant-seminary-dominated understanding of Hebrew and the Bible to a more secular, scientific understanding. This new secular orientation was organized under the rubric of "Semitic Studies" and it emerged at the end of the nineteenth and the beginning of the twentieth century. Second, in the mid-twentieth century a Jewish studies paradigm emerged; to a large extent this was energized by the entry of Jewish teachers of Hebrew into the academy and the establishment of the State of Israel. These Jewish teachers of Hebrew worked closely with their Christian counterparts in the formation of professional organizations that would promote high-level Hebrew studies in the academy. Most of the early members of the National Association of Professors of Hebrew, founded in 1950, were Christian professors of Hebrew in Protestant seminaries. Today, that organization is predominantly, though not exclusively, Jewish in membership.

The rise of Israeli Hebrew and Jewish studies classes didn't eclipse Protestant Hebraist traditions. These continued and at some schools flourished. What Arnold Band has identified as "Divinity School Hebrew" is still taught at the major Protestant seminaries. Harvard's Hancock Professorship, whose first incumbent was Stephen Sewall, is still a prestigious appointment at that university. Modern Israeli culture influenced the teaching and study of Hebrew in divinity schools as well, perhaps not in as direct a manner as it influenced many college Hebrew courses—where the instructor was often Israeli and the students are Jewish—but in a manner directly related to the theme of this book. The Hebrew Bible, and Judaic texts that touch on Christian origins (the Dead Sea Scrolls is the most obvious but not the only example), are widely studied and taught at American divinity schools. In addition, the archaeology of both the Old and New Testaments is an important component of seminary biblical studies programs. Many of these schools have study programs in Israel. In the 1970s the Mormon Church, whose founder Joseph Smith studied Hebrew with Joshua/James Seixas, built a School for Near Eastern Studies on the slopes of Jerusalem's Mount of Olives. That church's commitment to the State of Israel remains steadfast, and the establishment of the Jewish state is viewed by Mormons as the fulfillment of divine promise. For hadn't Joseph Smith, in 1841, sent his disciple Orson Hyde to Jerusalem to bless the Holy City and pray for the restoration of the Jews to their land?

At the Mormon School for Near Eastern Studies, at Jerusalem's American School for Oriental Research, at the Hebrew Union College Jerusalem campus, and at scores of other institutes throughout Israel, Edward Robinson's legacy, which tied together the study of the Bible and archaeology, is very much alive. Robinson's name is immortalized in Jerusalem's Old City, where "Robinson's Arch" is pointed out to tourists. More significantly, the legacy of Robinson's idea that the Bible cannot be understood without seeing and studying the remnants of the biblical world is stronger than ever before. Modern Israel and its archaeological sites constitute the "Third Testament" that Robinson and his followers spoke of. Remarkably, this concept has influenced Jews and Catholics as much as it has Protestants. Israeli archaeology—tied to national identity and the biblical past—is a direct outgrowth of American and European methods and theories of archaeological research. And for many secular Israelis, archaeology is a national pastime. Catholic scholars, most notably those associated with Jerusalem's Ecole Biblique, have made great contributions to biblical archaeology. The excavations at Qumran, under the direction of Father de Vaux, are a prime example. Americans continue to be fascinated with Holy Land archaeology. Witness the tours and the many excavations conducted every summer. The 2002 excitement over the so-called "Jesus Box," a first-century ossuary or bone box inscribed with the name of "James, brother of Jesus" is one illustration of that abiding interest.[14]

News of actual biblical artifacts attract wide attention; replicas of Holy Land sites and artifacts have long attracted Americans in droves. As early as 1874 Palestine Park emerged on the shores of New York State's Lake Chautauqua. Built by the founders of the highly influential Chautauqua adult education program, this park was designed to teach the basics of Holy Land geography and history. Scale models of Palestine's cities and towns were laid out on the shores of the lake, its "Mediterranean Coast." Most popular of Holy Land re-creations were replicas of Jerusalem's Old City, particularly of the Temple Mount. At the 1904 World's Fair, the Louisiana Purchase Exposition in St. Louis, Missouri, there was a massive model of Jerusalem's Old City. It sprawled over ten acres of the fairgrounds and included grand models of the Dome of the rock and the Church of the Holy Sepulcher. As Israeli scholar Rehav Rubin remarked: "the most astonishing fact about the enterprise is that several hundred people, Moslems, Jews, and Christians, were brought from Jerusalem to St. Louis. There they lived and worked within the model, dressed in their colorful costumes . . . and had to entertain and guide the visitors through its streets and sites."[15] Contemporary surrogate pilgrimage sites include Florida's Holy Land theme park (associated with Messianic Jews), and the Bridgeport, Connecticut, Holy Land (now fallen into disuse).

Though many Americans have visited Israel, the attraction of these home-made Holy Lands is still strong. And if the Middle East remains engulfed in war, these sites may serve as a viable alternative to seeing the real thing. Oddly, the recent inaccessibility of the Holy Land to travelers—an inaccessibility born of war—parallels the American situation before the Civil War and the advent of steamship travel. Palestine-mania had grabbed the imagination of mid-nineteenth-century America—but one couldn't get there. Simulations of Holy Land sites were constructed near urban centers and drew thousands of visitors. These models of the holy places served as a surrogate for travel to the Holy Land. By the 1870s when steamship travel was widely available and Jaffa could be reached in a three-week voyage, wealthy and influential Americans went to see the actual biblical sites. For those who couldn't—books, paintings, and theme parks were provided. In Part III of this book we saw how interest in Palestine generated changes in the work of American painters, among them Frederic Church. Today, television documentaries and websites provide virtual tours of the holy sites for those who can't visit either the Holy Land or American Holy Land theme parks.[16]

Throughout this book I have focused on American Christian engagement with Hebrew and the Bible—and with parallel or contrasting Jewish understandings of Hebrew and the Bible. For the most part my focus has been on Old Testament narratives. New Testament studies have also been revolutionized by Christian scholars' renewed engagement with Jewish languages and texts. One great reevaluation here has been in the study of the life of Jesus. The old model (European) downplayed Christianity's Jewish roots; the new model (American) confronted and emphasized the Judaic elements in Christian origins. I illustrated this clash of models with the Tillich-Niebuhr debate, in which the German theologian and his American colleague argued about the proper role of the Jewish past in the Christian present. Among the landmarks of this reassessment of the Jewish elements in early Christian thought was the 1922 publication of Strack's *Commentary on the New Testament*, which provided scholars of comparative religion with the opportunity to study the text of the New Testament against the background of rabbinic literature. In Strack's book, comparisons and parallels to the sayings of Jesus and the writings of the Evangelists were organized by New Testament book. For example, the context of "Repent, for the Kingdom of Heaven is at Hand," in Matthew 4:17, is provided by giving the reader references to scores of rabbinic statements on *Malkhut Shamayim*, the Hebrew phrase "Kingdom of Heaven." Over time, the effect of Strack's work was profound, especially in American Protestant circles, for it made claims about the rabbinic background of early Christianity that couldn't be ignored. Some more exegetically conservative scholars might try to refute these claims, but they couldn't ignore the textual evidence.

In Israel, too, there has been a reevaluation of Jesus. This engagement with a basic issue in Christian-Jewish relations began a quarter century before the establishment of the Jewish state. Joseph Klausner's 1922 Hebrew-language book, *Jesus of Nazareth* (published in the same year as Strack's commentary on the New Testament), began this process. In that study Jesus emerges as a rabbinic Jew whose parables and other teachings can only be understood against the background of Second Temple Judaism. Harvard's George Foot Moore read the book in Hebrew and praised it as a landmark study. Writing in the *Harvard Theological Review* of 1923, Moore noted that "the chapters on the teachings of Jesus are the part of the work in which Christian scholars would find the greatest intrinsic interest. . . . Unfortunately, a work written in Hebrew is a sealed book to most Christian readers. A translation of this part of the volume at least would be worth while." In 1925 a translation of the full text of Klausner's book was completed by Herbert Danby, Anglican bishop of Jerusalem and a twentieth-century exemplar of Christian Hebraist tradition. Danby, translator of the Mishna into English and friend of the Hebrew poet Haim Nahman Bialik, proudly notes in the preface that "this is probably the first time that a Modern Hebrew book of any considerable size has been translated into English." Danby then conveys a remarkable request from Klausner, the author: "He hopes that many of his fellow Jews, who are English speaking, may be helped by this translation to acquire a knowledge of present-day Hebrew." A remarkable notion: that a Hebrew book about Jesus will help American Jews learn the revived language of Jewish settlement in the Holy Land.[17]

Another area of inquiry in which the Jewish-Christian relationship was mediated and reevaluated was that of Kabbalism. A thread that weaves in and out of my narrative has been the persistence and centrality of Kabbalism, Jewish and Christian. The lives and writings of Judah Monis, Ezra Stiles, Jonathan Edwards, and the Mormon prophet Joseph Smith were influenced by kabbalistic ideas. Often presented in esoteric, recondite, hermetic form, these concepts have had a vigorous afterlife in American culture. Some mystical ideas and practices lived on in folkways of the nineteenth century and in popular culture of the twentieth. Today these mystical ideas are associated with the emergence of New Age religions, and with the infusion and inclusion of mystical ideas into established religious denominations. The last thirty years have seen the exponential growth of popular Kabbalah courses, institutes, books, and websites devoted to esoteric practices and ideas. These Kabbalah activities can be found in Jewish, Christian, and New Age contexts or settings. In all of these settings references abound to Hebrew language and Judaic concepts. In early-twenty-first-century America, Hebrew phrases and Jewish practices appear in the culture in unexpected and startling ways.

The Jewish-Indian theory, which figured so prominently in the early chapters of *God's Sacred Tongue*, has been consigned to the dustbin of antiquated ideas, but the search for the Ten Lost Tribes lives on in other forms. Eighteenth-century speculation that the Afghan tribes are descended from Judean exiles has been revived by Israeli anthropologists. According to these theorists, the Pashtun tribesman (the "Pathans" of the British) have many traditions that could be understood as Judaic. This is but one of many such identifications of Asian and African peoples with the Lost Tribes of Israel. What makes the modern situation radically different from the pre-modern period is that some of those identified as lost Jews have actually joined (or "rejoined") the Jewish people—and some have settled in the State of Israel. Other groups, including the Lemba of South Africa, have established ties with existing Jewish communities and do not plan to join the "Ingathering of the Exiles" in Israel. The largest and most famous Lost Tribe is from Ethiopia. Tens of thousands of Ethiopian Jews, the "Falasha" who identify themselves with the Tribe of Dan, were brought to Israel in the 1980s and 1990s. The airlifts by which the Ethiopians were transported to Israel were dubbed by the Israelis "Operation Solomon" and "Operation Moses," evoking biblical motifs in the service of modern politics. This situation provides a striking example of the potent mix of modern international politics and biblical literalism.

George Bush Revisited

Over the past three decades the careers of many American scholars, mystics, and prophets have been reevaluated. Among the cultural figures of the American past who have attracted recent attention is Professor George Bush, the early-nineteenth-century scholar who was the subject of a chapter in Part II. Until recently, Bush remained an obscure nineteenth-century figure. Just as Joshua/James Seixas was remembered in histories of the early Mormon Church, Bush was remembered by historians of the Church of New Jerusalem, the Swedenborgian church. As the translator and expounder of Swedenborg's ideas in both England and America, Bush had a role in the development of a new American form of mystical Christianity. The current rediscovery of Bush's work focuses not on his Swedenborgian efforts but on his writings on Israel, Judaism, and Islam. In his dispute with the teachings of Adventist William Miller, Bush argued against a dispensationalist interpretation of biblical prophecy and current events. The Millennium, said Bush, was not at hand. We cannot know or predict when it will arrive. But he did understand biblical prophecy to be quite specific about the return of the Jews to their land. The "dry bones" of Ezekiel 37 were the people of Israel, and at the end of time they would be restored to life and land. In his book on Ezekiel's prophecy Bush included a map of the Promised Land and its future settlement. But it would be hard to see this as a philo-Semitic notion. For the Jews would have to accept Christianity in the end of days. Swedenborg's writings on Jews and Judaism, in which Jews are essentialized as a dark force in history, precluded Bush from having a more irenic view of the Jewish future.

My rediscovery and reevaluation of Bush was an almost accidental discovery. In 1988 I was researching my first papers on American Hebraism and for that purpose rereading Raphael Loewe's magisterial article in the *Encyclopedia Judaica* on "European Christian Hebraism." Appended to Loewe's essay is a long annotated list of Christian Hebraists. Scanning it for an obscure seventeenth-century German scholar's name I noticed the name "George Bush (U.S.A.)." Intrigued by the appearance of the president's name on an academic roster I was diverted to investigate this George Bush's story. I found, by looking in the redoubtable *Dictionary of American Biography*, that Bush was a graduate of Dartmouth College, where I was then teaching Hebrew language and literature. Dartmouth's archives had a small file on Bush, an alumnus of whom the nineteenth-century historians of the school were somewhat embarrassed. They noted Bush's adoption of "the modern myth of spiritualism. These changes were much lamented owing to his high character and distinguished scholarship."

In 1989 I announced my "discovery" of Bush in *Newsday*, a New York newspaper. In that article I noted that Bush's engagement with the question of the Jewish return to Palestine was far from his only relevance to current events. For Professor George Bush wrote the first American book on Islam (published in 1830). As the war in the Persian Gulf loomed on the horizon, the revelation that one of Bush's ancestors wrote a book about Islam and its prophet got some media attention. Bush's book on Islam was, in the spirit of mid-nineteenth-century polemics against Islam and the Ottoman Empire, far from objective about Christianity's rival religion. The book's preface describes the work as "a selection and arrangement of the leading particulars of the Impostor's history." That Bush wrote in the 1840s a tract advocating the restoration of the Jews to the Holy Land was equally noteworthy. In that tract he called for "the literal return of the Jews to the land of their fathers." But his characterization of the Jews of his time was far from friendly. Jews will, he predicted, return to their land only if appeals are made to the "worldly and selfish principles of the Jewish mind."

In 1991 a scholarly journal, *American Jewish Archives*, published my article titled "George Bush, Nineteenth Century Scholar." To my surprise the White House took notice and wrote a letter confirming the president's connection to his illustrious, though sadly forgotten, ancestor. The artfully written letter even tried to make political capital out of Professor Bush's work—connecting it to the administration's "search for peace in the Middle East." Today, as the younger President Bush formulates his own policies on the Middle East, the writings of his ancestor have renewed relevance. Nineteenth-century scholar George Bush saw history through a biblical lens and viewed Judaism and Islam as threats to the Christian West. Some Americans may want the president to implement ideas advocated by his ancestor over a century and a half ago. Others, in search of new paradigms with which to understand the modern Middle East, are wary that he will do so.

NOTES

PROLOGUE

1. Cappon, *Adams-Jefferson Letters*, 305–8. The evaluation of the Adams-Jefferson correspondence is in Ellis, *Founding Brothers*, 223.

2. Manuel, *Broken Staff*, 66–82. The description of Divinity School Hebrew is that of Arnold Band in Mintz, *Hebrew in America*, 173.

3. Adams, *Education of Henry Adams*, 1. On Henry Adams's antipathy to Jews, see Grose, *Israel in the Mind of America*, 42.

4. Ariel, *Evangelizing the Chosen People*.

5. Dudman, *American Colony*, 27.

PART I

1. Meyer, *Hebrew Exercises*.

2. Morison, *Intellectual Life*, 20, 45.

3. Goldman, "Two American Hebrew Orations."

4. For the background of these complaints, see Thomas Siegel, "Professor Stephen Sewall," 237. For the text of Wigglesworth's comments, see de Sola Pool, "Hebrew Learning among the Puritans," 44–45.

5. Hertzberg, "New England Puritans," 105–21.

CHAPTER 1

1. Grafton, *New Worlds, Ancient Texts*, 148–49.

2. Godbey, *Lost Tribes a Myth*.

3. Grafton, *New Worlds, Ancient Texts*, 149.

4. Popkin, "Rise and Fall," 70–90.

5. For the context of Hakohen's book, see Yerushalmi, "Messianic Impulses."

6. Romm, "Biblical History and the Americas," 33.

7. Underwood, "Hope of Israel," 91–93.

8. Ibid.

9. Schoen, "The Circumcision Decision."

10. Popkin, "Rise and Fall," 78.

11. Ibid., 70–90.

12. Ibid., 71.

13. Ibid., 76 (my emphasis).

14. Berlin, "J. S. C. F. Frey," 41.

15. Smallwood, "Mormon Scholar."

16. On St. Jerome's ideas on language, see Larbaud, *Homage to Jerome*.

17. On Dante and Jewish texts, see Bevan and Singer, *Legacy of Israel*, 276.

18. *Encyclopedia Judaica* (1972), s.v. "Jerome."

19. Lloyd Jones, *Discovery of Hebrew in Tudor England*, 181–90; Goldman, "Spiritual Feminism and Christian Hebraism."

20. Stinson, "'Northernmost Israel,'" 14–42.

21. Yates, *Giordano Bruno*.

22. Lloyd Jones, *Discovery of Hebrew in Tudor England*, 22.

23. Yates, *Giordano Bruno*, 84.

24. Cassirer, "Pico Della Mirandola."

25. Jeremy Cohen, *Friars and the Jews*.

26. Bercovitch, *Typology and Early American Literature*.

27. Miller, "The Garden of Eden," 60.

CHAPTER 2

1. For details of Monis's baptism, see Lee Friedman, "Judah Monis," 1–24.

2. Manuel, "Israel and the Enlightenment."

3. Lee Friedman, "Cotton Mather and the Jews," 208 (Prayer of July 18, 1696).

4. On the Mather family and their ideas on Jewish conversion to Christianity, see Lee Friedman, "Cotton Mather and the Jews," 201–10.

5. Marcus, *United States Jewry*, 41. The Mather quote is further contextualized in Kohut, "Judah Monis, M.A."

6. See Silberschlag, "Judah Monis," 494–503.

7. Moore, "Judah Monis."

8. For a very useful 1985 survey of the literature on Monis, see Klein, "Jew at Harvard."

9. *Dictionary of American Biography* (1936), s.v. "Monis, Judah."

10. Klein, "Jew at Harvard," 143.

11. On Monis's tomb inscription, which could still be clearly read in the early 1990s, see Huhner, "Jews of New England," 80–105.

12. Reproduced in Marcus, *Colonial American Jew*, 318.

13. Meyer in "Hebrew at Harvard" (1637–1760).

14. Letter of May 22, 1722, in Moore, "Judah Monis," 294.

15. On the study of "oriental languages" at Harvard, see Morison, *Intellectual Life of Colonial New England*, 20, 44–45.

16. John Cotton quoted in Lee Friedman, "Judah Monis," 14.

17. Moore, "Judah Monis."

18. Kohut, "Judah Monis, M.A.," 217–26.

19. Ibid., 218–19.

20. Adams, *Founding of New England*, 1926.

21. On Kemper, see Lapide, *Hebrew in the Church*, 76.

22. Moore, "Judah Monis," 301–2.

23. Klein, "Jew at Harvard," 136–37.

24. Lee Friedman, "Contemporary Appraisal of Judah Monis," 146–48.

25. Thomas Siegel, "Professor Stephen Sewall," 234.

26. Ibid.

27. Ibid.

28. Ibid.

29. Ibid.

30. Stephen Sewall Lectures.

31. Siegal, "Professor Stephen Sewall," 237.

32. Ibid., 245.

33. Ibid., 234, 239.

CHAPTER 3

1. The standard biography of Stiles is Morgan, *Gentle Puritan*. An early-twentieth-century consideration of Stiles's writings on Hebrew and Jewish themes

is Kohut, *Ezra Stiles and the Jews*. In the 1970s Rabbi Arthur Chiel published a number of important papers on Stiles.

2. Oren, *Joining the Club*, 341.

3. Quoted in the preface to Taylor, *Upon the Types*, xx.

4. *Dictionary of American Biography* (1936), s.v. "Stiles, Ezra."

5. Dexter, *Literary Diary of Ezra Stiles*.

6. On this document, see Chiel, "Ezra Stiles and the Jews," 166.

7. Ibid., 156.

8. Morgan, *Gentle Puritan*, 68.

9. Chiel, "Ezra Stiles and the Jews," 157.

10. Manuel, *Broken Staff*, 31.

11. Morgan, *Gentle Puritan*, 93.

12. Kohut, *Ezra Stiles and the Jews*, 14.

13. Ibid.

14. Ibid.

15. *Dictionary of American Biography* (1936), s.v. "Stiles, Ezra."

16. Thomas Siegel, "Relationship," 3.

17. Dexter, *Literary Diary of Ezra Stiles*. Hereafter, quotations from this source will be followed by date of diary entry in parentheses.

18. Chiel, "Ezra Stiles, the Education."

19. Ibid., 238.

20. Kohut, *Ezra Stiles and the Jews*, 68, 49.

21. Chiel, "Rabbis and Ezra Stiles."

22. Ibid., 296.

23. On these letters, see Lee Friedman, *Rabbi Haim Isaac Carigal*, 23–25, and Kohut, *Ezra Stiles and the Jews*, 120.

24. Chiel, "Ezra Stiles, the Education," 241.

25. Moore, "Ezra Stiles Studies in the 'Cabala,'" 299.

26. Chiel, "Ezra Stiles, the Education," 239.

27. Chiel, "Ezra Stiles and the Jews" 157.

28. Lee Friedman, *Rabbi Haim Isaac Carigal*. 1.

29. Morgan, *Gentle Puritan*, 306.

30. Ibid., 302.

31. Lee Friedman, *Rabbi Haim Isaac Carigal*, 37.

32. For more on these lectures, see Morgan, *Gentle Puritan*, 382.

33. Chiel, "Ezra Stiles and the Jews," 165.

34. Morgan, *Gentle Puritan*, 310.

35. *Dictionary of American Biography* (1936), s.v. "Stiles, Ezra."

36. Morgan, *Gentle Puritan*, 432.

37. Kohut, *Ezra Stiles and the Jews*, 13.

38. Ibid., 12.

CHAPTER 4

1. Edwards, "To The Trustees of the College of New Jersey," 324.

2. Lowance, "'Images or Shadows of Divine Things.'"

3. Maclean, *History of the College of New Jersey*.

4. Johnson, "Jonathan Edwards' Background of Reading," 197 (emphasis added).

5. T. M. Davis, "Traditions of Puritan Typology."

6. Stein, "Spirit and the Word," 123.

7. Kimnach, *Sermons and Discourses*.

8. Elukin, "Jacques Basnage."

9. Smith, *Jonathan Edwards*, 143.

10. Quoted in Winslow, *Jonathan Edwards*, 371.

11. *Sibley's Harvard Graduates*, 93–98.

12. Winslow, *Jonathan Edwards*, 39.

13. Holbrook, *Original Sin*, 82.

14. Ramsey, *Ethical Writings*, 564.

15. Oviatt, *Beginnings of Yale*, 239.

16. Warch, *School of the Prophets*, 200.

17. Marsden, *Jonathan Edwards*, 47–48.

18. Oviatt, *Beginnings of Yale*, 416; Stokes, *Memorials of Eminent Yale Men*.

19. Smith, *Religious Affections*, 70; McDermott, "Possibility of Reconciliation"; Gale, *Court of the Gentiles*.

20. *Dictionary of American Biography* (1936), s.v. "Gale, Theophilus."

21. Preface to Gale, *Court of the Gentiles*.

22. Ibid.

23. Ibid.

24. McDermott, "Possibility of Reconciliation," 181.

25. Kimnach, *Sermons and Discourses*, 68.

26. Preface to Andrew Wilson, *Creation the Ground-Work*.

27. Ibid.

28. Perry Miller, *Jonathan Edwards, Images*, 156.

29. Holbrook, *Original Sin*, 102.

30. Ibid, 70.

31. Stein, "Spirit and the Word," 120–21.

32. Kimnach, "Jonathan Edwards's Pursuit of Reality," 113.

33. Introduction to Perry Miller, *Jonathan Edwards, Images*.

34. Anderson et al., *Typological Writings*, 25.

CHAPTER 5

1. Sarna, "American Jewish Response."

2. Berlin, *Defending the Faith*.

3. Hannah Adams, *History of the Jews*.

4. Lee Friedman, *Pilgrims in a New Land*.

5. *Dictionary of American Biography* (1936), s.v. "Boudinot, Elias," 477.

6. Boudinot, *Star in the West*.

7. Popkin, "Rise and Fall," 75.

8. Wosh, *Spreading the Word*.

9. Berlin, *Defending the Faith*.

10. Scult, *Millenial Expectations*.

11. Frey, *Narrative*, 11–12.

12. Scult, *Millenial Expectations*, 97.

13. Ibid., 122. The quote is from the pen of Moses Sailman, an opponent of Frey.

14. Eichhorn, *Evangelizing the American Jew*, 26.

15. Berlin, "Joseph S. C. F. Frey, the Jews," 36.

16. Frey, *Hebrew, Latin and English*, 3 (preface).

17. Preface to Frey, *Hebrew Grammar*.

18. Evearitt, "Jewish-Christian Missions to the Jews."

19. Eichhorn, *Evangelizing the American Jew*, 28.

20. Ibid., 37.

21. Frey, *Narrative*, 156.

22. Lee Friedman, *Pilgrims in a New Land*, 179.

23. Berlin, "Joseph S. C. F. Frey, the Jews," 36.

24. Grose, *Israel in the Mind of America*, 6.

25. Berlin, "Joseph S. C. F. Frey, the Jews," 45.

26. Frey, *Lectures on Baptism*, 6 (preface).

27. Ibid.

28. Ibid.

29. Ibid.

30. Berlin, "Joseph S. C. F. Frey, the Jews," 49.

31. Frey, *Narrative*, 162–63.

32. *Dictionary of American Biography* (1936), s.v. "Frey, JSCF."

33. Lapide, *Hebrew in the Church*, 51.

34. Shepherd, *Zealous Intruders*, 73.

35. Eichhorn, *Evangelizing the American Jew*, 68.

36. *Pontiac, Michigan, News*, June 1850.

CHAPTER 6

1. For the historical background of the conflict between "Russian" and "German" Jews, see Hertzberg, *Jews in America*.

2. Grinstein, *Rise of the Jewish Community*.

3. Ibid.

4. Hartstein, "Shearith Israel School."

5. Marcus, *Jew in the American World*, 115, 157.

6. Diner, *Time For Gathering*.

7. Kabakoff, "Use of Hebrew by American Jews," 191.

8. Hertzberg, *Jews in America*, 53.

9. Marcus, *Jew in the American World*, 41–44.

10. Goldman, "Vehu Shaul."

11. Kabakoff, "Biblical Exegete."

12. Kabakoff, "Use of Hebrew by American Jews," 194.

13. Epperson, *Mormons and Jews*.

14. Goldman, "Two American Hebrew Orations."

15. Ibid., 39.

16. Ibid.

17. Grinstein, *Rise of the Jewish Community*, 449–50.

18. Kohut, "Early Jewish Literature," 121, including preceding quote.

19. Kaganoff, "Hebrew and Liturgical Exercises," 186.

20. *Encyclopedia Judaica* (1973), s.v. "Divorce."

21. Kaganoff, "Hebrew and Liturgical Exercises," 188.

22. On Rabbi Aaronson and his career in New York, see Sherman, *Orthodox Judaism in America*.

23. Kabakoff, "Use of Hebrew by American Jews," 196.

PART II

1. Arnold, "Culture and Anarchy," 558, 571.

2. Trilling, *Matthew Arnold*, 216.

3. Fisk, "Holy Land," 3.

4. Stowe, Uncle Tom's Cabin, xviii.

5. Ibid., 422.

6. Raboteau, *Fire in the Bones*, 31–31.

7. L. Silberman, "Wellhausen and Judaism."

8. Merrill, "Report to the Assistant Secretary of State," 176.

9. Tuchman, *Bible and Sword*; an example of an anti-restoration tract is Eubank, *National Restoration of the Jews*.

10. Williams, *Times and Life*, 313.

CHAPTER 7

1. A recent full biography of Robinson is Williams, *Times and Life*.

2. Quoted in Handy, *Holy Land*.

3. Williams, *Times and Life*, 12; Obenzinger, American Palestine, 2.

4. Williams, *Times and Life*, 49.

5. Ibid., 67.

6. Ibid., 161.

7. Ibid., 159.

8. *Encyclopedia Judaica* (1972), s.v. "Neander, August."

9. On Stuart see Giltner, *Moses Stuart*.

10. Charles Wilson, *Elements of Hebrew Grammar*.

11. Thomas Siegel, "Relationship," 11–12.

12. Giltner, Moses Stuart, 16.

13. Ibid., 20.

14. Stuart, *Sermon at the Ordination*.

15. Giltner, *Moses Stuart*, 27. On Schauffler as Hebraist, see Nemoy, "William Gottlieb Schauffler."

16. Letter from Moses Stuart to J. Seixas, September 6, 1832, Seixas File.

17. "Fürst's Concordance," 226–27.

18. Ibid., 134.

19. George Adam Smith, *Historical Geography*, 91.

20. Ritter is quoted in Ibid., 91. On Robinson and Ritter, see Williams, *Times and Life*, 162.

21. Goren, *"Go View the Land,"* 63–64.

22. John Davis, *Landscape of Belief*, 48.

23. Williams, *Times and Life*, 198.

24. Robinson, *Biblical Researches*, 1:53.

25. "A Centenary Symposium on Edward Robinson," 384.

26. Ibid., 374.

27. Ben-Arieh, *Rediscovery of the Holy Land*, 89–90.

28. For the text and the story of the tunnel's discovery, see Pritchard, *Ancient Near East*, 1:212.

29. Robinson, *Biblical Researches*, 3:33.

30. On Clorinda Minor, see Kreiger and Goldman, *Divine Expectations*.

31. Williams, *Times and Life*, 313.

32. John Davis, *Landscape of Belief*, 36.

33. On Frederic Church in Beirut, see ibid., 176.

34. Twain, *Innocents Abroad*, 303.

35. "A Centenary Symposium on Edward Robinson."

CHAPTER 8

1. Chamberlain, *Universities and Their Sons*, 91. Tayler Lewis is there described by the editor: "He had the intense love of knowledge and the penetration and perseverance which rest content with nothing short of acquisition and first hand. His mastery of Greek went hand in hand with an absorbing study of Hebrew and other Oriental tongues which served a profound faith." The phrase "an Israelite truly in whom there was no guile" is an allusion to the text of John 1:47: "Jesus saw Nathaniel coming to him, and saith of him, Behold an Israelite indeed, in whom is not guile." Lewis's remark about Nordheimer is reproduced in Jones, *New York University*.

2. Robinson, "Notices of Nordheimer," 361, 390.

3. *Dictionary of American Biography* (1936), s.v. "Nordheimer, Isaac."

4. Chomsky, "Hebrew Grammar and Textbook Writing," 136. On Nordheimer's *Critical Hebrew Grammar*, see Fellman, "Notes Concerning Two Nineteenth Century Hebrew Textbooks," 75–77.

5. Marcus, *United States Jewry*, 375.

6. The biographical sketch that follows is based on Robinson, "Notices of Nordheimer"; *Dictionary of American Biography* (1936 ed.), s.v. "Nordheimer, Isaac"; and Neill, "Reminiscences."

7. *Dictionary of American Biography* (1936), s.v. "Grimké, Thomas S."

8. Ibid.

9. Grimké, *Reflections*, 139.

10. Ibid.

11. Ibid., 176. On the movement to "burn the classics" and on the effects of Grimké's ideas on this movement, see Fletcher, *History of Oberlin College*, 365–66. The description of the Grimké sisters is from Butler, *Awash in a Sea of Faith*, 281.

12. Grimké, *Reflections*.

13. Quoted in Neill, "Reminiscences," 508–9.

14. Robinson, "Notices of Nordheimer," 386.

15. Letter from Isaac Nordheimer to the Trustees of New York University, May 1838, Nordheimer File.

16. *Dictionary of American Biography* (1936), s.v. "Nordheimer, Isaac," 547.

17. Brown, *Rise of Biblical Criticism in America*, 111–18.

18. Robinson, "Notices of Nordheimer," 357.

19. Moshe Davis, *With Eyes toward Zion*, 41.

20. Robinson, "Notices of Nordheimer," 357.

21. The phrase is from Coffin, *Half Century of Union Theological Seminary*, 5.

22. *Dictionary of American Biography* (1936), s.v. "Nordheimer, Isaac," 547.

23. Handy, *History of Union Theological Seminary*, 13.

24. Stuart, *Grammar*, iv.

25. Bush, *Grammar of the Hebrew Language*, viii.

26. *Encyclopedia Judaica* (1972), s.v. "Neander, August," 910.

27. Neill, "Reminiscences," 511. According to the *Dictionary of American Biography*, Neill's article was "reprinted for private circulation by William Nordheimer, London, 1906."

28. Robinson, "Notices of Nordheimer," 385.

29. Marcus, *United States Jewry*, 376, lists Isaac Marcus Jost, Abraham Geiger, and Judah Loeb Rapoport among Nordheimer's influences.

30. Grinstein, *Rise of the Jewish Community*, 420; Nordheimer's participation in the school is mentioned on page 590, note 14.

31. Robinson, "Notices of Nordheimer," 388. Copies of this concordance are quite rare. I studied the copy in Yale's Sterling Memorial Library.

32. Neill, "Reminiscences," 507.

33. Moore, "Judah Monis," 285.

34. "Fürst's Concordance," 226–27.

35. Marcus, *United States Jewry*, 376.

36. Robinson, "Notices of Nordheimer," 389.

37. Postal and Kippman, *Jewish Landmarks*. The cemetery is described on page 170. On page 79 the authors erroneously describe Nordheimer as a professor of medicine.

38. De Sola Pool, *Portraits Etched in Stone*, 140.

39. Robinson, "Notices of Nordheimer," 389.

40. Letter from Isaac Nordheimer to the Trustees of New York University, May 1838, New York University Archives, Chancellor's Records.

41. *Semi Weekly Courier and New York Enquirer*, November 17, 1842. The poem is prefaced by the following note: "The following lines were mislaid, or would have been published at an earlier day." As Nordheimer died on November 3 and the poem is signed "Nov. 6, 1842 B.S.," the editors may have wanted to include it in the earliest possible edition. I have not been able to ascertain who "B.S." is.

CHAPTER 9

1. The scholarly literature on J. Seixas's life and work is limited. He is mentioned in Phillips, "The Levy and Seixas Families," 208, and in a short address by David de Sola Pool, "Joshua Seixas, Hebraist," delivered at the 1914 annual meeting of the American Jewish Historical Society. There have been a number of articles about Seixas in the Mormon popular press and in Mormon scholarly journals, and these will be cited in my discussion of Seixas and early Mormonism.

2. On G. Seixas see Marcus, "Handsome Young Priest in the Black Gown," 409–67.

3. Letter from N. Taylor Phillips to R. S. Fletcher, Oberlin College, Oberlin, Ohio, September 20, 1933, Prof. J. Seixas File (hereafter Seixas File).

4. Quoted in Snow, "Who Was Professor Joshua Seixas?"

5. Marcus, "Handsome Young Priest in the Black Gown," 413.

6. Grinstein, *Rise of the Jewish Community*, 230. On the shifting fortunes of this school, see also de Sola Pool and de Sola Pool, *Old Faith in the New World*.

7. Marcus, "Handsome Young Priest in the Black Gown," 442. For an evaluation of the Sampson Simson oration, see Goldman, "Two American Hebrew Orations."

8. Berman, *Richmond's Jewry*, 37.

9. These genealogical details of the J. Seixas family are from M. H. Stern, letter to L. G. Petersen, Latter Day Saints Church, Salt Lake City, Utah, May 9, 1954, Seixas File. For the full genealogical tables of J. Seixas's family, see Stern, *First American Jewish Families*, 264.

10. This circular was republished as the preface to the first edition of his *Manual Hebrew Grammar*. For a reproduction, see Snow, "Who Was Professor Joshua Seixas?," 68.

11. M. H. Stern, letter, 1954.

12. Seixas, *Manual Hebrew Grammar*, 3 (preface).

13. On Hebrew among the Puritans, see

de Sola Pool, "Hebrew Learning among the Puritans." The literature on Hebrew at the early American colleges is quite extensive, though not synthetic or analytical. For a review of the literature and for an attempt at analysis, see Goldman, "Biblical Hebrew in Colonial America," and "Hebrew at the Early Colleges."

14. Stuart graduated at the head of his class in 1799. See Giltner, *Moses Stuart*. Giltner points out that Stuart did not study Hebrew at Yale, though Hebrew was taught there when Stuart was an undergraduate.

15. Sarna and Sarna, "Jewish Bible Scholarship," 89–90.

16. George Bush and his associates are discussed in Chapter 10, while Isaac Nordheimer is discussed in Chapter 8. On Protestant attitudes toward Jewish scholars of this period, see Sarna and Sarna, "Jewish Bible Scholarship and Translations."

17. *Dictionary of American Biography* (1936), s.v. "Stuart, Moses," 174–75.

18. Brown, *Rise of Biblical Criticism in America*, 47–48.

19. Ibid.

20. Letter from Moses Stuart to J. Seixas, September 6, 1832, Seixas File.

21. On Stiles at Newport, see Chiel, "Rabbis and Ezra Stiles."

22. Stuart, *Grammar*.

23. Such "easy roads to Hebrew" had a venerable history in Protestant circles. As early as 1623, Schickard's *Horologium Hebraeum* promised mastery of the language in twenty-four hours! At Harvard, this text was the "beginning Hebrew" book from 1642 until late in the seventeenth century. Morison described the volume as "a manual which professed to teach students the elements of that sacred tongue in the surprisingly short space of twenty-four hours." See Morison, *Harvard in the Seventeenth Century*.

24. Stuart, *Grammar*, iv. On Seixas's use of Stuart's grammar as a source, see Chomsky, "Hebrew Grammar and Textbook Writing."

25. *New England Magazine* 5 (1833): 423.

26. Letter from Stuart to Seixas, September 6, 1832, Seixas File.

27. Seixas File.

28. Letter from J. Walker to M. Seixas, July 26, 1832, Seixas File.

29. *Encyclopedia Brittanica*, 15th ed., s.v. "Parker, Theodore."

30. Frothingham, *Theodore Parker*, 39.

31. *Dictionary of American Biography*, s.v. "Parker, Theodore," 329. Among the books that Parker bequeathed to the Boston Public Library was Seixas, *A Key to the Chaldee Landuage—Designed for Those Who Have Studied Hebrew with the Author*. The leaf of the book has Parker's signature on it and the title page is inscribed "the gift of Dr. Palfrey."

32. On American Jews and Unitarianism, see Kraut, "A Unitarian Rabbi?," 272–308. For the context of John Adams's remark, see Hertzberg, *Jews in America*, 86–87.

33. Parker, *Views of Religion*, 207; quoted in Feldman, *Dual Destinies*, 59.

34. Grodzins, *American Heretic*.

35. Phillips, "The Levy and Seixas Families of Newport," 198. We have here echoes of Heine's plaint about his own conversion to Christianity, which he called his "admission ticket to European culture."

36. Stuart, *Sermon at the Ordination*, 21. For further publication information, see Rosenbach, *American Jewish Bibliography*, item no. 338. On the American Jewish reaction to missionaries, see Sarna, "Impact of Nineteenth-Century Christian Missions," 232–54.

37. For reference to Seixas as "a Jewish rabbi," see Brodie, *No Man Knows My History*, 169.

38. Snow, "Who Was Professor Joshua Seixas?," 79.

39. Quoted in letter from A. L. White, Librarian, Western Reserve Historical Society, to J. R. Marcus, January 11, 1949, Correspondence File, American Jewish Archives.

40. Snow, "Who Was Professor Joshua Seixas?," 68.

41. Ibid., 69.

42. Ibid., 70. On Snow's conversion to Mormonism under his sister's influence, see *Dictionary of American Biography*, s.v. "Snow, Lorenzo," 386. At least one historian has suggested that Lorenzo Snow followed Seixas to Kirtland; and that it was thus Seixas who was responsible for Snow's initial contact with the Mormons. See Fletcher, *History of Oberlin College*, 75.

43. Brooke, *Refiner's Fire*.

44. Glanz, *Jew and Mormon*, 139–40.

45. Snow, "Who Was Professor Joshua Seixas?," 70–71. These diary entries of Smith were the subject of correspondence between Rev. L. G. Petersen, historian of the Latter Day Saints Church, and Rabbi Malcolm Stern, genealogist of the American Jewish Archives, where this correspondence is preserved. The early Mormon "romance" with Hebrew is discussed in Zucker, "Joseph Smith as a Student of Hebrew," 41–55. A more focused (and more technical) treatment is Walton, "Professor Seixas," 41–43. Walton's article is dedicated to Prof. Zucker. A facsimile of the second edition of Seixas's *Grammar* was published in Salt Lake City in 1981. A revised copy of Zucker's 1969 article, with a short preface by M. Walton, introduces the volume. My description of the founding of "the Hebrew School" is based on Backman, *Heavens Resound*, 270–72.

46. On D. M. Peixotto, see de Sola Pool and de Sola Pool, *Old Faith in a New World*, 51, 474.

47. Glanz, *Jew and Mormon*, 140.

48. Snow, "Who Was Professor Joshua Seixas?"; Stern, 1954.

49. Letter from F. C. Waite to J. R. Marcus, June 20, 1947, Seixas File.

50. De Sola Pool and de Sola Pool, *Old Faith in a New World*, 170–76. The Seixas-Peixotto marriage is mentioned in "Items Relating to the Seixas Family," 163.

51. Backman, *Heavens Resound*, 272.

52. Snow, "Who Was Professor Joshua Seixas?," 41.

53. B. Levinson, Seixas File.

54. Brodie, *No Man Knows My History*, 169–70.

55. Snow, "Who Was Professor Joshua Seixas?," 71.

56. Zucker, "Joseph Smith as a Student of Hebrew," 48.

57. Quinn, *Early Mormonism*, 181; Zucker, "Joseph Smith as a Student of Hebrew," 49.

58. Brodie, *No Man Knows My History*, 171.

59. Walton, "Professor Seixas," 43.

60. Zucker, "Joseph Smith as a Student of Hebrew," 53.

61. For the context of Joseph Smith's understanding of this "gathering," see Underwood, *Millenarian World*, 58–75.

62. Bush, *Grammar of the Hebrew Language*, viii.

63. Seixas, *Manual Hebrew Grammar*. Though his children's birth records indicate that Seixas lived in New York since 1838, it is striking that the family does not appear in the 1850 New York City Census. James's cousins, the children of Benjamin Seixas, do appear on the lists. It may be that James and his family were living outside of the city limits in 1850. See Jackson, *New York City 1850 Census Index*, 315.

64. M. H. Stern, Seixas File.

65. B. Moses quoted in Fletcher, *History of Oberlin College*, 1:370.

66. Personal communication from Dr. N. Kaganoff, American Jewish Historical Society, December 4, 1990.

67. See Heine's remarks as quoted in *Encyclopedia Judaica*, s.v. "Heine, H.," 272. The observation about the "price" of the ticket is Benjamin Braude's in Endelman, *Jewish Apostasy*, 189.

68. For a history and analysis of European Christian Hebraism see Manuel, *Broken Staff*.

CHAPTER 10

1. *Dictionary of American Biography*, 347.

2. Griswold, *Prose Writers of America*, 354.

3. On the phenomenon of "Christian Zionism," see *Encyclopedia Judaica* (1972), s.v. "Zionism," and Ariel, *On Behalf of Israel*.

4. Hayden, "Reminiscences," 186–89.

5. Bush, *Life of Mohammed*.

6. Ibid., 50.

7. Chase, *History of Dartmouth College*.

8. Goldman, "Biblical Hebrew in Colonial America," 173–80.

9. Jones, *New York University*.

10. Chamberlain, *Universities and Their Sons*, 91.

11. Hayden, "Reminiscences," 189.

12. Ibid.

13. Bush, *Treatise*, 260.

14. On Nordheimer, see Robinson, "Notices of Nordheimer," 379–90.

15. J. Friedman, *Most Ancient Testimony*, 15.

16. For a summary and review of the literature on Monis, see Klein, "A Jew at Harvard."

17. Bush, *Grammar of the Hebrew Language*.

18. Bush, *Valley of Vision*.

19. Warren, *Compendium of the Theological Writings of Emanuel Swedenborg*. On Bush on Swedenborg's writings, see *New Church Magazine* (London), no. 499 (January–March 1931).

20. Benz, *Emanuel Swedenborg*, 293.

21. Hayden, "Reminiscences," 186.

22. Ibid., 195.

23. Chapman, *Sketches of the Alumni of Dartmouth College*.

24. For the geneological information on the Bush family, see Prince, "Patrilineal Descent of Vice President Bush," 124. Vice President Bush's relationship to the Rev. George Bush was confirmed in a letter of February 18, 1989. For a full ancestral table of George Herbert Walker Bush, see Roberts, *Ancestors of American Presidents*, Reagan and Bush Tables.

25. Bush, *Valley of Vision*, 5.

CHAPTER 11

1. Report to the Assistant Secretary of State from the U.S. Consul in Jerusalem, October 3, 1891, National Archives, T471. The conclusion of the report appears in Moshe Davis, *With Eyes toward Zion*, 2:170–76. A discussion of Merrill appears in Kark, "Annual Reports of the U.S. Consuls in the Holy Land as a Source for the Study of Nineteenth Century Eretz Israel," in Moshe Davis, *With Eyes toward Zion*, 147–48. Kark, *American Consuls*, includes much valuable information on Merrill. My 1997 article "The Holy Land Appropriated" served as a draft for this chapter.

2. Grose, *Israel in the Mind of America*, 41.

3. Ibid.

4. *Encyclopedia Judaica*, s.v. "Hebraists, Christian," 8.

5. Ford, "Our American Colony."

6. Ibid.

7. On changes in the U.S. diplomatic and consular services, see Ilchman, *Professional Diplomacy in the United States*, 42–43, 85–89.

8. Manuel, *Realities of American-Palestine Relations*, 68.

9. Ibid.

10. Eliav, "Activities of Foreign Consuls in Erets-Israel."

11. Ben-Arieh, *Rediscovery of the Holy Land*, 90.

12. "A Merrill Memorial."

13. This biographical account is based on material in the Yale University Archives.

14. *A History of the Class of 1863, Yale College*, 247.

15. Ibid.

16. President's Correspondence File, Yale University Archives.

17. *Dictionary of American Biography*, s.v. "Merrill, Selah."

18. On Moses Stuart's Hebraic studies, see Chapter 7.

19. On Selma Lagerloff in Jerusalem, see *Encyclopedia Judaica*, 9:1577, 14:929. On the background of the Merrill-American Colony dispute, see Kark, *American Consuls*, 187–88, 214–15.

20. Vester, *Our Jerusalem*, 115.

21. Ford, "Our American Colony."

22. Vester, *Our Jerusalem*, 201.

23. Merrill, "Birds of Palestine," *P.E.F. Quarterly*, 1905.

24. Letter from Merrill to the Trustees of the Hartford Seminary, Merrill Collection.

25. Letter to Selah Merrill from the Trustees, February 1882, Merrill Collection.

26. *Boston Advertiser*, March 2, 1889.

27. Kark, *American Consuls*, 193, 80.

28. Moshe Davis, *With Eyes toward Zion*, 2:147–48.

29. Manuel, *Broken Staff*, 11.

30. Tuchman, *Bible and Sword*.

31. Matar, "Protestantism, Palestine."

32. Goldman, "Rev. George Bush."

33. *Encyclopedia Judaica*, s.v. "Hebraists, Christian."

PART III

1. Grose, *Israel in the Mind of America*, 82.

2. Bain, *March to Zion*.

3. Moshe Davis, *Christian Protagonists*.

4. McCullough, *Truman*, 231, 595–620.

5. For the context of this observation, see Kegley, *Reinhold Niebuhr*, 432–33.

6. Ariel, *Philosemites or Antisemites*.

CHAPTER 12

1. My portrayal of Harper is based on the following sources: *Dictionary of American Biography*, s.v. "Harper, W. R."; Wind, *Bible and the University*; and Kucklick, *Puritans in Babylon*.

2. Quoted in Wind, *Bible and the University*, 87.

3. Ibid., 103.

4. Giltner, *Moses Stuart*, 4–5.

5. Wind, *Bible and the University*, 90.

6. *Dictionary of American Biography*, s.v. "Harper, W. R."

7. Wind, *Bible and the University*, 28.

8. *Dictionary of American Biography*, s.v. "Harper, W. R."

9. *Hebraica* 7 (October 1890).

10. *Hebraica* 2 (January 1886): 117.

11. Cuddihy, *Ordeal of Civility*, 175–85.

12. *Hebraica* 8 (January 1891): 156.

13. *Hebraica* 5 (October 1888).

14. Philipson, *Reform Movement in Judaism*.

15. *Jewish Encyclopedia*, s.v. "Felsenthal, Bernard," 361.

16. M. Meyer, *Response to Modernity*.

17. Hirsch, *Dr. Emil G. Hirsch*.

18. *Encyclopedia Judaica*, s.v. "Bacher, Wilhelm," 52.

19. On Harper's methodology, see Wind, *Bible and the University*, 29.

20. Murphy and Bruckner, *Idea of the University of Chicago*, 7.

21. Rylaarsdam, *Transitions in Biblical Scholarship*.

22. Ibid.

23. Green's articles and Harper's responses appeared in *Hebraica* between 1888 and 1892.

24. M. Meyer, *Response to Modernity*.

25. Quoted in Wind, *Bible and the University*, 178.

26. *Dictionary of American Biography*, s.v. "Harper, W. R."

27. On Hirsch's eulogy, see ibid.

CHAPTER 13

1. Kegley, *Reinhold Niebuhr*, 3.

2. Bingham, *Courage to Change*.

3. My biographical portrait of Niebuhr is based on Fox, *Reinhold Niebuhr*;, Kegley, *Reinhold Niebuhr*; and Bingham, *Courage to Change*.

4. Fox, *Reinhold Niebuhr*, 28.

5. Ibid.

6. Ibid.

7. Ibid., 94.

8. Ibid., 283–323.

9. Bingham, *Courage to Change*.

10. Ibid.

11. On Niebuhr's complex relationships with Jewish scholars and Jewish communities, see Feldman, "Reinhold Niebuhr and the Jews"; Rice, "Niebuhr and Judaism"; and Fox, "Reinhold Niebuhr," 92–94.

12. Kegley, *Reinhold Niebuhr*, 3–23.

13. Ibid., 138; Edmund Wilson, *To the Finland Station*, 139.

14. Kegley, *Reinhold Niebuhr*, 43, 433.

15. Rice, "Niebuhr and Judaism," 109.

16. Feldman, "Reinhold Niebuhr and the Jews," 294.

17. Giardina, *Saints and Villains*.

18. Bennet, "Reinhold Niebuhr's Social Ethics"; Rice, "Niebuhr and Judaism."

19. Rice, "Niebuhr and Judaism," 110–11.

20. Fox, *Reinhold Niebuhr*, 209.

21. Ibid.

22. Rice, "Niebuhr and Judaism," 104.

23. Bingham, *Courage to Change*.

24. For Niebuhr's nuanced views on the prospects of political Zionism, see Rice, "Niebuhr and Judaism," 108–14.

25. *New York Times*, November 21, 1947, Letters to the Editor.

26. Stone, *Reinhold Niebuhr*.

27. Rice, "Niebuhr and Judaism," 111.

28. Ibid., 112–13.

29. Said, *Question of Palestine*, 31.

30. Fox, *Reinhold Niebuhr*, 209, 267.

31. Rice, "Niebuhr and Judaism," 136. And see Chilton, *Rabbi Jesus*, and Carroll, *Constantine's Sword*.

32. Rice, "Niebuhr and Judaism," 137.

33. Fox, *Reinhold Niebuhr*, 266, and Rice, "Niebuhr and Judaism," 137.

34. Feldman, "Reinhold Niebuhr and the Jews," 298.

35. Ibid.

36. Kegley, "Reinhold Niebuhr," 433.

37. Burnstein, "Niebuhr, Scripture, and Normative Judaism."

38. Seymour Siegel, "Reinhold Niebuhr."

39. Rice, "Niebuhr and Judaism," 136.

40. Fox, *Reinhold Niebuhr*, 283.

41. Seymour Siegel, "Reinhold Niebuhr," 57–58.

42. Heschel, "A Last Farewell," 63.

43. Ibid.

CHAPTER 14

1. In the years that have passed since Wilson's centenary, a number of new studies of the critic have appeared, among them a 1997 edited volume published by Princeton University Press. See Dabney, *Edmund Wilson*.

2. Dabney, *Viking Portable Edmund Wilson*.

3. "Genesis" appears in the "Viking Portable" volume.

4. Elena Wilson, *Edmund Wilson*, 521.

5. Edmund Wilson, *Piece of My Mind*, 87.

6. Douglas, *Edmund Wilson's America*. Douglas's 243-page book on Wilson's oeuvre makes only one passing reference to Wilson's *Scrolls from the Dead Sea*. Similarly, Janet Groth's, *Edmund Wilson: A Critic for Our Time*, does not discuss Wilson's Hebraic, Judaic, or Israeli interests.

7. Meyers, *Edmund Wilson*.

8. Elena Wilson, *Edmund Wilson*, 510.

9. Ibid., 521.

10. Krupnick, "Edmund Wilson and Gentile Philo-Semitism."

11. Edel, *Twenties*, 299–300.

12. Edmund Wilson, *I Thought of Daisy*.

13. Edmund Wilson, *To the Finland Station*, 118.

14. Kriegel, *Edmund Wilson*.

15. On Marx's rabbinical family, see Edmund Wilson, *To the Finland Station*, 112–13.

16. Edmund Wilson, "On First Reading Genesis."

17. On European Hebraism, see Manuel, *Broken Staff*. On American Hebraism, see Goldman, *Hebrew and the Bible in America*.

18. See Goldman, *Hebrew and the Bible*, 105–55.

19. See Edmund Wilson, *Patriotic Gore*, 785.

20. Edmund Wilson, *A Piece of My Mind*, 98–102.

21. Laor, *Agnon*, 511.

22. Dabney, "Philosopher and the Critic."

23. Quoted in *Forward*, December 1, 1995 (originally published in Yiddish *Daily Forward*, June 1992).

24. Dabney, *Edmund Wilson*, 153.

25. Ibid., 157.

26. Castronovo, "Edmund Wilson's Citizen Reader."

27. Ibid.

28. Ibid.

29. Dabney, *Edmund Wilson*.

30. Whitehouse, "Edmund Wilson's Jewish Ambassador."

31. Berryman, *Recovery*.

32. Ibid.

33. Dabney, *Edmund Wilson*.

34. Wain, *Edmund Wilson Celebration*.

35. *Times Literary Supplement*.

36. Wain, *Edmund Wilson Celebration*.

37. Dabney, *Edmund Wilson*.

38. Dabney, *Sixties*.

39. Said, *Question of Palestine*, 33–36.

40. Edmund Wilson, *A Piece of My Mind*, 108–35.

41. Elena Wilson, *Edmund Wilson*, 529.

42. Dabney, *Edmund Wilson*, 138.

43. Ibid.

44. Quoted in *Forward*, June 1992.

45. Kazin, *Lifetime Burning in Every Moment*, 200–201.

46. Meyers, *Edmund Wilson*.

EPILOGUE

1. For a more detailed treatment of this continuing debate, see Goldman, "Review of *With Eyes toward Zion*."

2. McCullough, *Truman*.

3. Ibid., 596; Miller, *Plain Speaking*.

4. M. Marty quoted in Goldman, "Review of *With Eyes toward Zion*."

5. Gorenberg, *The End of Days* provides a compelling picture of this alliance.

6. Malachy, *American Fundamentalism*, 99.

7. See Y. Ariel, *Evangelizing the Chosen People*, 273.

8. Gorenberg, *New York Times Sunday Magazine*, December 2002.

9. S. Y. Ariel, *Philosemites or Antisemites?*

10. *New York Times*, October 4, 2002, and December 18, 2002. On Jewish organizations and Christian Zionism, see K. Silverstein and M. Scherer, "Born Again Zionists."

11. On American Jewish participation in the academy, see Klingenstein, *Jews in the American Academy*.

12. Goldman, "Hebrew in America," 186.

13. Roth, *Operation Shylock*.

14. On this archaeological find, see *Biblical Archaeology Review* (December 2002). When, in June 2003, the Israeli Antiquities Authority declared that the inscription on the box was a forgery, there was great disappointment among Americans fascinated by biblical archaeology.

15. Rubin, "When Jerusalem Was Built in St. Louis."

16. Ibid.; Vogel, *To See a Promised Land*, 213–36.

17. Klausner, *Jesus of Nazareth*.

[*Notes to Pages 285–304*]

BIBLIOGRAPHY

MANUSCRIPT COLLECTIONS

Cambridge, Mass.
Harvard University Archives, Houghton Library
   Stephen Sewall Lectures
Cincinnati, Ohio
American Jewish Archives
   Prof. J. Seixas File
Hartford, Conn.
Hartford Seminary Archives
   Merrill Collection
New Haven, Conn.
Yale University Archives
   Jonathan Edwards Collection
New York, N.Y.
New York University Archives
   Chancellor's Records
   Nordheimer File
Washington, D.C.
National Archives

BOOKS AND ARTICLES

Adams, Hannah. *The History of the Jews from the Destruction of Jerusalem to the Nineteenth Century*. Boston: J. Elliot Jr., 1812.

Adams, Henry. *The Education of Henry Adams*. Boston: Houghton Mifflin, 1918.

Adams, James. *The Founding of New England*. Boston: Atlantic Monthly Press, 1921.

Anderson, Wallace E., Mason I. Lowance Jr., and David H. Watters, eds. *Typological Writings*. Vol. 2 of *The Works of Jonathan Edwards*. New Haven, Conn.: Yale University Press.

Ariel, Yaakov. *On Behalf of Israel: American Fundamentalist Attitudes towards Jews, Judaism, and Zionism, 1865–1945*. Brooklyn, New York: Carlson Publishing, 1991.

———. *Evangelizing the Chosen People*. Chapel Hill: University of North Carolina Press, 2000.

———. *Philosemites or Antisemites? Evangelical Christian Attitudes toward Jews, Judaism, and the State of Israel* Jerusalem: Hebrew University of Jerusalem, 2002.

Arnold, Matthew. "Culture and Anarchy." In *The Portable Matthew Arnold*, edited by Lionel Trilling. New York: Viking Press, 1949.

B. S. "The Tomb of Nordheimer." *Semi Weekly Courier and New York Enquirer*, November 17, 1842.

Backman, Milton V. *The Heavens Resound: A History of the Latter-Day Saints in Ohio, 1830–1838*. Salt Lake City, Utah: Dessert Book Co., 1983.

Bain, Kenneth Ray. *The March to Zion: United States Policy and the Founding of Israel*. College Station: Texas A&M University Press, 1979.

Baron, S. "Hebraic Heritage." In *Ancient and Medieval Jewish History*, edited by
L. Feldman, 332–35. New Brunswick, N.J.: Rutgers University Press, 1972.
———. *Steeled by Adversity: Essays and Addresses on American Jewish Life*. Philadelphia:
Jewish Publication Society, 1971.

Bartlett, S. C. *From Egypt to Palestine*. New York: Harper Brothers, 1879.

Ben-Arieh, Y. *The Rediscovery of the Holy Land in the Nineteenth Century*. Jerusalem: Magnes
Press, 1979.

Bennet, John C. "Reinhold Niebuhr's Social Ethics." In *Reinhold Niebuhr: His Religious,
Social, and Political Thought*, edited by Charles Kegley, 45–77. New York: Macmillan,
1950.

Benz, Ernst. *Emanuel Swedenborg: Visionary Savant in the Age of Reason*. West Chester, Pa.:
Swedenborg Foundation, 2002.

Bercovitch, Sacvan, ed. *Typology and Early American Literature*. Amherst: University of
Massachussetts Press, 1972.

Berger, David. *The Jewish-Christian Debate in the High Middle Ages*. Philadelphia: Jewish
Publication Society, 1979.

Berlin, George L. *Defending the Faith: Nineteenth Century Jewish Writings on Christianity
and Jesus*. New York: State University of New York Press, 1989.
———. "Joseph S. C. F. Grey, The Jews, and Early Nineteenth Century Millenarianism."
Journal of the Early Republic (1981): 27–49.

Berman, M. *Richmond's Jewry, 1769–1976*. Charlottesville: University Press of Virginia, 1979.

Berryman, John. *Recovery*. New York: Farrar, Straus and Giroux, 1972.

Bevan, Edwyn, and Charles Singer, eds. *The Legacy of Israel*. Oxford: Clarendon Press,
1928.

Bingham, June. *Courage to Change: An Introduction to the Life and Thought of Reinhold
Niebuhr*. New York: Scribners, 1961.

Blackman, M. V. *The Heavens Resound: A History of the Latter-Day Saints in Ohio: 1830–1838*.
Salt Lake City: Deseret Book, 1983.

Blau, Joseph. *The Christian Interpretation of the Cabala in the Renaissance*. New York:
Columbia University Press, 1944.

Bliss, Fredrick J. *The Development of Palestine Exploration*. London: Charles Scribner, 1903.

Boudinot, Elias. *A Star in the West; or, a Humble Attempt to Discover the Long Lost Ten
Tribes of Israel, Preparatory to Their Return to Their Beloved City, Jerusalem*. Trenton,
N.J.: D. Fenton, S. Hutchinson and J. Dunham, 1816.

Brodie, Fawn. *No Man Knows My History: The Life of Joseph Smith the Mormon Prophet*.
New York: Knopf, 1945.

Brooke, John L. *The Refiner's Fire: The Making of Mormon Cosmology, 1644–1844*.
Cambridge: Cambridge University Press, 1996.

Brown, Adna. *From Vermont to Damascus*. Boston: G. H. Ellis, 1890.

Brown, J. W. *The Rise of Biblical Criticism in America, 1800–1870: The New England Scholars*.
Middletown, Conn.: Wesleyan University Press, 1969.

Brumm, Ursula. *American Thought and Religious Typology*. New Brunswick, N.J.: Rutgers
University Press, 1970.

Burnett, Stephen. *From Christian Hebraism to Jewish Studies: Johannes Buxtorf and Hebrew
Learning in the Seventeenth Century*. Leiden: E. J. Brill, 1996.

Burnstein, Alexander J. "Niebuhr, Scripture, and Normative Judaism." In *Reinhold
Niebuhr: His Religious, Social, and Political Thought*, edited by Charles Kegley, 412–28.
New York: Macmillan, 1950.

Bush, George. *A Grammar of the Hebrew Language*. 2nd ed. New York: Leavitt, Lord,
1839.

———. *The Life of Mohammed*. New York: J and J Harper, 1830.

———. *A Treatise on the Millennium*. New York: Harper, 1832.

———. *The Valley of Vision; or, the Dry Bones of Israel Revived: An Attempted Proof of the Restoration and Conversion of the Jews*. New York: Saxton and Miles, 1844.

Butler, John. *Awash in a Sea of Faith: Christianizing the American People*. Cambridge, Mass.: Harvard University Press, 1990.

Cappon, Lester, ed. *The Adams-Jefferson Letters*. New York: Simon and Schuster, 1971.

Carroll, James. *Constantine's Sword—the Church and the Jews: A History*. Boston: Houghton Mifflin, 2001.

Cassirer, Ernst. "Pico Della Mirandola." *Journal of the History of Ideas* 3, no. 2 (1942).

Castronovo, David. "Edmund Wilson's Citizen Reader." *Forward*, November 6, 1992.

"A Centenary Symposium on Edward Robinson." *Journal of Biblical Literature* 58 (1939).

Chamberlain, J. L., ed. *Universities and Their Sons: New York University*. Boston: R. Herdon Company, 1901.

Chapman, G. *Sketches of the Alumni of Dartmouth College*. Cambridge, Mass.: Riverside Press, 1867.

Chase, E. *A History of Dartmouth College and the Town of Hanover, N.H.* Cambridge, Mass: J. Wilson, 1913–28.

Chiel, Arthur. "Ezra Stiles and the Jews: A Study in Ambivalence." In *Hebrew and the Bible in America: The First Two Centuries*, edited by Shalom Goldman, 156–67. Hanover, N.H.: University Press of New England, 1993.

———. "Ezra Stiles, the Education of an Hebrician." *American Jewish Historical Quarterly* 40 (1971): 235–41.

———. "The Rabbis and Ezra Stiles." *American Jewish Historical Quarterly* 41 (1972): 294–312.

Chilton, Bruce. *Rabbi Jesus*. New York: Doubleday, 2000.

Chomsky, William. "Hebrew Grammar and Textbook Writing in Early Nineteenth Century America." In *Essays in American Jewish History*. Cincinnati, Ohio: American Jewish Archives, 1958.

Clark, Christopher. *The Politics of Conversion: Missionary Protestantism and the Jews in Prussia, 1728–1941*. Oxford: Clarendon Press, 1995.

Coffin, Henry S. *A Half Century of Union Theological Seminary, 1896–1945*. New York: Scribner, 1954.

Cohen, Jeremy. *The Friars and the Jews*. Ithaca, N.Y.: Cornell University Press, 1982.

Cohen, Naomi, ed. *Essential Papers on Jewish-Christian Relations in the United States: Images and Reality*. New York: New York University Press, 1990.

Cooperman, B. D., ed. *Jewish Thought in the Sixteenth Century*. Cambridge, Mass.: Harvard University Press, 1983.

Cuddihy, James. *The Ordeal of Civility: Freud, Marx, Levi-Strauss, and the Jewish Struggle with Modernity*. New York: Dell, 1974.

Culver, Douglas. *Albion and Ariel: British Puritanism and the Birth of Political Zionism*. New York: P. Lang, 1995.

Dabney, Lewis M. "The Philosopher and the Critic." *New York Times Book Review*, November 29, 1998.

———, ed. *Edmund Wilson: Centennial Reflections*. Princeton, N.J.: Mercantile Library in association with Princeton University Press, 1997.

———, ed. *The Sixties*. 1st ed. New York: Farrar Straus Giroux, 1993.

———, ed. *The Viking Portable Edmund Wilson*. New York: Penguin Books, 1983.

Davis, T. M. "The Traditions of Puritan Typology." In *Typology and Early American*

Literature, compiled by Sacvan Bercovitch. Amherst: University of Massachussetts Press, 1972.

Davis, John. *The Landscape of Belief: Encountering the Holy Land in Nineteenth Century American Art and Culture*. Princeton, N.J.: Princeton University Press, 1996.

Davis, Moshe. *America and the Holy Land (with Eyes toward Zion—IV)*. Westport, Conn.: Praeger, 1995.

———, ed. *Christian Protagonists for Jewish Restoration*. New York: Arno Press, 1977.

———, ed. *With Eyes toward Zion*. Westport, Conn.: Praeger, 1977.

De Sola Pool, David. "Hebrew Learning among the Puritans of Early New England Prior to 1700." *Publications of the American Jewish Historical Society* (1911): 31–83.

———. *Portraits Etched in Stone: Early Jewish Settlers, 1682–1831*. New York: Columbia University Press, 1954.

De Sola Pool, David, and T. de Sola Pool. *An Old Faith in the New World: Portrait of Shearith Israel, 1654–1954*. New York: Columbia University Press, 1955.

Dexter, Franklin B., ed. *The Literary Diary of Ezra Stiles*. 3 vols. New York: Scribner's Sons, 1901.

Diner, Hasia R. *A Time for Gathering: The Second Migration, 1820–1880*. Baltimore, Md.: Johns Hopkins University Press, 1992.

Douglas, George H. *Edmund Wilson's America*. Lexington: University Press of Kentucky, 1983.

Dudman, Helga. *The American Colony: Scenes from a Jerusalem Saga*. Jerusalem: Carta Jerusalem, 1998.

Dunlap, William. *A History of New York Schools*. New York: Collin, Kesse, 1836.

Edel, Leon, ed. *The Twenties*. New York: Farrar Straus Giroux, 1975.

Edwards, John. *The Jews in Christian Europe, 1400–1700*. London: Routledge, 1988.

Edwards, Jonathan. "To the Trustees of the College of New Jersey." In *A Jonathan Edwards Reader*, edited by J. Smith, H. Stout, and K. Minkema, 321–25. New Haven, Conn.: Yale University Press, 1995.

Eichhorn, David. *Evangelizing the American Jew*. New York: Jonathan David Publishers, 1978.

Eliav, Mordechai. "The Activities of Foreign Consuls in Erets-Israel." *Cathedra* 26 (1982).

Ellis, Joseph J. *Founding Brothers: The Revolutionary Generation*. New York: Alfred A. Knopf, 2000.

Elukin, Jonathan. "Jacque Basnage and the History of the Jews." *Journal of the History of Ideas* 53, no. 4 (Oct.–Dec. 1992): 603–30.

Endelman, T., ed. *Jewish Apostasy in the Modern World*. New York: Holmes and Meier, 1987.

Epperson, Steven. *Mormons and Jews: Early Mormon Theologies of Israel*. Salt Lake City: Signature Books, 1992.

Eubank, Williams. *The National Restoration of the Jews to Palestine Repugnant to the Word of God*. London: F. and J. Rivington, 1849.

Evearitt, Daniel. "Jewish-Christian Missions to the Jews, 1820–1935." Ph.D. diss., Drew University, 1988.

Feldman, E. *Dual Destinies: The Jewish Encounter with Protestant America*. Urbana: University of Illinois Press, 1990.

———. "Reinhold Niebuhr and the Jews." *Jewish Social Studies* 46 (1984).

Fellman, Jack. "Notes Concerning Two Nineteenth Century Hebrew Textbooks." *American Jewish Archives* 32, no. 1 (1980): 75–77.

Fisk, Pliny. "The Holy Land: An Interesting Field of Missionary Enterprise." *Holy Land Missions and Missionaries*, edited by Moshe Davis. New York: Arno Press, 1977.

Fletcher, R. S. *A History of Oberlin College*. Vol. 1. Oberlin, Ohio: Oberlin College, 1943.

Ford, A. H. "Our American Colony." *Appleton's Magazine*, December 1906.

Fox, Richard Wightman. *Reinhold Niebuhr: A Biography*. Ithaca, N.Y.: Cornell University Press, 1985.

Frey, J. S. C. F. *Hebrew Grammar*. London: Baldwin, Cradock, and Joy, 1823.

———. *A Hebrew, Latin and Greek Dictionary*. London: Gale and Fenner, 1815.

———. *Lectures on Baptism*. New York: n.p., 1834.

———. *Narrative of JSCF Frey*. London: n.p., n.d.

Friedman, J. *The Most Ancient Testimony: Sixteenth-Century Christian Hebraica in the Age of Renaissance Nostalgia*. Athens: Ohio University Press, 1983.

Friedman, Lee M. "A Contemporary Appraisal of Judah Monis, Harvard's First Instructor in Hebrew." *Publications of the American Jewish Historical Society* 38 (1948): 146–48.

———. "Cotton Mather and the Jews." *Publications of the American Jewish Historical Society* 26 (1918): 201–10.

———. "Judah Monis, First Instructor in Hebrew at Harvard University." *Publications of the American Jewish Historical Society* 22 (1914): 1–24.

———. *Pilgrims in a New Land*. Philadelphia: Jewish Publication Society, 1948.

———. *Rabbi Haim Isaac Carigal*. Boston: Privately published, 1940.

Frothingham, O. B. *Theodore Parker: A Biography*. Boston: J. R. Osgood and Company, 1874.

"Fürst's Concordance." *Biblical Repertory and Princeton Review* (1839).

Gale, Theophilus. *Court of the Gentiles*. London: n.p., 1672.

Giardina, Denise. *Saints and Villains: A Novel*. New York: W. W. Norton and Co., 1998.

Gilmore, Myron. *The World of Humanism, 1453–1517*. New York: Harper and Brothers, 1952.

Giltner, J. H. *Moses Stuart: The Father of Biblical Science in America*. Atlanta: Society for Biblical Literature, 1988.

Glanz, R. *Jew and Mormon*. New York: n.p., 1963.

Godbey, Allen. *The Lost Tribes a Myth: Suggestions towards Rewriting Hebrew History*. Durham, N.C.: Duke University Press, 1930.

Goldman, Shalom. "Biblical Hebrew in Colonial America: The Case of Dartmouth." In *Hebrew and the Bible in America: The First Two Centuries*, edited by Shalom Goldman. Hanover, N.H.: University Press of New England, 1993.

———. "Hebrew at the Early Colleges." *American Jewish Archives* 17, no. 1 (1990).

———. "The Holy Land Appropriated: The Careers of Selah Merrill, Nineteenth Century Christian Hebraist, Palestine Explorer, and U.S. Consul in Jerusalem." *American Jewish History* 85, no. 2 (1977): 151–72.

———. "Rev. George Bush." *American Jewish Archives* 43, no. 1 (1991).

———. "Review of *Hebrew in America*." *Hebrew Studies* 35 (1994).

———. "Review of *With Eyes toward Zion*." *American Jewish History* (1995): 424–27.

———. "Spiritual Feminism and Christian Hebraism: Women and the Study of Hebrew in Seventeenth Century Europe." *Hebrew Studies* 39 (1998).

———. "Two American Hebrew Orations: 1799 and 1800." *Hebrew Annual Review* 13 (1991).

———. "Vehu Shaul: An Unknown American-Yiddish Polemic." *Jewish Book Annual* 51 (1993–94).

———, ed. *Hebrew and the Bible in America: The First Two Centuries*. Hanover, N.H.: University Press of New England, 1993.

Goren, H. *"Go View the Land": German Study of Palestine in the Nineteenth Century*. Jerusalem: Yad Ben Tzvi, 1999.

Gorenberg, Gershom. *The End of Days: Fundamentalism and the Struggle for the Temple Mount*. New York: Free Press, 2000.

Grafton, Anthony. *Defenders of the Text: The Traditions of Scholarship in an Age of Science*. Cambridge, Mass.: Harvard University Press, 1991.

———. *New Worlds, Ancient Texts: The Power of Tradition and the Shock of Discovery*. Cambridge, Mass.: Harvard University Press, 1992.

Grimké, Thomas S. *Reflections on the Character and Objects of All Science and Literature*. New Haven, Conn.: H. Howe, 1831.

Grinstein, Hyman. *The Rise of the Jewish Community of New York, 1654–1860*. Philadelphia: Jewish Publication Society, 1947.

Griswold, Rufus W. *Prose Writers of America*. Philadelphia: Carey and Hart, 1849.

Grodzins, Dean. *American Heretic: Theodore Parker and Transcendentalism*. Chapel Hill: University of North Carolina Press, 2002.

Grose, Peter. *Israel in the Mind of America*. New York: Alfred A. Knopf, 1983.

Groth, Janet. *Edmund Wilson: A Critic for Our Time*. Athens: Ohio University Press, 1989.

Gutjahr, Paul. *An American Bible: A History of the Good Book in the United States, 1777–1880*. Stanford, Calif.: Stanford University Press, 1999.

Handy, Robert. *A History of Union Theological Seminary in New York*. New York: Columbia University Press, 1987.

———. *The Holy Land in American Protestant Life*. New York: Arno Press, 1994.

Hartstein, S. "The Shearith Israel School." *Publications of the American Jewish Historical Society* 34 (1937).

Hatch, Nathan, and Harry Stout, ed. *Jonathan Edwards and the American Experience*. Oxford: Oxford University Press, 1988.

Hayden, W. B. "Reminiscences." In *Memoirs and Reminiscences of the Late Prof. George Bush*, edited by W. M. Fernald. Boston: O. Clapp, 1860.

Hertzberg, Arthur. *The Jews in America: Four Centuries of an Uneasy Encounter: A History*. New York: Simon and Schuster, 1989.

———. "The New England Puritans and the Jews." In *Hebrew and the Bible in America: The First Two Centuries*, edited by Shalom Goldman, 105–21. Hanover, N.H.: University Press of New England, 1993.

———, ed. *The Zionist Idea: A Historical Analysis and Reader*. New York: Atheneum, 1981.

Heschel, Abraham J. "A Last Farewell." *Conservative Judaism* 25, no. 4 (1971): 62–63.

Hirsch, D. E. *Dr. Emil G. Hirsch*. Chicago: Whitehall, 1968.

A History of the Class of 1863, Yale College. New Haven, Conn.: n.p., 1905.

Holbrook, Clyde A., ed. *Original Sin*. Vol. 3 of *The Works of Jonathan Edwards*. New Haven, Conn.: Yale University Press.

Huhner, Leon. "The Jews of New England Prior to 1800." *Publications of the American Jewish Historical Society* 9 (1903): 80–105.

Ilchman, W. F. *Professional Diplomacy in the United States, 1779–1939*. Chicago: University of Chicago Press, 1961.

"Items Relating to the Seixas Family." *Publications of the Jewish Historical Society* 27 (1920).

Jackson, R. V. *New York City 1850 Census Index*. Bountiful, Utah: Accelerated Indexing Systems, 1978.

Johnson, Thomas. *Jonathan Edwards's Background of Reading*. Boston: Colonial Society of Massachusetts, 1931.

Jones, T. J., ed. *New York University 1832–1932*. New York and London: New York City University Press and Oxford University Press, 1937.

Kabakoff, Jacob. "The Use of Hebrew by American Jews during the Colonial Period." In

Hebrew and the Bible in America: The First Two Centuries, edited by Shalom Goldman, 191–97. Hanover, N.H.: University Press of New England, 1993.

———. "A Biblical Exegete." *American Jewish Archives Journal* 69, nos. 1 and 2 (1997): 131.

Kaganoff, Nathan M. "Hebrew and Liturgical Exercises in the Colonial Period." In *Hebrew and the Bible in America: The First Two Centuries*, edited by Shalom Goldman, 184–90. Hanover, N.H.: University Press of New England, 1993.

Kark, Ruth. *American Consuls in the Holy Land, 1832–1914*. Detroit, Mich.: Wayne State University Press, 1994.

———, ed. *The Land That Became Israel: Studies in Historical Geography*. Jerusalem: Magnes Press, 1989.

Kazin, Alfred. *A Lifetime Burning in Every Moment: From the Journals of Alfred Kazin*. New York: HarperCollins, 1996.

Kegley, Charles, ed. *Reinhold Niebuhr: His Religious, Social, and Political Thought*. New York: Macmillan, 1950.

Kernohan, R. D. *The Road to Zion: Travellers to Palestine and the Land of Israel*. Grand Rapids, Mich.: Eerdmans, 1995.

Kimnach, Wilson. "Jonathan Edwards's Pursuit of Reality." In *Jonathan Edwards and the American Experience*, edited by N. Hatch and H. Stout. Oxford: Oxford University Press, 1988.

Kimnach, Wilson H., ed. *Sermons and Discourses, 1720–1723*. Vol. 10 of *The Works of Jonathan Edwards*. New Haven, Conn.: Yale University Press.

Klausner, J. *Jesus of Nazareth*. New York: Macmillan, 1925.

Klein, M. "A Jew at Harvard in the 18th Century." *Proceedings of the Massachusetts Historical Society* 97 (1985): 135–45.

Klingenstein, S. *Jews in the American Academy, 1900–1940*. New Haven, Conn.: Yale University Press, 1991.

Knight, Janice. "Learning the Language of God: Jonathan Edwards and the Typology of Nature." *William and Mary Quarterly* 48, no. 4 (1991): 531–51.

Kohut, George. "Early Jewish Literature in America." *Publications of the American Jewish Historical Society* 3 (1895): 103–47.

———. *Ezra Stiles and the Jews*. New York: P. Cowen, 1902.

———. "Judah Monis, M.A." *American Journal of Semitic Languages and Literatures* 14 (1898): 217–26.

Kraut, B. "A Unitarian Rabbi? The Case of Solomon H. Sonneschein." In *Jewish Apostasy in the Modern World*, edited by T. Endelman. New York: Holmes and Meier, 1987.

Kreiger, Barbara, with Shalom Goldman. *Divine Expectations: An American Woman in Nineteenth Century Palestine*. Athens: Ohio University Press, 1999.

Kriegel, Leonard. *Edmund Wilson*. Carbondale: Southern Illinois University Press, 1971.

Krupnick, Mark. "Edmund Wilson and Gentile Philo-Semitism." In *Edmund Wilson: Centennial Reflections*, edited by Lewis M. Dabney. Princeton, N.J.: Mercantile Library in association with Princeton University Press, 1997.

Kuklick, Bruce. *Puritans in Babylon: The Ancient Near East and American Intellectual Life, 1880–1930*. Princeton, N.J.: Princeton University Press, 1996.

Laor, Dan. *Agnon*. Jerusalem: Schocken, 1998.

Lapide, Pinchas. *Hebrew in the Church: The Foundations of Jewish-Christian Dialogue*. Grand Rapids, Mich.: Eerdmans, 1984.

Larbaud, Valery. *An Homage to Jerome: Patron Saint of Translators*. Marlboro, Vt.: Marlboro Press, 1984.

Le Beau, Byron, and Menachem Mor. *Pilgrims and Travellers to the Holy Land*. Omaha, Nebr.: Creighton University Press, 1996.

Lee, Sang Hyun, and Allen Guezlo, ed. *Jonathan Edwards and the Shaping of American Religion*. Grand Rapids, Mich.: Eerdmans, 1999.

Liebes, Y. "Mazmiah Qeren Yeshu'ah." *Jerusalem Studies in Jewish Thought* 3, no. 3 (1983): 324–25.

Lipman, Vivian. *Americans and the Holy Land through British Eyes, 1820–1917: A Documentary History*. Jerusalem: Hebrew University Press, 1989.

Lloyd Jones, G. *The Discovery of Hebrew in Tudor England: A Third Language*. Manchester: Manchester University Press, 1983.

Lowance, Mason. "'Images or Shadows of Divine Things' in the Thought of Jonathan Edwards." In *Typology and Early American Literature*, edited by Sacvan Bercovitch. Amherst: University of Massachusetts Press, 1972.

McCullough, David. *Brave Companions: Portraits in History*. New York: Simon and Schuster, 1992.

———. *Truman*. New York: Simon and Schuster, 1992.

McDermott, Gerald. "A Possibility of Reconciliation: Jonathan Edwards and the Salvation of Non-Christians." In *Jonathan Edwards's Writings: Text, Context, Interpretation*, edited by Stephen J. Stein. Bloomington: Indiana University Press, 1996.

McKane, William. *Selected Christian Hebraists*. Cambridge: Cambridge University Press, 1989.

Maclean, J. *History of the College of New Jersey*. New York: Arno Press, 1877.

Malachy, Y. *American Fundamentalism and Israel*. Jerusalem: Hebrew University Press, 1978.

Manuel, Frank. *The Broken Staff: Judaism through Christian Eyes*. Cambridge, Mass.: Harvard University Press, 1992.

———. "Israel and the Enlightenment." *Daedalus* (Winter 1982).

———. *The Realities of American-Palestine Relations*. Washington, D.C.: Public Affairs Press, 1949.

Marcus, Jacob R. *The Colonial American Jew, 1492–1776*. Detroit, Mich.: Wayne State University Press, 1970.

———. "The Handsome Young Priest in the Black Gown: The Personal World of Gershom Seixas." *Hebrew Union College Annual* 40–41 (1969–70).

———. *United States Jewry, 1776–1985*. Vol. 1. Detroit, Mich.: Wayne State University Press, 1989.

———, ed. *The Jew in the American World: A Source Book*. Detroit, Mich.: Wayne State University Press, 1996.

Marsden, George M. *Jonathan Edwards: A Life*. New Haven, Conn.: Yale University Press.

Matar, N. I. "Protestantism, Palestine, and Partisan Scholarship." *Journal of Palestine Studies* (Summer 1989): 52–70.

May, Harry. *The Tragedy of Erasmus: A Psychohistoric Approach*. Saint Charles, Mo.: Pireaus Publishers, 1975.

Merkley, Paul. *The Politics of Christian Zionism: 1891–1948*. London: Frank Cass, 1998.

Merrill, Selah. "Report to the Assistant Secretary of State from the U.S. Consul in Jerusalem." In *With Eyes toward Zion*, edited by Moshe Davis. Westport, Conn.: Praeger, 1977.

Meyer, I. *The Hebrew Exercises of Governor William Bradford*. Plymouth, Mass.: Pilgrim Society, 1973.

Meyer, Michael. *Response to Modernity*. New York: Oxford University Press, 1988.

Meyers, Jeffrey. *Edmund Wilson: A Biography*. Boston: Houghton Mifflin, 1995.

Miller, Merle. *Plain Speaking: An Oral Biography of Harry S. Truman*. New York: Berkley Publishing, 1974.

Miller, Perry. "The Garden of Eden and the Deacon's Meadow." *American Heritage* 7 (1955).

———. *Jonathan Edwards*. Cambridge, Mass.: Harvard University Press, 1948.

———, ed. *The American Transcendentalists: Their Prose and Poetry*. New York: Doubleday, 1957.

———, ed. *Images or Shadows of Divine Things / by Jonathan Edwards*. Cambridge, Mass.: Harvard University Press, 1948.

Mintz, Alan, ed. *Hebrew in America: Perspectives and Prospects*. Detroit, Mich.: Wayne State University Press, 1993.

Moore, George F. "Ezra Stiles Studies in the 'Cabala.'" *Proceedings of the Massachusets Historical Society* 51 (1918): 290–306.

———. "Judah Monis." *Proceedings of the Massachusets Historical Society* 52 (1919): 285–312.

———. "A Jewish Life of Jesus: A Review of J. Klausner, *Jesus of Nazareth*." *Harvard Theological Review* (1923): 93–103.

Morgan, Edmund. *The Gentle Puritan: A Life of Ezra Stiles*. New Haven, Conn.: Yale University Press, 1962.

Morison, Samuel Eliot. *Harvard in the Seventeenth Century*. Cambridge, Mass.: Harvard University Press, 1936.

———. *The Intellectual Life of Colonial New England*. Ithaca, N.Y.: Cornell University Press, 1936.

Murphy, W. M., and D. J. R. Bruckner, eds. *The Idea of the University of Chicago*. Chicago: University of Chicago Press, 1976.

Navert, Charles. *Agrippa and the Crisis of Renaissance Thought*. Urbana: University of Illinois Press, 1965.

Neill, H. "Reminiscences of Nordheimer." *New Englander* (July 1874).

Nemoy, Leon. "William Gottlieb Schauffler." *Publications of the American Jewish Historical Society* 35 (1939): 304–6.

Niebuhr, Ursula. *Remembering Reinhold Niebuhr*. San Francisco, Calif.: HarperCollins, 1991.

Obenzinger, Hilton. *American Palestine: Melville, Twain, and the Holy Land Mania*. Princeton, N.J.: Princeton University Press, 1990.

Oren, Dan. *Joining the Club: A History of Jews at Yale*. 2nd ed. New Haven, Conn.: Yale University Press, 2000.

Oviatt, Edwin. *The Beginnings of Yale (1701–1726)*. New Haven, Conn.: Yale University Press, 1916.

Parker, T. *Views of Religion*. Boston: American Unitarian Association, 1890.

Philipson, D. *The Reform Movement in Judaism*. New York: Ktav Publishing House, 1907.

Phillips, N. Taylor. "The Levy and Seixas Families of Newport and New York." *Publications of the American Jewish Historical Society* 4 (1897).

Popkin, Richard H. "The Rise and Fall of the Jewish Indian Theory." In *Hebrew and the Bible in America: The First Two Centuries*, edited by Shalom Goldman, 70–90. Hanover, N.H.: University Press of New England, 1993.

Postal, Bernard, and Lionel Kippman. *Jewish Landmarks in New York*. New York: Hill and Wang, 1964.

Prince, Elaine B. "The Patrilineal Descent of Vice President Bush." *NEXUS: The Bimonthly Newsletter of the New England Geneological Society* 3 (1986): 124–25.

Pritchard, James. *The Ancient Near East: An Anthology of Texts and Pictures*. Princeton, N.J.: Princeton University Press, 1958.

Quinn, D. Michael. *Early Mormonism and the Magic World View*. Salt Lake City: Signature Books, 1987.

Raboteau, Albert. *A Fire in the Bones: Reflections on African American Religious History*. Boston: Beacon Press, 1995.

Ramsey, Paul. *Ethical Writings*. Vol. 8 of *The Works of Jonathan Edwards*. New Haven, Conn.: Yale University Press.

Rice, Dan. "Reinhold Niebuhr and Judaism." *Journal of the American Academy of Religion* 45, no. 7, suppl. (1977).

Robinson, Edward. *Biblical Researches in Palestine, Mt. Sinai and Arabia Petraea*. 2 vols. Boston: Crocker and Brewster, 1841.

———. *Later Biblical Researches in Palestine, and in the Adjacent Regions*. Boston: Crocker and Brewster, 1856.

———. "Notices of Nordheimer." In *Bibliotheca Sacra: Or Tracts and Essays*. New York: Wiley and Putnam, 1843.

Romm, James. "Biblical History and the Americas." In *The Jews and the Expansion of Europe to the West, 1450 to 1800*, edited by P. Bernardini and N. Fiering, 27–46. New York: Berghahn Books, 2001.

Rosenbach, A. S. W. *An American Jewish Bibliography*. New York: American Jewish Historical Society, 1926.

Roth, P. *Operation Shylock: A Confession*. New York: Simon and Schuster, 1993.

Rubin, Rehav. "When Jerusalem Was Built in St. Louis." *Palestine Exploration Quarterly* 132 (2000): 59–70.

Rylaarsdam, J. Coert. *Transitions in Biblical Scholarship*. Chicago: University of Chicago Press, 1968.

Said, Edward. *The Question of Palestine*. New York: Times Books, 1979.

Sanders, Ronald. *Lost Tribes and Promised Lands: The Origins of American Racism*. New York: HarperCollins, 1992.

Sarna, J. D. "The Impact of Nineteenth-Century Christian Missions on American Jews." In *Jewish Apostasy in the Modern World*, edited by T. Endelman, 232–54. New York: Holmes and Meier, 1987.

Sarna, J. D., and N. M. Sarna. "Jewish Bible Scholarship and Translations." In *The Bible and Bibles in America*, edited by E. S. Frerichs. Atlanta: Scholars Press, 1988.

Sarna, Jonathan. "The American Jewish Response to Nineteenth-Century Christian Missions." *Journal of American History* (1981): 35–51.

Schoen, E. J. "The Circumcision Decision." *Moment Magazine*, October 1997.

Scult, Mel. *Millenial Expectations and Jewish Liberties*. Leiden: Brill, 1978.

Seixas, J. *A Key to the Chaldee Language—Designed for Those Who Have Studied Hebrew with the Author*. Andover, Mass.: Flagg, Gould, and Newman, 1833.

———. *Manual Hebrew Grammar*. Andover, Mass.: Flagg, Gould, and Newman, 1832.

Sewall, Stephen. "Draft of a Letter, 1767 or 1768." Cincinnati, Ohio: American Jewish Archives, 1954.

Shepherd, Naomi. *The Zealous Intruders: The Western Rediscovery of Palestine*. New York: Harper and Row, 1987.

Sherman, Moshe. *Orthodox Judaism in America: A Biographical Dictionary and Sourcebook*. Westport, Conn.: Greenwood Press, 1986.

Sibley's Harvard Graduates. Vol. 4 (1690–1700). Boston: Massachusetts Historical Society.

Siegel, Seymour. "Reinhold Niebuhr: An Appreciation." *Conservative Judaism* 25, no. 4 (1971): 57–61.

Siegel, Thomas. "Professor Stephen Sewall and the Transformation of Hebrew at Harvard." In *Hebrew and the Bible in America: The First Two Centuries*, edited by Shalom Goldman, 228–45. Hanover, N.H.: University Press of New England, 1993.

Silberman, L. "Wellhausen and Judaism." *Semeia* 25 (1982).

Silberman, N. A. *Digging for God and Country*. New York: Alfred A. Knopf, 1982.

Silberschlag, Eisig. "Judah Monis in Light of an Unpublished Manuscript." *American Academy of Jewish Research* (1979–80): 494–503.

Silverstein, K., and M. Scherer. "Born Again Zionists." *Mother Jones*, September–October, 2002, 56–61.

Smallwood, Robert. "Mormon Scholar." *Chronicle of Higher Education*, January 3, 2003.

Smith, George Adam. *The Historical Geography of the Holy Land*. London: Hodder and Stoughton, 1906.

Smith, John E. *Religious Affections*. Vol. 2 of *The Works of Jonathan Edwards*. New Haven, Conn.: Yale University Press.

———. *Jonathan Edwards: Puritan, Preacher, Philosopher*. Notre Dame: University of Notre Dame Press, 1992.

Smith, Winfred Cantwell. *What Is Scripture?: A Comparative Approach*. Minneapolis, Minn.: Fortress Press, 1993.

Snow, L. C. "Who Was Professor Joshua Seixas?" *Improvement Era* 34, no. 2 (1936).

Stein, Stephen. "The Spirit and the Word: Jonathan Edwards and Scriptural Exegesis." In *Jonathan Edwards and the American Experience*, edited by Nathan Hatch and Harry Stout. New York: Oxford University Press, 1984.

———, ed. *Jonathan Edwards' Writings: Text, Context, Interpretation*. Bloomington: Indiana University Press, 1996.

Stern, Malcolm H., comp. *First American Jewish Families: 600 Genealogies, 1654–1988*. Cincinatti, Ohio: American Jewish Archives, 1978.

Stinson, Charles. "'Northernmost Israel': England, the Old Testament, and the Hebrew 'Veritas' as Seen by Bede and Roger Bacon." In *Hebrew and the Bible in America: The First Two Centuries*, edited by Shalom Goldman, 14–42. Hanover, N.H.: University Press of New England, 1993.

Stokes, Anson Phelps. *Memorials of Eminent Yale Men; A Biographical Study of Student Life and University Influences During the Eighteenth and Nineteenth Centuries*. New Haven, Conn.: Yale University Press, 1914.

Stolz, Joseph. "Bernard Felsenthal." In *The Jewish Encyclopedia*. New York: Funk and Wagnalls, 1902.

Stone, Ronald. *Reinhold Niebuhr: Prophet to Politicians*. Nashville, Tenn.: Abington Press.

Stout, Harry. *The New England Soul: Preaching and Religious Culture in Colonial New England*. Oxford: Oxford University Press, 1986.

Stuart, Moses. *A Grammar of the Hebrew Language*. 6th ed. Andover, Mass.: Gould and Newman, 1838.

———. *A Hebrew Chrestomathy, Designed as the First Volume in a Course of Hebrew Study*. Andover, Mass.: Flagg and Gould; Codman Press, 1829.

———. *Sermon at the Ordination of the Rev. William G. Schauffler, as Missionary to the Jews*. Andover, Mass.: Flagg and Gould, 1831.

Taylor, Edward. *Upon the Types of the Old Testament*. Edited by Charles Mignon. Lincoln: University of Nebraska Press, 1989.

Trilling, Lionel. *Matthew Arnold*. Minneapolis, Minn.: Fortress Press, 1993.

Tuchman, Barbara. *Bible and Sword: England and Palestine from the Bronze Age to Balfour*. New York: New York University Press, 1956.

Twain, Mark. *The Innocents Abroad*. New York: Bantam Books, 1964.

Twersky, I., and B. Septimus, eds. *Jewish Thought in the Seventeenth Century*. Cambridge, Mass.: Harvard University Press, 1987.

Underwood, Grant. "The Hope of Israel in Early Modern Ethnography and Escatology." In *Hebrew and the Bible in America: The First Two Centuries*, edited by Shalom Goldman, 91–101. Hanover, N.H.: University Press of New England, 1993.

Vester, B. Spafford. *Our Jerusalem: An American Family in the Holy City, 1881–1949*. Salem, N.H.: Ayer, 1950.

Vogel, Lester. *To See a Promised Land: Americans and the Holy Land in the Nineteenth Century*. University Park: Pennsylvania State University Press, 1993.

Wain, John, ed. *An Edmund Wilson Celebration*. Oxford: Phaidon, 1978.

Walton, M. T. "Professor Seixas, the Hebrew Bible and the Book of Abraham." *Sunstone* (1981): 41–43.

Warch, Richard. *School of the Prophets: Yale College, 1701–1740*. New Haven, Conn.: Yale University Press, 1973.

Warren, Samuel M. *A Compendium of the Theological Writings of Emanuel Swedenborg*. New York: Swedenborg Foundation, 1974.

Wendell, Barrett. *Cotton Mather: The Puritan Priest*. New York: Harcourt, Brace, and World, 1963.

White, Andrew Dickson. *A History of the Warfare of Science with Theology*. New York: Dover Publications, 1896.

Whitehouse, Ann. "Edmund Wilson's Jewish Ambassador." *Forward* (1992).

Wilken, Robert. *The Land Called Holy: Palestine in Christian History and Thought*. New Haven, Conn.: Yale University Press, 1992.

Williams, Jay. *The Times and Life of Edward Robinson*. Atlanta, Ga.: Society for Biblical Literature, 1999.

Wilson, Andrew. *The Creation the Ground-Work of Revelation and Revelation the Language of Nature (A Brief Attempt to Demonstrate That the Hebrew Language is Founded on Natural Ideas)*. London: n.p., 1750.

Wilson, Charles. *Elements of Hebrew Grammar*. 3rd ed. Edinburgh: n.p., 1802.

Wilson, Edmund. *The Bit between My Teeth*. New York: Farrar Straus Giroux, 1965.

———. *I Thought of Daisy*. New York: Charles Scribner's Sons, 1929.

———. "On First Reading Genesis." In *The Viking Portable Edmund Wilson*, edited by Lewis M. Dabney. New York: Penguin Books, 1983.

———. *Patriotic Gore*. New York: Oxford University Press, 1962.

———. *A Piece of My Mind*. New York: Farrar, Straus and Cudahy, 1956.

———. *To the Finland Station: A Study in the Writing and Acting of History*. New York: Harcort, Brace and Company, 1940.

Wilson, Elena, ed. *Edmund Wilson. Lectures on Literature and Politics. 1912–1972*. New York, 1973.

Wind, James. *The Bible and the University: The Messianic Vision of William Rainey Harper*. Atlanta, Ga.: Scholars Press, 1987.

Winslow, Ola. *Jonathan Edwards: A Biography*. New York: Macmillan, 1940.

Wosh, Peter. *Spreading the Word*. Ithaca, N.Y.: Cornell University Press, 1994.

Yates, Frances. *Astraea: The Imperial Theme in the Sixteenth Century*. London: Ark Publishers, 1975.

———. *Giordano Bruno and the Hermetic Tradition*. Chicago: University of Chicago Press, 1964.

———. *The Occult Philosophy in the Elizabethan Age*. London: Ark Publishers, 1979.

———. *The Rosicrucian Enlightenment*. London: Routledge, Kegan Paul, 1972.

Yerushalmi, Y. H. "Messianic Impulses in Joseph ha-Kohen." In *Jewish Thought in the Sixteenth Century*, edited by Bernard Cooperman. Cambridge, Mass.: Harvard University Press.

Zucker, L. C. "Joseph Smith as a Student of Hebrew." *Dialogue: A Journal of Mormon Thought* 3, no. 2 (1969): 41–55.

UNPUBLISHED REFERENCES

"A Merrill Memorial." Typescript in Library of Congress.

Bassett, Joseph. Letter to the author on Judah Monis, May 20, 1990.

De Sola Pool, David. "Joshua Seixas: Hebraist." Paper presented at the American Jewish Historical Society annual meeting, 1914. Seixas File, American Jewish Archives, Cincinnati, Ohio.

Siegel, Thomas. "The Relationship between Christian Hebraists and Jewish Informants in New England." Unpublished paper, 1991.

INDEX

Anglo-American Commission on Palestine, 264
Anti-Defamation League (ADL), 296
Anti-Judaism, 3, 27, 48, 68, 186, 244, 269
Anti-Semitism: and British Israelite ideology, 20; Sewall and, 48; Wigglesworth and, 50; and European Jews, 112; and German Higher Criticism, 133; and Christian Hebraism, 211, 244; and Nazi Germany, 261, 265; and New Testament, 269–70; Wilson's reaction to, 278–79, 281
Arabic language: Harvard College and, 9, 38, 47; Native Americans and, 18; Stiles and, 61, 65, 67, 254; Frey and, 99; missionary activities and, 108; Calvin Stowe and, 133; Robinson and, 143, 157, 158; Andover Theological Seminary and, 147; Nordheimer and, 149, 167, 203; Eli Smith and, 154, 155, 157, 158, 159, 169; Stuart and, 182; Harper and, 235
Arab-Israeli conflict, 233, 263–64, 267, 281, 293, 295
Arabs of Palestine, 134–35, 229, 230, 263–64, 265, 267, 293
Aramaic language: Harvard College and, 9, 38; Jewish scholars and, 18; as original language, 23; Zohar and, 27; Pico della Mirandola and, 59; Stiles and, 60; Borrenstein and, 100; Andover Theological Seminary and, 147; Seixas and, 179, 194, 197; Mormon Church and, 191; Bush and, 200; Harper and, 235; seminary education and, 240
Archaeology: Near Eastern archaeology, 131, 237–38. *See also* Biblical archaeology
Ariel, Yaakov, 4
Aristide, Jean-Bertrand, 298–99
Arnold, Matthew, 130
Artas, 4–5, 160
Arthur, Chester A., 210, 219
Asia, 21, 23, 90
Assemblies of God, 294
Azulai, Hayyim Joseph David (rabbi), 68

Bacher, Wilhelm, 247
Balfour Declaration (1917), 232
Band, Arnold, 301
Baptist Union Theological Seminary, 241–42

Baron, Salo, 298
Baxter, Richard, 227
Bede, Venerable, The, 26
Beecher, Lyman, 132, 281
Begin, Menachem, 5, 294
Bellow, Saul, 277, 297, 300
Ben Gurion, David, 5, 230, 294
Bennet, John C., 261
Ben Yehuda, Eliezer, 115
Benz, Ernst, 206
Bercovitch, Sacvan, 29
Berlin, Isaiah, 282
Berryman, John, 277, 285–86
Bialik, Haim Nahman, 304
Bible: *sola scriptura*, 2, 17, 25; authority of, 2, 54, 55–56, 133, 153, 269; biblical history, 3, 17, 18–19, 54, 135, 141, 153, 154, 157, 161, 176; and origins of nations/peoples, 7, 15–16; biblical prophecy, 20, 72, 91, 142, 230, 262, 305; biblical typology, 29, 61, 74–75, 77, 82–85, 87, 88; King James version, 30, 276; and ancient learning, 80–81; tensions between Christian and Jewish understandings of, 134; and Jewish scholars, 147, 151, 163, 303; as product of Judaism, 246; and shared biblical tradition of Christians and Jews, 270, 271; literalist understanding of, 292, 293, 295, 305. *See also* Biblical studies; Hebrew Bible; New Testament; Old Testament
Biblia Hebraica: Jonathan Edwards copy of, 86
Biblical archaeology: Robinson and, 116, 137, 143, 155, 157–58, 215, 301; and Hebrew studies, 130–31; Merrill and, 209, 210, 214, 217, 220, 224; and concept of Holy Land, 210–11, 302
Biblical interpretation: and Christian Hebraism, 2, 125; and Jewish scholars, 12, 33, 45; and Hebrew studies, 25, 234, 244; and Kabbalism, 66; Robinson and, 140; Stiles and, 237; Harper and, 238, 244, 245, 249, 250
Biblical studies: and Hebrew language, 7, 9; and higher education, 9, 10, 60, 70, 235–38, 239; and Puritans, 12, 20, 201; Edwards and, 12, 77, 81–82, 84, 87, 88; and Lost Tribe theories, 17; and English language, 30, 75, 204, 235, 248;

and Jewish scholars, 48, 117, 162, 297; and science, 49, 152, 153, 154, 237–38, 242, 245, 250; Stiles and, 50, 55–56, 58–62, 67, 72, 119, 129; Wilson and, 118, 126, 234, 276, 277, 280, 284, 288; and Protestantism, 127, 130, 134, 142, 235, 237, 297; Stuart and, 131, 142, 148, 150, 182–83, 239; Robinson and, 131–32, 133, 134, 138, 139, 142, 152, 154, 157, 160, 161, 168, 203; and German Higher Criticism, 133, 250; Nordheimer and, 134, 163, 168, 169; Seixas and, 134, 181; Bush and, 134, 200, 204; Eli Smith and, 154, 157, 159; Grimké and, 165, 166; Merrill and, 210, 217, 219, 220, 226; and Zionism, 229; Harper and, 232, 234, 235–36, 237, 238, 239–40, 241, 242, 245; Niebuhr and, 234, 254, 255, 257; and seminary education, 239–40. *See also* Biblical archaeology

Bingham, June, 257, 264

Bishop, Albert Frederick, 260

Black Americans, 58, 71, 100, 133, 150, 166, 251, 256, 260, 298

Blackstone, William, 231, 232, 291, 292

Blackstone Memorial (1891), 208, 231, 291, 292

Blackstone Memorial (1916), 232, 291, 292

B'nai B'rith, 264, 296

Boerne, Ludwig, 41

Bonhoeffer, Dietrich, 260, 261, 262

Borrenstein, David A., 100

Boudinot, Elias: and Jewish-Indian theory, 21–22, 92, 93, 94; and ASMCJ, 89, 92, 102, 106; and Native Americans, 92–93, 94, 101; and American Bible Society, 94, 101, 159; and Frey, 101–2, 110

Boudinot, Elias (Cherokee), 94

Bradford, William, 7, 9, 126

Brainerd, David, 79

Brandeis, Louis D., 230, 231–32, 262–63

Breasted, James Henry, 138

Brewster, William, 7, 126

British Palestine Exploration Fund, 153

Brit Shalom, 264

Brodie, Fawn, 194

Buber, Martin, 264

Buchanan, Claudius, 108

Burnstein, Alexander J. (rabbi), 271

Bush, George: and Hebrew language instruction, 10, 169–70, 182, 195, 199, 203; and New York University, 10, 198, 199, 202, 207; and biblical studies, 134, 200, 204; and Nordheimer, 164, 169–70, 203; and Christian Zionism, 199, 207, 227; and Hebrew studies, 200, 201, 204; and Christian Hebraism, 201, 305–6; and Jews, 204; and Swedenborg, 205–7, 305

Bush, George H. W., 10, 207, 306, 315 (n. 24)

Bush, George W., 10, 207, 296, 306

Bush, Mary W. Fisher, 206

Buss, John, 189

Butzell, Fred, 257, 258

Buxtorf, Johann, 7, 57, 79, 80, 85, 86

Calvinism, 20, 32, 55, 60, 280

Cambridge University, 9, 10, 26, 57, 276

Carigal, Hayyim (rabbi), 63–66, 68, 119, 126

Carroll, James, 269

Case Western Reserve College, 129, 189, 191, 197

Cassirer, Ernst, 28

Castronovo, David, 283

Catholicism: and biblical history, 17; and Hebrew language, 25; Stiles and, 59; Catholic Church as "True Israel," 63; and missionary activity, 90; and Jews, 98, 268, 272; Robinson and, 156, 161; and Vatican II, 269; and biblical archaeology, 301

Chaldee language, 47, 60, 179, 181

Champollion, Jacques-Joseph, 142

Chapman, John Jay, 54, 281

Chauncy, Charles, 9, 13, 38

Cherokee language, 94

Chiel, Arthur (rabbi), 55, 56, 68

Chilton, Bruce, 269

Chomsky, William, 164

Christian Hebraism: and biblical interpretation, 2, 125; attitudes toward Jews, 3, 13, 20, 56, 198, 203, 210, 211, 225–26; and Christian Zionism, 4, 5, 229; in Holland, 11; European, 12, 15, 126, 130, 225; and Jewish scholars, 12, 33, 51, 56–58, 119, 198, 203, 210; and Puritans, 13, 14, 20, 60, 132, 147, 181, 227, 230; and higher education, 13, 26–27,

129, 140, 300, 301; ambivalence inherent in, 20, 24, 45, 68–69, 126, 198, 203, 211, 226, 297; roots of, 20, 25, 280; and King James Bible, 30; multifaceted interests of, 39; and study of Jews, 50; and Yale College seal, 53; and study as devotional act, 61; and transliterated texts, 82; and Jewish Hebraism, 111, 124, 125–27; and piety, 141; and Masorah, 146, 173; and Palestine exploration, 150–53; and anti-Semitism, 211, 244; and Zionism, 226, 227; and Bible-based education, 239; and American culture, 296–98. *See also* Biblical studies; Hebrew language; Hebrew language instruction; Hebrew studies

Christiani, Freidrich Albert, 43

Christian-Jewish relations: and Jewish-Indian theory, 89; Harper and, 245; Hirsch and, 246; Niebuhr and, 254, 257, 261, 269–71; and conversion of Jews, 268–70; Flusser and, 286; Wilson and, 287–88; Jesus and, 303; and Kabbalism, 304. *See also* Jewish-Christian scholarly cooperation

Christian Kabbalism: origins of, 27–28, 40–41; Monis and, 28–29, 31, 39–41, 87, 304; Stiles and, 28–29, 67, 87–88, 304; Edwards and, 29, 87, 304; and Trinitarian idea, 66; and mystical power of Hebrew language, 190. *See also* Kabbalism

Christians and Christianity: and American Jewish community, 3, 113; and restoration of Jews to Palestine, 4, 5, 103, 106, 134; and Holy Land, 4, 10, 110, 151; and Israel, 5, 25; and Zionism, 6, 227, 231; church/synagogue relationship, 12; Old and New Testaments fused in, 16; Judaic roots of, 20, 27, 259, 271, 303; and Jewish-Indian theory, 21; and Hebrew as original language, 23, 24–25; attitudes toward Jews, 24, 25, 54, 56, 126; and Christian Kabbalism, 28–29; Christianity as fulfilled Judaism, 32, 37, 94, 104; and Christian identity, 33, 34–35, 39, 41–44, 144, 187–89; and salvific function of Jews, 63; and role of transmitting Scripture, 81; and refu-

tations of Christian doctrine, 91–92; Jews' attitude toward, 96; and Hebrew language, 117, 122, 303; and Hebrew studies, 117, 297; and social justice, 256, 258. *See also* Catholicism; Christian Hebraism; Christian Kabbalism; Christian Zionism; Conversion of Jews to Christianity; Protestantism

Christian Zionism: and Christian Hebraism, 4, 5, 229; and evangelicals, 4, 233, 291, 294; and Israel, 5, 231, 266, 293–94; and rediscovery of Hebraic, 20; and Jewish Zionist ideas, 103; and politics, 160, 211; Joseph Smith and, 195; Bush and, 199, 207, 227; and Blackstone Memorial, 208, 231; and conservative ideologies, 233, 266; Niebuhr compared to, 261, 262, 267; and American Jewish community, 296. *See also* Restoration of Jews to Palestine; Zionism

Church, Frederic, 160–61, 302

Church of Jesus Christ of Latter-Day Saints. *See* Mormon Church

Cleveland, Grover, 220

Clifford, Clark, 292

Clinton, George, 124

Cohen, Morris, 281

College of New Jersey, 74–75, 78, 85, 86

Colman, Benjamin, 31, 33, 36, 38, 43

Columbia College, 120, 122

Columbia University, 115

Columbus, Christopher, 18–19

Committee of One Hundred, 257

Congregation Beni Abraham, 99–100

Congregation Bnai Jeshurun, 110

Congregation Mikve Israel, 115, 123–24

Congregation Mishkan Israel, 116–17

Congregation Ohavey Zedek, 110

Congregation Shearith Israel: Hebrew School of, 13, 114–15, 178; as early congregation, 110; and rabbinic texts, 117; and Simson family, 120, 121, 122; and English translations of Hebrew texts, 123; Nordheimer and, 172, 174; Seixas and, 177–78, 192, 196–97

Congregation Yeshuat Israel, 50

Conversion of Jews to Christianity: and Hebrew language as tool of conversion, 12, 27, 98–100, 108, 127, 131; and biblical prophecy, 20, 91; and millennial groups, 32, 95; and Puritans, 32, 211; and American colonies, 32–33, 43, 51; and European Jews, 42–43, 188; Frey and, 89, 90, 95, 96–97, 104, 106, 107, 109; and Lost Tribes theories, 92; and establishment of Jewish synagogues, 116–17; Robinson and, 143; Stuart and, 148; social stigma of, 187–88; Niebuhr and, 268, 269, 270–71; Ben Gurion and, 294. *See also* Missionary activity

Cowdery, Oliver, 191
Cresson, Warder, 213
Cromwell, Thomas, 57
Crossman, Richard, 264
Cuddihy, John Murray, 243

Dabney, Lewis, 275
Dalman, Gustav, 244
Damascus Affair (1840), 144, 172
Danby, Herbert, 303–4
Dartmouth College, 13, 199, 200, 207, 300, 306
Darwin, Charles, 152, 153, 237
Davis, John, 160
Davis, Thomas M., 77
Davis, W. D., 176
Dead Sea Scrolls, 234, 277, 281, 282, 283, 284, 286, 287, 301
Denison University, 241
De Sola Pool, David, 164, 168, 174, 185, 188, 196
Doctrinal issues: and legality of teaching Torah to non-Jews, 12–13; and Jewish-Christian scholarly cooperation, 13, 65–66; and Christian Kabbalism, 27–29, 40; and Jewish traditions of learning, 54; Stiles and, 55, 58; and missionary activity, 91–92; and Harvard College, 129; and Hebrew studies, 148; and biblical studies, 239
Donoghue, Denis, 285
Dos Passos, John, 276, 287
Dunster, Henry, 9, 38
Dwight, Timothy, 145

Eban, Abba, 282
Edel, Leon, 277, 287
Eden Theological Seminary, 255

Edwards, Esther Stoddard, 78
Edwards, Jonathan: and Hebrew studies, 11–12, 74, 77–80, 82, 84–86, 87, 88; and Christian Kabbalism, 29, 87, 304; and Stiles, 55, 73, 74, 78; Hebrew language knowledge of, 73, 75, 77–78; and typology, 74–75, 77, 82–85, 87, 88; and Hebrew language instruction, 75, 80; education of, 78–80; and Gale, 80–82; and William Robinson, 140
Edwards, Jonathan, Jr., 86–87
Edwards, Timothy, 78–79, 86
Egypt, 49, 131, 138, 142, 155, 156, 157, 159, 266
Ehrlich, Arnold, 118
Einhorn, David (rabbi), 246, 251
Eisenhower, Dwight D., 266
Elukin, Jonathan, 77
Emerson, Ralph Waldo, 206
End Time, 16, 21–22, 63, 81, 90, 103, 106, 231, 233, 262, 294–95
England: and Jewish history, 20–21; and Christian Hebraism, 25–26, 130; and Christian Kabbalism, 28–29; expulsion of Jews from, 57; and Hebrew printing, 99–100; and "return to the land" movement for Jews, 102; Frey and, 109; and Egypt, 142
English Civil War, 10
English Revolution, 41
English language: and Hebrew liturgy translations, 24; and biblical studies, 30, 75, 204, 235, 248; and Hebrew texts translations, 123
Enlightenment, 47, 49, 54, 283
Epstein, Jason, 287, 288
Ethiopia, 304–5
Ethiopic language, 9, 38, 47, 67
European Jews: and Lost Tribes theories, 17–18; conversion of, 42–43, 188; and missionary activity, 102, 116; and American Jewish community, 112–14, 151, 187, 188, 230; education of, 115; and American Jewish learning, 118; and religious tolerance, 119; and emigration to Palestine, 134, 138, 212, 214, 226; and Zionism, 230; and Nazism, 232; Niebuhr and, 260–61, 263, 266, 296
Evolution, 152, 153, 154, 237, 242

Ewald, H., 182
Ezekiel, Rabbi, 108

Falk, Joshua, 117
Falwell, Jerry, 5, 294, 295, 296
Fascism, 260–61, 264, 266
Fein, Leonard, 299
Feldman, Egal, 266
Felsenthal, Bernard (rabbi), 245–46
Female Society of Boston, 90, 100
Finch, Henry, 63
First Zionist Congress (1897), 230
Fisher, Jonathan, 10
Fisk, Pliny, 131
Flusser, David, 286
Folger, Peter, 29
Foot, Lucinda, 71–72
Ford, Alexander Hume, 212, 221–22, 223
Ford Motor Company, 256, 258–59
Fox, Richard Wightman, 256, 262, 263, 268
France, 93, 121, 143
Frank, Waldo, 278, 288
Franklin, Benjamin, 59, 61, 62, 139–40
Frey, Hannah Cohen, 97, 104
Frey, J. S. C. F.: and Hebrew language instruction, 12, 96, 105–6, 109; and conversion of Jews, 89, 90, 95, 96–97, 104, 106, 107, 109; and missionary activity, 89, 90, 95–102, 106–7, 109, 110; conversion of, 95, 96, 104–5, 110; and Hebrew translation of New Testament, 98–99, 100, 105, 107–8; and Jews' return to Zion, 103
Friedman, Jerome, 203
Friedman, Lee M., 91
Fuller, Thomas, 227
Fundamentalism, 4, 93, 296
Fürst, J., 172, 173

Gaelic language, 98
Gale, Theophilus, 80–82, 85
Gandhi, Mohandas, 257, 261
Geiger, Abraham, 171
Geography, 153
Geology, 152, 153, 154, 237, 242
Germany: and Hebrew studies, 2, 25, 26; scholars in, 25, 137, 142; and German Higher Criticism, 133–34; Robinson and, 137, 138, 143–44, 150, 153–54, 157,

168–69, 171; and graduate education, 137, 216, 245; philological method from, 142, 147, 150, 153–54, 163, 164–65, 168–69, 182, 240; Nordheimer and, 164–65, 169; and Nazism, 232, 261, 262, 265–66; and biblical scholars, 237; and seminary education, 239
Gesenius, Wilhelm, 147, 150–51, 174, 182
Giardina, Denise, 260, 261
Gilman, Henry, 214
Giltner, John, 145
Ginzberg, Louis, 40
Glanz, Rudolph, 191
Glazebrook, Otis A., 213
Godbey, Allen, 17
Goldwater, Barry, 287
Goodspeed, G. S., 238
Gorenberg, Gershon, 294–95
Gorham, John Warren, 213
Gottheil, Richard, 245, 297
Grafton, Anthony, 15, 17
Greek language: and Harvard College, 9, 11, 38; and Jewish-Christian scholarly cooperation, 57; Edwards and, 75, 77, 78, 80, 87; and higher education, 79, 120, 147, 201, 218, 241; Hannah Adams and, 101; and New Testament, 108, 241, 242, 253, 254; Calvin Stowe and, 132–33; Robinson and, 140, 141, 215; Stuart and, 144, 145; Lewis and, 163, 311 (n. 1); Bush and, 199, 203, 204; and New York University, 202; and Bible, 237; and seminary education, 280
Greek Orthodox Church, 156
Green, William Henry, 250
Grey, Richard, 46
Grimké, Angelina Emily, 166
Grimké, John Faucherand, 165
Grimké, Sarah Moore, 166
Grimké, Thomas, 165–66, 167
Grinstein, Hyman, 89, 172
Grose, Peter, 3, 209, 211
Gutjahr, Paul C., 110

Hakohen, Joseph (rabbi), 18
Hamlen, B. L., 168
Hancock, Thomas, 45, 46
Harper, Samuel, 241
Harper, William Rainey: and Monis, 44; and Hebrew language instruction, 129–

30, 232, 235, 236, 237, 239–42, 247, 248, 249, 251; and Christian Hebraism, 138, 232; and Hebrew studies, 219, 234, 238, 240–41, 242, 243–44, 247, 251; and biblical studies, 232, 234, 235–36, 237, 238, 239–40, 241, 242, 248, 249, 250, 251; and University of Chicago, 232, 236, 238, 239, 240, 244–45, 247–48, 251–52; and Jews, 232, 243, 244–48, 252

Harris, Thaddeus Mason, 45

Harris, William, 100

Harrison, Benjamin, 208, 231

Hart, Jeffrey, 271

Hartford Theological Seminary, 219, 224–25

Harvard College: and Hebrew studies, 9, 10–11, 29, 46–49, 281; and Hebrew language instruction, 11, 29–30, 31, 33, 34, 35, 36, 37–38, 45–51; rabbinic institutions as models for, 13, 70; and Christian Hebraism, 44, 140, 237, 280; Hebrew language insignia of, 52–53; Mather on, 54; Timothy Edwards and, 78; liberalism of, 140, 141, 142, 218; Seixas and, 197; Semitic Museum, 223, 225; Comparative Zoology Museum, 225; and comparative religion, 238; and graduate education, 245

Hayden, William, 199

Hebrew Bible: American engagement with, 2; and Harvard College, 9; and Puritans, 12; as universal history, 16; Stiles and, 66, 67; Edwards and, 79, 86; Frey and, 96, 100, 105; and American Jewish community, 115; Jewish-Christian arguments on, 134; and Siloam tunnel, 158; Nordheimer and, 172, 173; and Mormon Church, 176; Walker and, 186–87; Robinson and, 215; Niebuhr and, 234; Harper and, 252; and seminary education, 301

Hebrew language: Native American dialects descended from, 1–2, 17, 18, 86; Jews' use of, 2, 3, 124; rabbinic Hebrew, 2, 38, 39, 52, 60, 67, 77, 125–27, 147–48, 149, 243; divinity school Hebrew, 2, 52, 301; as original language, 10, 23–25, 33, 47, 49, 80–81, 190, 201, 280; as tool of conversion, 12, 98–100, 108, 127, 131, 148; American Jewish community's use

of, 13, 114, 117, 122–27; as tool of anti-Judaism, 27; and Old Testament, 37, 84, 99, 166, 241, 242, 248, 253, 254, 303; in letter writing, 66, 68, 118, 119, 120, 126; and typology, 84; and Gaelic language, 98; and tombstones, 126; Masorah, 146–47, 149–50, 173, 247; and Christian prayer, 243, 244; Israeli Hebrew, 298, 299, 300, 301; and Kabbalism, 304

Hebrew language instruction: Seixas and, 4, 149, 150, 176, 177–79, 181, 182–84, 189, 191–98; Bush and, 10, 169–70, 182, 195, 199, 203; and Harvard College, 11, 29–30, 31, 33, 34, 35, 36, 37–38, 45–51; and higher education, 12, 26–27, 29–30, 129, 147, 181, 197, 201, 218, 241; Frey and, 12, 96, 105–6, 109; Monis and, 31, 33, 34, 35, 36–37, 45–46, 47, 48, 188, 198, 203, 300; and Protestants, 45, 150, 151, 181, 182, 191, 203, 236–37, 249, 313 (n. 23); Stiles and, 53, 61–62, 70, 78, 116, 140, 181, 300; and Yale College, 53, 70, 78, 129, 140, 145, 181; Edwards and, 75, 80; and American Jewish community, 111, 114–16; Stuart and, 129, 146–47, 148, 150, 169–70, 173, 181, 182–83, 184; Harper and, 129–30, 232, 235, 236, 237, 239–42, 247, 248, 249, 251; Calvin Stowe and, 132–33; Robinson and, 140, 147, 168–69, 182; Jewish method of, 145–47, 181, 203; Nordheimer and, 149–50, 154, 164, 165, 166–68, 169, 170, 172–73, 203; Merrill and, 209, 217, 218, 220, 224, 226

Hebrew Literary and Religious Library Association, 172

Hebrew poetry, 123–24

Hebrew printing, 99–100, 123

Hebrew schools, 13, 114–15, 191–92, 299–300

Hebrew studies: in American colonies, 2, 7, 9, 10–11; and Germany, 2, 25, 26; and Harvard College, 9, 10–11, 29, 46–49, 281; and Cambridge University, 10; and Puritans, 10–11, 12, 20, 33, 37; Stiles and, 11, 19, 50, 52, 54, 58–66, 60, 67, 68–69, 72, 78, 124, 183, 254; and Yale College, 11, 52–53, 140; Edwards and, 11–12, 74, 77–80, 82, 84–86, 87, 88; and Lost Tribes theo-

modern Jewish history, 138; and Hebrew language, 141, 248; secular Israeli understanding of, 231; and Partition of Palestine, 232; and apocalyptic ideology, 233; American Christian support for, 263, 291–92; Niebuhr and, 266–67, 273; Wilson and, 281–82, 286, 287, 288; Truman and, 292; and Second Coming, 294–95; and Jewish studies, 300; and biblical archaeology, 301; Jesus and, 303

Italy, 26, 28, 59

Jaffa, 4–5, 213, 302
James, William, 55
Jarchi (Rashi), 85
Jastrow, Marcus, 245
Jastrow, Morris, 297
Jefferson, Thomas, 1–2, 21–22, 86–87
Jenkins, Jerry, 233
Jerome, Saint, 23–24, 25, 45
Jerusalem: biblical zoo of, 10; and Native Americans as Lost Tribes, 92; and missionary activity, 108; and conversion of Jews, 131; Merrill and, 134, 212, 213–15, 219, 220–21, 222, 225; Robinson and, 156, 158, 159; evangelical pilgrimages to, 294; replicas of, 302
Jesus: and Hebrew language, 24; and Yale College seal, 53; and Old Testament, 66, 75; Zohar and, 68; Edwards and, 84; and Lost Tribes theories, 93; and Reign of Christ, 95; and Palestine, 151; and Siloam tunnel, 158; and Jesus Seminar, 249; and Christian-Jewish relations, 269; and Jewish roots of Christianity, 303
Jewish-Christian scholarly cooperation: and doctrinal issues, 13, 65–66; opportunities for, 26, 51; and Hebrew studies, 56–58, 118–19, 151, 225–26; and Stiles, 59; and Jewish immigration, 113; Robinson and, 144; Niebuhr and, 272. *See also* Christian-Jewish relations
Jewish Community Relations Council, 298
Jewish Hebraism: and Christian Hebraism, 111, 124, 125–27; Simson and, 120; and facility with Hebrew language, 124; and American Jewish community, 151; Seixas and, 176. *See also* Hebrew language; Hebrew language instruction; Hebrew studies

Jewish identity: of Monis, 33, 35, 37, 39, 41, 42; and missionary activity, 91; and Hebrew schools, 114–15, 299–300; and Hebrew language use, 127; of Neander, 144; Robinson and, 144; of Seixas, 177, 189, 191, 193, 196, 197, 198; and conversion of Jews, 187–88; and Hebrew language study, 298, 299–300
Jewish-Indian theory, 1–2, 17–23, 72, 86–87, 89, 92–94, 102, 304
Jewish nationalism, 249, 263
Jewish scholars: and Christian Hebraism, 12, 33, 51, 56–58, 119, 198, 203, 210; and Torah, 12–13; and Kabbalah, 41; Monis and, 44; and biblical studies, 48, 117, 162, 297; Zohar and, 68; and origins of nations/peoples, 72; and American Jewish community, 113; and German Higher Criticism, 133–34; Robinson and, 162, 163; and higher education, 188, 197, 198, 203, 297–98; Harper and, 244–48
Jewish studies, 297–98, 300, 301
Jewish Theological Seminary, 272, 292
Jews and Judaism: and Jewish-Indian theory, 1–2, 17–23, 72, 86–87, 89, 92–94, 102, 304; use of Hebrew language, 2, 3, 124; Jewish role in history, 3, 19–20, 24, 63, 65, 93, 152, 230, 233, 295; anti-Judaism, 3, 48, 68, 244, 269; Stiles and, 11, 14, 50, 56, 58–60, 61, 62–65, 68, 69, 72, 116, 183; and Christian Hebraism, 12, 13, 56; and Puritans, 12, 33, 211; as Yale undergraduates, 14; and New World exploration, 15, 18; and Babylonian exile, 16, 18; and Return to Zion, 18, 63; and Jewish messianism, 20; and original language, 23; attitude toward missionary activity, 26, 103–4, 110, 127; mystical traditions of, 27; Reform Judaism, 40, 171, 243, 244–45, 246, 250; as preservers of sacred learning, 54; religious practices of, 56, 57, 58, 62, 65; Edwards and, 80, 85; and New Testament, 107; as distinct people, 131; Christian scholars and, 134, 152; and Israel and modern Jewish history, 138; Robinson and, 143–44; and

Hebrew language instruction, 145–47, 181, 203; and Holy Land exploration, 152; Joseph Smith and, 176; Parker and, 186; and higher education, 188; and Mormon Church, 191–93; Swedenborg and, 205–6; Merrill and, 208, 210, 211, 212, 214, 225; Harper and, 232, 243, 244; and Hebrew studies, 243, 247, 248–49, 303; Niebuhr and, 256; and social activism, 257, 259–60, 268. *See also* American Jewish community; Anti-Semitism; Conversion of Jews to Christianity; European Jews; Jewish identity; Restoration of Jews to Palestine

Jews Chapel, 99–100
Johns Hopkins University, 138, 245
Johnson, Samuel, 79, 116, 122, 129, 298
Johnson, Thomas, 75
Jones, William, 21
Josephson, Manuel, 117–18
Josephus, 156, 223
Joyce, James, 98

Kabakoff, Jacob, 127
Kabbalism: Pico della Mirandola and, 27–28; Lurianic Kabbalists, 39, 87; Stiles and, 63, 66–68, 88; Joseph Smith and, 177, 190, 193; and Christian-Jewish relations, 304. *See also* Christian Kabbalism
Kaganoff, Nathan, 125, 196
Kark, Ruth, 209
Kazin, Alfred, 277, 278, 282–83, 284, 288
Kegley, Charles, 271
Kemper, Johan, 42–43
Kennan, George, 254
Kimnach, Wilson, 77, 82, 87
King, Martin Luther, Jr., 257, 273
King, P. J., 156
Kingsborough, Lord, 21
King's College, 116, 129. *See also* Columbia College
Kitagawa, Joseph, 238
Klausner, Joseph, 303–4
Kohler, Kaufman (rabbi), 245
Kohut, G. A., 39, 40, 41–42, 44, 61–62, 72, 123, 223, 245
Kollek, Teddy, 262
Kriegel, Leonard, 279, 280

Krupnick, Mark, 278, 288
Kuklick, Bruce, 241

Ladino (Judaeo-Spanish), 65, 148
Lagerloff, Selma, 221
LaHaye, Tim, 233
Landau, Jacob, 284–85
Langdon, Samuel, 31
Language: Native American dialects descended from Hebrew, 1–2; Hebrew as original language, 23–25, 47, 49, 80–81; Sewall's lectures on, 47, 49; Stiles and, 54, 254; European Jews and, 57; Edwards and, 78, 80, 85, 86, 87; Protestants and, 116; Nordheimer and, 164; and heritage language teaching, 298. *See also* Philology; *entries for specific languages*
Las Casas, Bartolome de, 22
Latin language: and Harvard College, 9, 11, 38, 60; and Bible, 25; and Yale College, 52–53; Edwards and, 75, 77, 78, 79, 80, 87; and higher education, 79, 120, 147, 201, 218, 241; Hannah Adams and, 101; Calvin Stowe and, 133; Robinson and, 140; Stuart and, 145; Bush and, 199, 203, 204; and New York University, 202
Leeser, Isaac, 89–90, 95–96, 105, 151
Levita, Elijah (rabbi), 57
Lewis, R. W. B., 277
Lewis, Tayler, 163, 311 (n. 1)
Lindsey, Hal, 233
Loewe, Raphael, 211, 227, 305
London Missionary Society, 97
London Society for the Promotion of Christianity among the Jews, 97, 98, 99, 101, 105, 107, 108
Lord's Prayer, 38, 243
Lost Tribes: and origins of nations/peoples, 15–16, 22–23; Native Americans as descendants of, 15–16, 92–93, 94, 101; and New World exploration, 17, 18–19; and England, 20–21; Stiles and, 72–73; and Afghan tribes, 304; and Ethiopia, 304–5
Lowance, Mason, Jr., 75
Low Countries, 7, 26
Luncz, A. M., 220

Luria, Isaac, 40
Luther, Martin, 53, 237
Lyell, Charles, 237

Macdonald, Michael C. D., 283
Maclean, John, 75
Madrid Peace Conference (1991), 291
Magnes, Judah, 264
Maimon, Salomon, 280
Maimonides, 57
Malchi, Moses (rabbi), 63
Manual Hebrew Grammar (Seixas), 179, 181, 196, 197
Manuel, Frank, 32, 57, 210, 213, 214, 226
Marcus, Jacob Rader, 33, 115, 120, 164, 178
Margolioth, Naphtali, 43
Marty, Martin, 294
Martyn, John, 34–35
Marx, Karl, 259, 279–80
Marxist theory, 258–59, 268, 276
Mason, Jeremiah, 70
Matar, Nabil, 227
Mather, Cotton, 13, 29, 32, 50–51, 54, 90, 281
Mather, Increase, 32, 33
Mather, Nathan, 281
McClellin, William E., 191
McCullough, David, 293
McDermott, Gerald, 80
McGovern, George, 287
Melville, Herman, 5
Menasseh Ben Israel (rabbi), 17, 19–20, 22–23, 226
Merrill, Adelaide Brewster Taylor, 223
Merrill, Fanny Lucinda Cooke, 216
Merrill, Selah: as U.S. consul in Jerusalem, 134, 212, 213–15, 219, 220–21, 222, 225; and Jews, 208, 210, 211, 212, 214, 225, 226, 227; and Palestine, 208–12, 224, 230, 292; as archaeologist, 209, 210, 214, 217, 220, 224; as minister, 209, 216, 217, 220; and Hebrew language instruction, 209, 217, 218, 220, 224, 226; and American Colony of Jerusalem, 212; legacy of, 223–25
Mesopotamia, 131, 138, 142, 157, 219
Meyer, Michael, 246
Middle East: U.S. policy on, 5, 130, 232, 264, 265, 266–67, 296, 306; American

interest in, 10, 160–61; and origins of nations/peoples, 15; and University of Chicago, 138; geographical study of, 153; Eli Smith and, 154, 157; and Bible, 155; missionary activity in, 159, 229, 230; and American painting, 160, 161. *See also* Israel; Palestine
Millennial groups: and Jews, 2, 295; and Protestants, 3–4; and politics, 5; and Lost Tribes theories, 17–18, 21, 92; Las Casas and, 22; and conversion of Jews, 32, 95; and American Revolution, 93; and restoration of Jews, 103, 106; and United States, 233; and Israel, 294, 295
Miller, Perry, 11, 88
Miller, William, 4, 202, 305
Millerites, 4, 205, 212
Milton, John, 42, 227
Minor, Clorinda, 4–5, 159–60
Minority groups, 258, 259, 260, 263, 266, 273, 297
Missionary activity: and anti-Judaism, 3; and Hebrew language as tool of conversion, 12, 98–100, 108, 127, 131, 148; and Lost Tribes theories, 21, 92–93; Jews' attitude toward, 26, 103–4, 127, 159, 270; Frey and, 89, 90, 95–104; and American Jewish community, 89, 91, 99–102, 103, 105, 110, 113, 148, 187; and Jewish-Indian theory, 89, 92–94; and Palestine exploration, 100, 108, 159; and missionary societies, 100–107, 268; and European Jews, 102, 116; and New Testament in Hebrew, 107–8; Stuart and, 148, 236–37; Eli Smith and, 157, 159; in Middle East, 229, 230; Niebuhr's opposition to, 254, 270, 271; evangelicals and, 294
Monis, Abigail Marret, 32, 34
Monis, Judah: and Christian Kabbalism, 28–29, 31, 39–41, 87, 304; and Hebrew language instruction, 31, 33, 34, 35, 36–37, 45–46, 47, 48, 188, 198, 203, 300; baptism of, 31–34, 40, 43, 45, 52, 66, 99, 185, 188, 198, 203; Christian identity of, 33, 34–35, 39, 41–44; Jewish identity of, 33, 35, 37, 39, 41, 42; Harvard career of, 35–37, 51; and Hebrew studies, 38–41, 99; Sewall on, 45–46,

48; Sewall compared to, 47, 48, 50; and Jews as preservers of sacred learning, 54

Montezinos, Antonio, 17, 18, 19, 22, 23

Moore, Clement C., 100

Moore, George Foot, 34, 39–40, 42, 44, 67, 173, 218, 219, 238, 303

Morgan, Edmund, 58, 69

Morgan Park Seminary, 239

Morison, Samuel Eliot, 9, 38, 42

Mormon Church: and Jewish history, 4, 191; and Native Americans, 23; and Christian Hebraism, 119–20, 124; Seixas and, 149, 177, 188, 189–95, 197, 198; and Old Testament, 176; School for Near Eastern Studies, 301

Moses, Blanche, 196

Muller, Max, 238

Muskingum College, 240, 241

Muslims and Islam, 90, 108, 116, 200–201, 268, 296, 306

NAACP Legal Defense Fund, 257

Nabokov, Vladimir, 283–84

Nathan, Rabbi, 245

National Association of Professors of Hebrew, 249, 300–301

Native Americans: and Jewish-Indian theory, 1–2, 17–23, 72, 86–87, 89, 92–94, 101, 304; origins of, 7, 15–16, 17, 21, 92–93, 101; and missionary activities, 93–94; and Wilson, 286; and American West, 293

Neander, August, 143, 144, 170–71, 172

Near Eastern languages, 49, 148, 190, 215, 216, 238, 249

Neill, H., 170–71

Netanyahu, Benjamin, 5

Netherlands, 25

New Age religions, 304

New Haven Theological Seminary, 168, 212, 216

New Jerusalem Church, 206–7, 305

New Lights, 44, 212

New Testament: and Old Testament, 16, 45, 74–75, 99, 107; Hebrew words retained in, 24, 37; and "Israelite in whom there is no guile," 33; and Greek language, 38, 108, 241, 242, 253, 254; and Hebrew studies, 84; Cherokee translation of, 94; Hebrew transla-

tions of, 98–99, 100, 105, 107–8, 131; Ladino translation of, 148; and Holy Land, 151; Robinson and, 156; Mormon Church and, 176; Niebuhr and, 258; and anti-Semitism, 269–70; and biblical archaeology, 301; and rabbinic literature, 303

Newton, Isaac, 48, 55–56

New World, 15, 17, 18–19, 21, 22, 106, 130

New York University, 10, 149, 163, 167–68, 174, 198, 199, 202, 207

Niebaur, Alexander, 190, 193

Niebuhr, Gustav, 253, 254

Niebuhr, Helmut Richard, 253, 255, 264, 268–69

Niebuhr, Hulda, 253, 255

Niebuhr, Lydia, 253

Niebuhr, Reinhold: and Zionism, 232–33, 262–68, 295, 296; early life of, 253, 254–55; and social issues, 253–54, 256, 258, 260, 273; education of, 254, 255; and Jews, 256, 257–58, 260–63, 265, 266, 268; and Christian Pragmatism, 257–60, 261, 262, 264, 265, 266; and Tillich, 259, 261, 271, 303; and conversion of Jews, 268, 270–71; Jewish responses to, 271–74

Niebuhr, Ursula Keppel-Compton, 255, 262, 273

Nieto, Isaac, 123

Nordell, Philip, 244

Nordheimer, Isaac: and Christian Hebraism, 119, 163–64; and biblical studies, 134, 163, 168, 169; and Robinson, 149, 150, 154, 163, 164, 167, 168, 169, 173–74, 203, 272; and Stuart, 149, 150, 154, 182; and Hebrew language instruction, 149–50, 154, 164, 165, 166–68, 169, 170, 172–73, 203; and New York University, 163, 167–68, 174, 198; and Hebrew studies, 163, 173, 182, 201, 297; and Bush, 164, 169–70, 203; and Grimké, 165, 166, 167; and Union Theological Seminary, 169; and conversion issues, 170–71, 174; death of, 173–75

North American Relief Society for Indigent Jews in Jerusalem, 122

Obenzinger, Hilton, 139

Oberlin College, 129, 149, 189, 191, 197

Old Testament: and New Testament, 16, 45, 74–75, 99, 107; as sacred history, 16–17, 22; and American religious thought, 29; and Hebrew language, 37, 84, 99, 166, 241, 242, 248, 253, 254, 303; Stiles and, 56, 58, 62; Jesus and, 66, 75; Edwards and, 74, 86; and Documentary Hypothesis, 134; and proofs of biblical accuracy, 151; Robinson and, 156; Parker and, 187; Bush and, 204; and seminary education, 240; Harper and, 249; and Arabs of Palestine, 267; Wilson and, 276, 281, 288–89; and biblical archaeology, 301

Oslo Accords (1993), 291

Otto, Julius Conrad, 43

Ottoman Empire, 63, 213, 214, 221, 222–23, 306

Owens, Lance, 190

Oxford University, 26, 57, 276

Palestine: and Millerites, 4; and British Mandate, 10, 232; Carigal and, 63; Stiles and, 73; and missionary activity, 100, 108, 159; Robinson and, 100, 116, 131–32, 137–38, 139, 140, 142, 144, 151, 152, 153–62, 169, 215, 218, 240; opening to West, 108, 151; and American Bible Society, 110; as antidote to unbelief, 133; Jewish emigration to, 134, 138, 212, 226, 292; American perceptions of, 137, 138, 162; as Promised Land, 141; exploration of, 150–53; George Adam Smith and, 152; American travel to, 153, 221, 302; Merrill and, 208–12, 224, 225; and biblical archaeology, 210–11, 229; and American attitudes toward Jews, 211; and nationalism, 227; partition of, 230, 232, 265; refugees of, 233, 266; Niebuhr and, 261, 263; Shamir on, 291. *See also* Arabs of Palestine; British Mandate Palestine; Holy Land; Restoration of Jews to Palestine

Palestine Exploration Fund, 217, 218

Parker, Theodore, 185–87, 195

Partition of Palestine, 230, 232, 265

Pearson, Eliphalet, 218

Peixotto, Daniel Levy Maduro, 191

Peixotto, Rachel, 192

Phillips, Isaac, 178

Phillips, N. Taylor, 178, 187, 196

Philology: and Anglo-Saxons as descendants of Israel, 20; Monis and, 45; Sewall and, 46, 48; Stiles and, 60, 254; and Hebrew as original language, 81; Robinson and, 141, 142, 153–54, 169, 215, 240, 242; and Germany, 142, 147, 150, 153–54, 163, 164–65, 168–69, 182, 240; Stuart and, 142, 147, 150, 154, 168; Nordheimer and, 149, 163, 164–65, 166, 168, 203; Seixas and, 193, 194–95; Merrill and, 218; Harper and, 235, 238, 240, 241, 242, 249, 250; and anti-Judaism, 244; Niebuhr and, 253

Pico della Mirandola, Giovanni, 27–28, 41, 59, 81

Pinto, Isaac, 123

Pittsburgh Platform (1885), 246, 250–51

Politics: and Zionism, 4, 5, 211, 230, 263, 265; and Israel, 5, 295–96; and Lost Tribes theories, 18; and Bible, 30; and Christian Hebraism, 130, 226; and Christian Zionism, 160, 295–96; Nordheimer and, 172; Merrill and, 210; Niebuhr and, 257, 260, 263, 266–67, 269, 271; Wilson and, 279

Popkin, Richard, 17, 72

Pratt, Orson, 192, 194

Pratt, Parley, 194

Press, Samuel, 255

Princeton Theological Seminary, 200, 277, 280, 297

Princeton University, 278

Promised Land, 22, 29–30, 133, 139, 141, 234, 292, 305

Protestantism: American, 2, 3–4; and attitudes toward Jews, 2, 20, 134, 177, 181–82, 187, 210, 227, 245; evangelicals, 3–4, 5, 233, 262, 291, 292, 293–96; and function of Jews in history, 3, 63; and Hebrew studies, 26, 130, 133, 183, 242, 243; and Hebrew language instruction, 45, 150, 151, 181, 182, 191, 203, 236–37, 249, 313 (n. 23); Stiles and, 58; philanthropic work of, 90; and Native Americans, 92, 94; and *Princeton Review*, 100; denominational lines of, 104; and restoration of Jews, 106, 208, 209, 211; and American Jewish community, 113, 127; and *hazzan's*

Schwartz, Delmore, 277, 297
Science: and natural world, 10, 55, 82, 84; and biblical studies, 49, 152, 153, 154, 237–38, 242, 245, 250; Stiles and, 54, 55, 59; Wilson and, 84; and *Princeton Review*, 100; and religious worldviews, 152, 153; and New York University, 202
Scult, Mel, 97
Second Coming, 3, 4, 63, 90, 202, 205, 294–95
Second Temple Judaism, 303
Secularism: and higher education, 10, 117, 202; of American society, 91, 117; Nordheimer and, 164; and Zionism, 231, 266; Wilson and, 234, 279; and Jewish traditions, 244, 270, 296; and Jewish social activism, 257; Niebuhr and, 258, 266, 270; and Hebrew language, 300
Seixas, Benjamin, 192
Seixas, Gershom Mendes, 115, 120, 123–24, 149, 177, 178
Seixas, Hannah Manuel, 177
Seixas, Henrietta Raphael, 178, 196–97
Seixas, Isaac B., 178
Seixas, Joshua/James: and Joseph Smith, 4, 124, 176, 177, 189–90, 193, 301; and Hebrew language instruction, 4, 149, 150, 176, 177–79, 181, 182–84, 189, 191–98; and Stuart, 113, 148–49, 181, 182–85, 187–88, 195; and Christian Hebraism, 119, 181–85, 190, 195; and biblical studies, 134, 181; and Mormon Church, 149, 177, 188, 189–95, 197, 198; conversion of, 176, 179, 185–89, 193, 196, 197, 198; personal life of, 176–77, 195–98; and Hebrew studies, 197, 201
Selden, John, 62
Seminary education, 116, 129, 150, 218, 238–40, 248–49, 280, 300–302
Semitic languages, 138, 235, 238
Semitic studies, 300
Sewall, Samuel, 23
Sewall, Stephen, 37, 45–50, 60, 146, 300, 301
Shamir, Yitzhak, 5, 291
Sharon, Ariel, 5
Shearith Israel Hebrew School, 13, 114–15
Shepherd, Naomi, 108
Siegel, Seymour, 271–72, 273, 274
Siegel, Thomas Jay, 47, 60

Silberman, N. A., 217
Silberschlag, Eisig, 33
Simeon ben Jochai (rabbi), 67
Simon, Ernst, 264
Simon, Richard, 107–8
Simson, Joseph, 120
Simson, Sampson, 120–22, 123, 178
Simson, Solomon, 119, 120
Singer, Isaac Bashevis, 282–83
Slavery, 71, 100, 133, 150, 166, 251
Smith, Eli, 153–59, 162, 169
Smith, Eliza R. Snow, 190
Smith, George Adam, 152, 153, 154
Smith, John, 80–81, 300
Smith, Joseph: and Seixas, 4, 124, 176, 177, 189–90, 192–94, 301; and Christian Kabbalism, 29, 88, 304; and Christian Hebraism, 119, 124; and Hebrew studies, 176, 190, 191, 192–95; and Peixotto, 191–92
Snow, Lorenzo, 190, 314 (n. 42)
Snowman, Jacob, 21
Socialist Party, 258
Social justice, 246–47, 250–51, 256, 279
Soviet Union, 233, 259, 266–67
Spafford, Horatio, 220
Spafford family, 212, 221, 222
Spiegel, Shalom, 272
Sproul, William, 243
Stein, Stephen, 77
Stern, Malcolm, 196
Stiles, Ezra: and interest in Jews, 11, 14, 50, 54, 56, 58–60, 61, 62–65, 68, 69, 72, 116, 124, 126, 183, 226; and Hebrew studies, 11, 19, 50, 52, 54, 58–66, 67, 68–69, 72, 78, 124, 183, 254; and Kabbalism, 11, 63, 66–68; and Christian Kabbalism, 28–29, 67, 87–88, 304; visits with rabbis, 51, 62–66, 67; and Hebrew language instruction, 53, 61–62, 70, 78, 116, 140, 181, 300; family background of, 53–54; education of, 54–55, 58; and Edwards, 55, 73, 74, 78; as minister, 56, 60–61, 69; as pluralist, 56–58, 71, 72; and Christian Hebraism, 58, 60, 61, 66, 67, 69, 119, 129, 237; and Jewish scholars, 58, 118–19; and Yale College, 60, 68, 69–71; and Simson, 120; and America as God's Israel, 133, 139; and Stuart, 144–45

Stiles, Ezra (son), 62
Stiles, Isaac, 53–54
Stowe, Calvin, 132–33, 150, 218, 226, 281
Stowe, Harriet Beecher, 132–33, 218, 281
Straus, Oscar Solomon, 222–23
Stuart, Moses: and Seixas, 113, 148–49,
    181, 182–85, 187–88, 195; influence of,
    116, 218, 236–37, 240; and Jews, 124,
    144, 147–50; and Hebrew language
    instruction, 129, 146–47, 148, 150, 169–
    70, 173, 181, 182–83, 184; and biblical
    studies, 131, 142, 148, 150, 182–83, 239;
    and lower criticism, 133; and Robinson,
    142, 143, 144, 150, 151, 160, 168, 218; and
    Hebrew studies, 145–50, 151, 183, 201,
    218, 240; and Nordheimer, 149, 150,
    164, 169–70, 172–73
Suez Canal, 266
Suez Crisis of 1956, 266–67
Swedenborg, Emanuel, 205–7, 305
Syria, 47, 108, 157, 159, 160–61, 172
Syriac language, 67, 143, 147, 182, 200

Talmud: and observance of Sabbath, 13;
    and Aramaic language, 23, 60; Stiles
    and, 62, 67; Edwards and, 85; Ains-
    worth and, 86; Frey and, 96; American
    Jewish community and, 115; Nord-
    heimer and, 164, 173; and *Elohim*, 195;
    Felsenthal and, 245
Taylor, Edward, 53, 54
Taylor, Graham, 246–47
Taylor, J. M., 251
Taylor, John, 85
Theology: and Jewish history, 4; Edwards
    and, 11, 77, 80, 82, 84, 85; Jewish schol-
    ars and, 33, 45; and science, 55; and
    Aramaic language, 100; and Chris-
    tian Hebraism, 125; American Jewish
    community and, 127; Robinson and,
    133, 142; Stuart and, 142, 218; and
    Hebrew language instruction, 188;
    Mormon Church and, 190; Bush and,
    201; Swedenborg and, 205; and semi-
    nary education, 218, 239–40; Niebuhr
    and, 232, 234, 255, 261, 265, 271, 272,
    274; Stiles and, 237; Wilson and, 278;
    Israel and, 296
Thompson, William, 132, 162
Tillich, Paul, 259, 261, 271, 303

Torah, 12–13, 96, 178, 183, 247
Touro, Isaac, 61
Tower of Babel, 23, 24, 26, 190
Trilling, Lionel, 130
Tristram, Henry Baker, 224
Truman, Harry, 232, 292
Trumbull, Jonathan, 120
Tuchman, Barbara, 226–27
Turner, William, 168
Twain, Mark, 5, 161, 291, 292

Union College, 87
Union of American Hebrew Congrega-
    tions, 264
Union Theological Seminary, 138, 154,
    168, 169, 218, 260–62, 263, 272
Unitarianism, 129, 141, 186, 189
United Nations. *See* Partition of Palestine
United States: origins of American
    democracy, 1; national self-concept, 2,
    5, 30, 91–92; and American Hebraism,
    2, 15, 26, 227; American Revolution,
    69, 70, 93, 115, 120; as American Zion,
    75, 103, 205; and "return to the land"
    movement, 102–3; European Jews' at-
    titude toward, 118; religious tolerance
    in, 119; West, 129, 293; as God's Israel,
    133, 139, 293; geographical study of,
    153; State Department, 209, 213, 214,
    222, 292; ambivalence toward Jews
    in, 211; Civil War, 216, 281, 283; and
    British Mandate Palestine, 232; and
    millennialism, 233. *See also* American
    colonies
University of Berlin, 143, 144, 215, 216
University of Chicago, 138, 232, 236, 238,
    239, 240, 244–45, 247–48, 251–52
University of Munich, 164–65

Van der Hoeven, Jan Willem, 296
Vester, Anna Spafford, 221
Vester, Bertha Spafford, 222
Vietnam War, 287
Vital, Hayyim, 40
Viterbo, Egidio de, 57
Von Humboldt, Alexander, 143
Von Humboldt, Wilhelm, 143

Wadsworth, Benjamin, 37
Walker, Charley, 289

Walker, James, 185, 186–87, 195
Walton, Michael, 194
Warren, Charles, 153
Washington, George, 92, 124
Wellhausen, Julius, 133–34
Wheelock, Eliezer, 13
Whitefield, George, 44, 92
Whitney, William Dwight, 238, 241
Wigglesworth, Edward, Jr., 48, 50
Wigglesworth, Michael, 11
Willard, Sidney, 105–6
Williams, Charles, 256
Williams, Elisha, 79
Williams, Roger, 29
Wilson, Andrew, 82, 84, 85
Wilson, Charles, 145–46
Wilson, Edmund: and Hebrew studies,
   118, 126, 234, 275–78, 280–81, 282, 284–
   86, 288, 289, 297; and biblical studies,
   118, 126, 234, 276, 277, 280, 284, 288;
   and Jews and Judaism, 232, 275–78,
   281, 282–83, 284, 285, 287, 288, 289,
   296–97; and rabbinic aspect of leftist
   politics, 259, 287; Said on, 267; and
   Marx, 279–80; and Israel, 281–82, 287
Wilson, Elena, 276, 283, 289
Wilson, Thaddeus, 280
Wilson, Woodrow, 213, 232, 260
Wind, J. P., 235, 239
Winslow, Edward, 94
Winthrop, Elizabeth, 101
Winthrop, John, 47, 48
Wodrow, Robert, 43
Wolcott, S. W., 156
Wolfson, Harry, 44, 297–98
Women, 25, 26, 71–72, 90–91, 115, 166

Woolsey, Theodore, 217
World War I, 259–60, 265
World War II, 263, 264, 265–66, 296
Wosh, Peter, 94

Yadin, Yigal, 286
Yale College: and Hebrew studies, 11, 52–
   53, 140; rabbinic institutions as models
   for, 13, 70; Hebrew-language insignia
   of, 13–14, 52–53; and Hebrew language
   instruction, 53, 70, 78, 129, 140, 145,
   181; Stiles and, 60, 68, 69–71, 78, 129;
   women and, 71–72; Edwards and, 79;
   Merrill and, 216; Harper and, 235–36,
   239, 241; and biblical studies, 237
Yale Divinity School, 255
Yale Judaica Collection, 223
Yates, Frances, 27
Young, Andrew, 257

Zionism: and dispensionalists, 3–4; and
   Christian Zionism, 5; Stiles and, 72;
   and "return to the land" movement,
   102–3; American opposition to, 135;
   Merrill and, 210, 223; and Christian Hebraism, 226, 227; and American Jewish
   community, 229, 230, 293; American
   sympathy for, 230, 293; and secularism, 231, 266; Niebuhr and, 232–33,
   262–68, 271, 273; Truman and, 292–
   93; Jewish scholars and, 298. See also
   Christian Zionism; Restoration of Jews
   to Palestine
Zohar, 27, 28, 39, 59, 60, 62, 63, 66–68,
   86–88
Zucker, L. C., 195